Given By Inspiration

Also by William P. Grady:

FINAL AUTHORITY:
A Christian's Guide to the King James Bible

WHAT HATH GOD WROUGHT!:
A Biblical Interpretation of American History

HOW SATAN TURNED AMERICA AGAINST GOD

Given By Inspiration

*A Multifaceted Study on the A.V. 1611
with Contemporary Analysis*

William P. Grady, Ph.D.

GRADY
PUBLICATIONS, INC.

ISBN 978-0-9628809-0-2
Library of Congress Control Number: 2010913375
First Printing October 2010

For information, address:
GRADY PUBLICATIONS, INC.
P.O. Box 243
Swartz Creek, MI 48473
william.grady@gradypublications.com
www.gradypublications.com

Table of Contents

Dedication

This book is *lovingly* dedicated to "the saints at Macedonia Baptist Church" for standing with their pastor to make *Given By Inspiration* a spiritual reality. Thank you – *from the bottom of my heart* – for all of your prayers, input, and encouragement!

"For we are labourers together with God..."

(I CORINTHIANS 3:9)

Acknowledgments

I would like to thank the following people for their invaluable contribution to this book:

First and foremost would be my family, friends, and church members for their prayers and support throughout this *difficult* time (Psalm 119:71).

Jack Minor, Nick Cultrara, Mike Kee, Jeff Faggart, Mitch Canupp, and my son, Paul Grady, for research and proofreading (Bro. Canupp remains an untapped wealth of knowledge on the history of the King James Bible).

Tim Pye, of the British Library Reference Service in London, for his particular expertise.

Tammy Butler, for her excellent formatting skill and overall text design.

Tommy and Lori Ray, for the impressive cover (the *fourth* in seventeen years).

Eric Rishell and the staff at R. R. Donnelley & Sons, for their professional service during the printing phase of this project.

Finally, for the tireless proofreading and editorial assistance from my precious wife, Linda, who "celebrated" our 36th wedding anniversary by working at the computer until 2 a.m. (Proverbs 19:14).

Introduction

The Holy Spirit opened my eyes to the King James Bible in 1988 after reading *The Christian's Handbook of Manuscript Evidence*. I later published my *own* book, *Final Authority*, in March 1993 (the same month that *New Age Bible Versions* was released). Within three years a remarkable phenomenon had occurred. An article in the October 23, 1995, issue of *Christianity Today* reported, "Among conservative Christians, a grassroots backlash against contemporary English-language Bibles has triggered a renewed interest in the famed King James Version with its word-for-word translation and its longstanding authority." As Ecclesiastes 1:9 declares, *"The thing that hath been, it is that which shall be,"* history was evidently repeating itself, for in 696 BC, Hilkiah the high priest had declared unto Shaphan the scribe, *"I have found the book of the law in the house of the LORD."* (II Kings 22:8)

A lot of water has passed under the bridge since those early days. Unfortunately, as with that short-lived revival under King Josiah, the A.V. 1611 is once again at the center of controversy. This time, the issue concerns the doctrine of *inspiration*. I believe two factors are primarily responsible for this renewed contention. First, many of those in leadership positions who are now *crawfishing* (Southern colloquialism for "backing up") never *really* believed "The Book" to begin with. The worst offenders are invariably mega-church chameleons with schools and tuition money to raise. They constitute the point men for "*Pseudo* King James Onlyism." While some are merely pragmatic apostates *"going* along to *get* along," the rest would be characterized by the proverb, *"The dog is turned to his own vomit again."* (II Peter 2:22)

The second cause involves the degree of *depth* among the so-called "good guys" in the dispute. On April 8, 1984, Dr. Jack Hyles preached his famous sermon "*Logic* Must Prove the King James Bible." While practically all of his followers *embraced* the new position, few made it past "logic" as *their* reason for converting. In fact, few ever *reached* logic, as "Preacher" usually did the thinking for most of them. (My son-in-law, a faithful pastor for several years now, enrolled in Hyles-Anderson College in 1990, but quit after only seven weeks when a "Bible" teacher informed the class that they only "used" the King James Version because *Dr. Hyles said to* and would switch to *another* version the moment he instructed them otherwise.) Consequently, twenty-five years after that message, Dr. Hyles' *own* son-in-law, Jack Schaap, could stand in the pulpit of First Baptist Church and lead young preachers to question the very Bible that had birthed them into the Kingdom of God! Yet, the *bigger* crime was the collective passive reaction exhibited by the deacons, faculty, and administrators who showed themselves to be walking contradictions of the Bible they should have defended: *"For there must be also heresies among you, that they which are approved may be made manifest among you."* (I Corinthians 11:19)

To base one's faith in the King James Bible on "logic" is an invitation to disaster and an insult to the third member of the Godhead: *"Which things also we speak, not in the words which **man's wisdom** teacheth, but which the **Holy Ghost** teacheth; comparing spiritual things with spiritual."* (I Corinthians 2:13) In February 2009 Dr. Russell Anderson, co-founder of Hyles-Anderson College, addressed a letter of protest to Schaap, as well as the faculty and alumni of the school. The only problem was that he included the late *Dr. Hyles* in the salutation! Could we possibly imagine a more bizarre scenario than a *living* Christian writing a letter to a *dead* Christian? Dr. Anderson was literally trying to intimidate the members of the Body of Christ by invoking the attention of their departed leader. In his third paragraph he asks, "Dr. Hyles, do *you* think that I should have been notified by our college that they were going to make such a change?" Following logic rather than the Holy Ghost led the well-intentioned Christian philanthropist to *Endor*. (In *another* creepy form letter I received, dated August, 3, 2010, this time from Schaap himself, recommending Ray Young for speaking engagements, he glowingly stated – in the "spirit" of *The Tell Tale Heart* – "He keeps the heart of Bro. Hyles at Hyles-Anderson….")

I believe the Lord prompted me to write *Given By Inspiration* as a sincere challenge to preachers and church members alike to *rethink* their *true* relationship to the A.V. 1611. After thirty-seven years in the ministry, I can *assure* you that very few Christians have yet to scratch the surface of that blessed Authorized Version. While the majority of Schaap's detractors wave King James Bibles in the air, they remain oblivious to the countless doctrinal truths and exclusive perks that accompany a *genuine* Bible believer's experience (right division, cross-referencing, typology, numerology, similitudes, *English* word studies, etc.). As the gross heresy of necromancy reveals, most Baptists merely "gaze" into the Holy Bible (as the men of Beth-shemesh did with the Holy Ark) rather than "jump in" and *"search the Scriptures"* for themselves (in the spirit of those noble Bereans). We simply cannot afford to lose *another* quarter of a century leaning on *logic*. And don't bother waiting for the "Big Boys" to lead the way; the *"Pseudo* King James Only" camp is a politically-correct Laodicean rabble of pragmatic kingdom builders who will crusade for a "Book" in public which they refuse to study in private (II Timothy 2:15). Consequently, the divine author of the Holy Scriptures decrees: ACCESS RESTRICTED TO THOSE WHO *REALLY* BELIEVE. *"For this cause also thank we God without ceasing, because, when ye received the word of God which ye heard of us, ye received it not as the word of men, but as it is in truth, the word of God, **which effectually worketh also in you that believe."** (I Thessalonians 2:13)

For those familiar with my literary style, I have always been influenced by Spurgeon's admonition, "If a man would be *read,* he must *read*; if a man would be *quoted,* he must *quote.*" My three previous works reflect this advice (totaling over 2,000 pages with nearly 700 bibliography entries, citing everything from *Jet* magazine and the Black Bible Chronicles to privately taped CIA telephone recordings). However, *this* time my goal is to let the *Scriptures* speak for themselves; or, to "quote" the Orthodox Creed of 1679, written by the General Baptists in England, "...the holy Scriptures... is the best Interpreter of it self (sic)."

Yet, *God helping me*, I will remain as politically *incorrect* as possible. Take the Russell Anderson "letter bomb" fiasco, for instance. How could such a prominent leader force an entire mailing list of unsuspecting Baptists to witness a crime punishable by *death* in the Old Testament – in the name of the King James Bible, no less – *without* evoking a notable censure, *unless* it had something to do with *money*? (To give Dr. Anderson the benefit of the doubt, *technically,* he is not guilty of necromancy unless Dr. Hyles replied; so, do we laugh or cry?) By the grace of God, I have learned firsthand that religious "gurus" are no match for the Lord when *He* wants something to be said. For instance, after a well-known preacher "crawfished" from writing the foreword to my last book (*How Satan Turned America Against God*), the Holy Ghost replaced him with the esteemed Jewish physicist, Sam Cohen ("Father of the Neutron Bomb"), who supplied the afterword. When the *Sword of the Lord* refused to *sell* me a full-page ad, I received a *free* plug in the July 15, 2005, weekend edition of *USA Today.* And, while the book remains too controversial for the average *Christian* bookstore, it has been featured on *Barnes & Noble's* website for several years now with a *five*-star review.

The thesis for *Given By Inspiration* goes right to the heart of the matter and is presented here in no uncertain terms: THE DEBATE OVER WHETHER THE KING JAMES BIBLE IS INSPIRED IS A SATANIC ATTEMPT TO KEEP THE A.V. 1611 *SUBORDINATE* TO THE ORIGINAL MANUSCRIPTS. No matter *what* anyone tries to tell you, the *context* of II Timothy 3:15 *mandates* that Timothy's *copy* come under the heading of "Holy Scripture" with absolutely *no* distinction being made between *it* and the "venerable" autographs. And, if a *copy* can be liberated from the *illusion* of a superior original, then our King James English *translation* can be *just* as *"free indeed."* (John 8:32, 36)

Now, to defend my thesis and to further edify the Body of Christ, I have sought to define the doctrine of inspiration in its purest *biblical* context. To settle the contest between originals and copies, I have opted for the novel approach of pursuing "oldest *mention*" over "oldest *written*" (i.e., discovering the true purpose for inspiration by determining its original *usage* via the Law of First Mention). While scholars remain adamant that the *older* manuscripts are superior to the *younger* (e.g., codices *Vaticanus* and *Sinaiticus* being superior to the *Textus Receptus*), with the *originals* constituting the *ultimate* authority and sole recipient of inspiration, I prefer to follow the *same* approach—only, why stop with just *any* original? Why not go back to the *oldest* original of all? You see, the *first* appearance of the word "inspiration" is found in the book of Job, written 2,000 years *before* the autograph of II Timothy was composed. Thus, rather than confine our understanding of inspiration to the scholar's "private interpretation" of an original *manuscript* that *cannot* be seen, we will rely upon the original *mention* of that doctrine as preserved and taught by the Holy Ghost in a *translation* of a *copy* that *can* be seen. As the reader will soon discover, the Alexandrian scholar is slain by his own preference for "originals." II Samuel 23:20-21 says, *"And Benaiah...plucked the spear out of the **Egyptian's** hand, and **slew him with his own spear."***

One of the main criticisms for this book will undoubtedly be that my *expanded* view of inspiration is inconsistent with the past. Dr. Schaap is quick to insist that "400 years of orthodox Baptist positions" support *his* view of inspiration, etc. While there are certainly examples that could be cited to the contrary (such as the 1679 Orthodox Creed), I have no desire or need to subpoena these ancient witnesses; and, for a very specific reason, one that is beyond the grasp of "scholars" like Schaap. This "reason" concerns a statement that his father-in-law would often try to explain toward the closing years of his ministry: "Every generation has to rediscover the Bible for itself." In a second foreword to *Final Authority*, Dr. Hyles wrote:

> When I was a young preacher, the battle was over *how* to interpret the Bible. Now, almost half a century later, the battle is over the Bible *itself*. Then, the battle was over what the Bible TAUGHT. Today the battle is over what the Bible IS. Then, it was a battle over interpretation. Now, it is a battle over inspiration and preservation. Then, it was a battle over difference of doctrine. Now, it is a battle over where we get our doctrine. Then, it was a battle over the flow. Now, it is a battle over the source. Then, it was a battle over what Truth says. Now, the battle is over what truth is.... Bill Grady is right in his defense of the Bible.

What I believe Dr. Hyles was trying to say is that, while God's *truth* never changes, the amount of light He sheds *on* that truth *can* intensify from one generation to another (Daniel 12:4-9; Romans 16:25; Ephesians 3:5; Colossians 1:26; I Peter 1:10; Hebrews 11:29-30; etc.). Thus, any article in a "creed" formed by the spiritual perspective of *one* generation may not be strong enough for the particular needs of a *later* period. This is the very concept that was presented in the introduction to *Final Authority* almost twenty years ago. Having cited the works of John William Burgon (leading nineteenth-century advocate for the Traditional Text), I acknowledged that charges of inconsistency could be leveled at me since Burgon felt that the Authorized Version could possibly be revised in the future should the correct Greek text be employed. However, bear in mind that for nearly three centuries the A.V. 1611 was the *only* accepted Bible in the English-speaking world. The present "King James Only" position has been necessitated by the *unprecedented* modern "Bible" movement. Because twenty-first-century Christians are surrounded by literally dozens of corrupt versions – *unlike the time of Burgon* – we *must* hold to *one* Book and one Book *alone* for matters of final authority! We must follow the pattern of Benaiah's comrade, Eleazar, whose *"hand clave unto the sword."* (II Samuel 23:10)

All the rhetoric about creeds and orthodoxy is nothing more than a smoke screen to keep you from understanding *how* this unique problem came about. While the "historic Fundamentalist position" was emerging around the heavily promoted debut of the 1901 American Standard Version (ASV), the "new arrival" showed no aspiration for being used in the *sanctuary*, requesting only a humble abode in the pastor's *study* alongside his other reference tools. Having duped preachers on the merits of revision *per se*, the Devil laid low in patient anticipation of his carefully orchestrated end-day plethora of modern English translations. Had he dumped his entire truckload of over one hundred versions on the preachers of Burgon's day, they *never* would have taken his bait. While Satan got his foot *in* the door with the ASV, he *crashed* it down with the New American Standard Version, Living Bible, Reader's Digest Condensed Version, New International Version, etc. The growing alignment of frustrated independent Baptists behind the King James Bible is merely an attempt to *re-hang* the door on its hinges and SLAM it shut! A return to *one* Bible is a return to *the* Bible itself, for *"no man can serve **two** masters."* (Matthew 6:24)

The later chapters of this book offer a contemporary analysis of the King James Bible issue as set against the backdrop of Laodicean apostasy. As the reader will discover, this volume is not just another dry polemic on the doctrine of inspiration, but rather a multifaceted study promoting the untapped power and uncontested final authority of the A.V. 1611. Belief in the text itself is a natural prerequisite to understanding the process by which it was created (I Thessalonians 2:13). *Given By Inspiration* presents a scriptural definition of an eternal truth set in an ancient Hebrew text – preserved in a seventeenth-century English translation for a besieged remnant at the end of the Church Age – followed by a post-Rapture application to Tribulation saints.

I will now conclude these remarks with an insightful exchange that also occurred in seventeenth-century England between a scholar and a "tinker" (a mender of pots and pans). The Lord Jesus prayed, *"I thank thee, O Father, Lord of heaven and earth, because thou hast hid these things from the wise and prudent, and hast revealed them unto babes."* (Matthew 11:25) The tinker had been deprived of a formal education, spending only about three years in school. He had a prison record to boot, serving over a *decade* behind bars. However, the story has a happy ending, for the *tinker* was a *thinker*. While rotting in the loathsome Bedford jail, John Bunyan wrote his celebrated Christian allegory, *Pilgrim's Progress*, upon crumpled milk churn lids. Regarded as one of the most significant works of English literature, *Pilgrim's Progress* is second only to the Bible itself in numbers of copies sold worldwide. Bunyan's classic has been translated into 200 languages and has *never* been out of print since its release in 1678. The "unlearned" Baptist preacher would author *sixty* books before his death at age fifty-nine. The following "dispute with a scholar" is taken from *The Struggler*, and will serve as a most apropos transition to *Given By Inspiration*:

> As Mr. Bunyan was upon the road near Cambridge, there overtakes him a scholar that had observed him a preacher, and said to him, How dare you preach, seeing you have not the original, being not a scholar?
>
> Then said Mr. Bunyan, Have you the original?
>
> Yes, said the scholar.
>
> Nay, but, said Mr. Bunyan, have you the very self-same original copies that were written by the penmen of the scriptures, prophets and apostles?
>
> No, said the scholar, but we have the true copies of those originals.
>
> How do you know that? said Mr. Bunyan.
>
> How? said the scholar. Why, we believe what we have is a true copy of the original.
>
> Then, said Mr. Bunyan, so do I believe our English Bible is a true copy of the original.
>
> Then away rid [sic] the scholar.

"But God hath chosen the foolish things of the world to confound the wise...."

(I CORINTHIANS 1:27)

The *Authorized Version* maintained its effective dominance throughout the first half of the 20th Century. New translations in the second half of the 20th Century displaced its 250 years of dominance (roughly 1700 to 1950), but groups do exist – sometimes termed the King James Only movement – that distrust anything not in agreement with ("that changes") the *Authorized Version*.

— WIKIPEDIA

"I am as a wonder unto many;
but thou art my strong refuge."

(PSALM 71:7)

1

Forward to the Past

THE APOSTLE PAUL finished his course by recording specific warnings about the "last days" of the Church Age (II Timothy 3:1-4:5). It is highly significant that II Timothy 3:16, *the* text at the heart of the inspiration debate, was included in this very discourse. Now, after Paul had been *back* in Heaven for about thirty years (having been *"caught up to the third heaven"* following his stoning at Lystra), John suddenly pops up for *his* first visit in order to write the final book of the Bible (Acts 14:19; II Corinthians 12:2; Revelation 4:1-2). While Genesis reveals how all things *began*, Revelation shows how all things will *end*. Consequently, to understand how the doctrine of inspiration specifically relates to the "last days," we will *begin* at the *end*.

The book of Revelation has a lot to say about the Bible. The *"word of God"* appears in the second verse of the first chapter (just as the *"Spirit of God,"* the book's author, showed up in the second verse of the first chapter of Genesis). While God's word is mentioned *seven* times throughout the book, the final chapter makes *seven* references to the book of Revelation itself. The book *begins* with a special promise to bless all who read and hear, and *ends* with a promise to bless all who obey (Revelation 1:3; 22:7). Likewise, the book concludes with a special twofold promise to curse any who would add or take away from the same (Revelation 22:18-19). The most dramatic scene is Revelation 19:13 where the Lord Jesus Christ is introduced as *"The Word of God."*

Our specific need for light on the inspiration issue will be found in the exclusive, *prophetic* content of the book that begins as follows: *"The Revelation of Jesus Christ, which God gave unto him, to shew unto his servants things which must shortly come to pass; and he sent and signified it by his angel unto his servant John: Who bare record of the word of God and of the **testimony of Jesus Christ**, and of all things that he saw."* The cross-reference that identifies this "testimony" is Revelation 19:10, *"for the **testimony of Jesus** is the **spirit of prophecy**."* Thus, the "testimony of Jesus" is His ability to forecast the future with absolute certainty *and* to put it in writing (Isaiah 42:9).

While Paul uses "right division" in I Corinthians 10:32 to classify the human race into *Jews*, *Gentiles*, and *Christians*, John uses the "spirit of prophecy" in Revelation to forecast the future of each group through the natural threefold division of the book. In Revelation 1:19, John is commanded: *"Write the things which **thou hast seen**, and the things which **are**, and the things which **shall be hereafter**."* The Holy Spirit supplies the relevant dispensational coordinates: in Revelation 4:1-2, Heaven opens and someone goes *up*; in Revelation 19:11, Heaven opens and someone comes *down*. Ascribing to a *premillennial* eschatology (Christ's return *before* a literal 1,000-year Kingdom begins), the *prophetic* outline of Revelation unfolds as follows: chapters 1-3, *Church Age*; chapters 4-19, *Tribulation*; chapters 20-22, *Millennial Kingdom* and *Eternity*.

So far, so good; but now comes the *heavy* part (better "buckle up"). The average Christian forgets that Revelation is a *prophetic* book. In a supernatural setting, John was *literally* transported into the future to write the book. Though he woke up that morning *on* Patmos, he crossed over a *major* time zone at verse 10: *"I was **in the Spirit** on **the Lord's day**."* In a Bible *college*, "The Lord's *Day*" means *Sunday*; in a Bible *institute*, "The *Lord's* Day" means THE DAY OF THE LORD – as in the entire scope of apocalyptic terror, culminating at the Second Advent (Isaiah 13:6-11; Malachi 4:5). From John's perspective, then, he is writing with the Church Age *behind* him, the Tribulation *beneath* him, and the Millennium *before* him. (*His* present – the end of the Tribulation – is *our* future.) Although the autograph of Revelation was *officially* written roughly 2,000 years ago, the author was *actually* over 2,000 years *in the future* when he wrote it (i.e., *"Forward to the Past"* beats *"Back to the Future"*). Therefore, he could *technically* state, *"for the time is at hand"* – as it certainly *was* – *then* (Revelation 1:3). This is what Jesus was referring to when he replied to Peter's question regarding John's future – *"If I will that he tarry till I come, what is that to thee? follow thou me."* (John 21:22) And don't miss the beautiful devotional nugget; James 4:8 states: *"Draw nigh to God and he will draw nigh to thee."* Thus, we see that as the disciple drew nigh to his Saviour at *Calvary*, the Saviour drew nigh to His disciple at *Patmos*.

As the Lord's *first* command was to *"write the things which THOU HAST SEEN,"* the Holy Spirit utilizes the very next verse to restate *and* interpret what that vision included – *"and the SEVEN CANDLESTICKS which THOU SAWEST are the SEVEN CHURCHES."* Consequently, John is shown a panoramic view of the entire Church Age in the letters to the seven churches (each church constituting a unique prophetic type of a specific period of Church history in chronological sequence). To emphasize the reality that John is writing in "The Day of the Lord" – *with the Church Age behind him* – notice how John states, *"And I TURNED to see the voice that spake with me. And BEING TURNED, I saw seven golden candlesticks."* John had to *turn around* to see the seven churches (represented by the seven golden candlesticks) because they were *behind* him; i.e., in the past – positionally.

After completing this first task, he proceeds to take his second excursion *"in the Spirit,"* being called *up* to Heaven in Revelation 4:1, just as Christians will be raptured out when the Church Age is completed. It is *then* that he records the *"things which ARE"* – the events of Daniel's Seventieth Week. When he finishes chapter 19, he begins the third and final division, *"the things which SHALL BE HEREAFTER"* – from the Millennium to the Great White Throne Judgment and beyond.

It should be noted that the Scofield Reference Bible makes chapter 1 *"the things which thou hast seen"*; chapters 2 and 3, *"the things which are"*; and chapters 4-22, *"the things which shall be hereafter"* – erroneously combining the Tribulation *with* the Millennium and subsequent events. If we *really* want to get deep – though the phrase *"Come up hither, and I will shew thee **things which must come hereafter,"** could* give the impression that period three begins with Revelation 4 – one must understand that this section *would* constitute the "hereafter" to John *relevant to his arrival in Heaven* (ditto, Revelation 9:12). In any event, the One who *gave* John his instruction clarified the matter – *sixty years earlier* – connecting the **"hereafter"** with His Second Advent: *"**Hereafter** shall ye see the Son of man sitting on the right hand of power, and coming in the clouds of heaven."* (Matthew 26:64)

Now, wasn't *that* fun? (If anyone got "lost in the woods," just keep right on moving; you can always go back and review later.) Though this is about as heavy as it's going to get (well, for a *while*, anyway), this opening exercise is meant to serve as an important object lesson: *biblical* Bible study requires spiritual *labor.* Second Timothy 2:15 says: *"Study to shew thyself approved unto God, a **workman** that needeth not to be ashamed, rightly dividing the word of truth."* The only light this world can ever have will emanate from the *"church of the living God, the pillar and ground of the truth."* (I Timothy 3:15; Ephesians 3:10) Thus, the Holy Spirit used a "golden candlestick" as a type of the local assembly. And the *true* light will *always* come from the A.V. 1611; "John" was perfectly capable of telling us where he was all along – "in English."

"I John, who also am your brother, and companion in TRIBULATION...."

(REVELATION 1:9)

2

Seven Golden Candlesticks

THE MOST IMPORTANT truth to grasp at this juncture is that the seven literal churches of Asia Minor represent a prophetic profile of the entire Church Age. While the primary *doctrinal* application would be to the Tribulation saints, and while there would have been plenty of *devotional* application for the seven actual congregations that originally received the letters, the unique *prophetic* application constitutes a priceless asset for the Bible believer in the last days; particularly in light of the growing controversy over inspiration. When I taught Church History at Hyles-Anderson College (1986-1996), I would lecture from the second and third chapters of Revelation for sixteen weeks at a time. Obviously, we can barely do the subject justice in a single chapter here. However, the following synopsis will suffice, and will be amplified by a most profound postscript.

EPHESUS (AD 33-100)

The meaning of this name is "desirable one," or "fully purposed." (Note that dates and definitions given in this study are not dogmatic, but flexible, and can vary depending on perspective; some overlapping of the periods is also quite natural.) Ephesus portrays the Church of the Apostolic Age, ending with the death of the Apostle John near the close of the first century. This first letter is unique among the seven, as the period it entails is nearly over when John writes. While the salutation here is worded, *"Unto the angel of the church of Ephesus,"* subsequent greetings read, *"Unto the angel of the church in Smyrna...in Pergamos,"* etc. (i.e., *in* the Smyrna *Age, in* the Pergamos *Age...*). The Church at Ephesus was a hardworking, highly separated body that *hated* the things that Jesus *hated,* namely, *"the deeds of the Nicolaitanes."* The cause for this divine provocation can be understood by examining the word "Nicolaitanes." The compound root words are *nikao,* meaning "to conquer," and *laos,* meaning "the people," or "laity." Thus, the Nicolaitanes were a first-century sect which anticipated the Roman Catholic priesthood by dividing God's people into a *clergy/laity* relationship. (Baptists have historically rejected this unscriptural dichotomy.) By the time Revelation was completed, a spirit of complacency had set into the Church, resulting in the rebuke, *"thou hast left thy first love,"* and subsequent command to *"repent, and do the first works."* With the debate over inspiration centering on II Timothy 3:16, it is worth noting that Timothy was the pastor of the Church at Ephesus until his martyrdom in the year AD 97 (I Timothy 1:3).

SMYRNA (AD 67-313)

This name is derived from the root word "myrrh," an aromatic gum resin used for embalming the dead (John 19:39-40). The Smyrna Age is characterized by imperial Roman persecution. Consequently, John's letter deals with suffering, imprisonment, and pending martyrdom. As the believers were told that *"ye shall have tribulation ten days"* (the number of the Gentiles), *Foxe's Book of Martyrs* highlights *ten* major persecutions that occurred: Nero, AD 67; Domitian, AD 81; Trajan, AD 108; Aurelius, AD 162; Severus, AD 192; Maximus, AD 235; Decius, AD 249; Valerian, AD 257; Aurelian, AD 274; and Diocletian, AD 303. The most notable martyrs of this era (apart from the apostles) were two aged disciples of John, Polycarp and Ignatius; and two courageous young mothers, Perpetua and Felicity. When facing his approaching death in the Flavian amphitheater, Ignatius testified, "Gladly shall I welcome the wild beasts that are prepared for me, and I trust they will do their work quickly. I will lure them on to devour me. Even if they are unwilling, I will force them to it." History confirms that Ignatius did, indeed, experience his last request to depart this world as the "wheat of God," ground by the teeth of wild beasts. John's other "preacher-boy," Polycarp, was burned alive in the city where he was pastor – Smyrna *itself*. When pressed to recant, he boldly replied, "Eighty and six years have I served Him and He hath done me no wrong; how, then, could I do this great disservice against my King?" Surviving court documents reveal that the martyrs were slain for the "crime" of nonconformity, being charged with "*odio humani generis*" (literally, "hatred of mankind"). The entire Age is depicted by Tertullian's famous quote: "The blood of the martyrs is the seed of the church."

Two important doctrinal issues are also alluded to in this letter. The seeds of "replacement theology" can be discerned in the words, *"I know the blasphemy of them which **say they are Jews, and are not**, but are of the Synagogue of Satan."* A new faction of "Christians" had begun to assert that they were *spiritual* Jews; thus, heirs to the ancient promises of Israel. Here, we see the beginning of the Roman Catholic "priesthood" (designed to usurp the *Levitical* order), as well as the departure of premillennial teaching (no Jewish Millennium). On the other hand, the *"Synagogue of Satan"* concerns a legitimate body of Jewish apostates with a critical connection to the Bible issue itself. When a search of this period is conducted for a concentration of blasphemous Jews, a most enlightening discovery is made. A second-century census of Alexandria, Egypt, reveals that over 40% of the city's 800,000 residents were Jewish (the largest assemblage of Jews in the world at that time). The further confirmation of their defection from Judaism is striking. With their initial settlement occasioned by a rebellious flight from divine chastisement (Deuteronomy 28:68; Jeremiah 42 and 43), the later and larger waves of immigrants were enticed by the materialistic overtures (cucumbers, melons, leeks, onions, and garlic) of the epileptic sodomite, Alexander "the Great," himself. Within a generation, the destructive tenets of Greek philosophy had replaced the doctrine of Moses.

The leading apostate at this time was a Platonic Jewish scholar named Philo Judæus (20 BC - AD 54). It is no coincidence that this descendant of Aaron and contemporary of Jesus just "happened" to be the chief spokesman of his city's "Great Synagogue," a colonnaded basilica so immense that a system of relay signals was used to ensure a synchronized responsive reading. The all-important connection to the King James Bible has to do with the prestigious school of philosophy that Philo established in Alexandria. This very school was bequeathed to Philo's "Christian" comrades and became the "World's Most Unusual University" of antiquity. By the second century AD, the Catechetical School at Alexandria was in the hands of the self-emasculated Adamantius Origen, recognized by all modern scholars as *the* pioneer of the science of textual criticism. Every attack on the A.V. 1611 can be traced to this bastion of higher "Christian" education. The infamous codices *Vaticanus* and *Sinaiticus* were copied from copies that *originated* with *Origen*, the entire textual line being classified as "Alexandrian" in type. Whereas the Bible says, *"Who can bring a clean thing out of an unclean? not one* (Job 14:4), Dr. Ed Reese (a professor at The Crown College in Powell, Tennessee) labeled Origen "an influential biblical scholar" in his *Chronological Encyclopedia of Christian Biographies*; though he *did* acknowledge that Origen "defined amillennial views" (no literal 1,000-year reign), and that "his theology translated into a disbelief in the physical resurrection and an eternal hell."

PERGAMOS (AD 313-500)

Pergamos means "marriage and elevation." With the coronation of Constantine "The Great" – Rome's first "Christian" emperor – civil persecution of Christians was formally ended by the Edict of Milan in AD 313. (That "13" should have been an indication of things to come.) The price for this protection was the unholy marriage of the State to the visible, professing "Church" (the word "Church" used here more as a synonym for organized religion, *not* as a reference to the true New Testament Church). As the adage of "marrying *up*" goes, the new bride was subsequently "elevated" from the *catacombs* to the *cathedrals*. The Nicolaitanes are seen to reappear in this "Christian-friendly" environment, though now as an "enemy *within* the gates," having infiltrated the assembly: *"So **hast** thou also them that hold the doctrine of the Nicolaitanes."* Another ideological returnee is the replacement theology that began with Origen in the Smyrna Period; alluded to as Balac's having cast a *"stumblingblock before the children of Israel,"* it will manifest itself in the emperor's harsh anti-Semitic policies.

The majority of all Bible colleges will follow the party line in any standard textbook on Church History – that Constantine was a *great* Christian emperor, defender of the faith, etc. Unfortunately, the Holy Ghost would disagree, identifying the imperial throne room as *the* place *"where **Satan's** seat is"* (verse "13"). Now, if ol' "Connie" *was* a Christian, he was surely *one* of a kind. He consolidated his "Christian" reign by having scores of political rivals murdered, including a brother-in-law, an eleven-year-old nephew, and even his wife, Fausta, and eldest son, Crispus ("Focus on the Family," etc.). He then went on to postpone his "baptism" for a quarter of a century, believing that the water would wash away his sins. Consequently, he was sprinkled on the day of his death, and by an Arian heretic, no less. The "humble" servant was then placed in a golden coffin and positioned in the center of a dozen coffins in the Church of the Twelve Apostles. (Talk about the power of suggestion!) The sycophant, Eusebius, declared: "The blessed Constantine was the only mortal man who continued to reign *after* his death."

John's letter to Pergamos ends with a stern warning: *"Repent; or else I will come unto thee **quickly**, and will fight against them with the sword of my mouth."* (Note that qualifier, "quickly.") Church leaders were so elated that the *heat* was *off* and the *honor* was *on*, that they started preaching that the Kingdom had arrived.

But, then that *sword* came upon everyone, "quickly." Less than twenty-five years after Constantine's death, Europe is invaded in AD 360 by Attila the Hun, known as the "Scourge of God"; the Roman Emperor, Valens, is killed and his army routed by the Visigoths in AD 378; and, Rome herself is sacked in AD 410 (*the first time in 800 years*). The deluded Catholic theologian, Augustine, began his *City of God* the following year, explaining that *Rome* was now God's favorite place since He was "finished with the Jews *and* Jerusalem" (Psalm 122:6). In the midst of such widespread defection, however, a number of *real* preachers were following the example of "faithful Antipas"; men such as Athanasius and Chrysostom in the East, Patrick in Ireland, Columba in Scotland, and the Donatists in North Africa.

THYATIRA (AD 500-1500)

The message in the name of this "church" is a *dead* giveaway – "continual sacrifice." It is a reference to either the blasphemous mass of Romanism, or to the suffering of God's people at the hand of Rome itself. The letter to Thyatira provides much information about the Catholic Church in the Dark Ages. When Constantine deserted the "eternal city" for his new capital at Constantinople (which, of course, he named after himself), he left three vital things behind for the "up-and-coming" Bishop of Rome. The first was a *serious* power vacuum. The second was his personal title of *"Pontifex Maximus,"* or "Chief Priest" (of the pagan State religion), which is inscribed on the miter worn by every Pope in history. The emperor's third gift was that "SEAT"; you *do* recall – *"where Satan's seat is"*? All Popes would henceforth rule "ex-cathedra," i.e., from the "Chair of Peter" (though *we* know that the filthy gangsters *really* got their leg-up from "Connie's SEAT").

The letter begins by placing the Lord Jesus Christ as the *"Son of God"* (Acts 8:37; 9:20). The next verse is possibly a glancing reference to the "corporal works of mercy" provided through the area monastery in the best of medieval traditions (hospitals, schools, orphanages, "just war" theory, etc.) The pace picks up with the introduction of *Jezebel*. This evil Phoenician queen is an insightful correlation to the Vatican's infatuation with "all things female" (a holdover from the ancient vestal virgins): Mary, "Queen of Heaven"; the *ever*-virgin "Mother of God"; "Hail Mary"; Our Lady of Lourdes; Our Lady of Fatima; Our Lady of Guadalupe; Mother Superior; Mother Theresa; Mother Angelica; the sodomite "Singing Nun"; rosary beads; nuns in habits; harems called "convents"; Catholic women "confessing" in confessionals; celibate males dressing like "mothers" while calling themselves "Fathers"; altar *boys* in gowns; same-gender schools; the whole "Holy *Mother* Church" thing. And the Holy Spirit could not agree any more with the type, devoting two entire chapters to a religious whore (the obvious antithesis to the *"chaste virgin"* of Christ) – *"MYSTERY, BABYLON THE GREAT, THE **MOTHER OF HARLOTS** AND ABOMINATIONS OF THE EARTH."* Her address is duly noted, *"The seven heads are **seven mountains**, on which the **woman** sitteth"* (as in Rome's traditional title, "City of Seven Hills"), along with her powerful legacy, *"And the **woman** which thou sawest is that great **city**, which reigneth over the kings of the earth."* (Revelation 17:5, 9, 18; I Timothy 4:1-6)

As Jezebel introduced idolatry into Israel, Rome accomplished the same within the *professing* Christian "Church." The Vatican "wafer-god" of transubstantiation can be seen in the words, *"and to eat things sacrificed unto idols."* The harlot's incorrigible addiction to "spiritual" immorality is confirmed by the words, *"and she repented not."* The important cross-reference in Revelation 17:1-2 reveals that *"her fornication"* has taken place with *"the kings of the earth."* As this 1,700-year-long illicit relationship began with Rome's first "Christian" emperor, we discern an unmistakable bond between the two: "CONSTANTINE **THE GREAT**" and "MYSTERY, BABYLON **THE GREAT**."

There is so much historical corroboration for verse 23 that an entire book could be written on the subject. By every indication imaginable, *"the Son of God, who hath his eyes like unto a flame of fire"* was determined to *"kill"* Jezebel's *"children with **death**."* Over 50% of Europe's population consistently died before reaching their thirteenth birthday. Children in the Dark Ages were not even given names until they had reached the age of seven. The "staples" of the day were famine, drought, floods, pestilence, isolation, ignorance, fear, superstition, brigandage, warfare, depression, suicide, and genocide. Revelation 17:2 says, *"and the inhabitants of the earth have been made **drunk** with the wine of her fornication."* As the centuries rolled on, an extended review of the really big killing fields of Thyatira would include the Islamic and Viking invasions, the "Holy Wars" (including the insane Children's Crusade), the Hundred Years War, and the Black Death that wiped out one-third of Europe's population in the fourteenth century alone. Preferring a papal toe to a nail-scarred foot, Europe's benighted inhabitants got to experience the "joy" of a *satanic* Millennium.

Amidst the chaos, the Lord left our Baptist ancestors with His personal exhortation to *"hold fast till I come"* (i.e., no city-wide revival campaigns in the Dark Ages). An army of New Testament churches carried on by *whatever* name and reputation their particular Vatican antagonists decreed. A short list of these "sects" would include the Petrobrusians, Arnoldists, Cathari, Henericans, Paterines, Albigensians, Waldensians, and those ultimate advocates of "right division" – the *Paulicians*. Thankfully, however, help was *definitely* on the way. John's letter to Thyatira concludes with the Lord's promise: *"And I will give him **the morning star**."* In 1380, the first hand-written English language Bible manuscripts were produced by John Wycliffe at Oxford. As printing was yet to be discovered, the Wycliffe Bible had to be meticulously copied by hand, requiring about ten months of steady work by an experienced copyist to produce just one Bible. The rental fee for a single hour with so costly a treasure was an entire load of hay. I have always marveled that John Wycliffe came to be known as **"The Morning Star** of the Reformation."

Sardis (AD 1500-1611)

The word *Sardis* means "red ones," or more specifically, "bloodied ones." While the *"great whore"* spent the Dark Ages *"drunken with the **blood** of the saints, and with the **blood** of the martyrs of Jesus,"* the "mother of *all* blood baths" broke out when the nations of northern Europe decided to break away from *Pontifex Maximus* (Revelation 17:6). The catalyst for this revolt was that Morning Star of the Thyatira period. The Wycliffe Bible sparked a major revival that was quickly spread by his zealous disciples (known as Lollards). Twenty years after Wycliffe's death (in 1389), John Hus was already recognized as the outstanding advocate of "heretical Wycliffism" at the University of Prague, resulting in Bohemia's treasured legacy as "The Cradle of the Reformation." The influence of England's first Bible translator can also be traced, indirectly, to the Florentine reformer, Girolamo Savonarola. Placed at the feet of Martin Luther, and at the side of Wycliffe and Hus on the monument to the Reformation at Worms, the converted Dominican monk was reached primarily through the ministry of the *Bohemian* Brethren.

With so much influence stemming from a solitary English translation during the primitive manuscript era, the coming of Gutenberg's moveable type was destined to "blow the doors off." While Luther called the art of printing "the last and best gift of Providence," the Catholic Roland Phillips frightfully remarked (in a sermon preached at St. Paul's Cross, London), "We must root out printing, or printing will root *us* out." Meanwhile, the Rotterdam scholar, Desiderius Erasmus, was busy with his own epoch-making contribution to the history of the English Bible, producing the first printed copy of the Greek New Testament in 1517. Luther would later employ the work of Erasmus in his translation of the German Bible, inspiring the adage, "Erasmus laid the egg and Luther hatched it."

John's letter to the Church at Sardis marks the end of the Dark Ages and catalogues the turbulent times of the PROTESTANT

REFORMATION (that *"name"* referred to in the opening verse). The battle that began with Luther's *95 Theses* continued for over a century, finally ending in 1648 with the Peace of Westphalia, which concluded the horrific Thirty Years War. Though "victorious," the Protestant forces constituted a "bloodied remnant" indeed. The slain on both sides numbered in the millions; the combined populations of Germany and Austria being reduced by at least one-half (some say by two-thirds). However, their *spiritual* losses were far more telling. While the Lord informed the Church at Sardis that *"thou livest,"* He was also quick to add, *"and art **dead**."* The most significant shortcoming of the Protestant Reformation is contained in the rebuke, *"for I have not found thy works **perfect** before God."* Though the Reformers did *some* "reforming" (by way of certain individual doctrines within a corrupt, unscriptural religious system), they never went far enough. By refusing to reject infant "baptism," for instance, the Protestant denominations would never be able to perpetuate a regenerate membership. As such, their "churches" were *"ready to die."*

The *Baptist* remnant in this period can be discerned in the words, *"Thou hast a few names even in Sardis which have not defiled their garments."* Called *Anabaptists* ("*re*-baptizers") by their enemies, a *"few"* of these *"names"* would include Balthasar Hubmaier, Felix Manz, Conrad Grebel, and Menno Simons. Our spiritual ancestors were no doubt the "bloodiest remnant" of all! Whereas the *Protestants* were attempting to break away from *Rome*, the *Baptists* were constantly persecuted by *both*. The Protestant decree at the Diet of Speyer in 1529 proclaimed: "All Anabaptists and rebaptized persons, male or female, of mature age, shall be judged and brought from natural life to death by fire, or sword, or otherwise, as may befit the persons." For the "crime" of immersing their converts, Baptist preachers were often specifically drowned, or as their "Christian" tormentors would say, *"permanently* immersed." While Balthasar Hubmaier was spared this indignity, *being burned at the stake* (his beard caked with sulfur and gunpowder), his courageous wife, Elizabeth, was not, being thrown from a bridge into the Danube with a stone around her neck three days later – *"and they shall walk with me in white: for they are worthy."* (Revelation 3:4)

PHILADELPHIA (AD 1611-1901)

We have now arrived at the most fruitful period in Church history (to be followed by the *worst* period). This is *the* Age that produces the greatest pastors, evangelists, missionaries, and soul winners of all time; and it is built upon a "flawed" *translation* of "inferior" *copies*. As nearly everyone knows, *Philadelphia* means "brotherly love." Named after Attalus II Philadelphus (its second-century BC founder), the connection to America's first capital is surreal. Three powerful themes are contained in this letter: the *word* that is kept; a *door* that is opened; and the *key* that is used. The Lord's specific commendation to the Church at Philadelphia was *"thou…hast kept my **word**"* (with a second reference, *"thou hast kept the **word** of my patience"*). Consequently, I have chosen to date this era from the A.V. 1611 to the arrival of the American Standard Version of 1901. To vindicate them for their fidelity to His word, the author Himself promised: *"I will make them of the **synagogue of Satan**…to come and worship before thy feet, and to know that I have loved thee."* We note that those ancient Alexandrians from the Smyrna period are shown to reappear *between* the two verses that mention God's word; but their efforts go nowhere in the Philadelphia Age. In *A Brief History of English Bible Translations*, Dr. Larry Vance highlights forty innocuous attempts at improving the Authorized Version before 1881.

However, while the subjects of King James *were* given the *right* Bible, they were *not* given the *right* to follow its precepts, *vis-à-vis* England's ironclad church-state relationship. Edward Wightman, a Baptist minister, was burned at the stake in 1612 for opposing infant baptism. One could say that the problem was genetic, for every Protestant nation was "its mother's daughter." The Roman Catholic Church is not only called a "HARLOT" (for committing fornication with the *kings* of the earth), but a *"MOTHER OF HARLOTS,"* as well. Post-Reformation Europe had become a continent of "little harlots." Thus, we perceive that the death count suffered by the Protestants in the Sardis period was a direct fulfillment of the promise Jesus made to Thyatira: *"And I will kill her children with death."* Thankfully, all of this was destined to change as the "Philadelphia" of Revelation 3:8 was on the *other* side of the "Great Pond."

In the fullness of time, America would become the final "enlargement of Japheth," providing mankind with the greatest exhibition of God's nation-building power in all of history (Genesis 9:27). While no "scholar" in his right mind could accept the thesis of my chapter, he would do well to check out a simple fifth-grade textbook on American history, for the widest "open door" in the annals of man's struggle for freedom of conscience was opened by the Bill of Rights to the United States Constitution – and the paperwork was finalized in a place called PHILADELPHIA. Over half-a-century earlier, the famous Anglican evangelist, George Whitefield, had seen the glorious day approaching, recording in his diary for November 28, 1739: "Blessed be God, for the great work begun in these parts. Oh, that what God says of the Church of Philadelphia in the Revelation, may be now fulfilled in the city called after her name! *'I know thy works: behold I have set before thee an open door, and no man can shut it.'*" (But, why pay any attention to what *that* guy thought? His preaching from the steps of the Philadelphia courthouse could "only" draw about 20,000 listeners when the city's entire population was *only* 14,000.)

The words *"thou hast a little strength"* reflect the little-known background that intensified the demand for a First Amendment. Like Bunyan of old, scores of Baptist ministers in Virginia chose jail rather than to accept a license to preach the Gospel. As "truth is stranger than fiction," congregations would literally assemble beneath the cell grates on Sunday morning so their pastors could preach to them. (This phenomenon was known as "denying the prison bounds.") The accumulating bad press and remonstrances of Patrick Henry, James Madison, George Washington, Thomas Jefferson, and other outraged Virginians eventually brought about those fateful words: "Congress shall make no law respecting an establishment of religion, or prohibiting the free exercise thereof." And so, 1,757 years after the Lord's *first* preachers were confronted by local authorities who *"laid hands on them, and put them in hold unto the next day,"* the dawn of a new era had *finally* arrived. Thanks to the words "freedom of speech," no American minister would be burned at the stake for preaching on the streets. And, owing to the "free press" clause, none would be burned for printing the Holy Bible, either. With those two divine safeguards in place, an army of Baptist soul-winners rushed through that Philadelphia door with hearts of "brotherly love" to obey the scriptural charge on the Liberty Bell (displayed in *Philadelphia's* Independence Hall) to *"proclaim liberty throughout all the land unto all the inhabitants thereof."* (Leviticus 25:10)

Finally, we note that the cross-reference to Revelation 3:7 is Isaiah 22:22: *"And the key of the house of David will I lay upon his shoulder; so he shall open, and none shall shut; and he shall shut, and none shall open."* The immediate context (as shown in the preceding verse) is millennial blessings on Israel, with the LORD declaring about Jesus (through Eliakim) that He will commit the *"government into his hand"* (Isaiah 9:7). The combined application, as taken from John's text, *"These things saith he that is holy, he that is true, he that hath the key of David,"* is that *the* KEY which opened the door to America's unparalleled religious liberty was a *JEWISH* KEY. Though *Plymouth* Rock may have been built on a *Geneva* Bible, it was a King *James* Bible that Andy Jackson pointed to when he exclaimed from his death bed – *"That Book, Sir, is 'The Rock' upon which our Republic rests."* The English name "James" is a transliteration of the Greek name *Jacobos*, which in turn is a transliteration of the Hebrew name *Yaakov* for "Jacob." The *"Jacobean* Age" refers to the period in English and Scottish history that coincides with the reign of King James I (1603-1625) of England who was also King James VI of Scotland, encompassing the style of architecture, visual arts, decorative arts, and literature that dominated the period. Thus, the

Key to America's unrivaled power would be a *"Jewish* Book" (authorized by a *Gentile* king with a *Hebrew* name) for – *"Where the word of a king is, there is power."* (Ecclesiastes 8:4)

America was destined to prosper *primarily* because Jehovah's covenant people would be drawn to her shores by the fledgling nation's unique policy of religious freedom. As the doctrine of "soul liberty" was brought to the New World by the Baptists, it is no coincidence that the oldest Jewish synagogue in America – Touro Synagogue of Congregation Jeshuat Israel in Newport, Rhode Island – "just happens" to be located *around the corner* from the first *Baptist* church in America (United Baptist Church, John Clarke Memorial).

Unlike the intolerant monarchical policies of Old World Europe, America would be a nation of written laws. While Thomas Hooker observed that "the law is not subject to passion," Thomas Jefferson's remedy for tyrants was to "bind them down with the chains of the Constitution." It is believed by some that William Penn, who came to America with a friend named *Key*, said that "by the use of the *Key* and *Pen*, the Everlasting Kingdom of God would be set up and triumph over all opposition." We marvel that the state of Pennsylvania was founded by that *"Pen"* with *Philadelphia* as its capital. And though the Kingdom would not materialize here, America's critical support for the newly formed State of Israel in 1948 would certainly keep the prophetic clock ticking. And, as *twelve* is the Bible number for Israel, we note that there are *twelve* letters in PHILADELPHIA.

That *"key of David"* would have been the first truth that greeted the waves of European immigrants as they passed by the Statue of Liberty; for those immortal lines, "Give me your tired, your poor, your huddled masses…," were written by a young *Jewess*, Emma Lazarus. And, of course, there would *never have been* a Statue of Liberty without a Revolution in the first place. Unbeknown to most, a core of patriotic Jewish businessmen actually helped to precipitate the conflict. On October 25, 1765, no less than eight Jewish merchants threw potential profits to the wind by affixing their signatures to the incendiary Non-Importation Agreement aimed squarely at Great Britain. They were Benjamin Levy, Samson Levy, Joseph Jacobs, Hyman Levy, Jr., David Franks, Michael Gratz, and, get this – a *Moses* Mordecai *and* a Mathias *Bush*. By the way, that agreement was signed in PHILADELPHIA.

But then, Lady Liberty *never would have arrived* if General Washington hadn't prevailed. And General Washington *never would have prevailed* had it not been for that "Jewish Key" – the generosity of a single Hebrew benefactor, Haym Salomon, who practically bankrolled the entire war, advancing Congress the incredible sum of $658,007.13. Anti-Semitic kooks like Texe Marrs are referred to the U.S. Postal Service, which in 1975 issued a commemorative stamp in Salomon's honor, stating on the reverse side: "Financial hero—Businessman and broker Haym Salomon was responsible for raising most of the money needed to finance the American Revolution and later to save the new nation from collapse." In 1941, the city of Chicago erected a statue in Salomon's honor, positioning him to the left of George Washington (with Treasury Secretary Robert Morris to the president's right). The inscription reads: "Haym Solomon – Gentleman, Scholar, Patriot. A Banker whose only *interest* was the *interest* of his Country." This must surely have been the case; for less than two years after the Treaty of Paris, America's banker of providence succumbed to tuberculosis at the age of forty-five, dying *penniless* on January 6, 1785. He was buried by his Hebrew congregation in the Mikveh Israel cemetery in PHILADELPHIA.

LAODICEA (AD 1901-?)

The name *Laodicea* means "rights of the people," or "civil rights." Whereas the Church of the "*Open* Door" is easily discerned against the historical backdrop of the Bill of Rights, the Church of the "*Closed* Door" is equally conspicuous, being defined by the modern age of unprecedented materialism. Our Lord's specific indictment against Laodicea – *"thou sayest, I am **rich**, and increased* *with **goods**"* – mandates an exclusive application to the twentieth and twenty-first centuries. Bunyan's "Vanity Fair" could not begin to compare with the mega-mall mentality of American shopaholics; buying things they *don't* need, with money they *don't* have, to impress people they *don't* like. Our present "culture of entitlement" was forecast and recorded 2,000 years ago through the name *Laodicea* – "*RIGHTS* OF THE PEOPLE."

As the Philadelphia Church Age began with the 1611 Authorized Version, the Laodicean Age can be dated from the American Standard Version of 1901. The ASV was the American facsimile of Britain's corrupt Revised Version of 1881. As noted in the introduction to this book, the advent of "*dual* authority" signaled a repudiation of "*final* authority," for our Lord declared: *"No man can serve **two** masters."* The competing authority will *always* be money: *"Ye cannot serve God and **mammon**."* (Matthew 6:24) Hence, Laodicea's distraction with "things" results in her unmistakable profile as *"**lukewarm**, and neither cold nor hot,"* having one eye on the Church and one eye on the World. As lukewarm water is used to induce vomiting, the lovely Lord Jesus adds: *"I will **spue** thee out of my mouth."* (Revelation 3:16)

We discern, therefore, that the current unparalleled variety of "Bibles" just happens to coincide with an unparalleled age of materialism – which brings us full circle as to the part this chapter plays in the thesis of my book. It has been said that there are three groups of people in the world: the first group *makes* things happen; the second group *watches* things happen; while the third group *doesn't know* what's happening. The average Baptist of today appears to be in group three. The King James Bible is under attack because the majority of professing Christians are *Laodicean* in temperament: *"Having a form of godliness, but denying the power thereof."* (II Timothy 3:5) Because *"no man can serve two masters,"* the person who chooses to sell out for materialism becomes incapable of submission to God. He who woefully succumbs to the *"care of this world, and the deceitfulness of riches"* could *not* submit to God if he *wanted* to, as *"No man can serve two masters."*

(Matthew 13:22) Because the rich young rulers of our day have become spiritually incapacitated, they will not embrace a Bible that lays exclusive claim to the English-speaking world. Instead, they will take cover behind the assurances of "Christian" scholarship that one conscientious translation is as good as the next. They will embrace *anything* but a dreaded submission to *one* book.

The Laodicean apostasy is also the main cause for the decline of American liberties in general. God's formula for freedom has always been simple: To whatever degree the local New Testament Church would keep the *word*, the Lord would keep the *door*. Obviously, Laodicea has a problem, as Jesus is depicted standing on the *wrong* side of a *closed* door. In the Philadelphia Age, *He* sends the *Christians* out; in Laodicea, *they* keep *Him* out! The salutation to Laodicea is the only text that reads, *"And unto the angel of the church OF THE LAODICEANS"* (i.e., as opposed to *"in* Laodicea"). So, why should a Bible believer be surprised when Fundamentalists "crawfish" around the inspiration issue? The Holy Spirit has already confirmed that the average Christian in Laodicea would be *spiritually* blind: *"Because thou sayest, I am rich, and increased with goods, and have need of nothing; and knowest not that thou art wretched, and miserable, and poor, and BLIND, and naked."* What a contrast to John's description of the Church in Smyrna: *"I know thy works, and tribulation, and poverty, (but thou art rich)."* One church is poor, but *actually* rich; the other is rich, but *actually* poor. Thus, the Lord counsels Laodicea to *"anoint thine eyes with eyesalve, that thou mayest see."* In New Testament times, the city of Laodicea was a wealthy community, boasting a prestigious medical school with a renowned ophthalmologist in residence. The region's second-most widely exported product was an eye salve (collyrium) known as "Phrygian Powder."

Perhaps the greatest illustration of spiritual blindness in our day concerns former Alabama Chief Justice Roy Moore and the infamous removal of his Ten Commandments monument from the State Judicial Building on August 26, 2003. The attendant imagery is powerful. As Laodicea means "civil rights," we marvel that the

Dexter Avenue King Memorial Baptist Church (Martin Luther King's former pastorate) is located just 0.13 of a mile from the site of the Ten Commandments travesty. However, there is something far more portentous here. The text on Judge Moore's monument was taken from the King James Bible. *It does not match the wording in the Bibles used in Judge Moore's Southern Baptist Church.* Before the Ten Commandments were ever yanked out of Judge Moore's *court* house, they were yanked out of Judge Moore's *church* house. Now *that's* blindness!

MY FAVORITE OUTLINE

Given By Inspiration is an *eleventh*-hour clarion call for Baptists to acquaint themselves with the Bible they profess to believe and presume to defend. An important subliminal theme that will permeate this book is the untapped power of the English text. For instance, while the foregoing material should have been spiritually stimulating (especially in light of Revelation 1:3), there is *far* more than meets the eye. The prophetic content of the *"seven churches which are in Asia"* can be gleaned through other scriptural means, as well. In his monumental work, *Dispensational Truth*, Clarence Larkin developed an elaborate chart integrating the seven churches with the Kingdom of Heaven parables in Matthew 13:1-50. Another outline based on numerology would be as follows: ONE = Unity: The phrase "one accord" appears numerous times in Acts, characterizing the Apostolic Age; TWO = Division: The Apostolic Age is divided from Church history proper (final link severed with death of Polycarp); THREE = Trinity: church, state, and Satan; FOUR = Earth: *"that great city, which reigneth over the kings of the earth"*; FIVE = Death: *"and art dead"*; SIX = Man: "Brotherly Love"; SEVEN = Completeness: *"After this I looked, and, behold, a door was opened in heaven."*

However, my personal favorite is the amazing correlation between the seven churches and the first seven books of the Bible:

EPHESUS .... Left First Love...Fallen
GENESIS .... Adam and Eve Fell

SMYRNA .... Persecution under Rome
EXODUS .... Persecution under Egypt

PERGAMOS .... Religious State under Constantine
LEVITICUS .... Theocracy under Jehovah

THYATIRA .... Judgment in Europe
NUMBERS .... Judgment in the Wilderness

SARDIS .... Remnant from Reformation
DEUTERONOMY .... Remnant from Wandering

PHILADELPHIA .... Spiritual Conquest
JOSHUA .... Spiritual Conquest

LAODICEA .... Spiritual Apostasy
JUDGES .... Spiritual Apostasy

The spiritual value in the preceding outline is related to a well-established maxim in Bible study: The Old Testament is the New Testament *concealed*; the New Testament is the Old Testament *revealed*. This simply means that many Church Age doctrines are often illustrated in Old Testament stories and events. For instance, Enoch is a type of the Rapture, while Noah pictures Israel in the Tribulation. Thus, Paul writes: *"For whatsoever things were written aforetime were written for our learning."* (Romans 15:4) Applying this principle to our study, the book of Judges will uniquely illustrate numerous truths that pertain to the Laodicean Church Age. As modern Christianity repudiates the **King** James Bible, the *last* verse in Judges says, *"In those days there was no **king** in Israel."* The last Judge dies *blind*, so don't miss that *last* word in the book:

"...every man did that which was right in his own EYES."

(JUDGES 21:25)

3

No King in the Land

ILES SMITH WROTE in the Preface of the A.V. 1611 (also known as "The Translators to the Reader"), "Translation it is that openeth the window, to let in the light, that breaketh the shell, that we may eat the kernel; that putteth aside the curtain, that we may look into the most Holy place; that removeth the cover of the well, that we may come by the water." Charles Spurgeon, known as the "Prince of Preachers," would often say, "Illustrations are the windows into our sermons." Matthew 6:22 teaches that the eye is the window into a man's soul. When we want to catch a glimpse of our coming Saviour, we peer through the "lattice" of God's word (Song of Solomon 2:9). Similarly, the Book of Judges is the Bible's unique prophetic window into the Laodicean Church Age. As *Laodicea* means "**rights** of the people," the key verse of the book states that *"every man did that which was **right** in his own eyes."* (Judges 21:25) The major types of this chaotic period can be figuratively viewed through the "lattice" in Sisera's house (Judges 5:28).

The spiritual conquests recorded in the *sixth* book of the Bible revolve around a central *human* authority, Joshua, the son of Nun. (As *six* is the number of *man*, Joshua is the first book named after a *man* and spelled with *six* letters.) The Lord had specifically promised him: *"Every place that the sole of **your** foot shall tread upon, that have I given unto **you**, as I said unto Moses."* (Joshua 1:3) However, there would be no question that all subsequent gains would be tied to the *word* of Joshua's God: *"This **book of the law** shall not depart* *out of thy mouth; but thou shalt meditate therein day and night, that thou mayest observe to do according to all that is written therein: for then thou shalt make thy way prosperous, and then thou shalt have good success.* " (Joshua 1:8) Likewise, the victories in the Philadelphia Age would be attributed to the Lord's commendation – *"thou...hast kept my word."* Thus, we read the telling account: *"And the people served the LORD **all the days of Joshua.**"* (Judges 2:7) Israel's problems were destined to begin *after* Joshua's departure; and, just as the bridge to the Apostolic Age did not totally close until the deaths of John's last surviving converts (Ignatius and Polycarp), the Holy Spirit adds the clarifier: *"**and** all the days of the **elders that outlived Joshua**, who had seen all the great works of the LORD, that he did for Israel."*

The nineteenth and twentieth centuries divide as perfect antitypes of Joshua and Judges. Before the arrival of the American Standard Version in 1901, God's men were able to minister effectively with a central authority, the A.V. 1611. However, with the passing of "Joshua" (i.e., the age of a central *written* authority), pragmatic Laodiceans placed Jesus "outside the *Church*" so they could start thinking "outside the *box*." The greatest application of an elder who outlived "Joshua" was the influential Baptist pastor, Dr. J. Frank Norris, whose ministry spanned both periods of Church history.

Born in 1877, Dr. Norris was well acquainted with the power of the Philadelphia Church Age. Back then, there was no question in anyone's mind that the results were being produced *solely* by the King James Bible. The man known as "The Texas Tornado" didn't pastor the two largest churches in America *simultaneously* (First Baptist in Fort Worth and Temple Baptist in Detroit) by using a carnal, "Joel Osteen" approach ("Your Best Life Now," etc.). He did it by *losing* "his best life now" through the power of a King James Bible, stating: "What is needed is a school that teaches the whole English Bible....What is needed is a school that will teach a man how to go out with the Bible under his arm, faith in his heart, and in the power of the Holy Spirit begin in a vacant lot and build a church to the glory of God." (And we all know that he wasn't talking about a bunch of nonexistent original manuscripts in a language that no one could read.)

As Dr. Norris had helped stem the tide of iniquity from the "Roarin' Twenties" to the "Rockin' Fifties" (including numerous assaults on "Hell's Half Acre," Fort Worth's infamous haunt of desperadoes like Butch Cassidy and the Sundance Kid), his death in 1952 marked *the* spiritual watershed of the century. Hell's *fullest* fury would now be unleashed on America's churches. The "last days" of the "last days" had finally arrived (II Timothy 3:1). Although many spiritual pastors were still on the scene, Dr. Norris had been one of the remaining titans *"who had seen all the great works of the LORD, that he did for Israel."* (In 1999, *The City's Magazine* of Fort Worth declared, "A true hellfire and damnation preacher, J. Frank Norris could easily be called the most controversial man who ever lived in Fort Worth.")

And so, with the passing of Dr. Norris, the lingering effects of the Philadelphia Church Age faded away, as well. As if to mark the occasion, the apostate National Council of Churches published their blasphemous Revised Standard Version that very year. (Zondervan would mark the 400th anniversary of the A.V. 1611 by releasing their perverted revision of the New International Version; the first complete update of the NIV since 1984.) Other foreboding "highlights" of 1952 would include the world's first gender-change operation (in Denmark); the United Nations taking up their permanent residence in New York City; Norman Vincent Peale publishing *The Power of Positive Thinking*; and, dope-head Hank Williams releasing his all-time classic, "Your Cheatin' Heart."

As noted, the Devil's prototype of "delayed action" occurred fifteen centuries earlier: *"And Joshua...died...and they buried him... And also all that generation were gathered unto their fathers: and there arose another generation after them, which knew not the LORD, nor yet the works which he had done for Israel."* (Judges 2:8-10) The very next verse reads: *"And the children of Israel did evil in the sight of the LORD, and served Baalim: **And they forsook the LORD God of their fathers.**"* Thus, what you read in the book of Judges is what you are surrounded by in the closing days of Laodicea. *And it has **everything** to do with why your King James Bible is under attack.* While there are nine direct references to "the word" (or words) of God in *Joshua*, there is but one *indirect* reference in *Judges* (a "word" from the angel of the Lord). Furthermore, the phrase *"In those days there was no king in Israel"* appears three times in Judges (18:1; 19:1; and 21:25). As the *seventh* book of the Bible, Judges represents the final apostasy that *completes* the Church Age. Consequently, the book records *seven* apostasies, *seven* servitudes to *seven* heathen nations, and *seven* deliverances. (Brother Lester Roloff used to say, "The Church in the last days is just a mop-up crew.") And, as *thirteen* is God's number for sin and rebellion, there are *thirteen* judges, with the birth of the *thirteenth* judge (Samson) recorded in chapter *thirteen*.

IDOLATRY

There are at least *seven* sins in the Book of Judges that apply to the spiritual declension of Laodicea. The *first*, as mentioned above, was the gross sin of *idolatry*. Judges 10:6 lists *seven* gods, or groups of gods, worshiped by Jehovah's covenant people: *"And the children of Israel did evil again in the sight of the LORD, and served Baalim, and Ashtaroth, and the gods of Syria, and the gods of Zidon, and the gods of Moab, and the gods of the children of Ammon, and the gods of the Philistines, and forsook the LORD, and served not him."* In spoiled America, the Lord also takes a back seat to a unique pantheon of modern "gods": cell phones; iPods; McDonald's; video games; *Facebook*; blue jeans; and let's not forget good ol' "Wally-World" (a.k.a. "All things Chinese" – Revelation 16:12). As the King James Bible declares in I Timothy 6:10, *"For the love of money is **the** root of **all evil**,"* the text has been corrupted in every English version on the planet (e.g., "For the love of money is **a** root of **all kinds** of evil" – NIV).

COMPROMISE

The *second* sin of this period is related to the first – a lucre-driven *hireling ministry*. Judges devotes nearly two chapters to a bizarre story about a wandering Levite who is hired to be the personal priest of a man named Micah. As the young man was looking for "a place," Micah says, *"Dwell with me, and be unto me a **father** and a **priest**, and I will give thee **ten** shekels of silver by the year, and a suit of apparel, and thy victuals"* (the number *ten* being another prophetic reference to the Gentile Age, as noted in Acts 14:27). The verse concludes, *"So the Levite went in."* (The roots of the pagan Roman Catholic priesthood are discerned by the proximity of the words **father** and **priest**, proscribed in Matthew 23:9, not to mention Micah's garage full of graven images). We then read the shocking words: *"And Micah consecrated the Levite; and the young man became **his priest**, and was in the house of Micah."* (Judges 17:10, 12) However, in the following chapter, a band of Danites searching for a homestead drop in on "Father Jonathan" and "make him an offer he can't refuse." With 600 armed men outside, the "negotiator" says, *"Hold thy peace, lay thine hand upon thy mouth, and go with us, and be to us a father and a priest: is it better for thee to be a priest unto the house of one man, or that thou be a priest unto a tribe and a family in Israel?"* With Micah away at the moment, his hireling takes a powder: *"And the priest's heart was glad, and he took the ephod, and the teraphim, and the graven image, and went in the midst of the people. So they turned and departed."* (Judges 18:19-21)

Many pastors in Laodicea share a similar experience with the Levite in our story. Armed with intimidating financial clout, today's affluent parishioners have reduced their *pulpit* ministries to *puppet* ministries. In dramatic fulfillment of Paul's departing admonition, *preachers* proclaiming sound doctrine have been replaced by *teachers* sharing fables (II Timothy 4:1-6). There is also a profound application to the logic behind the Levite's decision for the better "place." Paul warned preachers about *"perverse disputings of men of* *corrupt minds, and destitute of the truth, **supposing that gain is godliness.*** " (I Timothy 6:5) Influenced by "Japhethic genes," as per Genesis 9:27, the mindset of Laodicea is – "Bigger is better" – thus, the trend to pragmatism; growth at *any* cost (e.g., *The Purpose **Driven** Church*).

Then, just when I thought I had seen *everything*, a preacher friend sent me a copy of a promotional flyer from an independent Baptist church in Florida. Under a color picture of Dr. Martin Luther King, Jr., waving to the masses at the Lincoln Mall (August 28, 1963), the following statement appears: "This Sunday, August 29, 2010, at 11 am we welcome you to hear _____ recite Martin Luther King Jr.'s, 'I Have A Dream' speech during our morning service. A gift will be given to all who attend as we honor the life of Dr. King. An original copy of the Chicago Tribune from the morning after Dr. Kings (sic) assassination will be awarded to the person with the most visitors in the service. Make plans to be with us!"

JEALOUSY

The *third* sin in Judges is likened to the second – *jealousy*, especially in the ministry. On two separate occasions, Gideon and Jephthah were hindered by the men of Ephraim while attempting to deliver Israel from their oppressors. In both instances, the Ephraimites feigned righteous indignation over not being invited to join the campaign. Preachers who buy into the "bigger is better" mentality will often succumb to a spirit of jealousy when unwisely *"comparing themselves among themselves."* (II Corinthians 10:12) Laodiceans have it all backward, *"supposing that **gain** is **godliness**,"* when the *true* formula for success is, *"**godliness** with **contentment** is great **gain**."* (I Timothy 6:5-6) "Just" *two* verses are devoted to a judge named Tola; about the only thing we know about him was that he was *"the son of Dodo."* The same would apply to other lesser-known, though faithful, judges such as Jair, Ibzan, Elon, and Abdon. We can all take comfort in the promise of Hebrews 6:10 – *"For God is not unrighteous to forget your work and labour of love, which ye have* *shewed toward his name, in that ye have ministered to the saints, and do minister."*

INTIMIDATION

The *fourth* problem area is also a result of the preceding issues – *intimidation*. With occupying forces coming and going for over three centuries, many of the Jews had developed PPS (*Perennial Paranoia Syndrome*). Even Gideon was a little shaky on his trial mission to destroy his father's groves (Judges 6:27). When preparing for the Midianite campaign, he instructed his assembled army of 32,000 men: *"Whosoever is **fearful** and **afraid**, let him return and depart early from Mount Gilead."* (Judges 7:3; Deuteronomy 20:8) When the dust settled, "General Gideon" got the shock of his life, as a throng of *22,000* had taken him up on his offer. Similarly, the average Christian in Laodicea is like the typical American citizen – *scared of his own shadow*. Political correctness rules the day, and rare is the believer who is willing to tell the proverbial emperor that he's "naked." While a slip of the "N" word can bring the death penalty, "Oh, my G-d!" has become the most popular cliché in American culture (Exodus 20:7). The problem is that boldness is a by-product of holiness, a spiritual trait that is woefully lacking in our time. *"The wicked flee when no man pursueth: but the righteous are bold as a lion."* (Proverbs 28:1) From issues ranging from *Romanism* to *racism*, *"The fear of man bringeth a snare,"* while *"The fear of the LORD prolongeth days."* (Proverbs 10:27; 29:25)

IMMORALITY

The *fifth* sin is the so-called "scarlet sin" of *immorality* (Isaiah 1:18; Proverbs 6:32-33; I Corinthians 6:18). In 1850, Nathaniel Hawthorne published *The Scarlet Letter*, an explosive novel revolving around the adulterous relationship of Hester Prynne and the esteemed minister, Reverend Mr. Arthur Dimmesdale. The fallen pastor asks, "What can a ruined soul, like mine, effect towards the redemption of other souls?" After describing the agony of standing in his pulpit and seeing the naïve admiration of his flock, he groans, "I have laughed, in bitterness and agony of heart, at the contrast between what I seem and what I am! And Satan laughs at it!" Judges 16:25 reads: *"And it came to pass, when their hearts were merry, that they said, Call for Samson, that he may make us **sport**. And they called for Samson out of the prison house; and he made them **sport**: and they set him between the pillars."*

Tragically, the man about whom it was said, more than any other Old Testament character, *"The spirit of the LORD came upon him,"* was reduced to the sad state of affairs described in Judges 16:21: *"But the Philistines took him, and put out his **eyes**, and **brought him down** to Gaza, and **bound** him with fetters of brass; and he did **grind** in the prison house."* Thus, we have the well- known sermon outline: "Sin *blinds*, Sin *binds,* and Sin *grinds*." As Proverbs 6:26 reads, *"For by means of a whorish woman a man **is brought** to a piece of **bread**,"* it is not without significance that Samson "is brought" to a prison to grind *meal*, the hardest and lowest kind of slave labor. (Exodus 11:5) What a marked contrast to Ignatius as the "wheat of Christ." And, as Samson was probably naked in his ordeal, he would have perfected the Laodicean type – *"wretched, and miserable, and poor, and blind, and naked."*

When the *thirteenth* judge, with *six* letters in his name, loses his *seven* locks of hair – the Church Age is just about *complete* (Judges 16:19). As Proverbs 7:27 says of the strange woman: *"Her **house** is the way to hell, going **down** to the chambers of death,"* it was fitting that Samson "brought the house down," killing more of God's enemies in his death than in his life (Judges16:30). Many years later, Samson's epitaph would be penned by another vanquished womanizer – *"many **strong** men have been slain by her."* (Proverbs 7:26) So, do we *really* need to dredge up the numerous moral failures of our time, particularly in the ministry? Suffice it to say that the "standard" immorality of the Bakker and Swaggart era has not caused half the reproach that the growing sodomite phenomenon has, epitomized by Charismatic weirdos like Ted Haggard. (And, can you *even* imagine how many times you were blessed by the songs, "Thank You for Giving to the Lord," "The Anchor Holds," and "I Pledge Allegiance to the Lamb," before you found out they were written by another "Christian twinkie"?)

FEMINISM

Number *six* represents a major reflection of God's disfavor with Israel in general. The ultimate degradation for any culture was given in Isaiah 3:12 – *"As for my people, children are their oppressors, and **women rule over them**."* In *our* time it is Sandra Day O'Connor; Ruth Bader Ginsburg; Sonia Sotomayor; Elena Kagan; "Judge Judy"; Michelle Obama; Hillary Rodham Clinton; Nancy Pelosi; Barbara Boxer; Dianne Feinstein; Jennifer Granholm; Condoleezza Rice; and, *especially*, Sarah "You Betcha!" Palin – darling of the Tea Party movement and self-proclaimed leader of the up-and-coming "Mama Grizzlies." (The unprecedented slate of *female* Republicans in the 2010 election – more accurately reflecting a *"Ladies'* Tea" movement – signaled an ominous repudiation of Proverbs 31:3, *"Give not thy strength unto **women**."*) The obvious rub comes from Genesis 3:16, where the first woman was told in no uncertain terms – *"thy desire shall be to thy husband, and **he shall rule over thee**."* Then, out of nowhere we read: *"And Deborah, a **prophetess**, the **wife** of Lapidoth, **she** judged Israel at that time...and the children of Israel came up to **her** for judgment."* (Judges 4:4-5) While it was specifically said of the first two judges that the Lord "raised them up," the Holy Spirit simply says of Deborah that *"**she** judged Israel at that time."*

One of the greatest sins of the last days is the abomination of "Christian feminism," the *"silly women"* of II Timothy 3:6. Deborah is the major type of this unscriptural practice of female leadership in the work of God. In New Testament times, Christian women were not even permitted to ask questions in public service, much less assert visible authority in the same. (While the context in I Corinthians 14:34 is tongues, that was *not* the case in I Timothy 2:11-12: *"Let the woman* *learn in silence with all subjection. But I suffer not a woman to **teach**, nor to usurp **authority** over the man, but to be in silence."*)

There are several long *overdue* observations to make regarding Deborah, Barak, and Jael. To begin, the case is often made that Barak was a wimp, based on his insistence that Deborah join the expedition. I beg to differ. The name BARAK means "thunder bolt" or "lightning." (Politics aside, Israel's greatest living commando is former Prime Minister Ehud BARAK, who led several highly acclaimed missions and was the chief architect of the famed July 4, 1976, "Operation Entebbe.") As a seasoned warrior, what possible military advantage could Barak have hoped to gain by Deborah's presence on the battlefield? There are at least two explanations to consider. If he had doubted Deborah's legitimacy, he would have naturally called her hand on the matter (i.e., "I'm right behind ya'"). On the other hand, if he *did* believe in her divine appointment, he might have felt that her visible presence would have enhanced God's favor on the operation. Thus, the worst-case scenario would have been Barak's desire to cover all the bases. I repeat, as Judges 9:54 illustrates, no normal, red-blooded alpha male of antiquity would have gone on record desiring the military prowess of *any* woman. (The *Boadiceas* of history are merely the exceptions that prove the rule.)

Then, we have the prophetic record to evaluate. Deborah appears to have been fixated by "honor." Besides holding court under a tree named "Deborah," her "Song of *Deborah* and Barak" is a little heavy on the narcissistic side (Judges 4:5; 5:7). Her attempt at intimating Barak with the prophecy, *"notwithstanding the journey that thou takest shall **not** be for **thine honour**,"* assumes that he was motivated by personal glory. (Judges 4:9) However, the story shows otherwise. Having seen that the "Big Kahuna" had *"lighted down off **his** chariot and fled away on his feet,"* the Bible says, *"**But** Barak pursued after **the chariots**."* (Judges 4:15-16) The "honor" connected with killing the fugitive in that *single* chariot was not *nearly* as important as stopping those other *899* chariots of iron that threatened the security of his fellow countrymen! If Barak *was* a "wimp," at least he was able to accomplish what the entire tribe of Judah could not

(Judges 1:19). And besides, as things turned out, the *Lord* got the credit: *"So **God** subdued on that day Jabin the king of Canaan before the children of Israel."* (Judges 4:23)

Deborah's second prophecy was that Sisera would be done in by a woman. Her third prediction concerned the heroine herself, a gal named Jael (meaning "wild she-goat"). For one thing, Jael and her Midianite husband, Heber, had been in cahoots with King Jabin for several years (Judges 4:17). Consequently, Jael's nail was just the smart move, considering what Barak would have done had she been found harboring the hated enemy commander. Notwithstanding, Deborah prognosticated: *"Blessed above women shall Jael the wife of Heber the Kenite be."* (Judges 5:24)

So, how did Deborah the "prophetess" do? Well, Sisera *definitely* got "hammered" by a woman (constituting a type of Christ's *warrior* Bride at Armageddon, described in Song of Solomon 6:10 as *"an army with banners"*). However, with regard to that "shoo-in legacy," most people are a tad more familiar with *Mary*, the "mother of Jesus," than with *Jael*, the "wild she-goat" – Elisabeth declaring to Joseph's wife, *"**Blessed art thou among women**, and blessed is the fruit of thy womb."* (Luke 1:42) And with regard to Barak losing his honor, remember that God always writes the last chapter, or, as Paul put it: *"**JUDGE** nothing before the time."* (I Corinthians 4:5) The Holy Ghost set the record straight in Hebrews 11:32 – *"And what shall I more say? for the time would fail me to tell of Gedeon, and of **BARAK**, and of Samson, and of Jephthae."* While Barak exhibited enough *faith* to be inducted into the Hebrews 11 "Hall of Fame" (e.g., taking on those chariots of iron), his two female antagonists were no-shows and also-rans. *"When a prophet speaketh in the name of the Lord, if the thing follow not, nor come to pass, that is the thing which the Lord hath not spoken, but the prophet hath spoken **presumptuously**."* (Deuteronomy 18:22)

Perhaps the best illustration of the feminism projected in the Book of Judges would be the city of Gideon's birth and final resting place. As the name of this city appears *five* times in Judges ("five" being the number for death), we are not surprised that the place literally flowed with blood. While Gideon is considered to be the greatest of the judges, his offspring did not fare as well. For some strange reason, Gideon celebrated his victory over the Midianites by erecting a golden ephod in this city – *"and all Israel went thither a whoring after it: which thing became a snare unto Gideon, and to his house."* (Judges 8:27) Gideon's "house" consisted of *"threescore and ten sons of his body begotten: for he had many wives,"* and at least one other son from *"his concubine that was in Shechem."* (Judges 8:30-31) After Gideon's death, number "71" made Emperor Constantine look like an amateur. In a horrific bid for power, Abimelech forms a conspiracy with his mother's people and slays 69 of his half-brothers in the city in question; only one sibling survives the slaughter, Jotham, the youngest. Three years after this ghastly fratricide, Abimelech is himself overthrown and assassinated.

Now, an indirect, tongue-in-cheek connection of this city to the reigning "Queen of Feminism" in America is uncanny. According to Oprah Winfrey, she was supposed to have been named after the Bible character *Orpah* (Ruth's sister-in-law), but the name was misspelled on the birth certificate. As one spelling mistake is as "good" as another, *we* recognize that adding the letter "h" (as in HELL) makes the *better* spelling, for the *hellish* philosophy of "Oprah" was forecast in the Book of Judges over 3,200 years ago. Thus, she is more "accurately" misnamed after a *place*: *"And he went unto his father's house at* OPHRAH, *and slew his brethren."* (Judges 9:5) *"'O' – my* G-d!"

DECEPTION

There are many strange accounts in the book of Judges to be sure. Even the detailed Scofield Reference Bible had a difficult time outlining all the chaos, relegating the last five chapters of the book to the singular heading: *"Confusion, civil and religious."* As the Bible says, *"For God is not the author of confusion,"* we know that Satan was running full throttle during this period. (I Corinthians 14:33) For instance, in one of the wilder stories, several thousand men lose their lives for mispronouncing a *single* word. The incident involves the second jealousy of the Ephraimites. Having accosted Gideon for slighting their services in his campaign against the Midianites, they pull the same routine on Jephthah following his victory over the Ammonites. *"Wherefore passedst thou over to fight against the children of Ammon, and didst not call us to go with thee?"* They then inform Jephthah: *"we will **burn** thine house upon thee with fire."* (Judges 12:1) This particular threat would have been especially painful in view of Jephthah's awful vow to offer up his daughter *"for a **burnt** offering."* (Judges 11:31)

In any event, the Lord decides it's time to take Ephraim to the woodshed: *"Then Jephthah gathered together all the men of Gilead, and fought with Ephraim: and the men of Gilead smote Ephraim."* (Judges 12:4) As the battle appears to have been fought in Gilead, the retreating Ephraimites had to pass back over the Jordan to make it home safely. However, Jephthah's men gained the advantage, as *"the Gileadites took the passages of Jordan before the Ephraimites."* (Judges 12:5) WHAT HAPPENED NEXT HAS A VITAL APPLICATION TO *EVERY* FUNDAMENTAL BIBLE COLLEGE IN AMERICA – *"and it was so, that when those Ephraimites which were escaped said, Let me go over; that the men of Gilead said unto him, Art thou an Ephraimite? If he said, Nay; Then said they unto him, Say now **Shibboleth**: and he said **Sibboleth**: for he could not frame to pronounce it right. Then they took him, and slew him at the passages of Jordan: and there fell at that time of the Ephraimites forty and two thousand."* (Judges 12:5-6) Even if this figure should represent *all* of the slain in the campaign, *including* those killed at the Jordan, the reality remains that *thousands* of soldiers perished with a lie upon their lips; or, as Luther wrote, "One little word shall fell him."

The *seventh*, and final, sin of our survey is *deception*. The application for the Bible believer in Laodicea should be obvious – stuttering *Ephraimites* trying to pass themselves off as *Gileadites*. Just because someone *says* they "believe" (or "use") the King James Bible means absolutely nothing. The entire next chapter will deal with that all-important password – *Shibboleth*, but before we go, the following story will serve as a fitting conclusion to the consequences of spiritual anarchy.

"The Sinister Minister"

As previously noted, the book of Judges covers some pretty *far out* material. While Abimelech slays 69 of his half-brothers, as many as 42,000 other men are slaughtered over a three-syllable word. And then, there is the tragic story of Jephthah and his daughter. Though not the most popular view, there is no reason to believe that Jephthah did not fulfill his vow in the literal sense (Judges 11:31-39). Such are the consequences of *"no king in the land."* And, as if all this carnage was not enough, the Holy Spirit apparently saved the "best" for last. The key incident involving the closing two chapters of the book was *so* insane that the writer states that *"it was so, that all that saw it said, There was no such deed done nor seen from the day that the children of Israel came up out of the land of Egypt unto this day."* (Judges 19:30)

To make a long story short, a certain Levite was journeying with his concubine and servant when an elderly stranger in Gibeah gave them lodging for the night. Before long, a mob of sodomites surround the house intent on assaulting the male guests. However, the Levite's concubine is offered in exchange and is subsequently violated throughout the night. The next morning the woman is found dead on the doorstep. Her worthless "husband" then puts her lifeless body on his donkey and returns home to Ephraim. Upon his arrival, he cuts the corpse into twelve parts, sending a piece to each of the twelve tribes in a demand for justice. As a result of this macabre action, the Israelites assemble and march against the men of Benjamin (the atrocity having occurred within their borders). In the ensuing genocide, nearly the entire tribe of Benjamin is wiped out. (Judges 21:3)

According to the theme of this chapter, the book of Judges is a precursor to the Laodicean Age. During my five years as a student at Hyles-Anderson College, one faculty member remained in a class by himself. Joe Combs was without a doubt the most popular teacher in the school. (What we didn't know at the time was that much of his lecture material was not his own.) *He was also the most outspoken critic of the King James Bible on campus.* For instance, he loved to harp on the italicized words in Psalm 14:1, telling us that the *correct* reading should be, "The fool has said in his heart, NO, God." In the course of events, I became his main assistant, doing everything from grading test papers to washing his car and even grocery shopping for his wife, Evangeline. Stranger yet, when I later became a teacher at Hyles-Anderson myself (1986), Combs was just leaving, and I distinctly remember him cornering me over "Dr. Hyles' nutty *new* position on the King James Bible issue," etc. After leaving the school, Joe eventually wound up in Bristol, Tennessee, pastoring a small church. (By then, their family had grown to six children, four biological and two adopted.)

On March 24, 2000, the Fundamentalist world was shocked as "Brother" Combs and his wife were sentenced to *179 years* behind bars for the horrific crime of *torturing their adopted daughter, Esther, for nearly two decades.* My favorite Bible teacher received 114 years for a litany of offenses, including aggravated kidnapping, aggravated assault, and *seven* counts of aggravated rape. (His "helpmeet" got off lightly, getting "only" 65 years for aggravated kidnapping and aggravated child abuse.) The medical record confirmed that *layers* of scar tissue appeared over most of the victim's body, revealing over *400* scars from burns and cuts! According to official transcripts, every imaginable thing was done to this poor girl (short of death): her skin was ripped open with pliers and sewn back together with darning needles; she was burned with scalding water; hung by her neck until unconscious; thrown down a flight of stairs while strapped in a highchair; beaten with ball bats and hoses; her teeth were knocked out and her bones were broken. While she was told by her mother that her scars were the "Mark of the Beast," her father supposedly told her that "David had concubines, too." (How ironic, having named her after a queen.) The jury was out for less than four hours. Needless to say, this surreal blockbuster created a media circus for several years with Combs billed as the "Sinister Minister" on such programs as *ABC's Primetime* and *20/20*. (For the record, I visited the pair in prison and they both "assured" me of their complete innocence, etc.)

As we learned from that slaughter at the Jordan, it is dangerous to "profess" one thing while *really* believing something else. I can still recall Combs' favorite advice (the quote that always appeared with his picture in the college yearbook): *"What you do with the Bible determines what God does with you."* His signature on my ordination certificate will always serve as a grim reminder of Laodicean deception; for, try as they will, *"Pseudo* King James Onlyites" *cannot* pronounce *"Shibboleth,"* the best they can do is *"Sibboleth."* In classic poetic justice, while modern Ephraimites insist on limiting *God's* breath to original manuscripts, their apostate ancestors could not even formulate their *own* breath flow of words. And I'm sure it was just a "coincidence" that the number-one Bible critic at Hyles-Anderson College "just happened" to have a distinct *speech impediment*, as well!

"My breath is corrupt...."

(JOB 17:1)

4

Shibboleth

$\mathfrak{F}$OLLOWING THAT 1995 *Christianity Today* article acknowledging the "renewed interest in the famed King James Version," several prominent Bible colleges suddenly morphed into bastions of "King James Onlyism." After years of ignoring, avoiding, contradicting, ridiculing, or outright rejecting this position, Fundamental schools were now assuring prospective students that their faculties had *really* been champions of the "Old Black Book" all along, etc. (A whole lot of folks were trying to cross that Jordan.) However, beaten and battered from over a quarter century in the trenches, the old guard viewed their new "allies" with understandable skepticism. As *"the love of money is the root of all evil,"* many questioned if tuition income was the *real* catalyst. In the process of time, Bible believers would have their suspicions confirmed by various "business as usual" developments.

In 1998 Pensacola Christian College attempted to cash in on the prevailing momentum by releasing a three-part video series entitled *The Leaven in Fundamentalism: A History of the Bible Text Issue in Fundamentalism.* Dr. Dell Johnson, who conducted the seminar (assisted by the late Dr. Theodore Letis), ended his remarks by ridiculing *Final Authority*, misrepresenting the author, maligning other KJB advocates, and blatantly contradicting himself. (By the time PCC had decided to jump on the bandwagon, *Final Authority* was already in its ninth printing, being used as a textbook in scores of Bible schools throughout the nation.) Every student who attends a Bible college that promotes the King James Bible has a *right* to expect their faculty to know the password – "SHIBBOLETH." If all they can say is "SIBBOLETH," they should be *FIRED* ON THE SPOT!

On Friday, September 16, 2005, I was the guest speaker for the chapel service at Crown College in Powell, Tennessee. (At the time I had also been invited to preach at Temple Baptist Church on the following Sunday evening.) I began the message with a brief history of the King James issue from my own vantage point of thirty-plus years as both an alumnus and former faculty member of Hyles-Anderson College. In my earlier student days (1976-1981), Dr. Hyles would preach blistering chapel messages out of the King James Bible while his professors would correct the text in the classrooms on a daily basis. Of course, Dr. Hyles had already set the pace by correcting "The Book" himself in his *own* books (i.e., Revelation 22:14 in *Let's Study the Revelation*).

I then traced the fatal error all the way back to Drs. Westcott and Hort in the nineteenth century. The trail begins with Dr. John R. Rice (1895-1980), founding editor of the *Sword of the Lord*. Dr. Hyles often referred to his beloved mentor as "The Captain of Our Team." Well, in 1969 "The Captain" went on record recommending the 1901 American Standard Version in his definitive work, *Our God-Breathed Book: The Bible*. Dr. Rice's link to the Devil was his *own* mentor, the Protestant theologian, Dr. R. A. Torrey (1856-1928). While I was delivering this message, Dr. Ed Reese (a notorious critic of the KJB himself) was listening from the faculty section. He wrote about Torrey: "Not satisfied with the training he received in the States, he studied at the German universities of Leipzig and Erlangen in 1882-83....Early in his studies he was pronounced a higher critic." Reese makes the claim that Torrey "swung gradually back to old conservative doctrines," though he apparently never swung all the *way* back, as his subsequent writings were consistently tainted by readings from the 1881 Revised Version (e.g., in his famous sermon, "Ten Reasons Why I Believe the Bible is the Word of God," Torrey quotes the corrupt RV rendering in John 7:17, "If any man willeth to do his will, he shall know of the teaching, whether it be of God, or whether I speak from myself.") Thus, we understand that the attack on the King James Bible has crept along from *Satan > Origen > Westcott & Hort > R. A. Torrey > John R. Rice > Jack Hyles*, and continues with modern-day stuttering Ephraimites such as *Clarence Sexton* and *Jack Schaap*.

At this point I related the account of Dr. Hyles' dramatic epiphany in 1984 ("Logic Must Prove the King James Bible"). After sounding the alarm regarding the many *superficial* conversions to the A.V. 1611, I suggested the need for a litmus test based on the practical wisdom in the twelfth chapter of Judges. (As the sermon was broadcast live over the Internet, I specifically stated that my "advice" was being providentially offered to college students *everywhere*; two of my own children, plus my son-in-law, are graduates of Crown). The second half of the message consisted of the following outline, entitled "Seven Signs of *Pseudo* King James Onlyism."

CLOSET "TR" POSITION

The most deceptive ploy of "*Pseudo* King James Onlyites" is their ability to promote the King James Bible as the "word of God" in *public* while accepting the *Textus Receptus* as the higher authority in *private*. Nearly every Bible college in the Fundamentalist orbit pursues this duplicitous strategy. Their campus bookstores belie their true convictions, however. While Greek and Hebrew "study aids" abound, one will search in vain for a book *specifically* about the King James Bible. (Any exceptions to this rule will be offset by the author's affiliation as a "*TR* Man.") The school catalogue is another indicator. While the rhetoric used in student recruitment may have changed, the doctrinal statements have not. All of the standard jargon continues to be printed. Such holdover phraseology from the "pre-KJV Only" era would include "verbal and plenary inspiration of the autographs"; or, "The King James Bible is the *most* accurate translation," etc. The best way to demand a password from a "*TR* Man" is to ask him if he believes he can hold a literal copy the "Holy Scriptures" in his hands. Ask him if he owns a copy of the preserved "words" of God (plural, with a lower case "w").

When you confront a modern Ephraimite at the Jordan, his true doctrinal convictions will read as follows:

A) No one has a copy of the "Holy Scriptures" in their possession.

B) The word of God is not the words found in any one "book"; it is a message found in several hundred books.

C) All books that uneducated Christians call "the word of God" are full of mistakes, but godly men will correct them for you.

D) No book on earth is *the* "final authority" for *anything*, but we will profess that *a* book we never saw (and one that never even existed, for that matter) *is* our final authority.

E) As man is the *real* final authority: *use* what works (pragmatism); *use* what you prefer (humanism); come to *me* for *my* authoritative opinion (egotism) and *I* will base all *my* authoritative opinions upon the authoritative opinions of those authorities who taught *me* to replace the authority of the Holy Bible with the preferences and opinions of *my* fellow human authorities.

AVERSION TO REPROACH

All "*Pseudo* King James Onlyites" are driven by a fleshly desire to appear scholarly or intellectual. Isaiah 66:1-2 reads: *"Thus saith the LORD, The heaven is my throne, and the earth is my footstool: where is the house that ye build unto me? and where is the place of my rest? For all those things hath mine hand made, and all those things have been, saith the LORD: but to **this** man will I look, even to him that is poor and of a contrite spirit, AND TREMBLETH AT MY WORD."* Now, whoever heard of a Hebrew or Greek professor *trembling* at God's word? How *can* they, when *they don't even believe it exists*? Whenever Christians become infatuated with intellectual power, the Devil has a field day, foisting scams like – THE Greek text, or THE *Textus Receptus* (as if there was only *one*). The truth is, there are at least *three* major editions of the *Textus Receptus* currently in print: F. H. A. Scrivener's 1894 *Annotated Greek New Testament*, reprinted by the Trinitarian Bible Society; Jay Green's *Interlinear Hebrew-Greek-English Bible*, published by Hendrickson (another version of Scrivener); and the *Interlinear Greek-English New Testament*, published by Baker Book House (an exact copy of the *Stephanus* 1550 edition). Furthermore, there were at least *sixteen* "*TRs*" in circulation during the Reformation, ALL *DIFFERING SLIGHTLY FROM ONE ANOTHER*: *Erasmus* 1516, 1519, 1522, 1535; *Beza* 1565, 1582, 1589, 1590, 1598; *Stephanus* 1546, 1549, 1550, 1551; *Colinaeus* 1534; and, *Elsevier* 1623, 1624.

The King James Bible is an *eclectic* text, which means that it was produced from a *variety* of underlying sources. While *Beza's* 1598 edition was the *predominant* text, the appendix in Scrivener's 1859 edition listed *190* references where the A.V. 1611 departed from *Beza*. Generally, the translators simply opted for a different Greek text, with a *minority* reading occasionally preferred to a *majority* reading (as in the case of I John 5:7). Sometimes they bypassed the Greek altogether in favor of a Latin text. Occasionally, God forbid, they even had the "audacity" to insert an English idiom, with *no* manuscript authority whatsoever, such as the phrase – *"God forbid"* (used fifteen times in the New Testament). The bottom line is that the King James Bible *cannot* be matched to *any* single Greek text or *Textus Receptus*. Thus, the Holy Spirit has the Christian in a corner; either he believes the *English* text of the A.V. 1611, *unequivocally*, or he must choose between three *different* Greek *Textus Receptus* manuscripts for his *final* authority. (And, should he want to cover *all* the bases, he can even choose between two "Majority Texts," a different animal altogether – *The Greek New Testament According to the Majority Text*, edited by Zane C. Hodges and Arthur L. Farstad; or, *The New Testament in the Original Greek: Byzantine Textform 2005*, edited by Maurice A. Robinson and William G. Pierpont).

The problem with stuttering Ephraimites is that they simply refuse to *believe* the word of God, *especially* the verse that so accurately identifies their root problem – *"Knowledge **puffeth** up"* (I Corinthians 8:1). The Lord's reaction to these conceited scholars is given in Psalm 10:5 – *"as for all his enemies, he **puffeth** at them."* His reason for doing so follows in Psalm 12:5, *"I will set him in safety from him that **puffeth** at him."* And for a final "nugget" in the *English*, don't miss the immediate context: *"The words of the LORD are pure words: as silver tried in a furnace of earth, purified seven times. Thou shalt keep them, O LORD, thou shalt preserve them from this generation for ever."* (Psalm 12:6-7)

COUTH OVER TRUTH

Dr. Bob Jones, Sr., used to say, "I'd rather hear a man say 'I seen' something, who *did*, than a man say 'I saw' something, who *didn't*." Such was the wisdom of an Alabama peanut farmer born in the Philadelphia Church Age (who passed the majority of his ministry *before* the King James Bible became an issue). With thousands seated before him in his 1916 New York City crusade, Dr. Bob thundered: "The only difference I could see between New York and Hell was that New York was completely surrounded by water!" His son, Bob, Jr., devolved to a Shakespearean aficionado; hence, perfecting his father's expression about "carpeting the sawdust trail." And then we have "Bob the Third" providing the key jacket endorsement for the 1999 anti-KJV book *"From the Mind of God to the Mind of Man"* (compiled by nineteen faculty members, alumni, and friends of Bob Jones University), labeling it "one of the ten most important books published for believers in the twentieth century." The "Fourth" must have suffered an identity crisis, for in 1999 he earned a Master's degree from Notre Dame University. At "The World's Most *Unusual* University," CULTure reigns as *the* "final authority"; the predominant philosophy being *couth* over *truth*.

The inspired profile for these culture-worshiping "*Pseudo* King James Onlyites" was given in II Timothy 3:5 nearly 2,000 years ago: *"Having a **form** of godliness, but denying the **power** thereof."* (Who doesn't know that the *Holy Scriptures* constitute the power of godliness?) When attempting to say "Shibboleth," modern Ephraimites will invariably give themselves away with effeminate statements like: "Well, it's not *what* he says that bothers me, but rather *how* he says it" (i.e., that hayseed who "seen" something). Dr. Bob would also remark: "If a man wants truth bad enough, he'll crawl though any muck and mire necessary to get it; if he *doesn't* want it, he'll not take it no matter *how* much you sugar coat it."

Do you seriously think the Apostle Paul would have lasted 30 seconds at a BJU vesper service? *"And my speech and my preaching was **not with enticing words** of man's wisdom, but in demonstration of the Spirit and of power."* Again: *"Seeing then that we have such hope, we use **great plainness of speech**."* And again: *"For his letters, say they, are weighty and powerful; but his bodily presence is weak, and **his speech contemptible**."* At *least* Paul was man enough to admit that he wasn't effeminate: *"But though I be **rude in speech**, yet not in knowledge."* (I Corinthians 2:4; II Corinthians 3:12; 10:10; 11:6) Notice *how* the Holy Spirit led him to describe his own "ministerial personality" – Noah Webster's 1828 *American Dictionary of the English Language* (hereafter referred to as *"Webster's"*) defines "rude" as: "Rough; uneven; rugged; unformed by *art* (*that* was a funny one); of coarse manners; harsh; unpolished; savage; raw; *artless* (another funny one); inelegant; not polished." *Brother*, talk about being handicapped; how do you suppose the Lord ever used *him* to write one-third of the New Testament?

SHALLOW BIBLE KNOWLEDGE

Whenever the King James Bible is undermined by the *Textus Receptus*, serious consequences will follow. When Jesus was rebuking the Pharisees for their policies concerning designated offerings, He said to them: *"Thus have ye made the commandment of God of **none effect** by your tradition."* (Matthew 15:6) As the word of God continues to be corrected in our Bible colleges, "The Book" literally begins losing its effect on the hearers. David wrote: *"Yea, they turned back and tempted God, and **limited the Holy One of Israel**."* (Psalm 78:41) Paul made it clear that a divine correlation exists between how much Bible you *know* and how much Bible you *believe*: *"For this cause* *also thank we God without ceasing, because, when ye received the word of God which ye heard of us, ye received it not as the word of men, but as it is in truth, the word of God, **which effectually worketh also in you that believe.** "* (I Thessalonians 2:13)

"*Pseudo* King James Onlyites" are some of the shallowest Bible students in the Body of Christ. They are always lacking in two areas – right division and cross-referencing. Consequently, they never get to the real "meat" of any issue. There is a marked difference between pastors who were trained by "*TR* men" and pastors who were trained by "KJB men." The sermon content of the *former* generally revolves around topical themes, devotional areas, the home, biographical sketches, patriotism, and "revival," while the sermon content of the *latter* encompasses verse-by-verse Bible teaching and preaching (affording both doctrinal and devotional application), along with plenty of Baptist history and current events. Ministries that are built on the A.V. 1611 have two other noticeable advantages. First, as their people have more *meat* in their diet, they have more energy to serve the Lord; thus, the "burn-out" factor is considerably reduced. Second, the giving is generally much higher, especially with regard to the pastor's needs; as the adage goes: "Feed the *sheep* and the sheep will feed *you*."

FUNDAMENTALIST VS. BIBLE BELIEVER

Though the *Fundamentalist* desperately wants to be identified with the King James Bible (for various ulterior motives), he doesn't realize that his outdated Protestant sobriquet is just one more sign that's he's caught in a serious time warp. As noted in the Introduction, the "Fundamentalists" of the first half of the twentieth century did not have to contend with the "Bible of the Month Club." Unbeknown to many, the Holy Spirit has long since picked a new *fight* with a new *tag* in vogue. Not only am I a "KJB Man," as opposed to a "*TR* Man," but I am also a "Bible believer," as opposed to a "Fundamentalist." This ideological shift could not have come at a more critical time, as a Bible believer is exactly *that,* and a Fundamentalist is exactly *that*; a Bible believer holds to *"the whole counsel of God,"* while the Fundamentalist holds to five or six "fundamentals." Contending for the "fundamentals" is much easier than contending for the "faith," especially if you're in a building program or have a typical suicide budget to maintain. "Fighting Fundamentalists" get to dodge a lot of bullets that Bible believers have to take. *Any* preacher can contend for the "vicarious death," or the "bodily resurrection," but try contending against wimpy husbands and unsubmissive wives *"that the word of God be not blasphemed."* (Titus 2:5) At its inception, Fundamentalism was a conservative ecumenical movement pioneered by baby-sprinkling Protestants who never fulfilled the Great Commission a day in their lives (i.e., *"...**baptizing** them in the name of the Father..."*), timed around the arrival of the blasphemous American Standard Version of 1901. Doesn't *Bible-believing Baptist* sound a whole lot better?

CUTE CLICHÉS

David noted that the most dangerous enemy he faced was the *two*-faced kind: *"The words of his mouth were smoother than butter, but war was in his heart: his words were softer than oil, yet were they drawn swords."* (Psalm 55:21) Jesus said of his enemies: *"This people draweth nigh unto me with their mouth, and honoureth me with their lips; but their heart is far from me."* (Matthew 15:8) Paul warned the end-day believers that *"evil men and seducers"* would go about *"deceiving, and being deceived."* (II Timothy 3:13) The *sixth* sign of *"Pseudo* King James Onlyism" is the use of cute clichés to subtly ridicule both the A.V. 1611 and those who believe it. While Paul wrote in Philippians 2:9, *"God also hath highly exalted him, and given him a name which is above every name,"* David declared in Psalm 138:2, *"thou hast magnified thy word above all thy name."* Yet, Fundamentalist pinheads will shoot off their mouths with such foolish statements as: "Well, I *believe* the Bible, but I don't *worship* the Bible"; or, "Don't preach the cover; preach what's between the covers." Other phonies will ask Bible believers if they think the King James Bible "parachuted down from Heaven"; or, was "typed out on Paul's typewriter," etc.

While attending Hyles-Anderson College, I worked at a foundry in East Chicago, Indiana. As the plant employed over a hundred students, we were given special permission to spend our lunch breaks together while holding a fifteen-minute preaching service, as well. One of the students was a King James Bible believer; and, *boy*, did he *ever* stick out in those days. I can still remember how several "preachers" would ridicule him by literally bowing down to his Bible as it lay on the lunchroom table.

THE "R" WORD

When the Apostle Paul gave his testimony before the multitude, an amazing response established the defining moment: *"And he said unto me, Depart: for I will send thee far hence unto the **GENTILES**. **And they gave him audience unto this word**, and then lifted up their voices, and said, Away with such a fellow from the earth: for it is not fit that he should live. And as they cried out, and cast off their clothes, and threw dust into the air."* (Acts 22:21-23) These nice religious folks were willing to give Paul a hearing *until* he crossed the line with a particular word; *then* a veritable *BOMB* went off in the room!

My eyes were opened to the supremacy of the King James Bible back in 1988. Ever since that time, I have discerned an insightful modern application to Paul's experience. With first-century Jews, it was the "G" word; for twenty-first-century Fundamentalists, it is the "R" word. Though 2,000 years have passed, when the name "Ruckman" is cited in "polite Christian circles," that *same* bomb goes off: the *same* voices are lifted up; the *same* epithets are hurled; the *same* clothes are torn off; and the *same* dust is thrown into the air. It is really something to behold, being "recognized" as an unofficial psychosomatic disorder known as – "Ruckmanitis."

When it comes to Dr. Peter Ruckman, the "brethren" are at the top of their game with hypocrisy and inconsistency. There is no escaping this reality, as it constitutes the 800-pound gorilla in the room that will *not* go away; for no one is talking about wearing "100% for Ruckman" buttons (as with the "100% for Hyles" buffoonery of the 1990s). What I *do* insist on discussing is basic Christian ethics as defined by Scriptures, such as: *"Finally, brethren, whatsoever things are **true**, whatsoever things are **honest**, whatsoever things are **just**...**think on these things**"* (Philippians 4:8); *"Provide things **honest** in the sight of all men"* (Romans 12:17); and, *"Let the elders that rule well be counted worthy of **double honour**, especially they who **labour in the word and doctrine**"* (I Timothy 5:17).

At the end of the day, Dr. John R. Rice was *wrong* on the Bible, but *right* on the *home*; Dr. Peter S. Ruckman was *right* on the *Bible*, but *wrong* on the *home*. (One does not have to be a rocket scientist to take it from here.) So, why has "The Captain" been elevated to sainthood while "Ruckman" has been consigned to the abyss? If Fundamentalists can give Dr. Rice a pass for recommending the ASV while continuing to promote everything else he has in print, why can't Dr. Ruckman be given the same grace? Are we to conclude that being a *right* husband is *more* important than contending for the *right* Bible?

For the record, I will tell you *exactly* what they have against Dr. Ruckman. And it has *nothing* to do with the marriage and divorce issue (or else his critics would have to throw away their Scofield Reference Bibles, as "Pastor Scofield" was a "double-married preacher" himself). The *main* problem with Dr. Ruckman is the amount of *light* he is able to shed on the King James Bible! Because most pastors in Laodicea never study, they live in constant fear that their people will one day discover how shallow they really are. Any honest Christian who has taken the time to read Dr. Ruckman's material will come to the same conclusions: He reinforces what he teaches with multiple cross-references; the Holy Spirit bears witness to these references; and, he makes no claim to papal infallibility. And, as Baptists hold to *soul liberty*, once again, "100 % for Ruckman" buttons are not required to profit from his lifetime of *"labor in the word and doctrine"* (as illustrated by nearly six feet of printed material, including the 1,864-page Ruckman Reference Bible). Even *Jesus* appealed to the visible fruit of His own ministry: *"Believe me that I am in the Father, and the Father in me: **or else believe me for the very works' sake.**"* (John 14:11)

The key connection between "Ruckmanism" and "*Pseudo* King James Onlyism" is the *unnatural* way in which Dr. Ruckman has been "*left* under the bus" in the wake of the so-called "KJV revival." If we are now all one big happy "King James family," why would the person *most* responsible for this "awakening" continue to be viewed as the Antichrist? (This would be analogous to the liberated Europeans of World War II complaining about General Patton's coarse language.) Do you think many preachers even know *what* led Dr. Hyles to preach his watershed sermon, "Logic Must Prove the King James Bible"? When Dr. Mark Rasmussen was on the faculty at Hyles-Anderson College, he told me personally that his pastor-father, Dr. Roland Rasmussen (a renegade BJU alumnus) had mailed Dr. Hyles a significant amount of pro-KJB material representing Dr. Peter Ruckman's position. (While Dr. Hyles obviously never really "got it," the point should be duly noted for the record.)

So, let me say for the *third*, and final, time – this has *nothing* to do with a sweeping endorsement of Dr. Ruckman's views or mannerisms. We have been searching out things that are *true*, *honest*, and *just*. Consequently, it would be *false*, *dishonest*, and *unjust* to vilify a *man* of God who was *used* of God to open our eyes to the *word* of God! When the Pharisees tried to intimidate the man who was healed concerning his association with the "J" word, he simply replied: *"Whether he be a sinner or no, I know not: **one thing I know, that, whereas I was blind, now I see.**"* (John 9:25)

POSTSCRIPT

That same afternoon, Dr. Sexton called my home to politely inform me that my Sunday evening invitation to speak at Temple Baptist Church was cancelled. He said, "I'm sure you want what's best for Crown College"; whereupon, I replied, "I want the will of God." To Dr. Sexton's "credit," he did offer me a $3,000 check (though I declined to accept). Yet, the one thing I *did* request was ultimately denied – a simple copy of my own sermon. (*Now* I know why the Holy Ghost specifically impressed me to have the message recorded live off the Internet, and later, posted on my own website to verify what was said.)

The following week I received a snarky note from Dr. Ed Reese. (Like Joe Combs, Reese is another Bible-correcting former professor of mine at Hyles-Anderson College.) His mailing included a booklet entitled *Trusted Voices on Translations*, containing statements from various personalities in Church history that would be inconsistent with a King James Only position today. It also contained the "official" resolution passed at the 75th annual meeting of the *Fundamental Baptist Fellowship* in 1995. If you want to know what *Pseudos* like Clarence Sexton *really* believe, consider the following excerpts from this typical Fundamentalist dictum:

> In light of the considerable discussion among fundamentalists about the issue of manuscripts and textual theories, no particular belief about the best textual theory should be elevated to the place of becoming a core fundamentalist belief....Additionally, proper evaluation of the doctrinal integrity of any particular English translation can only be done by examining its faithfulness to the original languages, not by comparing it to another English translation....In a day when translations abound, fundamentalists must exercise careful discernment in both the selection and rejection of translations. Some professing fundamentalists have wrongfully declared one translation to be the only inspired copy of God's Word in the English language and have sought to make this a test of fundamentalism. **Since no translation can genuinely claim what only may be said of the original, inspired writings, any attempt to make a particular English translation the only acceptable translation of fundamentalists must be rejected.**

As for Ed's personal comments to his old student, they were limited to a *single, scribbled* line on a *used* piece of stationery: "Bill, I realize you are more knowledgeable on translations than Spurgeon,

Moody, Wesley, Ironside, Scofield, Torrey, Burgon, and all the rest, but as a historian, my vote goes for the enclosed 31 enteries (sic). Ed"

"SCHOLARSHIP ONLYISM"

If one rejects "King James Onlyism" as his final authority, the *only* alternative is *"Scholarship* Onlyism." While Bible believers are perceived to be *"unlearned and ignorant men"* (like Peter and John in Acts 4:13), a look at the other crowd "ain't" much better. For instance, in 2007 the long-awaited *Reese Chronological Encyclopedia of Christian Biographies* was finally published. An excerpt from the endorsements of this 1,389-page tome hailed the monumental achievement as "the culmination of fifty years of research," describing the content as "an index of biographical sketches for nearly every major person who has come and gone throughout Christian history...the most complete compilation of Christian personalities ever assembled...a virtual 'Who's Who' of Christian History from the First Century AD to Today." *Wow* – that's *some* build up! Dr. Sexton could not be more proud of his famous professor, stating on a promotional brochure: "These sketches will inspire Christian workers, student and layman alike, and immensely help our Christian heritage to be passed down to the next generation." Bill Gothard even jumped on board, stating: "To honor these courageous heroes of the faith is appropriate."

So, who are these "courageous heroes of the faith"? The *first* sentence of the *first* sketch on the *first* page pretty well sets the pace for the credibility of this "scholarly" work: "Veronica – Woman whose veil retained impression of Christ. Veronica was a *legendary*, pious, and renowned woman of Jerusalem." The Roman Catholic fairy tale continues: "According to French *legend* (thirteenth century), she took the cloth wrapped around her head and gave it to Jesus that He might wipe His face as He carried the cross to His crucifixion on Calvary." (Notice how the word "legend" appears twice in the opening two sentences of this book – marking the author as one who has been *"turned unto **fables**"* after having *"turn*[ed] *away* [his own] *ears from the **truth**,"* as prophesied in II Timothy 4:4.) Ed's opening profile concludes: "When Jesus returned it to her, the impression of His features were upon it." (*Excuse* me? Chapter and verse, please?) While the average Baptist wouldn't have a clue regarding the identity of this purely mythical woman, former Roman Catholics like myself recall hearing about good ol' "Saint" Veronica at our first participation in the pagan "Stations of the Cross."

As Reese gave *me* 31 testimonials to prove that *I* was "wrong" concerning the Bible issue, I will leave my readers with a similar number of witnesses from *his* attempt at Christian scholarship. The following is what you can expect at The Crown College (and believe me – it all goes *south* from here): Johnny Cash ("Folsom Prison Blues"); "Colonel" Harland Sanders ("extra crispy or regular?"); Norman Vincent Peale (*The Power of Positive Thinking*); Kathryn Kuhlman (Charismatic, faith-healing "evangelist," labeled by *Time* magazine as "a veritable one-woman Shrine of Lourdes"); "Saint" Francis of Assisi (Rome's prototype of the satanic *stigmata* and co-founder of the "Holy Inquisition"); Martin Luther King, Jr. (*his* "Dream" – *our* "Nightmare"); Roy Rogers ("Happy Trails to You"); Karl Barth (founder of Neo-Orthodoxy, i.e., "The Bible *contains* the Word of God"); Ruth Carter Stapleton (Jimmy Carter's whacked-out, faith-healing sister who "led" pornographer Larry Flynt "to the Lord" in 1977 while the two were "hanging out" in a discothèque); Sister Gertrude "The Great" (German nun who labored on behalf of the suffering souls in "Purgatory"); Pepin "The Short" (a 4' 6" Catholic king who personified the "small man syndrome," dragging his 6-foot sword everywhere he went); Saint Simeon Stylites (another "piece of work" whose 15 minutes of fame resulted from sitting atop a 60-foot pillar for 36 years).

Then we have: Richard "The Lion Hearted" (no doubt a cool guy like General Patton, but *probably* not a "courageous hero of the faith," etc.); Richard "Tricky Dick" Nixon ("Watergate ministry"); Aimee Semple McPherson (faith-healing career ended by overdose of pills); Adamantius Origen (most infamous Bible corrector in history, excommunicated from the Catholic Church for *castrating* himself); Westcott and Hort (duh!); John Wimber (founder of the Vineyard Ministries, spawning such heresy as the Joel's Army movement, Latter Rain theology, Laughter Revivals, and "Holy Ghost Glue"); Henry Ford (notorious anti-Semite); Roy Acuff (described as a "Christian Hillbilly," whatever *that* is); Harold J. Ockenga (coined the term "New/Neo Evangelicals/ism"); "Reverend" Eldridge Cleaver (former Black Panther activist who traced his "spiritual journey" – *from* Islam *through* Marxism, "Moonyism," and his own mutation of "Christ-lam," *to* Mormonism – to a "mystical vision" he received of Jesus' face appearing in the moon); George Bernard Shaw (alcoholic, vegetarian, and moral deviant who believed he was a reincarnation of William Shakespeare); Alphaeus H. Zulu (South African former President of the World Council of Churches); Marga Buhrig (another former President of the WCC, recognized by the liberal *Anglican Journal* as "one of Switzerland's pioneering feminist theologians"); "Saint" Bernadette Soubirous ("saw" the Virgin Mary at Lourdes); and, Mother Teresa. (Who could *possibly* say anything bad about *her*?)

One of the more bizarre sketches in the entire book is Edward I; the infamous English monarch also known has "Longshanks" (featured in the Hollywood film, *Braveheart*). Among his many "contributions" to the cause of Christ, we read: "In 1290, he banished 16,000 Jews charged with organized extortionate usury" (*there's* the Mel Gibson connection). Of course, he is much better known for having drawn and quartered the beloved Scottish patriot, Sir William Wallace, in 1305. Incidentally, neither Wallace nor his protégé, "Robert the Bruce," made the cut in Ed's "Christian" encyclopedia.

Coming in at Number 31 in our countdown is the most *outstanding* example of "spirituality" and "scholarship" offered at *any* Bible-correcting school. (*Better sit down for this one, folks!*) On page 106, Reese states: "Lady Godiva – Honorable and *compassionate* member of the English Nobility, wife of Leofric (earl of Mercia)." He then gives further insight regarding the "compassionate" nature of this eleventh-century diva, the original "Lady Ga Ga": "There is a *legend* (Here we go, again!) of her riding *naked* through the streets of Coventry, covered only by her flowing hair" (i.e., Peter & Gordon, 1966). "It is *alleged* that this happened on January 6th." (Note the "accuracy" of this "important, historical resource.") "The term 'peeping Tom' *was to have originated* for a townsperson who was miraculously blinded for looking upon her during this ride. However, this story is presumed to be false." (*Boy* – do I feel better now!) "*Supposedly*, she was carrying out an ill-advised agreement with her husband to lower burdensome taxes." For *obvious* reasons, unlike most of Ed's profiles, "Lady G's" sketch does *not* include a picture. (As a "fighting Fundamentalist" with "strong convictions," etc., if Reese was thinking of I Corinthians 11:15, he might have chosen a more *modest* "heroine of the faith" like *Rapunzel*.)

Finally, not only does his book woefully miss the mark because of its countless *idiotic* entries, but because of the many *legitimate* "heroes of the faith" who were shamefully excluded! In his foreword, the late Ted Engstrom wrote: **"You will be hard-pressed to find someone of note that he has omitted."** While Ed featured scores of Bible correctors, he missed 42 of the 47 esteemed translators of the Authorized Version, men like *Miles Smith*, renowned as "a very walking library"; John Bois, who was reading Hebrew at age five; and Andrew Downes, described by Milton as "chief of learned men in England." Their slots were apparently taken by the likes of William E. Crumes, life-long civil rights activist recognized for his career transition from a *barber* in Cincinnati to a *bishop* in the Church of the Living God; Elijah Muhammad, leader of the Nation of Islam; and Frances X. Cabrini, the first American to be canonized as a "Saint." Thus, Winston Churchill would write of the A.V. 1611, "The scholars who produced this masterpiece are mostly unknown and unremembered. But they forged an enduring link, literary and religious, between the English-speaking people of the world."

One is also hard-pressed to learn about that great host of *Baptist* preachers who forged the political and religious culture of this once-great land. This subtle *anti-Baptist bias* is simply an extension of Ed's workplace. While Sexton tries to pitch his school as

"A Distinctive Baptist College," he has no problem sending mixed signals to his students by repeatedly scheduling *Protestant* speakers in Chapel (ditto his own engagements at various Protestant institutions, including the notoriously pro-Westcott and Hort *Bob Jones University*). Our Baptist ancestors are *conspicuous by their absence*, and the contrast afforded by so many "blanks" only makes the conspiracy even worse. For instance, while the pagan Greek philosopher Aristotle *is* noted for being a "Great Thinker," *no* mention is given to the nineteenth-century Baptist minister, Dr. Jabez Lamar Monroe Curry, a graduate of *Harvard University* whose lifetime achievements required *three* columns of print in the prestigious *Dictionary of American Biography*, as well as the commissioning of a marble statue in Washington's *National Statuary Hall*.

Ed's readers may be "inspired" to learn that Buddha "was the founder of Buddhism," but will look in vain for the name John Gano, the American Revolutionary chaplain who baptized George Washington. We also learn that "St. Stephen I of Hungary [the patron saint of my Catholic elementary school in Manhattan] received a crown...for his coronation from Pope Sylvester II," though fail to hear about Andrew Tribble, the Baptist pastor who dined with Thomas Jefferson, influencing his political thinking on autonomous government. According to Ed's "scholarly" work, we discover that "Reverend" James Cleveland, the "African-American" music icon known as the "King of Gospel," taught nine-year-old Aretha Franklin how to sing; yet, we read *nothing* about the brutal beating, in 1651 Boston, of Obadiah Holmes – *constituting the first blood shed on American soil for the cause of religious liberty*. Ed tells us that Charles F. Gounod wrote "*Ave Marie*," yet fails to mention that Francis Bellamy wrote the *Pledge of Allegiance* to our flag.

We are reminded that Tennessee Ernie Ford "sold over 20 million copies of his famous album *Sixteen Tons*," though *no* space is given to Tidence Lane, the fruitful Baptist evangelist and church planter who founded the *first* church *of any denomination* in Ernie's home state – Buffalo Ridge Baptist Church in Gray, Tennessee. While Ed *remembered* to include several "legends" of Southern Gospel music, such as George Younce, W. Jake Hess, and that iconic duo Howard & Vestal Goodman, he "somehow" *forgot* to mention the name of Shubal Stearns – *the Baptist preacher credited with singlehandedly birthing the entire Bible Belt itself.* (Fortunately, the North Carolina Historical Society *has* preserved Stearns' legacy on a highway gravesite marker, stating of his pioneering work: "Sandy Creek Baptist Church – Mother of all Separate Baptist Churches in the South.") And, though I "suppose" there is *some* enduring "spiritual" benefit in knowing that Sister Anne Javouhey "trained 900 nuns," *somehow* I just can't help wondering whether the students at Crown would be better served learning about *any* of the *hundreds* of Baptist preachers who endured such *"cruel mockings and scourgings, yea, moreover of bonds and imprisonment"* in eighteenth-century Virginia for the cause of *their* current religious liberty.

Dr. Reese has often said, "Books are not for reading; they're for filing." Should we be surprised, therefore, that he missed *three* of the most important Baptist historians in his encyclopedia? Ignoring Dr. David Benedict, he enlightens us about Benedict of Nursia – Founder of monasteries in Western Europe – "A pet raven snatched a poison slice of bread from Benedict's hand, just in time to save his life." In the place of Dr. John T. Christian, we have Christian II – King of Norway, Denmark, and Sweden – "known as 'The Cruel' for his massacre of Scandinavian nobility." Finally, while "somehow" forgetting to cite Dr. William Cathcart (editor of a *real* research work – the two-volume, 1,323-page *Baptist Encyclopedia*), Ed *did* include William de la Mare, William I of England, William I of the Netherlands, William I "The Pious," William III, William of Auvergne, William of Champeaux, William of Corbeil, William of Ockham, William of St. Carilef, William of St. Thierry, William of Tyre; and last, but not least, William of Wickham!

Well, *enough* is *enough*; we *cannot* go on forever.

> "When you mess with 'The Book,'
> God messes with your mind."
>
> (Anonymous)

5

Given By Inspiration

WHEN CHRISTIANS BECOME infatuated with culture, any number of telltale signs will arise. Nearly three years after my sermon at The Crown College, a large painting of Adamantius Origen was on display at the school. (It was eventually removed after an alumnus complained that Origen was the greatest Bible critic in history.)

Since the lingering controversy over the doctrine of inspiration centers on II Timothy 3:16, a study of the general context is in order. Before the Apostle Paul ever mentions the word "inspiration," he directs Timothy: *"Of these things put them in remembrance, charging them before the Lord that they **strive** not about **words** to no profit, but to the **subverting** of the hearers."* (II Timothy 2:14) Whenever someone tells you that the King James Bible is *not* the *"inspired* word of God," the scorner will build his entire argument around a solitary word – "inspiration." For the record, this word is found only *two* times in the entire Bible, while the sacrosanct underlying Greek – *theopneustos* – appears only *once*. Conversely, the words "Scripture" and "Scriptures" are used fifty-three times in the "Holy Scriptures."

The Holy Spirit reveals that the goal of these spiritual parasites is the *"**subverting** of the hearers."* In their letter of conciliation, the Jerusalem Elders reassured their Gentile brethren: *"Forasmuch as we have heard, that certain which went out from us have troubled you with **words**, **subverting** your souls, saying, Ye must be circumcised, and keep the law: to whom we gave no such commandment."*

(Acts 15:24) *Webster's* defines "subvert" as: "to overthrow from the foundation; to overturn; to ruin utterly." David assures us that the Bible issue is no light matter; for, *"If the **foundations** be destroyed, what can the righteous do?"* (Psalm 11:3)

The Apostle Peter gave a similar warning when addressing opposition to Paul's letters. As if to mirror **II *Timothy* 3:16**, **II *Peter* 3:16** states: *"As also in all his epistles, speaking in them of these things; in which are some things hard to be **understood**, which they that are unlearned and unstable **wrest**, as they do also the other **scriptures**, unto their own destruction."* *Webster's* defines "wrest" as: "to distort; to turn from truth or twist from its natural meaning by violence." We should also note that this is the last mention of the word "Scripture(s)" in the Bible.

It was Martin Luther's observation that the first time the Devil appears in Scripture it is under the *"tree of **knowledge**."* Sadly, one of the "best" places for a young preacher to lose his faith in the Bible is in "Bible" college. (It has often been said that a Bible *college* teaches you *about* the Bible, while a Bible *institute* teaches you *the* Bible.) As noted in chapter one, our Lord had nothing but contempt for intellectual intimidation, stating: *"But this thou hast, that thou hatest the deeds of the Nicolaitanes, **which I also hate**."* (Revelation 2:6) Having instructed Timothy in verse 14 as to what his *"faithful men"* of verse 2 should *not* do – *"strive,"* Paul declares what they *should* do in verse 15 – *"study."* The reason pastors are admonished to *"**strive** not about **words** to no profit"* is so they may be free to *"**study**...the **word** of truth,"* becoming *"approved unto God"* in the process. (Obviously, Timothy *must* have had the *"word of truth"* in order to have complied.) The apostle then imparts the all-important key to proper study – *"rightly dividing the word of truth."* As II Timothy 2:15 is the only verse in Scripture that commands the believer to *study*, as well as the only text that tells him *how*, we are not surprised to learn that the verse has been shamefully adulterated in every modern version (e.g., "Do your best to present yourself to God as one approved, a workman who does not need to be ashamed and who correctly handles the word of truth" New International Version).

Consequently, by the time we "fast forward" to the twenty-first century, we encounter a bunch of dry theologians who know nothing of studying the word of truth (much less right division) *striving* about the word *"theopneustos."* Thus, we conclude that the Hebrew and Greek departments of our so-called "Christian" colleges and universities will *"strive"* about *"words to no profit"* (Thayer's *Lexicon*, Vincent's *Word Studies*, Trench's *Synonyms*, Wilson's *Old Testament Word Studies*, Zodhiates' *Bible Study Helps*, Vine's *Expository Dictionary of New Testament Words*, etc.) in order to *"subvert the hearers"* by bringing them under the authority and control of someone *other* than the Holy Spirit. In a sad play on words, while their *"striving"* produces no *spiritual* profit, the detestable operation produces plenty of *financial* profit. Paul informed Titus that the *"liars, evil beasts"* and *"slow bellies"* that were *"subvert[ing] whole houses"* on Crete, were doing so *"for filthy lucre's sake."* (Titus 1:11)

While there was a priest class in the Old Testament to determine the inspiration of the canon (Deuteronomy 31:25-26; 33:8-10; II Chronicles 17:8-9; Ezra 7:11-12; Malachi 2:4-7), no such arrangement has ever existed in the Church Age, as every individual in the Body of Christ is a "voting" member of a *"royal priesthood"* and collectively responsible for guarding the *"royal law"* (James 2:8; I Peter 2:9). With no apologies to those who spend *"their time in nothing else, but either to tell, or to hear some new thing,"* the *Holy* author of the *Holy* Scripture, God the *Holy* Ghost, bears witness to the inspiration of His *own* work (Acts 17:21; John 16:13). Levite "wannabes" in the New Testament Church betray their true identity as Vatican change agents for "replacement theology."

For all his authoritative warbling about "historic positions," however, the professional Christian scholar doesn't know half as much as you think. Although he is quick to define the limitations of inspiration (i.e., to the original manuscripts), he cannot begin to

explain the doctrine itself. As I noted in *Final Authority*, a survey
of such intellectual "mumbo jumbo" would include:

> Were we asked, then, how this work of divine inspiration has
> been accomplished in the men of God, we should reply, that we
> do not know. (Louis Gaussen)

> The doctrine of inspiration, because it is supernatural, presents
> some problems to human understanding. (Lewis Sperry Chafer)

> Accepting the above as the best definition of inspiration, we
> observe that we do not know the mode of inspiration. (Henry C.
> Thiessen)

> Of course there is a mystery connected with a product that is the
> result of the confluence of the human and the divine. (Harold
> Lindsell)

> What is declared is that the Scriptures are a divine product
> without any implication of how God has operated in producing
> them. (Philadelphia Biblical University class notes)

These are the very men exposed by Paul (less than ten verses
from their pet word *theopneustos*) as being *"heady"* and *"highminded"*
while *"Ever learning, and never able to come to the knowledge of
the truth."* (II Timothy 3:4, 7) One of their consistent arguments is
that the King James translators never *stated* the conviction that
their work was "divinely inspired," etc. The simplest answer is that
the supernatural process of inspiration (including preservation)
would not apply to the translators' "non-canonical words" (while
the Holy Spirit chose to hover over the text, He was under no
obligation to do the same for anything the translators may or may
not have said, *or* professed to believe; e.g., the error of infant
sprinkling). Yet – call it what you may – these intellectual giants
were smart enough to believe that "their" work had been undertaken
by divine guidance, Dr. Miles Smith writing in "The Translators
to the Reader": "And in what sort did these assemble? in the trust
of their knowledge, or of their sharpnesse of wit, or deepnesse of
judgement, as it were in an arm of flesh? At no hand. **They trusted
in him that hath the key of *David*, opening and no man shutting;**

they prayed to the Lord the Father of our Lord...." (Note that unmistakable cross-reference to the Philadelphia Church Age.)

Another objection is that the Bible itself is silent on the claim of "inspired translations." However, this same charge could be leveled at the critic. Suffice it to say that there is not a single verse in either Testament that supports the relegation of inspiration to autographs. Furthermore, in similar fashion to the total blackout of *Catholic* "Christianity" in Acts (robed, bingo-playing, celibate priests being called "Father"; prayers to Mary; statues, candles, incense pots, etc.), there are *no* examples in God's word of *anyone* questioning the Scriptures they were reading, much less employing the scholars' scientific rhetoric in the process. In nineteen encounters with the "Holy Scriptures," the Lord Jesus never showed a Nicolaitane preference for a verbally inspired autograph, an older manuscript, or a more accurate reading, etc. *"Having never learned,"* the carpenter from Nazareth never made a single confusing reference to interpolations, glossas, eclecticity, scholia, kepholia, colophons, neumes, or "even" onomostics (John 7:15). Yet, despite this less-than-intellectual approach, His listeners *"were astonished at his doctrine."* (Mark 1:22)

With this brief introduction concluded we will now delve into the "official" *scholarly* position on II Timothy 3:16. Dr. James M. Gray, former dean of the Moody Bible Institute and contributing editor to the Scofield Reference Bible, has written: "Let it be stated further in this definitional connection, that the record for whose **inspiration** we contend is the **original** record—the **autographs** or **parchments** of Moses, David, Daniel, Matthew, Paul, or Peter, as the case may be, and **not** any particular **translation** or **translations** of them whatever."

Let it be stated further in *this* definitional connection that the scholars cannot even agree as to *where* inspiration lies; while some say the *authors* were inspired, others say the *words*; some, the *finished product*, others, the *process* itself; though, again, ALL *agree* that the King James Bible cannot *possibly* be identified with inspiration. *"And the same day Pilate and Herod were made friends*

together: for before they were at enmity between themselves."
(Luke 23:12) Having defined *theopneustos* as "God-breathed," the
scholar will then explain that inspiration occurred only once when
God mysteriously breathed out the very words comprising the
original manuscripts. However, this theory breaks down whenever
the *first* copy of the *first* original was penned, for *if* inspiration is
confined to the originals, *then* the "laity" must conclude that God's
breath somehow "evaporated" with the deterioration of His
autographs! The historic *Fundamentalist* position implies that
theopneustos "was" a quick *round* trip, while the historic *scriptural*
position reveals that inspiration "is" an extended *one-way* trip (at
least until the believer makes it Home).

At this point, allow me to say that I have no problem with the
"B" word. Some King James advocates feel compelled to remove
God's *breath* from the standard definition of *theopneustos*. This
view depicts Scripture being given by God's *Spirit*, as opposed to
His *breath*. In my opinion, this is splitting hairs. If the Scriptures
are *alive* (and they *are*), it would not be unnatural to associate
God's *breath* with them, as all *living* things are *breathing* things,
including "words" (Acts 17:25; John 6:63). The Law of First Mention
reveals God quickening the first man by BREATHING *"into his*
nostrils *the* ***breath*** *of life."* (Genesis 2:7) And this process did not
cease in the Garden, as men in Job's time were receiving *their* life
the same way (Job 33:4).

Then, the Bible will often present God's *breath* and *Spirit* "in
the *same* breath" (no pun intended). For instance, while Isaiah 2:2
states, *"Cease ye from man, whose* ***breath*** *is in his* ***nostrils,"*** Job 27:3
states, *"All the while my* ***breath*** *is in* ***me,*** *and the* ***Spirit*** *of God is
in my* ***nostrils.***" Job 33:4 "clarifies" matters with, *"The* ***Spirit*** *of God
hath made me, and the* ***breath*** *of the Almighty hath given me* ***life."***
The phrase *"And God* ***said***" appears eight times in the opening chapter
of the Scriptures (referring to the *act* of Creation), confirming that *"the*
Word" literally *spoke* the world into existence (John 1:10). Yet,
notice how WORD, SPIRIT, and BREATH are used *interchangeably*
by the CREATOR Himself: *"BY HIS SPIRIT he hath* ***garnished***

the heavens" (Job 26:13); *"*BY THE *WORD of the* LORD *were the heavens* **made;** *and all the host of them* BY THE *BREATH* OF HIS MOUTH*"* (Psalm 33:6).

And, as man was *made* in the image of God, *his* words and breath are *also* inseparable; "words" being formed by *breath* resonated over vocal chords and shaped by the tongue, teeth, and lips (Exodus 4:11). But, even though *garnishments* are secondary to the *salad* itself (or, in this case, *"the heavens"*), obviously (and at the risk of sounding *silly*) – should "push come to shove" – God's *breath* would *have* to be subordinate to His *Spirit.* And *whenever, wherever,* or, *however* He would choose to use "it," we can rest assured the results will be just fine (Isaiah 42:5). Therefore, rather than getting further bogged down "rightly dividing" God's *Spirit* from His *breath*, let us resume our focus on the more pressing subject at hand (Luke 10:41).

CONTEXT

Now when the so-called "historic Fundamentalist position" is examined in the light of the Scriptures themselves, at least *three* major problems arise. The *first* obstacle is occasioned by the *immediate* context. If *"**all** scripture is given by inspiration of God,"* would that not have to also include the *"Scriptures"* that were providentially mentioned in the *preceding* verse? II Timothy 3:15 reads: *"And that from a child thou hast known the **Holy scriptures,** which are able to make thee wise unto salvation through faith which is in Christ Jesus."* How could any *thinking* person suppose that Timothy ever *saw* an Old Testament original, much less that his mother possessed any? Eunice obviously reared her boy on *copies* of *copies.* And notice how the omniscient Holy Spirit was able to head Satan's minions off at the pass by elevating the status of *copies* to *"Holy Scriptures"* in verse 15, having anticipated the train wreck of equating *"Scripture"* with autographs in verse 16. While scholars suggest that these Scriptures may have been a Greek translation of the Old Testament (given that Timothy's father was a Greek), I reject this theory, as Timothy's mother was a saved *Jewess,* the context indicating that her husband was a heathen (Acts 16:1).

The nexus between the two verses cannot be emphasized enough. While a seminary professor will tout II Timothy 3:16 (like a Campbellite elder pontificating over Acts 2:38), he wouldn't *dare* touch verse 15 with a 15-foot pole. His antipathy (and/or ignorance) for right division is revealed by his *"wrongly* dividing" verse 16 away from its providential precursor – a blatant disregard of the adage, "A text without a context is a pretext." The consequence of this presumption is preposterous! Are we to believe that the *"Scriptures"* Timothy read as a child exhibited *less* of God's life-giving breath than the two "fresh" manuscripts he received from Paul? Did the *copies* require an oxygen tent to make Timothy *"wise unto salvation"*? Were they weakened by some spiritual form of COPD? Did Paul place a higher textual status or reliability on his pastoral epistles than he did on Timothy's Old Testament facsimiles? Perhaps Dr. Gray was full of hot air.

But, the case is stronger yet. While there is not a single verse in the Bible that specifically limits inspiration to the autographs, *every* reference to the word "Scripture" is a reference to a *copy.* In John 5:39, Jesus told His listeners to *"Search the **scriptures**,"* a ridiculous charge if He was referring to originals; in Acts 8:32, the Ethiopian eunuch is seated in his chariot reading a copy of Isaiah, the *"place of the **scripture**"* being duly noted; in Acts 17:2, Paul is in Thessalonica reasoning with the Jews *"out of the **scriptures**"*; in Acts 17:11, the Bereans are commended for having *"searched the **scriptures** daily."* The ultimate example is found in Luke 4:16-22, where the *incarnate* "**W**ord of God" stood up to **read** the *written* "**w**ord of God" in His hometown synagogue. His sermon from Isaiah began when He *"opened the **book**"* and ended when He *"closed the **book**."* Well, what about that! The "human" reaction was predictable: *"And all bare him witness, and wondered at the gracious **words** which proceeded out of his **mouth**."* Not one of these Jews was any less affected than their ancestors were in

Isaiah's day. If anything, they were *more* affected: ***"This day* is *this scripture** fulfilled in **your** ears."*

Could we find a *better* illustration of *Webster's* definition for the word "wrest" than we have in the modern scholars' treatment of the word "inspiration": "To distort; to turn from the truth or twist from its natural meaning by **violence**"? To *make* the only verse in the New Testament where "inspiration" is found equate to "autographs," the *opposing* manuscript evidence displayed in 53 verses (where "Scripture" is *always* a reference to a copy) *had* to be resisted with the *utmost* of **violence**. So, what else is new? *"And from the days of John the Baptist until now the kingdom of heaven suffereth **violence**, and the **violent** take it by force."* (Matthew 11:12)

GRAMMAR

The *second* problem concerns grammar. Most Greek and Hebrew scholars seem to have real difficulty when it comes to reading simple English. But, then again, the explanation might have more to do with deceit than anything else. For instance, former President William Jefferson Clinton, a.k.a. "Slick Willie," has been one of the more unsavory characters in recent American history. While that incredible remark, "I didn't inhale," revealed how far we had fallen from more innocent times ("I cannot tell a lie," etc.), it was the Monica Lewinsky fiasco that would take Bill to a whole new level. When laboring to enlighten a grand jury as to why he hadn't *really* lied when he initially told his aides (regarding Miss Lewinsky), "There's nothing going on between us," the wordsmith extraordinaire replied – "It depends upon what the meaning of the word 'is' is."

Now, as badly as President Clinton performed that day on national television, he *pales* in comparison to the professional "Christian" scholar. While Clinton was at least *attempting* to hide a "was" behind an "is," the modern Bible critic insists on blatantly changing an "is" to a "was." The Holy Spirit wrote: *"All scripture **is** given by inspiration of God."* If inspiration was something that related *only* to the originals, you would expect the text to read exactly as it appeared in Kenneth Taylor's perverted *Living Bible*: "All scripture **was** given by inspiration of God." While past action may sometimes be described with present tense usage ("All construction *is* done according to a blueprint," etc.), and while some New Testament autographs had yet to be penned at the time of Paul's death, the fact *is* that "is" *is* the normal meaning for "is." (David declared in Psalm 119:89, *"For ever, O LORD, thy word is settled in heaven."*) Thus, *whatever* inspiration "is," it *is* certainly a process that appears to *include* the present.

But, just before we go, note further that there are *two* "ises" in the verse (just six words apart). And to make things really interesting, they are both in *italics*. The reason that the translators had to add the word "is" is because there is no predicate in the underlying Greek. We then observe that the two Greek words translated *"given by inspiration"* and *"profitable"* are connected by the conjunction "and." This all-important conjunction requires that both words be preceded by the verb "is," as one cannot say, *"All Scripture **was** given by inspiration AND **is** profitable."* The "and" makes both sides of the equation equal. Any question *is* removed by the reinforcing word "that," which begins the very next verse. Thus, it *is* inspiration that makes Scripture *profitable*, so *"**That** the man of God may be perfect, throughly furnished unto all good works."*

Like I said, too much time in the Hebrew and Greek will mess up one's English. For instance, every opponent of the King James Bible will eventually jump from II Timothy 3:16 to II Peter 1:20-21. This time he will get the right tense but get caught red-handed trying to change another word into an entirely different one. Dr. Gray said that the only inspiration worth contending for concerns the "autographs or parchments," i.e., the *Scriptures* (from the Latin *scriptura*, "written material"; from *scriber*, "to write"). While Paul was referring to the ongoing effects of inspiration via tangible documents (i.e., the *copies* that had made Timothy *"wise unto salvation"*), Peter takes us back to the genesis of inspiration – which did not have *anything* to do with *anyone* WRITING *anything* down on *anything*: *"Knowing this first, that no prophecy of the* *scripture is of any private interpretation. For the prophecy came not in old time by the will of man: but **holy** men of God **SPAKE** as they were **moved** by the **Holy Ghost.**"* (II Peter 1:20-21)

Notice how the Holy Ghost is perfectly capable of differentiating between tenses – *"no prophecy of the scripture is"* (present) as opposed to *"holy men of God spake"* (past). And look how the words *"old time"* make the distinction even more obvious. However, the scholar crashes and burns when he comes to that word *"spake,"* for he *thought* it read "wrote." Thirty years earlier, the future author of II Peter *spake: "Men and brethren, this **scripture** must needs have been fulfilled, which the **Holy Ghost** by the **mouth** of David **spake** before concerning Judas, which was guide to them that took Jesus."* (Acts 1:16) Apparently, inspiration – *whatever* it is – does not begin with a pen. By the time the prophet's words reach the ears of the *amanuensis* ("50-cent" word for "scribe") they are already inspired, having left the lips of *"**holy** men of God...moved by the **Holy Ghost.**"* You might call the ethereal transmission a *"flying roll"* (Zechariah 5:1).

Of course, this is too deep for *heady, high-minded* "Athenians," as the subject of inspiration cannot be dissected in a language lab. Furthermore, according to Hebrews 4:12-13, if there's any *dissecting* to be done, it will be done by the Scripture itself/Himself. (As former New York Mayor Ed Koch used to say, "I don't *get* ulcers; I *give* 'em.") The scholar is always out of his league whenever he attempts to mess with "The Book." If he wants to dissect a text, let him start with Job 38:4, *"Where wast **thou** when I laid the foundations of the earth?"* The second verse in Genesis tells us that *"the Spirit of God **moved** upon the face of the waters,"* and He has been *moving* upon everything else ever since: *"And he is before all things, and by him all things **consist.**"* (Colossians 1:17)

Now this is where the hated doctrine of *preservation* comes in: *"The **words** of the LORD are pure **words**: as silver tried in a furnace of earth, purified seven times. Thou shalt **keep** them, **O LORD,** thou shalt **preserve** them from this generation **for** ever."* (Psalm 12:6-7) The word "preservation" is composed of three parts: *pre-*, a prefix meaning "before"; *serve*, a verb meaning "to hold as a slave"; and, *-ion*, a suffix meaning "the act of." When we cross-reference to Psalm 119:89, *"For ever, O LORD, thy **word** is **settled** in heaven,"* the *spiritual* definition becomes: "The act of holding as a slave since before the foundation of the world." As the author of the *Holy* Scriptures, the *Holy* Spirit was responsible for *preserving* that "flying roll" *from* the *lips* of a *holy* man *to* the *ears* of a ready scribe. Sometimes, as in the case of Paul and Tertius, it was a short trip – across a room, if you will (Romans 16:22). Other times, the journey could be much further – *centuries* between the words spoken by Adam through Joseph to Moses – while *millenniums* from Enoch to Jude (Jude 14).

A preacher friend of mine, Dr. J. Wendell Runion, has stated that "the doctrines of inspiration and preservation are as inseparable as a pair of Siamese twins with one heart." If inspiration is confined to the penning of words on paper, one is forced to conclude that preservation can *precede* inspiration (analogous to the evolutionists' worst nightmare of RFSO – *reverse fossil strata order*). Jesus, as the living *"Word"* (with no beginning or end), summarized the doctrine of preservation by declaring that *"the **scripture** cannot be **broken**,"* and then illustrated the same at Calvary: *"For these things were done, that the **scripture** should be fulfilled, **A bone of him** shall not be **broken**."* (John 10:35; 19:36)

Another disconcerting mystery confronting the scholar concerns the matter of translations. Dr. Gray was adamant in divorcing inspiration from "any particular translation or translations." For the sake of illustration, translations can be viewed as the "transfers" or "connecting flights" required along the way of preservation. While the critic is quick to sit in judgment on any translation from the Old and New Testament languages into English, he has obviously never considered the "switches" that were made closer to the point of embarkation. The second book in the Bible provides many insightful examples. In Exodus 10:7, we have Moses recording the words of Pharaoh's servants, spoken *after* he left the room. To begin with, how did Moses know what they said? Next, do you suppose these Egyptians spoke Hebrew to one another? Obviously, the Lord gave Moses the content, but in which language? In any event, Moses eventually inserted the translated discussion into the Hebrew "autograph." The question then arises, was the Hebrew *original* inspired, or just the *spoken* Egyptian that Moses *didn't* hear?

And then we have the peculiar order of transmission that arose because of Moses' "panic attacks" about public speaking. If we take Exodus 4:12-15 and 7:2 as our guide, much of the dialogue we read in Exodus would have run: God to Moses; Moses to Aaron; Aaron to the Israelites, and to Pharaoh. (Personally, I think the text implies that Moses eventually made a comeback.) So, where did the inspiration begin and end? Yet, we know it had to be *somewhere*, because *"all scripture is given by inspiration of God"* and Paul makes it clear that the "Scripture" was *definitely* there; only, the Lord gets a little "carried away," calling *Himself* the Scripture. Citing Jehovah's "take" on Exodus 9:16, Paul records: *"For the **scripture** saith unto Pharaoh, Even for this same purpose have I raised thee up, that I might shew my power in thee, and that my name might be declared throughout all the earth."* (Romans 9:17) By the way, in case you didn't catch it, while penning his inspired epistle to the Gentile church at Rome, Paul did a "no-no" by creating and inserting an inspired translation of Exodus 9:16 into his Greek autograph. How's *that* for "double inspiration"?

One of my favorite "paper" trails is the text, *"Thou shalt not kill."* (Exodus 20:13) The process begins with the LORD *speaking* these words to Moses (along with the other nine commandments), then *personally inscribing* them in a complimentary two-volume set of stone tablets (Exodus 31:18). These Hebrew originals are subsequently destroyed when Moses has a "holy hissy" over the golden calf (Exodus 32:19). Moses then goes back up the mountain and receives a *second* set of "originals" (Exodus 34:1-4, 29). He later makes an "inspired *copy*" of the *second* set of tablets along with the entire Torah, placing both in the Holy Ark for safekeeping (Exodus 40:20-21, Deuteronomy 31:24-26). In the process of time, the Ark and its contents are lost, probably during the destruction of

Jerusalem in 586 BC under Nebuchadnezzar, as Josephus notes that there was no Ark in the post-exilic temple (and "Indiana Jones" has *yet* to find them). Several centuries later, Jesus shows up preaching and teaching out of preserved copies of copies of the original Hebrew. In Luke 18:18-23, the beloved physician records our Lord's conversation with the rich young ruler. Here, we have Dr. Luke inserting an "inspired translation" of Jesus' citing of the Ten Commandments in Hebrew into his "former treatise" in Greek. (*Phew!*) In the middle of verse 20 we read the slightly altered, *"Do not kill."* And, to whatever degree He may have addressed any non-Hebrew speaking listeners in Aramaic, the picture gets wilder yet. So, I ask ya', "Doc": *Where's the inspiration?* And don't look now, but in Matthew's Gospel, Jesus takes further editorial liberty by tweaking *"Thou shalt not **kill**"* to *"Thou shalt do no **murder**"*; thus paving the way for Gentile nations to understand His Father's attitude toward capital punishment, national defense, and personal protection. (Matthew 5:21; 19:18)

CONTENT

The scholars' *third* dilemma is likened to the other two; *they can't read simple English.* After all the rancor, where does II Timothy 3:16 say the Scripture(s) was/is/are, or *whatever* – INSPIRED? I *believe* it says: *"All scripture is GIVEN BY inspiration."* The editors of the New International Version understood the difference, substituting their own perverted rendition, "All scripture is God-breathed." Paul directed Titus: *"A man that is an heretick after the **first** and **second** admonition reject."* (Titus 3:10) Even the *world* understands "three strikes and you're *out*." (We will examine this third point more thoroughly in chapter seven.)

These are the issues that require answers *before* any attempt is made to distance inspiration from the A.V. 1611. However, don't hold your "breath," as *"Wisdom is too high for a fool."* (Proverbs 24:7) Solomon provided an inspired profile of the professional scholar in Proverbs 18:1-2: *"Through desire a man, having separated himself, seeketh and intermeddleth with all wisdom. A fool hath no delight in understanding, but that his heart may discover itself."* A timely exegesis by any Bible believer would read: *"Through desire* (to replace the Holy Spirit as the final authority on all questions of biblical authority) *a man* (Hebrew and/or Greek scholar), *having separated himself* (from the real world to his air-conditioned study or library cubicle), *seeketh and intermeddleth with all wisdom* (pursues any and all information that can be used to intermeddle with "The Book"). *A fool hath no delight in* **understanding** (the very *fruit* of inspiration), *but that his heart may discover itself* (through the invigorating experience of lording over God's people by his "ability" to sit in judgment on the Holy Scriptures)."

In the final analysis, the unregenerate egghead is *"**snared** in the work of his own hands,"* having *forgotten* the very warning of his second-favorite text – *"no prophecy of the scripture is of any* **private interpretation**.*"* (Psalm 9:16; II Peter 1:20) Thus, he is snared by his own *"private interpretation"* of II Timothy 3:16. *"Through desire"* for *preeminence* he "forgot" to heed the hymn, "Take Time to Be **Holy**." He "forgot" that the *Holy* Ghost moved *holy* men to produce the *Holy* Scriptures for *holy* brethren with a *holy* calling, lifting up *holy* hands, and greeting one another with a *holy* kiss. And, alas, he "forgot" that *"It is a **snare** to the man who* **devoureth** *that which is* **holy**.*"* (Proverbs 20:25) Most significantly, he "forgot" that the idea of a *"Bible* scholar" is a gross misnomer to begin with, the standard definition for scholar being: "One who has gained *mastery* in one or more disciplines." We will return to the scholar and his "issues" in chapter seven with the following chapter forming an important linkage between the two.

> *"Neither be ye called masters:*
> *for one is your Master, even Christ."*
>
> (MATTHEW 23:10)

6

The Two-Edged Sword

NE OF THE major goals of this book is to convert *Textus Receptus* Fundamentalists into King James Bible believers by weaning them from the "milk" of *Greek* and *Hebrew* to the "meat" of the *English* text. In order to do this, the "*TR* Man" must close his lexicon long enough to take a prayerful look at what the *words* in the A.V. 1611 actually say. And if the "scales" ever *do* fall off, the so-called "nuggets" from the original languages will be seen to possess the "nutritional" value of *chicken* nuggets by comparison (Acts 9:18). But this is entirely between the Fundamentalist and the Holy Ghost; for, *"Do not interpretations belong to God?"* (Genesis 40:8) While I am not a Calvinist, I have profited from selected portions of the writings of Arthur Pink. Commenting on John 8:28, *"as my Father hath taught me, I speak these things,"* he writes:

> This discourse He had delivered originated not in His own mind. His doctrine came from the One who sent Him. It was the same with the apostle Paul. Hear him as he says to the Galatians, "But I certify you, brethren, that the gospel which was preached of me is not after man. For I neither received it of man, neither was I taught it, but by the revelation of Jesus Christ" (1:11, 12). And these things, dear brethren are recorded for our learning. No one *has to* take a course in any Bible School in order to gain a knowledge and insight of the Scriptures. The man most used of God last century – Mr. C. H. Spurgeon – was a graduate of no Bible Institute! We do not say that God has not used the Bible schools to help many who have gone there; we do not say there

may not be such which He is so using today. But what we *do* say is, that such schools are not an *imperative* necessity. You have the same Bible to hand that they have; you have the same Holy Spirit to guide you into all truth. God may be pleased to use human instruments in instructing and enlightening you, or **He may give you the far greater honor and privilege of teaching you** *directly*. That is for *you* to ascertain. Your first duty is to humbly and diligently look to HIM, *wait* on Him for guidance, *seek* His will, and the sure promise is, *"The meek will he guide in judgment: and the meek will he teach his way"* (Psalm 25:9).

I would add I John 2:27 – *"But the anointing which ye have received of him abideth in you, and ye need not that any man teach you: but as the same anointing teacheth you of all things, and is truth, and is no lie, and even as it hath taught you, ye shall abide in him."* Clarence Larkin, the preeminent American Bible teacher and contemporary of Charles Spurgeon, wrote several monumental works, including: *Dispensational Truth*; *Rightly Dividing the Word*; and, *Why I Am A Baptist*. Yet, his formal "theological" training consisted of a secular degree in mechanical engineering. I fear that the Body of Christ has lost sight of the fact that the command to *"study"* in II Timothy 2:15 applies to *every* generation. If our Bible is supposed to be inexhaustible, then where are the fresh truths for today? I'll tell you where they are – they're lying *undiscovered* in the Bibles being carried by the unfortunate underlings of Nicolaitane kingdom builders who hide their own shallowness behind cries of *"no new thing under the sun,"* etc. The material presented in this chapter has *nothing* to do with Greek or Hebrew. It will serve as an important foundation for the chapter to follow.

"WHAT IS MAN?"

In order to understand the doctrine of inspiration in its *widest* application one must have a scriptural grasp of the human composition. David asked, *"What is **man**?"* (Psalm 8:4). The answer to this question will shed light on II Timothy 3:16, for the context of "inspiration" (as we shall see in chapter seven) is the

Creator communicating with His creation, and ultimately, with man's supernatural capacity to receive that communiqué. Ironically, while many of "the brethren" feel competent to sit in judgment on the King James Bible, they don't even *know* that they don't even *know* their unique scriptural identity, as the answer to David's question is found in the "elusive" English. The Apostle Paul wrote in I Thessalonians 5:23, *"And the very God of peace sanctify you wholly; and I pray God your whole **spirit** and **soul** and **body** be preserved blameless unto the coming of our Lord Jesus Christ."* This makes man a *tripartite* being, comprised of a spirit, soul, and body. Genesis 1:27 states that *"God created man in his own image."* Thus, man is a trinity, because God is a trinity: The Holy Spirit is the *spirit* of the Godhead; the Father is the *soul*; and Jesus is the *body*.

As to their individual components, the Holy Spirit is always likened to *wind.* When God appeared to Ezekiel in the valley of dry bones, He directed him to *"say to the **wind**...**breathe** upon these slain, that they may live,"* and then, *"prophesy...unto them...ye shall know that I am the LORD, when I...shall put my **spirit** in you."* (Ezekiel 37:9, 13-14) Jesus told Nicodemus, *"The **wind bloweth** where it listeth, and thou **hearest the sound thereof**, but canst not tell whence it cometh, and whither it goeth: **so is every one that is born of the Spirit**."* (John 3:8) Thus, the third member of the Trinity is like wind; you can *hear* it, but cannot *see* it. Consequently, the first of twenty-one definitions for *spirit* in *Webster's* states: "Primarily, wind; air in motion; hence, breath." ("Discovering" that the Greek *pneuma* is the source for several words involving air, such as "pneumonia" and "pneumatic drill," is simply a nice afterthought.)

With regard to God the Father, while John 1:18 reads: *"No man hath seen God at any time,"* Jesus adds, *"Ye have neither heard his voice at any time, nor seen his **shape**."* (John 5:37) Consequently, a human soul also has a shape (II Corinthians 12:3). From the account of the rich man and Lazarus we learn that it is *bodily* in form. Jesus described the rich man: *"And in hell he lift up his **eyes**, being in torments,"* while also relating his request to *"send Lazarus, that he may dip the **tip** of his **finger** in water, and cool my **tongue**;*

for I am tormented in this flame." (Luke 16:23-24) John testifies in Revelation 6:9, *"I saw under the altar the* **souls** *of them that were slain for the word of God."* Two verses later, he adds, *"And white* **robes** *were given unto every one of them."* Apparently, a soul can wear a robe. Of course, any heathen Hollywood producer knows that a *real* ghost needs a sheet. Thus, the Holy Spirit reveals that souls comprise the features of their physical bodies. Finally, the Lord Jesus represents God's *body*, Paul writing: *"For in him dwelleth all the fullness of the Godhead* **bodily**,*"* with John identifying Him as *the* one *"from the beginning...which we have* **looked** *upon, and our* **hands** *have* **handled**.*"* (Colossians 2:9, I John 1:1)

Though not very spiritual, a common football is the best illustration that ties the three concepts together—the leather pigskin representing the *body*; the bladder, the *soul*; and the air, the *spirit*. The more detailed account of man's creation in Genesis 2:7 shows how they all coalesced: *"And the LORD God formed man of the* **dust** *of the ground, and breathed into his nostrils the* **breath** *of life; and man became a living* **soul**.*"* Thus, when dust from below makes contact with breath from above, MAN becomes a *"living soul."* As a tripartite being, man is fully equipped to relate to his Creator through his *spirit*; to his fellow humans through the mind, emotion, and will of his *soul*; and to the physical world through the five senses of his *body*.

Adam was immediately put on notice that his privileged status of being in the very image of God was not to be taken lightly: *"And the LORD God commanded the man, saying, Of every tree of the garden thou mayest freely eat: But of the tree of the knowledge of good and evil, thou shalt not eat of it:* **for in the day that thou eatest thereof thou shalt surely die**.*"* (Genesis 2:17) Quite naturally, this is the first mention of the word "die" (or any other derivative of *death*) in Scripture. The one who *"had the power of death"* shows up in the very next chapter. (See also Hebrews 2:14) A former student of mine, Dan Goodwin, made the astute observation that the serpent's initial approach to Eve not only questioned the *content* of God's message – *"Yea, hath God said"* – but more precisely, her husband's *preservation* of the *"oral* original." Remember, Genesis 2:16 stated: *"And the **LORD***

*God commanded the **man***" (I Corinthians 14:35). Eve had received God's word *secondhand*. By the time we arrive at verse 6 (the number of man) we discover that the entire human race fell because a woman had doubted the veracity of a preserved "copy." Satan gained the advantage by convincing her that the secondary message was not as reliable as the "inspired original." There is a timely lesson here, as Eve constitutes the first major type of the Church in Scripture (Ephesians 5:31-32). Adam is subsequently informed that he is now destined for the dirt from whence he came (Genesis 3:19). The final scene in "Paradise Lost" reads: *"So he drove out the man; and he placed at the east of the garden of Eden Cherubims, and a flaming **sword** which turned every way, to keep the way of the tree of life."* (Genesis 3:24) This sword is not wielded by the Cherubims, but turns independently – *"without hands"* (the significance of which will be noted later).

At this juncture it is necessary to reexamine the traditional conclusions drawn from the wording of Adam's death sentence – *"**in the day** that thou eatest thereof **thou shalt surely die**."* Because Adam did not experience *physical* death *that same day*, the natural assumption is that he died *spiritually*. This has led many to further assume that Adam's *spirit* died. While not wanting to give the appearance of splitting hairs myself (and while making no claims to having "all knowledge"), I *do* believe this view could use some "tweaking." First, the Bible attributes significant activity to man's spirit, which would hardly be possible if it was *dead*. Proverbs 20:27 states: *"The **spirit of man** is the candle of the LORD, **searching** all the inward parts of the belly."* Paul adds: *"For what man **knoweth** the things of a man, save the **spirit** of man which is in him?"* (I Corinthians 2:11) Another problem concerns the physiological reality that the spirit is *the* essential for physical life: *"If he set his heart upon man, if he gather unto himself his **spirit** and his **breath**; All flesh shall **perish** together, and man shall turn again unto **dust**"*; and, *"For as the body without the **spirit** is dead."* (Job 34:14-15; James 2:26)

Remember – the *real* "you" is your *soul*, with the *pre*-Fall designation specifying *"a **living** soul."* (Genesis 2:7) Consequently, the prophet draws the distinction that *"the **soul** that sinneth, it shall die."* (Ezekiel 18:4) Jesus warned: *"fear him which is able to destroy both **soul** and body in hell."* (Matthew 10:28) Again, there is no question that a lost man is spiritually dead – *"And you hath he quickened, who were **dead** in trespasses and sins."* (Ephesians 2:1) However, when John 3:6 says *"**that** which is born of the Spirit is **spirit**,"* the object in view is a *spiritual* creation; namely, *"the **new man**"* of Ephesians 4:24, *"which after God is **created** in righteousness and true holiness."* (The reason I am being so particular will become apparent in the following chapter when the critical relationship between inspiration and the human spirit is analyzed.)

When Adam was driven away from the life-sustaining properties of God's presence, his entire tripartite nature was adversely affected. Though his spirit may not have died, it was certainly *deadened* to its original purpose, i.e., the capacity to discern all *spiritual* data, as *"the things of the Spirit of God knoweth no man, but the Spirit of God."* (I Corinthians 2:11) The most telling loss of all was the forfeiture of God's image. After reiterating, *"In the day that God created man, in the likeness of **God** made he him,"* the Bible records, *"And Adam...begat a son in **his** own likeness, after **his** image."* (Genesis 5:1, 3) For what it's worth, only two verses removed, the Lord drops some *"handfuls of purpose"* as if to illustrate, *"Touching the Almighty, we cannot find him out."* (Job 37:23) With *five* being the number of *death* (contrary to what we heard in Bible college about "grace"), we are not surprised to find the first recorded *natural* death in history showing up in Genesis 5:5. However, it is the *age* of the "deceased" that we are interested in here: *"And all the days that Adam lived were **nine hundred and thirty years**: and he died."* As II Peter 3:8 states that *"**one day** is with the Lord as **a thousand years**,"* we *understand* that Adam *did* in fact expire the selfsame day that he ate thereof. He just did so according to *God's* calendar.

In II Corinthians 5:1-4, Paul likened the Christian's *"earthly house"* to a *"tabernacle,"* as the *"tent of the **testimony**"* bore advanced *testimony* to the restored tripartite being of the believer: the *"courtyard,"* a type of the *body*; the *"Holy Place,"* of the *soul*; the

"Most Holy Place," of the *spirit* and the *"glory of the LORD"* of the indwelling *Holy Spirit* (Numbers 9:15). As our first parents began their earthly pilgrimage, their tripartite nature resembled the tabernacle *minus* the *"glory of the LORD."* (Exodus 40:35) Yet, despite this *"Ichabod"* status, the key truth to see is that fallen man was *still* in possession of his tabernacle, *including* the *"Most Holy Place."* While unsaved Jews and Gentiles alike would henceforth be incapable of knowing the *"deep things of God"* without *"the Spirit of God,"* the *"things of a man"* would still be discernable by the *"spirit of man which is in him."* (I Corinthians 2:11)

As there are very few atheists in foxholes, the book of Job gives three of the most commonly asked questions that mortals from Plato and Pilate to "P. Diddy" have pursued through the ages – *"how should man be just with God?"*; *"yea, man giveth up the ghost, and where is he?"*; and, *"If a man die, shall he live again?"* (Job 9:2; 14:10, 14) These inquiries are often the natural result of that *"candle of the LORD"* interacting with *"that which **may** be known of God...even his eternal power and Godhead."* (Romans 1:19) This *"candle,"* identified as *"the spirit of man,"* would also be involved with the conditions Paul went on to describe: *"For when the Gentiles, which have not the law, do by nature the things contained in the law, these, having not the law, are a law unto themselves: Which shew the work of the law written **in their hearts**, their **conscience** also bearing witness."* (Romans 2:14-15)

While the initial work of this candle is the elementary function of bearing an internal witness to human *consciousness*, the ultimate attainment is to perfect the sensitivities of the *conscience* itself as it comes in contact with everything from *stars* to *Scripture*. How else are we to account for anyone in the Old Testament acting "spiritual" without the permanent indwelling Holy Spirit? (See Genesis 20:6; II Chronicles 7:14; John 8:9) In any event, we can all rejoice for the way in which that candle wrought conviction in our *own* souls. And praise God for the One who lit the wick: *"That was the true Light, which **lighteth** every man that cometh into the* *world....For the grace of God that bringeth salvation hath appeared to all men."* (John 1:9; Titus 2:11)

SPIRITUAL CIRCUMCISION

After Adam's tripartite descendants put nearly 2,000 weary years behind them (including the Flood of Noah's day), the Lord calls a Shemite out of *Iraq* by the name of Abram (meaning "High Father"). He informs Abram that he will be a blessing to all families of the earth and that the land of Canaan will be deeded to a particular line of his posterity as an everlasting possession. The only problem is that Abram and his wife are childless senior citizens. Then, one evening the Lord points Abram's attention to the heavens and instructs him to *"tell the stars, if thou be able to number them,"* adding, *"So shall thy seed be."* To Abram's eternal credit, the Bible says, *"And he believed in the LORD; and he counted it to him for righteousness."* (Genesis 15:5-6) When Abram later hit the "Big 99," he got some *good* news and some *bad* news. The *good* news was that God was going to reconfirm His covenant with him and change his name to Abraham in the process (meaning "Father of many nations"). The *bad* news was that Abraham would have to perform a painful operation on himself as a token of this special covenant: *"And God said unto Abraham...This is my **covenant**, which ye shall keep, between me and you and **thy seed** after thee; Every man child among you shall be **circumcised**. And ye shall **circumcise the flesh of your foreskin;** and it shall be a **token of the covenant** betwixt me and you."* (Genesis 17:9-11)

Although a bit "intense" in appearance, the rite of circumcision was charged with spiritual imagery. With another 2,000 years until Calvary, Abraham would have to "get a knife," for *"without shedding of blood is no remission."* (Hebrews 9:22) The "point of contact" indicated that the problem with the human race was connected with their *seed.* Men are lost because they are born in the image and likeness of Adam. (This is why the *"last Adam"* had to be *virgin* born.) Paul would later reveal that Abraham's circumcision served as an important picture of the saving faith he displayed on that starry night: *"And he received the sign of circumcision, a seal of the righteousness of the **faith** which he had yet being uncircumcised: that he might be the father of all them that **believe**, though they be not circumcised; that righteousness might be imputed unto them also."* (Romans 4:11)

Now this is the station where all Greek and Hebrew experts get off the train. Remember, Bible colleges only teach you *about* the Bible, while Bible institutes teach you *the* Bible. "*Allllll* Aboard!" The main truth about *physical* circumcision in the Old Testament is that it pictures *spiritual* circumcision in the New Testament. There is a major theological reason as to *why* Abraham was commanded to separate himself from a portion of his own flesh. Before the Cross, all men were condemned, primarily because they were stuck with their father's image, *literally*. (WARNING: Close all lexicons!) When Adam fell, his seed went bad and his flesh became corrupt. The problem is that Adam's *soul* was attached to his *body* like the *bladder* is to the *pigskin*. (I can already hear a few Athenian stowaways mumbling the words of Acts 17:20 – *"thou bringest certain strange things to our ears."*)

A simple reading of the *English* text reveals that Abraham's descendants had a terrible time under the Law as they were always *touching* something that would get them into trouble. (See Genesis 3:3 for the Law of First Mention regarding "touch.") Leviticus 22:6 says, *"The **soul** which hath **touched** any such shall be unclean until even, and shall not eat of the holy things, unless he wash his **flesh** with water."* Paul referred to this spiritual roller coaster climate as the *"**Touch** not; **taste** not; **handle** not"* syndrome (Colossians 2:21). Prior to Calvary, the most common synonym for "man" was "soul." The word "soul" is used 426 times in the Old Testament, though, notably, only *five* times in the Pauline epistles. There's a reason church visitation is called "***soul*** winning," for *"the **soul** that sinneth, it shall die."*

The problem that *"wretched"* men have endured, being attached to the *"body of this death,"* was solved by the death and Resurrection of the Lord Jesus Christ (Romans 7:24). Because of Him, we can now "loose" more than just *foreskin*. Paul described this procedure in detail in his letter to the Colossians. The moment an unsaved man yields his will to the convicting power of the Holy Spirit and believes the Gospel of the grace of God, the most amazing process occurs. As God initially withdrew His presence from Adam the moment his "primary residence" got contaminated, the Lord must separate the soul of man from *his* corrupt flesh so that the Holy Spirit can reenter his spirit. While most Christians are familiar with the *fact* of that glorious reunion – *"The Spirit itself beareth witness with our spirit, that we are the children of God"* – few have ever discovered *how* the encounter was permitted to occur: *"And ye are complete in him, which is the head of all principality and power: In whom also ye are **circumcised** with the **circumcision made without hands**, in **putting off the body of the sins of the flesh** by the **circumcision of Christ**."* (Romans 8:16; Colossians 2:10-11) Do you see that *"**putting off the body**"* business? Isn't that *incredible*?

But it gets better yet. Notice how the Holy Spirit calls it an *"**operation** of God"* (Colossians 2:12). And what kind of operation is done *"**without hands**"*? The first *sword* that is mentioned in Scripture was also able to turn *"without hands."* (Genesis 3:24) This leads us to *the* most important surgical instrument of all: *"For the **word of God** is quick, and powerful, and sharper than any twoedged sword, **piercing even to the dividing asunder of soul and spirit, and of the joints and marrow**, and is a discerner of the thoughts and intents of the heart."* (Hebrews 4:12) *Wow*, talk about "cutting-edge" laser surgery! How's *that* for *"rightly **dividing**"*? (And, can you believe that we haven't even consulted the Greek yet?)

Now the main advantage of being *loosed* from our flesh is that we get to reattach elsewhere. *"Know ye not, brethren...how that the law hath dominion over a man as long as he liveth? For the woman which hath an husband is **bound** by the law to her husband so long as he liveth; but if the husband be dead, she is **loosed** from the law of her husband...Wherefore, my brethren, ye also are become dead to the law by the body of Christ; that ye should be **married to another**, even to him who is raised from the dead, that we should bring forth fruit unto God. For **when** we were **in the flesh**...but **now** we are* *delivered.*" (Romans 7:1-2, 4-6) This is what Genesis 2:24 is all about – *leaving* and *cleaving*. *"But he that is **joined** unto the Lord is **one spirit**.*" (I Corinthians 6:17) When the Holy *Spirit* is finally reunited with man's *spirit* in the Most Holy Place, the believer is simultaneously baptized into Christ's spiritual body. Thanks to the *"Last Adam"* (I Corinthians 15:45), man is once again a perfect tripartite being in the likeness and image of the Godhead: *"Lie not one to another, seeing that ye have **put off the old man** with his deeds; And have **put on the new man**, which is renewed in knowledge **after the image of him that created him**.*" (Colossians 3:9-10)

The most remarkable perk about spiritual circumcision is that the Lord no longer sees us as sinners! Notice how the Holy Spirit leads Paul to present this truth as though he could hardly fathom it himself: *"If then I do that which I would not, I consent unto the law that it is good. **Now then it is no more I that do it, but sin that dwelleth in me**. For I know **that in me (that is, in my flesh,)** dwelleth no good thing...Now if I do that I would not, **it is no more I that do it, but sin that dwelleth in me**.*" (Romans 7:16-20) The Apostle John expressed this spiritual phenomenon in I John 3:9 and 5:18 – *"Whosoever is born of God **doth not commit sin**; for his seed remaineth in him: and **he cannot sin**, because he is born of God...We know that whosoever is born of God **sinneth not**.*" (How many times have we heard Fundamentalist scholars butcher these verses with the Greek?) Unlike the "souls" in the Old Testament, we are *in* our bodies but no longer *attached* to them. A common ice tray is the best illustration to comprehend this concept. The tray holds frozen cubes of ice. However, when warm water is applied and the tray is twisted slightly, the cubes break loose but *remain* in the tray. While you and I are *in* the tray, we're not stuck *to* the tray. *Praise God*, one day we're going to leave these old ice trays behind, preferring *"rather to be absent from the body, and to be present with the Lord."* (II Corinthians 5:8) And it won't be long before we get *new* "ice trays" to boot! *"It is sown a natural body; it is raised a spiritual body...as we have borne the image of the earthy, we shall also bear the image of the heavenly."* (I Corinthians 15:44, 49)

"TEN...NINE...EIGHT...SEVEN...SIX..."

However, in the midst of all our rejoicing, we must never forget about the lost. Have you ever considered what takes place when an unsaved person dies? While *we* get to retain *our* restored tripartite nature forever, our unconverted friends and loved ones will have a different ending altogether. Rush Limbaugh has spent a career joking about having "talent on loan from God." If he *only* knew! El Rushbo (along with every *other* unconverted sinner) *does* have something "on loan from God," but it's not *talent*. (Remember that *"candle of the LORD, searching all the inward parts of the belly"*?) We are all familiar with that somber ICU bed scene alongside the foreboding heart monitor. Well, guess what happens to that *candle* when the screen goes **Beep, Beep, Beep, Beep,** *Beeeeeeeeeeeep....................* *"Or ever the silver cord be **loosed**, or the golden bowl be **broken**, or the pitcher be **broken** at the fountain, or the wheel **broken** at the cistern.* **THEN** *shall the **dust return to the earth** as it was:* **AND THE SPIRIT SHALL RETURN UNTO GOD WHO GAVE IT.***"* (Ecclesiastes 12:6-7)

With "all due respect" to Dr. Jack Van Impe and his "Doggies-and-Kitties-Go-*Up*-At-the-Rapture" fantasy, the Lord only breathed into *Adam's* nostrils. *"Who knoweth the **spirit of man** that goeth **upward**, and the spirit of the beast that goeth downward to the earth?"* (Ecclesiastes 3:21) Like a man who died broke with only half a treasure map in his pocket, the spirit *was* the only part of his being that was capable of reconnecting him to the divine nature of his Creator; and, as the prophet cried to Elisha: *"Alas, master! for it was **borrowed**."* (II Kings 6:5)

While the mighty in *this* life may have caused Wall Street to tremble, when it's *"yo'* time to *go,"* then it's *"yo'* time to *go!"*; for, *"There is no man that hath power over the **spirit** to retain the **spirit***; *neither hath he power in the day of death: and there is no discharge in that war."* In one of the most insightful passages on the subject of human nature, Solomon tells us why *"the misery of man is great upon him"* – because he *cannot* control the future – *especially* with regard to when the Grim Reaper will come knocking: *"For he knoweth not **that** which shall be: for who can tell him **when** it shall be?"* (Ecclesiastes 8:6-8) *"Seeing his days are determined, the number of his months are with thee, **thou hast appointed his bounds that he cannot pass.**"* (Job 14:5) Moral of the story: Don't let all that celebrity bravado fool you. The "stars" who *"through **fear of death** were **all their lifetime** subject to **bondage**,"* chant, "Oh, my G-d!" in their *subconscious*. (Hebrews 2:15)

So the next time you have an opportunity to talk with a lost person, just remember that the very *breath* of God permeates their soul. (In Mr. Limbaugh's case, the very *breath he mingles with his cigar smoke* is what he "has on loan from God.") Just as *our* soul and spirit, *joined* unto the Lord by the Holy Spirit, will one day "fly away" like a s*pace shuttle stack* that will *never* disengage or explode – the *Lord's "candle"* stands on the launching pad of every *lost* man's soul like a solitary external tank ready to unite with those two rocket boosters to take *him* home, as well. With the "some glad morning" of *our* departure drawing ever nearer, let us do our best to ensure that the *spirit* of some unsaved friend or loved one does *not* return to God like an unmanned *drone* – *"My **spirit** shall not always strive with man."* (Genesis 6:3)

"AND *AWAY* WE GO"

(JACKIE GLEASON'S EPITAPH)

7

The Inspiration of the Almighty

ELUSIONAL SCHOLARS EMPLOY an array of scientific methods to "discover" the exact wording of original manuscripts that disappeared millenniums ago. Yet, the very authors of those documents are presented as being incapable of comprehending them without special assistance from God. Though David could pen the 23rd Psalm – the most recognized passage of the Bible – even *he* had to pray, *"Open thou mine eyes, that I may behold wondrous things out of thy law."* (Psalm 119:18) Sometimes those petitions went unanswered. With the ink still wet on Daniel's original, the prophet was told to *"shut up the words, and seal the book,"* prompting the exchange: *"And I heard, but I **understood** not: then said I, O my Lord, what shall be the end of these things? And he said, Go thy way, Daniel: for the words are closed up and sealed till the time of the end"* (Daniel 12:8-9). If you were blessed from the Bible study on spiritual circumcision, it was because the Holy Spirit enabled you to *understand* the doctrine. The ability to comprehend the Scripture is not an automatic perk that should be taken lightly. Peter himself acknowledged that the Pauline epistles contained *"some things **hard** to be **understood**."* (II Peter 3:16) When Jesus advanced to the meat of the word, *"many of his disciples went back, and walked no more with him,"* muttering, *"This is an **hard** saying; who can hear it?"* (John 6:60-66)

So the obvious question is: How could many of "the brethren" read the same material concerning spiritual circumcision and scoff? How could the identical truth be "edifying Scripture" to some, while "nutty Ruckmanite doctrine" to others? How are we to account for such irreconcilability when the author of the Bible is *supposed* to be indwelling both groups? Well, for one thing, "division" is nothing new and is often "inspired" by Jesus: *"So there was a **division** among the people **because of him**...And there was a **division** among them...There was a **division** therefore again among the Jews for these sayings."* (John 7:43; 9:16; 10:19) But then, who said the word "division" is always a *bad* word? Jesus was extremely candid with His fair-weather listeners, declaring: *"Suppose ye that I am come to give peace on earth? I tell you, Nay; but rather **division**."* (Luke 12:51) The reason these Jews were having an audience with their unrecognized Messiah in the first place was because of their own unique status, the "I AM" having previously informed Pharaoh, *"And I will put a **division** between **my** people and **thy** people."* Division isn't wrong – as long as it's *"right* division."

Take this matter of the A.V. 1611 and the *endless* debate over the doctrine of inspiration, structured around a single Greek word – *theopneustos*. Why are so many Christians "divided" in *this* area? (And don't forget that it's the "King James Only" crowd that is constantly being accused of "causing unnecessary *division* in the body," etc.) Jesus unraveled the mystery when He declared, *"If any man **will do** his will, he **shall know** of the doctrine, whether it be of God, or whether I speak of myself."* (John 7:17) Thus, a direct correlation exists between a person's *willingness* to *do* God's *will* and his *ability* to *understand* God's *word*. It is no coincidence that the greatest opponents of the King James Bible are self-promoting kingdom builders who are not about to surrender their own preeminence to *any* "book," especially one that will expose their unmistakable profile (III John 9). Notice how Jesus nails their hides in the very next verse: *"**He that speaketh of himself seeketh his own glory**: but he that seeketh his glory that sent him, the same is true, and no unrighteousness is in him."* Paul adds: *"**For we preach not ourselves, but Christ Jesus the Lord.**"* (II Corinthians 4:5) The major cross-reference for John 7:17 is II Timothy 4:3-4 – *the* single-most important verse in the New Testament to understand the current apostasy. *"For the time **will come** when they **will not endure** sound doctrine; but after their own lusts shall they heap to themselves teachers, having itching ears; **And they shall turn away their ears from the truth, and shall be turned unto fables**. "* Note the striking connection to Jesus' words: *"If any man WILL DO his will, he SHALL KNOW of the doctrine. "* Thus, Christians who will *not* do, will *not* know – it's as simple as that.

Paul confirmed this principle in his salutation to Titus: *"Paul, a servant of God, and an apostle of Jesus Christ, according to the faith of God's elect, **and the acknowledging of the truth which is after godliness.** "* (Titus 1:1) The apostle *understood* that his only "ministerial credentials" stemmed from the *"faith of God's elect"* (i.e., that he was *who* and *what* he professed to be), and that their *"acknowledging of the truth"* (concerning *what* he preached) stemmed from "godliness" – *their* godliness (*godliness* being a prerequisite to *understanding*). Should we really be surprised that the same generation that turned away their ears *from* the *King James Bible* has also *been* turned *unto* fables like *The Chronicles of Narnia*? Sadly, the average Baptist is far more familiar with C. S. Lewis than he is with Dr. John Clarke or Shubal Stearns. Thus, the need of the hour is divine *illumination*, for what good is an "inspired" text – whether *autograph*, *copy*, or *translation* – if the reader is unable to understand it's content? So, the question becomes: What part, if any, does inspiration itself play in this important process? It is the thesis of this book that whenever the Scripture is allowed to speak for itself, the doctrine of inspiration will be seen to have a wider jurisdiction than the scholar is willing to concede.

ENTER ELIHU

The main problem with confining inspiration to the autographs is caused by the scholar confining his exegesis to II Timothy 3:16. In their rush to maintain job security, modern Nicolaitanes ignore one of the most important keys to proper Bible study – the "Law of First Mention." As previously discussed, the word "inspiration" occurs only twice in the entire Bible. The *first* and more critical usage is found in Job 32:8 – *"But there is a spirit in man: and the **inspiration** of the Almighty giveth them **understanding**."* When both verses are examined and compared, Job 32:8 will be seen to reveal the *definition* and *purpose* for inspiration, while II Timothy 3:16 provides the major *illustration* of *theopneustos* in action.

In its most basic exegesis, *inspiration* gives man *understanding* as it is received and employed by his *spirit*. This simple truth was provided by the Holy Spirit nearly 1,800 years before Paul ever discussed the subject with Timothy. It is also highly significant that these words constitute the *first* utterance by Elihu, the human author of the book itself. (Note the abrupt shift from the *third* to the *first* person, in verses 14-16.) As Job is the oldest book in the Bible, we marvel that the *first* writer of Scripture "just happens" to record *the* definitive statement on inspiration, as well! And the authoritative nature of Elihu's pronouncements could not be stronger – as Job had requested, *"Oh that one would hear me! behold, my desire is, that the Almighty would answer me"* – Elihu informs him, *"Behold, I am according to thy wish in God's stead."* (31:35; 33:6) In keeping with the promise, *"Delight thyself also in the LORD; and he shall give thee the desires of thine heart,"* Elihu fulfills Job's burden: *"Oh that my **words** were now **written**! oh that they were **printed in a book**!"* (Psalm 37:4; Job 19:23) It is also worth noting that, as we cannot know for sure what language Elihu would have used during this post-Babel era, his autograph was probably translated into Hebrew by Moses (Acts 7:22). This would make the entire first book in the canon an *inspired* translation. (*Tell* me that God doesn't have a sense of humor.)

As mentioned in the previous chapter, *inspiration* – as the very breath of Jehovah – constitutes the infusion of human life itself, with God's breath and man's breath frequently presented as one and the same: *"All the while my **breath** is in me, and the **spirit** of God is in my **nostrils**"* (Job 27:3). Note the important cross-reference to Job 32:8 (just *across* the page): *"The **Spirit** of God hath made me, and the **breath** of the Almighty hath given me **life**."* (Job 33:4)

Thus, we *understand* that the *Spirit* of God positioned the words *"inspiration of the Almighty"* and *"breath of the Almighty"* within a mere eighteen verses of one another. To the consternation of higher Christian education, the chronological usage in the *English* text connected inspiration to God's breath long before any recourse to the Greek was needed at II Timothy 3:16. (Ah, but *"wisdom is too high for a fool."*) However, to throw a "bone" to the *Gentile* scholars, whereas *theopneustos* made only *one* appearance in the New Testament, the Hebrew *nĕshamah* (translated "inspiration" in Job 32:8) was employed 24 times throughout the Old Testament, Genesis 2:7 being the *first* mention – *"And the LORD God formed man of the dust of the ground, and breathed into his nostrils the **breath** of life; and man became a living soul."* In 17 of these instances, the English text reads "breath."

From Genesis 1:27, 2:7, and I Thessalonians 5:23, we deduce further that this divine breath forms the essence of man's *spirit.* The key in all of this is to realize that the *"understanding"* of Job 32:8 is designed to go far beyond mere human instincts. When unsaved men pursue their search for *"glory and honour and immortality,"* the Lord has obligated Himself to reciprocate: *"And ye shall seek me, and find me, when ye shall search for me with all your heart."* (Romans 2:7; Jeremiah 29:13). In the book of Proverbs, God promised to respond to any who would respond to *Him*: *"Turn you at my reproof: behold, I will pour out my **spirit** unto you, I will **make known my words unto you.**"* (Proverbs 1:23) Note how this "inspiration" results in a greater "understanding" of his *words*; and what a blessed circle indeed: *"The entrance of thy **words** giveth **light**; it giveth **understanding** unto the simple."* (Psalm 119:130)

This all has to do with that *"**candle** of the LORD"* business; the *light* being employed to find "something" that was *lost*. *"Either what woman having ten pieces of silver, if she **lose** one piece, doth not **light a candle**, and sweep the house, and seek diligently till she **find** it?"* (Luke 15:8) Thus, the cycle would appear to run: Basic *inspiration* to man's spirit – resulting in greater *understanding* – resulting in greater *desire* for *more* inspiration, and so forth. *"Draw* *nigh to God, and he will draw nigh to you."* (James 4:8) Every searching Cornelius will eventually meet his Apostle Peter, *"for he that cometh to God must believe that he is, and that he is a rewarder of them that diligently seek him."* (Acts 10; Hebrews 11:6)

The Bible also reveals that God can extinguish a man's candle for spiritual indifference: *"The light of the righteous rejoiceth: but the **lamp of the wicked** shall be **put out**."* (Proverbs 13:9) And, *"The light shall be dark in his tabernacle, and his **candle shall be put out with him**."* (Job 18:6) Paul described end-time defectors as *"having their **conscience** seared with a hot iron."* (I Timothy 4:2) *Webster's* defines *seared* as "to make callous or insensible" (a most accurate depiction of the professional *"highminded"* scholar, being *"without natural affection"* – II Timothy 3:3-4). After the heathen came to know the Lord's *"eternal power...being **understood** by the things that are made...they glorified him not as God, neither were thankful; but became vain in their imaginations, **and their foolish heart was darkened**."*

Someone has said, "Light rejected becomes *lightening*." When that candle goes out, the capacity for understanding goes with it. *"And even as they did not like to retain God in their **knowledge**, God gave them over to a **reprobate mind**...being filled with all unrighteousness...**without understanding**."* (Romans 1:20-21, 28, 31) Job adds, *"For thou hast hid their heart from **understanding**."* (Job 17:4) After describing a bunch of benighted souls roasting their meat and warming themselves by the fire generated by the left-over wood from the tree that had just provided their latest "god," Isaiah 44:18 renders God's condemnation of the heathen: *"They have not known nor **understood**: for he hath shut their eyes, that they cannot see; and their hearts, that they cannot **understand**."* (Southern Baptist Bill "is/is" Clinton heard *many* a sermon in his younger days).

Now, while *inspiration* appears only twice in Scripture, the word *understanding* (the very *fruit* of inspiration) appears *160* times. As we have limited use for lexicons, the Bible provides its own two-part definition for this important English word. In Job 28:28, we read, *"to **depart from evil** is **understanding**,"* with Proverbs 9:10

adding, *"the **knowledge** of the **holy** is **understanding**."* Note how the first condition is a prerequisite to the second. Paul recorded the New Testament equivalent of this spiritual correlation in Acts 20:21 when he described his dual message as *"testifying both to the Jews, and also to the Greeks, **repentance** toward God, and **faith** toward our Lord Jesus Christ"* (a far cry from "one-two-three, repeat after me" soul winning). Again, the *first* action leads to the *second*.

JOB 32:8 AND I TIMOTHY 3:16

The most striking connection between the two appearances of "inspiration" can be viewed in the context of their respective chapters. There are at least *seven* amazing similarities between the two settings. *Both* Elihu and Timothy are described as young men prone to intimidation (Job 32:6; I Timothy 4:12); *both* have a unique relationship with an afflicted mentor; *both* are mentioned alongside of wisdom (Job 32:7, 9, 13; II Timothy 3:15); *both* are confronted by age without understanding (Job 32:3, 9, 12; II Timothy 3:7-8); *both* mentors were falsely slandered (Job 32:3, 13; Philippians 2:14-16); while *both* appealed to their personal track record (Job 32:1; II Timothy 3:10-12).

The seventh parallel is the most pertinent to this chapter. Both Elihu *and* Timothy are seen to be *"inspired* through *inspiration."* Elihu testified that he had remained quiet before his elders, for he thought *"multitude of years should teach wisdom."* (Job 32:7) However, as he perceived that Eliphaz, Bildad, and Zophar were clueless regarding Job's true plight, the "juices started to flow," *inspiring* him to declare in Job 32:17-19: *"I said, I will answer also my part, I also will shew mine opinion. For I am full of matter, the **spirit within me constraineth me**. Behold, my **belly** is as wine which hath no vent; it is ready to burst like new bottles."* (Did you notice that important cross-reference between **spirit** and **belly**, as in, *"The **spirit** of man is the **candle of the LORD**, searching all the inward parts of the **belly**"*?) Elihu says that his *spirit* literally "constrained" him to speak, despite his youth and inexperience. *Webster's* defines *constrain* as: "To compel or force, to urge with irresistible power, or with a power sufficient to produce the effect." Thus, Elihu's surge of holy boldness is the all-important context of Job 32:8. While verse 9 declares that Job's "friends" failed to *"understand judgment,"* Elihu would set them straight over the next *five chapters*, being "constrained" by the "inspired understanding" he received from that key verse directly preceding: *"But there is a **spirit** in man: and the **inspiration** of the Almighty giveth them **understanding**."*

The comparison with Timothy's need for spiritual "inspiration" is striking. Like Elihu, Timothy must have viewed himself as a neophyte, for Paul encouraged him: *"Let no man despise thy **youth**."* (I Timothy 4:12) And, though *Paul* was the one awaiting execution in the Mamertine dungeon, *he* attempted to reassure *Timothy*: *"I have remembrance of thee in my prayers night and day…being mindful of **thy** tears,"* exhorting, *"Wherefore I put thee in remembrance that thou **stir up the gift of God**, which is **in thee** by the putting on of my hands. For God hath not given us the spirit of **fear**."* (II Timothy 1:3-4, 6-7) As Timothy's ultimate need was also one of "understanding," the apostle directs him accordingly: *"Consider what **I** say; and the Lord give thee **understanding** in all things."* (II Timothy 2:7) Furthermore, it is no coincidence that this very Scripture is the *key* to *"rightly dividing the word of truth,"* Paul being the central spokesman for the Church Age. The root word *"know"* appears five times within the first fifteen verses of the third chapter of II Timothy.

Then, whereas Elihu was the literal human progenitor of God's word, Paul reminded Timothy that *"from a **child** thou hast **known** the **holy scriptures**, which are **able** to make thee **wise** unto salvation through faith which is in Christ Jesus."* (II Timothy 3:15) And herein lies the *ultimate* context for *theopneustos* – that the *"holy scriptures"* are *"given"* to men with their own intrinsic *ability* to impart the *ability* to *know* their *holy* content; i.e., the *"holy scriptures"* are *able* to impart *"understanding,"* which *is "the knowledge of the holy."* The Lord declares: *"So shall **my word** be that **goeth forth out of my mouth**: it shall not return unto me void, but it shall* *accomplish that which I please, and it shall prosper **in the thing** whereto I sent it."* (Isaiah 55:11)

The ultimate accomplishment of this process is to *make* the *one* into whom it was sent *"wise unto salvation."* Notice how the Holy Spirit positioned the words *"wisdom"* and *"wise"* in the verses immediately before and after Job 32:8. Thus, we are not surprised that "wisdom" and "understanding" fit together like a hand in a glove, appearing 54 times *each* in Proverbs. As 5 plus 4 equals 9 (the number of *fruit bearing*), we "understand" that their combination will impart a *double* fruit-bearing experience. At *99* years of age, Abraham was told by God, *"And I will make thee **exceeding fruitful.**"* (Genesis 17:1, 6) Paul later reveals that Abraham became *"the father of **all** them that believe,"* both Jews *and* Gentiles. (Romans 4:11) After God asks Job, *"Who hath put **wisdom** in the inward parts? Or who hath given **understanding** to the heart?"* the final chapter declares, *"And...the LORD gave Job **twice** as much as he had before."* (Job 38:36; 42:10) You would think that any scholar who could count to *ten* would have enough "wiggle room" to *understand* such things: *"and - the - inspiration - of - the - Almighty - giveth - them - **understanding.**"*

When Jesus needed to "inspire" a bunch of shaky apostles for their future ministry, He simply stated to them: *"Peace be unto you: **as** my Father hath sent me, **even so** send I you. And when he had said this, he **breathed** on them, and said unto them, Receive ye the **Holy Ghost.**"* (John 20:22) Just as His *own* descent from Heaven into Mary's womb as *"that holy thing"* had been occasioned by the *"The Holy Ghost,"* the eleven would likewise be commissioned by "holy breath" (Luke 1:35). And, of course, within days that same Holy Ghost would arrive with the sound of *"a rushing mighty **wind.**"* (Acts 2:2)

INSPIRATION
REVELATION • PRESERVATION • PROPAGATION • ILLUMINATION

It would therefore appear that the doctrine of inspiration involves far more than merely the production of original manuscripts. In any standard theological presentation on *Bibliology* (the study of the Bible), inspiration is presented as *one* of five related sub-topics: revelation, inspiration, preservation, propagation, and illumination. Reviewing them in their suggested sequence, *revelation* would involve the initial sending of God's message into the spirit of His human instrument of choice; *inspiration* would be the infallible recording of that revelation; *preservation*, the divine safekeeping of that inspired revelation; *propagation*, the spirit-led dissemination of that preserved message; and *illumination*, the supernatural ability to discern the delivered message. (While "illumination" is not a Bible word *per se*, it serves the same purpose as other non-scriptural terms such as "Trinity" and "Rapture" in describing a clear truth – Psalm 119:18; Luke 24:31-32.)

Considering this "traditional" outline in the light of ever-increasing attacks on the King James Bible, the time has come for believers to heed Colossians 2:8 and exchange the *tradition* of *men* for the *truth* of *Christ*. As "eight" is the Bible number for "new beginnings," we understand that there are *eight* words in the text that require a *new* interpretation: *"All scripture is given by inspiration of God."* In short, like the blind man in John 9:23, the Scripture must *finally* be permitted to speak for itself. When *inspiration* is viewed *solely* as that second stage – responsible only for creating the autographs – it automatically relegates all subsequent copies and translations to an inferior status under *preservation*. Dr. Stewart Custer, former chairman of the Bible department at Bob Jones University wrote: "As much as Fundamentalists have loved and defended a great translation like the King James Version, they *must* remember that the court of last resort in doctrinal matters is not any translation, *but the wording of the original Greek and Hebrew texts....*" (Emphasis mine)

I would submit to Dr. Custer that the *English* text is plain enough to "understand," the breath of God's Spirit being directly involved with the *entire* transmission process (or, as they say down in *Greenville*) – "From the *first* hallelujah to the *last* amen." Given that the Scripture is frequently identified with God *Himself* (Romans 9:17; Galatians 3:8; Hebrews 4:12-13), one *could* say that inspiration is the *Alpha* and

Omega of Bibliology *itself.* When the *receiving* and *recording* phases are combined under the initial stage of *revelation, inspiration* can then be seen as the actual driving engine of the other four stages. This is the very relationship that we find in Job 32; Elihu, one of five characters in the book, separates himself in order to set the other four parties straight (including Job) concerning their "words." (Job 32:11, 12, 14)

Now, I am well aware that this expanded approach to inspiration *must* (as the Stewart Custers of "Christendom" would say) be rejected out of hand as unorthodox nonsense for opposing "conventional wisdom." But isn't that the very focus of the chapter we have been studying? As I understand it, the first human "author" of Holy Scripture had gotten a *belly full* of "conventional wisdom" and decided that *his* opinion was as good as anyone else's, declaring, rather contemptuously: *"**Great men are not always wise:** neither do the aged **understand** judgment. Therefore I said, Hearken to me; **I will also shew mine opinion.** "* (Job 32:9-10)

I can empathize with Elihu in this dramatic scene, for while he is *absolutely convinced* that Job is innocent of the charges against him, yet he offers his reasoning as *opinions* (Job 32:12-13). Likewise, *I* am absolutely convinced that my King James Bible is innocent of *all* charges made against *it.* And yet, while I have tried to saturate this book with prayer and Scripture, I would be a fool if I pretended to be an infallible pope. (Dr. Jack Schaap "eulogized" the departed John Paul II in his Sunday evening sermon on April 3, 2005, stating: "The man did his best. **I think he was a sincere man**. I read his articles, and I read many of his sermons and I tried to get a feel for the man.") Let me say again that I have *zero* reservations about my King James Bible, though the "court of last resort" (as Dr. Custer put it) with regard to my pertinent "opinions" will be the Judgment Seat of Christ. (And, for the record – "His Holiness," John Paul II, *wrote the book* on unmanned drones, and any Baptist Pastor who would praise a Roman Catholic pope from a Baptist pulpit had better check out his *own* launch pad!)

Allow me to proceed, therefore, in the spirit of Elihu: *"I will speak, that I may be refreshed: I will open my lips and answer."* (Job 32:20) To begin, though my *scriptural* thesis is not very "scientific," it *will* offer a stimulating perspective to that unresolved "is/was" dilemma. For when the *breath* of God, the Holy Ghost, is *understood* to be actively blowing in a single, continuous stream – first, *into* the spirit of one of those *"holy men of God"*; next, *into* a piece of parchment; then, *into* multiplied copies and translations; then, off the page and *into* some soul through the eye and/or ear gate; and then, finally, *into* the terminus of the spirit itself – *then*, that "dissonant" grammatical construction – *"All scripture is given by inspiration of God"* – takes on a *whole* new meaning!

While the immediate context of II Timothy 3:16 is the critical preceding verse, the context for *that* verse is found in the apostle's opening remarks: *"When I call to remembrance the unfeigned faith that is in thee, which dwelt first in thy **grandmother Lois**, and thy **mother Eunice**; and I am persuaded that in thee also."* (II Timothy 1:5) The reason Timothy had known the Holy Scriptures from childhood was because they had been "given" to him by his mother and grandmother, as in – *"All scripture is given by inspiration of God and is profitable."* And the reason they were *able* to make Timothy *"wise unto salvation"* was because *"There is a **spirit** in man: and the **inspiration** of the Almighty **giveth** them **understanding**."* (Job 32:8) Paul's "son in the faith" could *understand* the Scriptures because they had been "given to him" through inspiration. This is precisely why the only two verses in Scripture that mention "inspiration" use the word "give" in the present tense – *"giveth them"* and *"is given."* We conclude, therefore, from the *English* that "inspiration" *gives* man two essential things: *"all Scripture"* (i.e., *autographs*, *copies*, and *translations*) and *"understanding."*

Once Timothy's *"candle"* was in full fellowship with the *big* "candle" he could advance past salvation to *"know the things that are freely given to us by God,"* the so-called *"deep things of God,"* defined as *"doctrine...reproof...correction, and instruction in righteousness."* (Romans 8:16; I Corinthians 2:10; I Timothy 3:17)

In the interim, he would have to contend with the *"candle of the wicked,"* Paul warning his son in the faith, *"But **evil** men and seducers shall **wax** worse and worse, deceiving, and being deceived."* (II Timothy 3:13) However, their end would be certain – *"as **wax melteth** before the fire, so let the **wicked** perish at the presence of God."* (Psalm 68:2)

PERSONAL TESTIMONY

As Paul shared his testimony on three occasions, I will do the same here. My own "dungeon flamed with light" following a marvelous sequence of providential events. Born on Thanksgiving Day 1952 (three months after Dr. Norris died), I was christened in St. Monica's Roman Catholic Church at 413 East 79th Street in New York City. As only God can so arrange our lives, the historic First Baptist Church, founded by John Gano, is located on this same street at 265 *West* 79th Street. Following my mother's suicide in 1964, our family moved to Wilmington, Delaware, where I later enrolled in the largest Catholic high school in the state. I can still recall, as a despondent youth, sleeping off a drunk "under the boardwalk" at Rehoboth Beach. In yet another twist of "fate," the man God would later use to make this book possible, frittered away *his* unsaved years as a lifeguard on that very beach, over two decades earlier. A Wilmington native, Peter Ruckman entered this world on the family couch at his parents' residence on Gilpin Avenue. Well, "it just so happens" that Gilpin dead-ends at Woodlawn Avenue, with 2010 Woodlawn Avenue being *my* first Delaware address. (Dr. Ruckman's father, Colonel John Hamilton Ruckman, a World War I veteran and distinguished member of the Manhattan Project, is buried in Rehoboth, Delaware.)

In the ensuing years, the Holy Scriptures were *given* to me on several occasions by faithful soul-winning Christians. Finally, in 1974 the Holy Ghost "cranked things up" through the radio speakers of my Toyota Corolla during a morning commute to work. For the next five months, Pastor Randy Carroll of Marcus Hook Baptist

Church in Lynwood, Pennsylvania, proceeded to *give* me the Holy Scriptures through his daily, fifteen-minute broadcast. My wife, Linda, and I were married at Holy Cross Roman Catholic Church in Dover, Delaware, on August 17th of that same year. At *my* request, Mary was duly "honored" with *Ave Marie.* (Though Linda had been saved in a Baptist revival meeting as a child, her parents soon divorced and she was not fully grounded spiritually.) The typical Catholic reception, featuring an open bar and a live band, followed at a local dining establishment. The Polish priest who married us (my homeroom teacher in high school) livened things up with his accordion by leading a conga line to the tune of "When the Saints Go Marching In." (Of course, little did I know at the time that we were actually "marching to *Hell.*") While my fellow Catholics and I "congaed" around the dining room, my Baptist in-laws gasped in disbelief!

Thankfully, the Lord showed up later that afternoon during the drive to our hotel. My lovely bride and I were exchanging wedding gifts in the back seat of the limousine: I presented her with a romantic charm bracelet; she *gave* me a giant print King James Bible – my first-*ever* copy of the Holy Scriptures! And, believe it or not, as truth is stranger than fiction, she purchased the Bible at the Delaware State Fair *after attending a Beach Boys concert.* Like Romans 5:20 says, *"But where sin abounded, grace did much more abound"* (i.e., the book you are reading can literally be traced to a Beach Boys concert in Harrington, Delaware, a mere 33 miles from that boardwalk at Rehoboth).

After a weeklong honeymoon in Hawaii, we made a *beeline* for Pastor Carroll's church that first Sunday morning home. And you'll never guess what happened – the Scriptures were *given* to me *again,* this time through a sermon on Acts 10. By invitation time, "It was all over but the shoutin'!" *Eight* days after that infamous conga line it was time for a "new beginning." You would have to be a student of Baptist history to appreciate *my* experience: The Lord *gives* me a *Baptist* wife, born in *Virginia,* who *gives* this Catholic city boy his first *King James Bible,* who then gets saved in one of the oldest *Baptist* churches in the *Philadelphia* area. Then, to top things off, my good friend, Pastor Jeff Faggart (founder of the Baptist History Preservation Society), informs me that the premier Bible teacher of the early twentieth century, Clarence Larkin, became a Baptist upon joining Marcus Hook Baptist Church in 1882 (being ordained into the ministry two years later). "Well, *Glory!*" Have the Holy Scriptures ever been GIVEN to YOU? If so, they were GIVEN by inspiration and *"the inspiration of the Almighty GIVETH [YOU] understanding."*

INSPIRATION IN MOTION

I would now like to illustrate the entire process. Paul informed the Galatians: *"But I certify you, brethren, that the **gospel** which was preached of me is not after man. For I neither received it of man, neither was I taught it, but by the **revelation** of Jesus Christ."* (Galatians 1:11-12) Paul's ministry began with special revelation directly from God. My "opinion" is that his *ability* to "understand" the revelation would have been the first occurrence of inspiration based on the scriptural definition of the word – *"the **inspiration** of the Almighty giveth them **understanding**."* Having carried this "inspired" revelation in his heart for some time, Paul is then *moved* by the Holy Ghost (while ministering in Corinth) to author the book of Romans. (As previously mentioned, Paul *quotes* his message to Tertius, who pens the actual epistle.) When the words, *"Paul, a servant of Jesus Christ, called to be an apostle, separated unto the **gospel** of God,"* leave Paul's mouth, they are conveyed to Tertius in such a manner that he is able to "understand" and record the quoted text precisely. My "opinion" is that the breath of God would have ensured such a transaction, as *"the **inspiration** of the Almighty giveth them **understanding**."* Whoever delivered Paul's original to Rome did so under the watchful eye of divine providence (Acts 27). Now, it's just my "opinion," but I wouldn't be surprised if the "breath of God" had availed the courier with the necessary *understanding* for his precarious journey, as *"the **inspiration** of the Almighty* *giveth them* **understanding.** *"* Thus, we see *preservation* before the original ever reaches the intended recipients.

Then, when the first Gentile believers in Rome read those opening words, *"Paul, a servant of Jesus Christ,"* theopneustos had to be all over the place; otherwise, no one would have been able to *understand* a single word, for *"the* **inspiration** *of the Almighty giveth them* **understanding.** *"* Here, we have "inspired illumination" at work. Regardless of what you choose to call it, Paul was burdened that believers *"might be filled with the knowledge of his will in all* **wisdom** *and spiritual* **understanding.** *"* (Colossians 1:9) And, of course, we know *"the* **inspiration** *of the Almighty giveth them* **understanding.** *"* As David testified, *"Thy* **word** *have I hid* **in** *mine* **heart,** *that I might not sin against thee,"* God's will is for the **in**spired word to *penetrate* and *permeate* His children, transforming them into "transparent theopneustos" in the process – *"Forasmuch as ye are manifestly declared to be the* **epistle of Christ** *...written not with ink, but with the* **Spirit** *of the living God; not in tables of* **stone,** *but in fleshy tables of the* **heart.** *"* (Psalm 119:11; II Corinthians 3:3; Romans 12:1-2)

Having devoured the contents of Paul's *original*, the believers in Rome would have naturally dispatched any number of *copies* to their brethren in outlying churches. When these copies were made and sent out, would it not be natural to assume that God's breath accompanied them as well? Would a believer in a distant city have experienced *less* conviction from a "mere" copy of Romans than had been generated by the autograph itself? If the Christians who received the first *copy* were able to "understand" its content, would it not be reasonable to conclude that *inspiration* was involved, for *"the* **inspiration** *of the Almighty giveth them* **understanding** *"*?

But, now we are about to encounter a *supposed* "bump in the road." When the vast array of extant Greek manuscripts is collated, some variant readings appear. This demonstrates human "error" in the transcription process, analogous to the harmless *printing* mistakes in the early editions of the King James Bible. To illustrate, should one decide to make a handwritten copy of the Bible for a missionary in an English-speaking field, wouldn't some "eye-to-hand" mistakes likely occur? Now, this is where FAITH comes in, and *"without faith it is impossible to please God."* (Hebrews 11:6) *How* the Holy Spirit chose to *preserve His* words would have fallen under *His* jurisdiction and expertise, not *ours* (Isaiah 55:8). Many Christians are like Martha, *"careful and troubled about many things"* (Luke 10:41). In 1742, George Whitefield would have been *too* preoccupied – *preaching to over 100,000 people on a mountainside in Cambuslang, Scotland* – to be worrying about any remaining errata in his King James Bible; while, likewise, oblivious to the *future* significance of the celebrated Bishop Blayney edition of 1769 (his death occurring the following year while laboring in America). The only thing that puzzles me about the transmission process is how the Lord was able to "limp along" for so many centuries without the aid of modern textual critics. (His *breath* was "probably" involved, for *"the **inspiration** of the Almighty giveth them **understanding**."*)

There were, of course, many additional areas that required a superintending *theopneustos*. For instance: How many Greek professors would associate inspiration with "propagation"? Do you think that Paul and Silas received any unique "understanding" when it came to transporting the apostle's inspired revelation into Europe? The same Holy Ghost who twice *"suffered them not"* to "waste" any more time in Asia, later drew them across the Aegean Sea via the "Macedonian Call" (Acts 16:6-11). Obviously, Paul's heavenly GPS had something to do with the routing, for *"the **inspiration** of the Almighty........*OH WELL, YOU PROBABLY HAVE THE IDEA BY NOW.

The Holy Spirit would also have breathed life into the many powerful ancient translations, such as the *Peshitta* (AD 145), the *Italia* (AD 157), the *Gothic* (AD 330), the *Ethiopian* (AD 350), and the *Armenian* (AD 400). Paul implied that he fully expected the autographs and copies to be translated, declaring: *"But now is made manifest, and by the **scriptures** of the prophets, according to the **commandment** of the everlasting God, **made known to all nations** for the obedience of faith."* (Romans 16:26) My friend, Evangelist Phil Schipper, has made the astute observation that

Revelation 9:11 is another proof text that the Holy Spirit never intended to restrict the *"word of truth"* to the original languages. If that had been the case, why tell the reader, *"And they had a king over them, which is the angel of the bottomless pit, whose name in the Hebrew tongue is Abaddon, **but in the Greek tongue hath his name Apollyon**"*? (The foreboding reference of "9:11" constitutes a subliminal rebuke to the *"Pseudo* King James Onlyism" that has helped to facilitate the end-day destruction of America.)

Then, while the Lord was obviously willing to tolerate occasional copyists' "typos," He would have certainly put the "kibosh" on the various mutilated manuscripts of heretics and apostates alike. His "holy breath" would have also been the key ingredient in establishing the canon of sixty-six books, leaving junk like the "Gospel of Mary," "III Corinthians," and the "Epistle of Pontius Pilate" for the fools on the *History Channel*. (I once had the unforgettable experience of having to listen to a barber who "professed" to be a Christian rant and rave about the "Book of Enoch.")

Contrary to all "conventional wisdom," the greatest gust of *theopneustos* occurred with the rise of the West and the enthronement of *English* as the world's language of choice. By the year 1800, the Caucasian race occupied or controlled 35% of the land surface of the world; by 1914 this figure had peaked at 84% (as per Genesis 9:27). This "politically incorrect" empire has dominated everything from the international banking system and all capital markets through the most advanced technical research and development venues, including international communications, aerospace, and the high-tech weapons industry. Over 80% of the world's electronically stored data on the Internet is contained in *English*. For the first time in history, one language is spoken in every country on the planet. Linguists now estimate that over 25% of the world's population can communicate in some degree of English. Even *time* and *location* are determined by Greenwich, England. So, the question naturally arises – Any "chance" the Lord saw *this* one coming? Four centuries ago, the same God who could boast in Isaiah 42:9, *"new things do I declare: before they spring forth I tell you of them,"* bestowed upon mankind the *greatest* gift this side of the empty tomb – The HOLY BIBLE – 1611 Authorized King James Version, *affectionately* regarded as "THE MONARCH OF BOOKS."

The most profound illustration I ever heard connecting *inspiration* with the King James Bible was given to me by Dr. Wendell Runion. *Webster's* third definition for inspiration reads, "The infusion of ideas into the mind by the Holy Spirit; the conveying into the minds of men, ideas, notices or monitions by extraordinary or supernatural influence; or the communication of the divine will to the *understanding* by suggestions or impressions on the mind, which leave no room to doubt the reality of their supernatural origin." While this more than adequately complements the scriptural definition provided in Job 32:8 (especially the reference to *understanding*), it is when we "rightly divide" the actual word itself that the *English* nuggets appear. This noun is comprised of three parts: *in – spire – ion*. While *in-* is a preposition meaning "within," *-ion* is a suffix meaning "the act of." *Webster's* first definition for *spire* is "To shoot; to shoot up *pyramidically*." Inspiration, therefore, would be "The act of spiraling up *pyramidically* from within." The similitude of a *pyramid* opens an insightful vista, indeed.

As the *"oracles of God"* were initially committed to the Jew, the Hebrew Masoretic text forms the base of the pyramid (Romans 3:2). Next, we have the four-sided structure itself. Psalm 12:6 states: *"The **words** of the LORD are pure **words**: as silver tried in a furnace of earth, **purified seven times**. Thou shalt keep them, O LORD, thou shalt **preserve** them from this generation for ever."* There were six major English translations of the Bible preceding the A.V. 1611: Tyndale (1525); Coverdale (1535); Great (1538); Matthew (1539); Geneva (1560); and, Bishops' (1568). Thus, we see that following a thousand years of darkness, six English translations of the Holy Scriptures *suddenly* "shoot up" in less than *half* a century! Then, as *spire* calls for an upward movement that is "pyramidical" in trajectory, we understand that a *capstone* must eventually be used (see any dollar bill). Consequently, the King James Bible – as the *seventh* major English translation – *completes* the building, *"purified* *seven times."* Thus, *Elihu* sits at the *top* as the source of *all* inspiration, while the other *four* character types in book of Job are positioned at *their* respective corners *below*.

This similitude is further magnified when compared to the architectural type depicted by modern translations – the SKY SCRAPER – Paul, writing in II Timothy 3:7, *"Ever learning, and never able to come to the knowledge of the truth."* (See the twentieth-first century *Burj Dubai,* which eclipses the Empire State Building by 1,466 feet.) In *The English Bible from KJV to NIV: A History of Evaluation,* Jack Lewis acknowledged that "the sky's the limit," writing: "A translation starts to become outdated from the moment it is completed. Information from new manuscript materials, new insights into the languages in which the Bible was first written, and new data concerning biblical history need to be communicated to the reader. Changing ideas about translations and changes in the English language itself all outdate a version, thus preparing the way for the process to be started all over again."

Finally, not only did inspiration impart the needed understanding for the translators, but for the readers, as well. Since those holy days at Hampton Court, the A.V. 1611 has been *reverently* followed by *"a band of men, whose hearts God had touched"* (I Samuel 10:26). Having now encountered the predicted apostasy of II Timothy 4:3, thankfully, another *"band of men"* is receiving the necessary *understanding* to *"turn away"* from the corrupt "skyscraper" versions (II Timothy 3:5). As the previously cited article in *Christianity Today* was willing to concede, "Among conservative Christians, a grassroots backlash against contemporary English-language Bibles has triggered a renewed interest in the famed King James Version with its word-for-word translation and its long standing authority." And, in more recent times, even *Wikipedia* could discern, "The *Authorized Version* maintained its effective dominance throughout the first half of the 20th Century. New translations in the second half of the 20th Century displaced its 250 years of dominance (roughly 1700 to 1950), but groups do exist – sometimes termed the King

James Only movement – that distrust anything not in agreement with ('that changes') the *Authorized Version*."

THE OLD SHIP OF ZION

Now, of course, the "scholars union" would ridicule these analogies as ludicrous. Their ancestors were no different, calling Paul a *"babbler."* (Acts 17:18) And they *sure* wouldn't have any use for Elihu, *especially* given the way he ended his definitive chapter on inspiration: *"Let me not, I pray you, accept any man's person, neither let me give flattering titles unto man. For I know not to give flattering titles; in so doing my maker would soon take me away."* (Job 32:21-22) I will, therefore, close *my* own chapter on this expanded view of inspiration by employing (and tweaking) *the* favorite illustration of every Greek professor who has ever undermined a King James Bible.

The Greek word *phero* is translated *"moved"* in II Peter 1:21. As previously noted, this text is the scholars' second-favorite stronghold when attempting to humble the A.V. 1611. According to *Strong's Greek Lexicon* (entry #5342), *phero* is defined as: "To be conveyed or borne with the suggestion of force or speed: 1) *of persons borne in a ship over the sea.* 2) of a gust of wind, to rush. 3) of the mind, to be moved, to be moved inwardly, prompted." The last application was already conveyed in the English when Elihu described himself as *"ready to burst"* (Job 32:19). However, it is the first definition (supported by the second) that so aptly pictures the all-encompassing work of divine inspiration. As the autographs were christened by those *"bottles* of *wine"* in Job 32:19, they *"phero*-ed" out of God's harbor with *"theopneustos"* behind their sails, "to be conveyed or borne with force or speed over the sea." Does the scholar seriously believe that the *wind* ceased after the first vessel was retired into dry dock (i.e., after the autographs disintegrated)? Does he have a problem with the same freight being carried by a *new* ship (Jeremiah 36:28)? Thus, the saying goes – "A *Bible* that's falling apart is often owned by a *Christian* who's not."

As previously displayed with the nation of Israel, the New Testament Church, and the born-again believer, "The Master of the Sea" is *more* than capable of *keeping* the necessary wind at the back of *His* vessels. No sooner does Elihu utter his last word in Job 37:24 than the Lord "blows in" at Job 38:1 – *"Then the LORD answered Job out of the **whirlwind**."* Though the Old Ship of Zion and her precious cargo have endured many a storm, believers can rejoice that "Captain Holy Ghost" is at the helm. One day we will all experience those precious words, *"He maketh the storm a calm, so that the waves thereof are still. Then are they glad because they be quiet; **so he bringeth them unto their desired haven.**"* (Psalm 107:29-31) Praise God for that "Haven of Rest!"

When that blessed day comes and we all *spiral* up with a shout, many a scholar will be left behind to sift through millions of King James Bibles *dropped* at "blast off." Those cutesy clichés won't seem nearly as funny then; like that one about the King James Bible "parachuting down from Heaven," or "being typed out on Paul's typewriter," etc. However, as "truth *is* stranger than fiction," the wildest imaginable scenario yet may be just around the corner. After all, Paul reminds us: *"Eye hath not seen, **nor ear heard**, neither have entered into the heart of man, the **things** which God hath prepared for them that love him."* (I Corinthians 2:9) Don't you know "there's gonna be a *whole* lot of shoutin' goin' on" in the Millennial Kingdom! Do you recall when Jesus said, *"if these should hold their peace, the **stones** would immediately **cry** out"*? (Luke 19:40) Well, wouldn't it be *something* if Moses' *second* "original" tablets showed up and started *testifying*? Like Dr. B. R. Lakin used to say, "Hold my mule while I shout!" But let me leave you with a nugget from the *English* that is far more surreal than that. While I don't know how many King James Bibles will survive the Tribulation intact, I *do* know what they'll be *doing*:

*"Let every **thing** that hath **breath** praise the LORD.*
Praise ye the LORD."

(PSALM 150:6)

8

Seven Pillars In the House of Wisdom

𝕿HE TWOFOLD PURPOSE of this book is to present an expanded view of the doctrine of inspiration as defined by Job 32:8, and to illustrate the inexhaustible riches of the A.V. 1611. For, whenever the King James Bible is given exclusive *recognition* as Holy Scripture, the *"inspiration of the Almighty"* will give exclusive *understanding* of its text, Hebrew and Greek "nuggets" becoming moot in the process. The current chapter will offer a further devotional study on the relationship between *wisdom* and *understanding* as contained in the *original* "English."

The spiritual adage goes, "If you *are* what you ought to *be,* you'll *do* what you ought to *do.*" There are many biblical traits that need to be incorporated into our lives along with many actions we need to employ as a result. However, one particular set would appear to represent the most important correlation. Proverbs 4:7 states: *"**Wisdom** is the **principal** thing; **therefore get wisdom.**"* Every schoolchild knows that the *principal* is the head of the school. Solomon cannot say enough about the value of wisdom: *"Happy is the man that findeth wisdom...She is more precious than rubies... Length of days are in her right hand; and in her left hand riches and honour...Exhalt her, and she shall promote thee...a crown of glory shall she deliver to thee...Wisdom is better than strength... Wisdom is better than weapons of war,"* etc. (Proverbs 3:13-16; 4:8-9; Ecclesiastes 9:16, 18)

With regard to our many spiritual responsibilities, the Bible again points to *one* as being most significant. Paul instructed the

Colossians: *"Put on therefore, as the elect of God, holy and beloved, bowels of mercies, kindness, humbleness of mind, meekness, longsuffering; Forbearing one another, and forgiving one another, if any man have a quarrel against any: even as Christ forgave you, so also do ye. **And above all these things** put on **charity**, which is the bond of **perfectness**."* (Colossians 3:12-14) Thus, *wisdom* is the *"**principal** thing,"* while *charity* is the *"bond of **perfectness**."* Notice how the Holy Spirit led Peter to give charity the identical preeminence: *"But the end of all things is at hand: be ye therefore sober, and watch unto prayer. **And above all things** have fervent **charity** among yourselves: for **charity** shall cover the multitude of sins."* (I Peter 4:7-8) In his first epistle to Timothy, Paul summed up the purpose for the Law in a single verse: *"Now the **end** of the commandment is **charity** out of a pure heart, and of a good conscience, and of faith unfeigned."* (I Timothy 1:5) He then devotes an entire chapter of the New Testament to this subject with the familiar conclusion: *"And now abideth faith, hope, charity, these three; **but the greatest of these is charity**."* (I Corinthians 13:13) Thus, "wisdom" is our main *provision*, while "charity" is our main *priority*. To attain the *"bond of **perfectness**,"* we must avail ourselves to the *"**principal** thing."*

UNDERSTANDING • WISDOM • CHARITY

Now, if *wisdom* produces *charity*, the next step would naturally be to discover the catalyst for wisdom. Not surprisingly, the answer to this question is related to the doctrine of inspiration. As we learned from Job 32:8, the *scriptural* definition of "inspiration" encompasses far more than the creation of original manuscripts: *"But there is a spirit in man: and the **inspiration** of the Almighty giveth them **understanding**."* The book of Proverbs reveals that *understanding* is the primary facilitator of *wisdom*. As previously noted, their unique correlation is seen by the fact that both words appear 54 times *each* in Proverbs. While Solomon declared: *"**Wisdom** is the **principal** thing; therefore get **wisdom**,"* he concluded by stating, *"and* *with all thy getting get **understanding**.* " The pair is often inseparable, appearing together in 24 separate verses (e.g., Proverbs 3:13, *"Happy is the man that findeth **wisdom**, and the man that getteth **understanding**.")* You *could* say they are twins, for in Proverbs 8:14, *wisdom* cries: *"I am understanding"* (John 10:30). However, the text is precise, in that *understanding* is the spiritual prerequisite to *wisdom*: *"a man of understanding hath wisdom"*; *"Wisdom resteth in the heart of him that hath understanding"*; and, *"Wisdom is before him that hath understanding. "* (Proverbs 10:23; 14:33; 17:24)

The special "working" relationship between the two doctrines is revealed by the way they are defined in Scripture. True to form, the definitions for both words appear side-by-side and in two *parts* over two *verses*. In Job 28:28, we read: *"Behold, the **fear of the Lord**, that is **wisdom**; and to **depart from evil is understanding**. "* Then, in Proverbs 9:10, the Holy Spirit supplies the completed definitions: *"The **fear of the LORD** is the **beginning** of wisdom: and the **knowledge of the holy** is understanding. "* While *wisdom* is synonymous with the *"fear of the Lord,"* it obviously encompasses far more in the believer, culminating with the mind of Christ itself (Philippians 2:5). And, as noted in the previous chapter regarding *understanding*, one cannot turn *to* a *"knowledge of the holy"* until he has first turned *"from evil. "* Putting it all together, the appropriate sequence would be: Departing from *evil* enables a pursuit of *holiness*, which produces the *fear* of the Lord, which motivates a life characterized by *charity*; *"O that there were such an heart in them, that they would fear me, and keep all my commandments always, that it might be well with them, and with their children forever!"* (Deuteronomy 5:29)

With the doctrinal material in the Old Testament generally presented through stories, similitudes, and types, Proverbs 9:1 states: *"**Wisdom** hath builded her **house**, she hath hewn out her **seven pillars**. "* This personification would constitute the ideal habitation for the child of God in this life: The table is spread, *"She hath killed her beasts; she hath mingled her wine; she hath also furnished her table"*; the invitation is unequivocal, *"Come, eat of my bread, and* *drink of the wine which I have mingled. Forsake the foolish, and live; and go in the way of understanding"*; while the alternative is deadly, *"A foolish woman...sitteth at the door of **her house**...the dead are there...her guests are in the depths of hell."* (Proverbs 9:2-18; 7:27) Notice that the Holy Spirit specifies that the house of wisdom is held together by *"seven pillars."* We then read in Proverbs 24:3, *"Through wisdom is an house builded; and by **understanding** it is **established."*** Thus, we see that the longevity of the structure is "established" through *understanding – seven* pillars of *understanding*, to be exact.

We have now arrived at the primary focus of this chapter. A second principle regarding Old Testament theology is conveyed by the saying, "The *Old* Testament is the *New* Testament *concealed*, while the *New* Testament is the *Old* Testament *revealed"* (e.g., Genesis 5:24 is the New Testament doctrine of the Rapture *concealed*, while I Thessalonians 4:17 is the Old Testament story of Enoch *revealed*.) Applying this truth to our present study points us to the New Testament in search of *seven* "things" that would specifically apply to *understanding* (i.e., to an enhanced *"knowledge of the holy"*). While Christian apologists waste their life in pursuit of Noah's ark, the greatest discovery one could *ever* make is resting atop the *"holy mount"* of II Peter, chapter one. Of course, the scholar is too preoccupied "intermeddling" with verses twenty through twenty-one to notice that amazing list of *"seven* things" in verses five through seven.

As a *"knowledge of the holy"* would translate into a greater knowledge of *God* Himself, a check of the immediate context confirms that we are hot on the trail. Only two verses into the chapter we read: *"Grace and peace be multiplied unto you through the **knowledge** of God, and of Jesus our Lord."* The next verse confirms that *knowing* God is the key to acquiring all things spiritual: *"According as his divine power hath given unto us all things that pertain unto life and godliness, through the **knowledge** of him that hath called us to glory and virtue."* After listing these *"seven* things," Peter states in the next verse: *"For if **these things** be in you, and abound, they make you that ye shall neither be barren nor unfruitful* *in the **knowledge** of our Lord Jesus Christ."* This concept of "understanding" as the *"knowledge of the holy"* continues throughout the epistle; II Peter 2:20 refers to those having *"escaped the pollutions of the world through the **knowledge** of the Lord and Saviour Jesus Christ,"* while the book ends with the admonition, *"But grow in grace, and in the **knowledge** of our Lord and Saviour Jesus Christ."* All told, the word "knowledge" appears *seven* times in II Peter, one reference for each pillar.

Being *"moved by the Holy Ghost,"* Peter *"spake"* much about these *"seven* things" in verses five through seven. After making the aforementioned promise in verse eight regarding *"**these things**,"* he issues a warning in verse nine: *"But he that lacketh **these things** is blind, and cannot see afar off, and hath forgotten that he was purged from his old sins."* An amazing guarantee is then given in verse ten, *"for if you do **these things**, ye shall never fall."* In verse twelve, he says, *"Wherefore I will not be negligent to put you always in remembrance of **these things**."* Approaching his own martyrdom, the apostle concludes in verse fifteen, *"Moreover I will endeavour that ye may be able after my decease to have **these things** always in remembrance."*

The main reason "these *things*" are so important is because they constitute the "seven *pillars*" in the house of wisdom, for *"by **understanding** it is established."* Each pillar serves a unique purpose toward gaining an *understanding* of the *"knowledge of the holy."* When all seven are acquired, the Christian will then have the *wisdom* of God (Proverbs 8:14). The subsequent view from the house of wisdom is unlike any other vista on earth. With the *"knowledge of the holy"* having developed into *wisdom*, the Christian can now see life from God's perspective. The hymnist, Helen Lemmel, described the transition thusly: "Turn your eyes upon Jesus, look full in His wonderful face; and the things of earth will grow strangely dim in the light of His glory and grace."

Upon receiving his *first* anointing from Jesus, the blind man said: *"I see men as trees, walking"* (illustrating how carnal believers will *use* their fellow man for whatever selfish benefit they can attain – shade, fuel, fruit, swings, shelter, etc.) However, after the *second* anointing, *"he was restored, and saw every man clearly."* (Mark 8:24-25) Looking through the bay window in the house of wisdom, men will always be seen clearly for what they are – never-dying souls created in the image and likeness of God. Consequently, though the Christian may be grounded by the *"fear of the Lord,"* the ultimate end of wisdom is always *charity*, the *"bond of perfectness."* And it *all* has to do with the scriptural definition of "inspiration," for *"the **inspiration** of the Almighty giveth them **understanding.**"* (Job 32:8)

To profit from this study one must envision the applicable Old Testament structure in mind. According to Bible archeology, Solomon is describing a "mansion" built around an open courtyard. Architecturally, the pillars of the *inner* court are meant, which supported the gallery of the first story (and, sometimes, a second). Four of these were in the corners, with one in the middle of each of three sides, while the entrance of the court was through the fourth side of the *square* (Revelation 21:16). The imagery is holy, Paul telling the Corinthians, *"ye are God's **building,**"* with the entire edifice resting on Christ, *"For other **foundation** can no man lay than that is laid, which is Jesus Christ."* (I Corinthians 3:9, 11) In the Church Age, we dwell in the *courtyard*, a "waiting" area with an entrance *opened* by the owner's Son; our "mansion" awaits us *above* (John 14:1-2). And, as *wisdom* declares in Proverbs 8:14, *"**I am** understanding"* – lest we forget the third member of the Godhead, the "speaker" adds in verse twelve, *"I wisdom dwell with **prudence"*** (a most fitting type of the Holy Spirit; *prudence* applying to the discretionary use of wisdom as illustrated in Romans 8:14).

With this introduction behind us, we are now prepared to enter the sacred courtyard. Pillar number *one* is situated to our immediate left (with two and three directly behind it). All seven will exhibit their own unique relationship to *truth* as the *"knowledge of the holy."* They will also be positioned in the sequence of our normal growth in grace. Finally, as noted above, *everything* in II Peter 1:5-6 is *added* to our *faith*, for "On Christ, the solid Rock, I stand; all other ground is sinking sand."

VIRTUE

The Holy Spirit begins: *"And beside this, giving all diligence, add to your faith virtue...."* There are only eleven references to virtue in the entire Bible; four of these describe the ideal woman, while three depict the spiritual power that left Christ's body when He healed the sick. The word also appears in Peter's introduction, reminding us that we have been called to *"glory and virtue."* (II Peter 1:3) Virtue is often defined as "moral excellence." Being the *first* pillar in our Christian life, virtue constitutes the *"preparation* for truth." It has everything to do with our spiritual *character*, especially *attitude*. The Lord said, *"I will pour water upon him that is thirsty, and floods upon the dry ground."* (Isaiah 44:3) In the Sermon on the Mount, Jesus assured His followers, *"Blessed are they which do hunger and thirst after righteousness, for they shall be filled."* (Matthew 5:6) Bob Jones, Sr., said, "When gratitude dies on the altar of a man's heart, that man is well nigh *useless*." Virtue is the veritable gatekeeper for the house of wisdom; without it, we become "street people for Jesus." While all Christians receive the Rock foundation of Matthew 7:24, many have not fulfilled *their* responsibility to erect a shelter *on* that Rock (i.e., the "house of wisdom"). Yes, they will still be there *after* the storm passes, *but* they will get soaked in the process. How many ruined testimonies come to *your* mind? (The Baptist deacon who led me to Christ *blew his own brains out*.) *"I had rather be a doorkeeper in the house of my God, than to dwell in the tents of wickedness."* (Psalm 84:10)

KNOWLEDGE

"...and to virtue knowledge..." Whereas *virtue* generates an *appetite* for truth, *knowledge* follows as the *"reception* of the truth" itself. Pillar *two* represents the practical step to pursue every scriptural

learning opportunity – *"Wise men lay up **knowledge**: but the mouth of the foolish is near destruction."* (Proverbs 10:14) The standard list would include attending all scheduled church services (including special meetings); regular Bible study; Scripture memorization; reading spiritual books; and, counseling with the pastor and other seasoned believers, etc. Notice how pillar *one* will automatically lead to pillar *two*: *"Yea, if thou **criest** after knowledge... **Then** shalt thou...find the knowledge of God."* (Proverbs 2:3, 5) Like *wisdom* and *understanding*, spiritual *knowledge* is a priceless commodity, indeed: *"There is gold, and a multitude of rubies: but the lips of **knowledge** are a precious jewel."* (Proverbs 20:15) The word appears 42 times in Proverbs and is presented as one of the *nine* major goals of the book: *"The proverbs of Solomon...To know wisdom and understanding; To receive the instruction of wisdom, justice, and judgment, and equity; To give subtilty to the simple, to the young man **knowledge** and discretion."* (Proverbs 1:1-4) Finally, as *"wisdom is too high for a fool,"* the professional "Christian" scholar is exposed at this juncture for attempting to proceed directly to pillar *two* – *without* stopping at pillar *one* – resulting in a head-on collision at I Corinthians 8:1, *"Knowledge [minus virtue] puffeth up."*

TEMPERANCE

*"...and to knowledge **temperance**..."* The word *temperance* has to do with a controlling influence from without, primarily directed at the human appetites (e.g., the *American Temperance Society* was formed in the early nineteenth century to combat the evils of drunkenness). *Webster's* second definition says, "patience; calmness; sedateness; and moderation of passion." In Galatians 5:22, *temperance* is listed as the last of the nine fruit of the spirit. At pillar *two*, the Christian learns what God expects of him. At pillar *three*, he begins to *allow* the Holy Spirit to alter his lifestyle accordingly. Thus, the trip between the two points is characterized by meditation (Joshua 1:8; Psalm 1:2). For instance, at pillar *two* the believer hears a sermon on the text, *"Take heed, and beware of*

covetousness: for a man's life consisteth not in the abundance of the things which he possesseth." (Luke 12:15) By the time he gets to pillar *three*, he decides to have a garage sale for missions. Whatever truth you imbibe at *two* is put into action at *three*. Consequently, pillar three is the *"effect* of the truth."

Now, try to envision your location in the courtyard. You have moved inward as far as possible and are presently at the far left corner. It is time to pivot 90° to the right and face the *center* pillar of the structure. *Better hold on......*

PATIENCE

*"...and to temperance **patience**... "* The first thing you will see as you turn to the right is a massive pillar of fire! This is one of two places where the believer is tempted to turn back. We have all heard the caution – "Don't pray for patience." God's poster child for suffering and heartache was identified and characterized accordingly: *"Ye have heard of the **patience of Job**. "* (James 5:10) The Heavenly Father knows us far better than we can ever know ourselves. Remember all that "truth" you took in at pillar *two*? Well, just because you "received" it does not mean you "understand" it; *that's* what the *fire* is for. At pillar *two* a Christian reads the verse, *"But my God shall supply all your need according to his riches in glory by Christ Jesus. "* (Philippians 4:19) However, with his bills current, cash reserves in the bank, and all the overtime he could desire – the *depth* of this verse might not mean as much to him as to someone else. Consequently, he will often experience a "change of fortune" and find himself on the unemployment line at pillar *four*. Thus, the all-important center pillar in the house of wisdom becomes the *"refining* of the truth."

> When thro' **fiery** trials thy path-way shall lie,
> My grace, all-sufficient, shall be thy supply;
> The **flames** shall not hurt thee, I only design
> Thy **dross to consume**, and thy **gold to *refine*.**

While the heat at pillar *four* is surely intimidating, I can offer two good incentives as to why you should not shrink back. The first has to do with *who* awaits you *in* the flames. According to the quintessential encounter of God's people with *fire*, Daniel 3:24-25 records King Nebuchadnezzar declaring in astonishment: *"Did not we cast* **three** *men bound into the midst of the* **fire**? *They answered and said unto the king, True, O king. He answered and said, Lo, I see* **four** *men loose, walking in the midst of the* **fire**, *and they have no hurt;* **and the form of the fourth is like the Son of God.**" Many commentators have noted that the only things that burned were the ropes that had bound the three men. However, the most important insight is often missed in the euphoria of the moment: *"Then* **Shadrach, Meshach,** *and* **Abed-nego,** *came forth of the midst of the fire."* As the saying goes, "Do the math" – *Three* go in; *four* are seen; *three* come out. Guess where Jesus is!

The second incentive has to do with *what* awaits you *past* the flames.

GODLINESS

"...and to patience **godliness**...*"* Though *temperance* is a good thing, it cannot compare with *godliness*. We all know of successful men and women who have allowed the "outside influence" of a materialistic world view to motivate them to live a disciplined life, yet know *nothing* about spirituality. Paul wrote: *"For bodily exercise profiteth little: but* **godliness** *is profitable unto all things, having promise of the life that now is, and of that which is to come."* (I Timothy 4:8) One cannot reach the pillar of *godliness* without passing *through* the pillar of *patience*. That brother who lost his financial security at pillar *four* will often discover that he has gained a few pounds by the time he reaches pillar *five*, as the Lord supplied *all* his need – *and then some* (Ephesians 3:20). The Christian who lost a loved one at pillar *four* advances to pillar *five* fully aware that *"My grace is sufficient for thee"* – a text he merely *filed* at pillar *two*. *Godliness* is the *"comprehension"* of the truth."

It is at pillar *five* that Job declared: *"I have heard of thee by the hearing of the ear: but **now** mine eye seeth thee. Wherefore I abhor myself, and repent in dust and ashes."* (Job 42:5-6) Likewise, David testified: *"It is good that I have been **afflicted**; that I might **learn** thy statutes."* (Psalm 119:71)

Having attained a level of spiritual maturity in the far *right* corner, you must now pivot once again in order to start making your way *out* of the courtyard. While the house of wisdom is intended to be our primary residence, we are commanded to minister to those less fortunate *without*. Jesus prayed in the upper room: *"I pray not that thou shouldest take them out of the world, but that thou shouldest keep them from the evil."* (John 17:15) After entering the courtyard as a hungry neophyte, you were blessed to *experience* life-changing truths at pillar *four;* truths that you may now share with *authority*. The Apostle Paul declared: *"And not only so, but we glory in tribulations also: knowing that tribulation worketh patience; and patience **experience**."* (Romans 5:3-4) Thus, he could testify, *"for when I am **weak**, then am I **strong**."* (II Corinthians 12:10) However, before *anyone* can descend the *"holy mount"* to help the "lunaticks" at Matthew 17:15, he must *first* heed the admonition, *"As we have therefore opportunity, let us do good unto all men, **especially** unto them who are of **the household of faith**."* (Galatians 6:10)

BROTHERLY KINDNESS

*"...and to godliness **brotherly kindness**..."* As the *sixth* church of the book of Revelation was characterized by "brotherly *love*," the *sixth* pillar in the house of wisdom is likewise defined by "brotherly *kindness*." Accordingly, before we can exit the *"**house** of wisdom,"* we must extend *kindness* to our own *brethren* within the *"**household** of faith"*; for even the world understands that "**charity** begins at **home**." Pillar *six* is the *"application* of the truth." Paul reminded the Corinthians that they were stewards of God's comfort: *"Blessed be God, even the Father of our Lord Jesus Christ, the Father of mercies, and the God of all comfort: Who comforteth us in all our*

tribulation, **that we may be able to comfort them which are in any trouble,** *by the comfort wherewith we ourselves are comforted of God."* (II Corinthians 1:3-4) The main responsibility for Christians at pillar *six* is to steady their fellow believers who are approaching pillar *four.* A godly widow can be a powerful encouragement to a sister in Christ who is burdened with a terminally ill husband, etc.

We have now arrived at the moment of truth. As previously stated, pillar *four* is one of two places where the Christian is tempted to turn back; pillar *six* is the other. It is here that all believers share the same inevitable experience that will determine whether or not they make it to the final pillar. With *six* being the number of man and *seven* being God's perfect number, we *know* that something is bound to happen at this critical point. It has been said that "the best of men are but men at best." The crisis that occurs at pillar *six* can be described in many ways, but basically boils down to a sincere Christian being deeply hurt by someone he or she has previously helped. And, to add insult to injury, their motives are often questioned, as well. Unfortunately, it is a never-ending scenario; one with deadly consequences. But, if we are to *"follow his steps,"* then we must *also* be willing to be "kissed in a garden," for *"the servant is not greater than his lord."* (I Peter 2:21; Luke 22:48; John 15:20).

So the closing scene is as follows: You are ministering to the brethren at pillar *six.* And then it happens – BAM! What you do next may very well determine the outcome of your entire Christian life. You can either go *back;* or, you can go *forward.* If you quit, your house of wisdom will remain unfinished (Luke 14:28-30). If you go forward, you will advance to the last pillar. Regardless of your direction, you *will* leave pillar six with an *axe* in your back.

CHARITY

"...and to brotherly kindness **charity***..."* Ironically, in the face of Hebrews 10:25, the believer who reaches pillar *seven* will do so in *spite* of the body of Christ. As followers of Jesus, we are to know the *"power of his resurrection"* through the *"fellowship of his suffering."*

(Philippians 3:10) Hence, *His* experiences must be *our* experiences. Zechariah 13:6 tells us that at the Second Advent, *"And one shall say unto him, What are these wounds in thine hands? Then he shall answer, Those with which I was **wounded** in the **house of my friends**."* (The perverted *Living Bible* translated this passage, "And if someone asks, 'Then what are these **scars** on your **chest** and your **back?**' he will say, '**I got into a brawl** at the home of a friend!'") Sadly, the greatest wounds *you* will ever suffer in this life will be received *in* the *"**house of wisdom**."*

Samson perished between two pillars in the temple of Dagon. Likewise, many believers in the Laodicean Age commit *spiritual* suicide between "brotherly kindness" and "charity." Nothing short of the grace of God can carry you from pillar *six* to pillar *seven*. The two numbers total 13 – the number of *rebellion*. Thus, it will take nothing short of a *spiritual* rebellion to survive. The reason that the modern Christian refuses to *"take up his **cross**"* is because a *cross* symbolizes the *crossing* of *God's* will with *our* will, and Paul has already told us, regarding the last days: *"For the time will come when they **will not** endure sound doctrine."* (Matthew 16:24; II Timothy 4:4) Ultimately, the victory *will* come when the believer is *willing* to embrace the truth of his "exalted" title: CHRIST-I-A-N – CHRIST is everything; *I am nothing*.

So, with that axe in your back, take a good look at the prize before you. There are *seven* letters in the *seventh* pillar, as C-H-A-R-I-T-Y is that *"bond of **perfectness**."* (Colossians 3:14) Note the incredible *cross*-reference that highlights the prerequisite of unconditional love: *"If we love one another, God dwelleth in us, and his love is **perfected** in us…God is love; and he that dwelleth in love dwelleth in God, and God in him. Herein is our love made **perfect**."* (I John 4:12, 16, 17) As charity is the ultimate goal of the Christian life, we are not surprised that every modern translation has eliminated the word. They all change "charity" to "love," destroying the most important truth *about* love in the process. Without the use of a Greek lexicon, the English of I John 4 tells us that love can be *perfected*. That is precisely what charity is all about. Charity is *perfected* love. First, charity constitutes love in *action – "For God so loved the world, **that he gave** his only begotten Son."* Second, and most critically, charity is love in *perpetuity – "Charity suffereth long and is kind...Beareth all things...endureth all things.* CHARITY NEVER FAILETH.*"* (I Corinthians 13:4, 7-8) Christians who walk away from pillar *six* in disillusionment may do so with *"the love of God...shed abroad in* [their] *hearts."* (Romans **5:5**) However, I John 3:14 tells us: *"He that loveth not his brother abideth in death."* It is at pillar *seven* that *love* becomes *charity* – the veritable *"bond of perfectness."*

Thus, Paul concludes his treatise on charity with the words, *"And now abideth faith, hope, charity, these three; **but the greatest of these is charity.**"* (I Corinthians 13:13) Faith says, "I *know* God can deliver me; Hope says, "I *hope* God will deliver me"; but *Charity* says, "Whether God delivers me or not, I will *still* do right!" Or, like the three Hebrew children testified: *"If it be so, our God whom we serve **is able** to deliver us from the burning fiery furnace, and **he will** deliver us out of thine hand, O king. **But if not**, be it known unto thee, O king, that **we will not** serve thy gods, nor worship the golden image which thou hast set up."* (Daniel 3:17-18) Charity is love that *never* quits on God, faithfully declaring, *"If I perish, I perish"*; *"Should such a man as I flee?"*; *"Though he slay me, yet will I trust in him,"* etc. (Esther 4:16; Nehemiah 6:11; Job 13:15) Is it any wonder, therefore, that the professional "Christian" scholar hates that word? You would almost think that those two *13s* in the Scripture address anticipated his *sin* and *rebellion* in the Laodicean Age. Of course, the Holy Spirit had his "number" all along: *"Knowledge puffeth up, **but charity edifieth.**"* (I Corinthians 8:1)

In closing, the greatest manifestation of charity that the world has ever seen was displayed on an old rugged Cross "roughly" 2,000 years ago. While I Timothy 1:3 says, *"Now the **end** of the commandment is charity,"* Romans 10:4 confirms, *"For **Christ** is the **end** of the law."* Where *Moses* stumbled as a type of the Law – being denied the Promised Land for a *single* offense – *Joshua*, as a type of Christ, replaced Moses and led the people in

(Numbers 20:12; Galatians 3:10; 5:3; James 2:10). Thus, we have that amazing revelation in Acts 7:45 (or, "glaring error," according to the scholars' union) where the Holy Ghost identifies *Jesus* as the great antitype of *Joshua*: *"Which also our fathers that came after brought in with **Jesus** into the possession of the Gentiles."* The Hebrew construction for *Joshua* means "Jehovah saves" and comes up *Jesus* after passing *through* the Greek *into* English.

The lovely Lord Jesus Christ became the epitome of charity when He fulfilled the *Ten* Commandments in *ten* simple words – *"Father, **forgive them**; for they know not what they do."* (Luke 23:34) As *ten* is the number of the *Gentiles*, Matthew 27:54 subsequently records the first *Gentile* profession of Christ's deity: *"Now when the centurion, and they that were with him, watching Jesus, saw the earthquake, and those things that were done, they feared greatly, saying, **Truly this was the Son of God**."* If we assume that the dying thief was a *Jew*, then the order fulfills Romans 1:16 – *"to the Jew **first**, and also to the Greek."* Thus, we see Jesus in every phase of the "house of wisdom": He is *understanding*, being born without sin and described as a *"holy thing,"* Luke 2:47 telling us, *"And all that heard him were astonished at his **understanding**";* He is *wisdom*, as Luke 2:40 states, *"And the child grew, and waxed strong in spirit, filled with **wisdom**";* and finally, He is *charity*, being *wounded* by his own *brethren*, then forgiving them, and then stepping *out* of the house to begin reaching those *"other sheep... which are not of this fold."* (John 10:16)

Whoever makes it to that *last* pillar and *beyond* morphs into the very truth itself – *"Ye are our epistle written in our hearts, known and read of **all** men."* (II Corinthians 3:2) Thus, pillar *seven* becomes the *"display* of the truth."

*"...*TRULY *this was the Son of God."*

(MATTHEW 27:54)

9

How to Study the Bible

A "*PSEUDO* KING JAMES Only" church in my area posted a sermon on their website entitled "How to *Read* the Bible." The pastor's three-point outline was as follows: *Read* the Bible *prayerfully*; *Read* the Bible *thoughtfully*; and, *Read* the Bible *obediently*. Now, in the first place, most of us learned how to *read* in elementary school. Secondly, God's specific command is to "*Study*... *the word of truth.*" (II Timothy 2:15) When I was a lost Roman Catholic, the "clergy" made sure that the "laity" never came into contact with the Bible. For example, every Pope's worst nightmare has been that some "good Catholic" would stumble upon an enlightening verse like Mark 6:3, where the "ever-Virgin" Mary's *other* children are named. Sadly, many Baptist pastors employ a similar quarantine of the Scriptures, lest one of *their* uninformed parishioners discover something that flies in the face of *Fundamentalist* tradition. (*Given By Inspiration* will undoubtedly be condemned in no time for this very reason.) But then, these men are merely passing along that which *they* received in "Bible" college (Acts 4:20). For instance, every ministerial student is told that Satan's head was bruised at *Calvary*. Yet, in Romans 16:20, we read, "*And the God of peace shall bruise Satan under your feet shortly*" (Psalm 68:21; Habakkuk 3:13).

Enshrined within the hallowed halls of militant Fundamentalism is the sacrosanct cliché that "Old Testament saints looked *forward* to the Cross, while New Testament saints look *back* to the Cross." Yet – *What saith the Scripture?* If people living *hundreds* of years before the time of Christ were saved by comprehending the *identical*

Gospel which Paul received and established (Galatians 1:11), why does the Holy Spirit tell us – *in the clearest possible manner* – that the most informed disciples were totally *clueless* regarding a bodily resurrection? *"And as they came down from the mountain, he charged them that they should tell no man what things they had seen, till the Son of man were risen from the dead. And they kept that saying with themselves, questioning one with another* WHAT THE *RISING FROM THE DEAD* SHOULD MEAN.*"* (Mark 9:9-10) The last time I "checked," the *Resurrection* was a vital part of the Gospel (I Corinthians 15:4).

So, how could some Gentile child in 150 BC be expected to understand what was hidden from *Christ's own apostles* less than a week before the Crucifixion? *"Then he took unto him the twelve, and said unto them...concerning the Son of man...he shall be delivered unto the Gentiles...and they shall...put him to* DEATH: *and the third day he shall* RISE *again.* AND THEY UNDERSTOOD *NONE* OF THESE THINGS: AND THIS SAYING WAS *HID* FROM THEM, NEITHER KNEW THEY THE THINGS THAT WERE SPOKEN.*"* (Luke 18:31-34) Had they *been* anticipating a bodily resurrection, how are we to account for their reaction to the women's initial report of this very event? *"And their words seemed to them as idle tales,* AND THEY BELIEVED THEM *NOT.*" (Luke 24:11) The answer is given in John 20:9 – "FOR AS *YET* THEY KNEW NOT THE SCRIPTURE, THAT *HE MUST RISE AGAIN FROM THE DEAD.*"

Should any "*Pseudo*" be interested, the disciples on the road to Emmaus "cleared the air" concerning *exactly* what Old Testament saints *were* expecting: *"But we trusted that it had been* HE WHICH SHOULD HAVE REDEEMED ISRAEL*" – precisely* as Zacharias had declared – *"That we should be* SAVED FROM OUR ENEMIES.*"* (Luke 24:21; 1:71) Only *afterward* are the disciples enlightened by their resurrected Messiah: *"These are the words which I spake unto you,* WHILE I WAS YET WITH YOU, *that all things must be fulfilled, which were written in the law of Moses, and in the prophets, and in the psalms, concerning me. THEN* OPENED HE

THEIR *UNDERSTANDING,* THAT THEY MIGHT *UNDERSTAND* THE SCRIPTURES.*"* (Luke 24:44-45) This is what the Holy Ghost is talking about in I Corinthians 2:8 – *"Which none of the princes of this world knew:* FOR HAD THEY KNOWN IT, *they would not have crucified the Lord of glory."* Thus, the "greatest *secret* ever kept" became the "greatest *story* ever told."

But there is more. Not only was the particular *redemptive* mission of Israel's Messiah "hid" from Old Testament Jews, but the *name* of their Prince, as well. While the nation was informed of their God's personal name in Exodus 3:14, and while Psalm 2:12 reveals that He has a "Son," the *name* of that Son was presented as a mystery of sorts, Proverbs 30:4 asking, *"what is his son's name, IF* THOU CANST TELL?*"* When Manoah met *"the angel of the Lord"* (an Old Testament appearance of Jesus Himself), he asked him directly, *"What is thy name?"* – whereupon the Son of God replied, *"Why askest thou thus after my name,* SEEING IT IS A *SECRET?"* (Judges 13:17-18)

Thus, in retrospect, verses such as John 8:56 and Acts 10:43 merely refer to the coming of Israel's King, with occasional *veiled* glimpses of His passion, such as Psalm 22 and Isaiah 53. Any question on the matter is settled by I Peter 1:10-12, where the Holy Ghost makes it clear that the Old Testament prophets did not understand *what* they were prophesying about. Sadly, however, most Fundamentalist pastors are too *insecure* to acknowledge their woefully inadequate training in the "English," preferring rather to condemn revealed truth as heresy by citing some "good, Godly authority"; or wresting another verse out of *its* context; or, simply, by "submerging" to the Greek.

On March 20, 2010, Dr. Jack Schaap brought the closing message for the annual Pastor's School convention at First Baptist Church of Hammond. Only eight months after conducting his highly promoted "King James Summit," Schaap made a stunning concession that represents a most insightful glimpse into the world of *"Pseudo* King James Onlyism." (Unfortunately, it sailed right over the heads of his likeminded constituents.) "Pastor" Schaap informed the delegates that the single greatest pressure on his life was *finding* three new sermon "ideas" each week. He then went on to bring a message on missions that revolved around *Coca Cola* and *McDonald's* hamburgers. Apparently, it has never occurred to Dr. Schaap that a pastor is supposed to *"preach the word,"* not "search for ideas" (II Timothy 4:2). But, then again, according to Jeremiah 23:28, one would have to *believe* "The Book" in order to *preach* "The Book" – *"and he that **hath** my word, let him **speak** my word faithfully."* (If Schaap ever got *converted* to the King James Bible, he would *quit* reading sermons by Catholic popes and preaching sermons about Ronald McDonald and company.)

In Nehemiah 8:8, the Holy Spirit gave His own three-point outline on how God's *men* are to communicate the Scripture to their people: *"So they read in the book in the law of God **distinctly**, and gave the **sense**, and caused them to **understand** the reading."* Preachers are to *begin* by reading the Scripture clearly and distinctly. Thus, Paul instructs Timothy: *"Till I come, give attendance to **reading**."* (I Timothy 4:13) The next step is to make sense out of the passage; to *explain* what it means. Finally, the text must be personally applied to the listeners. When Philip asked the Ethiopian eunuch, *"**Understandest** thou what thou readest?"* the eunuch replied, *"How can I, except some man should **guide** me."* (Acts 8:30-31) Thus, we see another practical application of inspiration at work. (*"But there is a spirit in man: and the **inspiration** of the Almighty giveth them **understanding**."*)

Spirit-led pastors are to elucidate the Scriptures so that God's people may gain the necessary *understanding*. There can be *no* excuse for *any* shepherd who falls short of his basic responsibility to *"Study to shew thyself approved unto God, a **workman** that needeth not to be **ashamed**, rightly dividing the word of truth."* (II Timothy 3:15) A local congregation must be properly instructed in order to obey the charge in I Peter 3:15: *"But sanctify the Lord God in your hearts: and be ready always to give an answer to every man that asketh you a reason of the hope that is in you with meekness and fear."* Consequently, the following outline is offered as a primer to profitable Bible study. It has *nothing* to do with "cute ideas." And when God's *methods* are employed, God's *results* will always occur: *"For all the people **wept**, when they heard the words of the law."* (Nehemiah 8:9)

FIRST MENTION

The Law of First Mention teaches that the primary meaning of any word (or phrase) is revealed by the way it is used the *first* time it appears in Scripture. While subsequent usage may add further clarification, the original mention will always set the tone for the basic understanding of the word throughout the rest of the Bible. A sample of such occurrences would include the following: The *first* mention of the word "sinner" is found in Genesis 13:13, *"But the men of **Sodom** were wicked and **sinners** before the LORD exceedingly."* Thus, the first representatives of Adam's fallen race to receive this infamous title are *sodomites.* As Romans 1:26 will isolate this perversion as being *"**against** nature,"* the Holy Spirit adds the modifier *"exceedingly."* Also, the conspicuous Scripture address establishes *13* as the number for *sin* and *rebellion* (the verse being comprised of *13* words for added emphasis). Finally, as if to underscore *how* "exceedingly" wicked things had become, the *first* mention of the word "fire" is Genesis 19:24 – *"Then the LORD rained upon **Sodom** and upon Gomorrah brimstone and **fire** from the LORD out of heaven."*

Deuteronomy 32:22 is the *first* mention of the word "Hell." Because this doctrine constitutes one of the most uncomfortable subjects in sophisticated Laodicean society, the New International Version deletes the despised word in 40 of its 54 references. Billy Graham made everyone relax when he told *Time* magazine in 1993, "The only thing I could say for sure is that hell means separation from God...When it comes to a literal **fire**, I don't preach it because I'm not sure about it." Too bad Billy didn't follow the Law of First Mention. Deuteronomy 32:22 is the *only* reference to Hell in the Old Testament that includes the word "fire" in the same verse: *"For a fire is kindled in mine anger, and shall burn unto the lowest hell, and shall consume the earth with her increase, and set on fire the foundations of the mountains."* The perverted NIV reads: "For a **fire** has been kindled by my wrath, one that **burns** to the realm of **death** below....") In the *first* reference to "Hell" in the New Testament, Jesus contradicts the hireling Graham, even placing the words side-by-side – *"but whosoever shall say, Thou fool, shall be in danger of hell fire."* (Matthew 5:22)

As the context of Deuteronomy 32:22 deals with the Tribulation judgments involving Israel and her enemies, we are not surprised to learn that Exodus 3:5 is the *first* mention of the word "holy." The world certainly has its own icons, running the gamut from Amos and Andy (Kingfish's "Holy mackerel there, Andy!"), Batman & Robin (Robin's "Holy *this*" or "Holy *that*"), and legendary baseball announcer Harry Caray (*"Holy Cow!"*) to the more "serious" usage of *"Holy* Father," *"Holy* Mother of God," and *"Holy* Koran." However, in *God's* Book, the first thing *He* calls "holy" is *dirt* – *"And he said, Draw not nigh hither: put off thy shoes from off thy feet, for the place whereon thou standest is* HOLY GROUND.*"* This is why 3,500 years later *Israel* is still called the "Holy Land."

For additional study see: *blood* (Genesis 4:10); *believed* (Genesis 15:6); *love* (Genesis 22:2); *worship* (Genesis 22:5); *salvation* (Genesis 49:18); *miracle* (Exodus 7:9); *faith* (Deuteronomy 32:20); *prayer* (II Samuel 7:27); *preach* (Nehemiah 6:7); and last, but not least, the first mention of *Scripture* (Daniel 10:21).

SIMILITUDES

In Hosea 12:10, the Lord said, *"I have also spoken by the prophets, and I have multiplied visions, and used **similitudes**, by the ministry of the prophets."* The use of *similitudes* is one of the most basic methods of Bible instruction employed by the author Himself. *Webster's* defines the word as "1) Likeness; resemblance; likeness in nature, qualities or appearance; 2) Comparison; simile." The purpose of a similitude is to help you comprehend what you do *not* understand by comparing it to that which you *do* understand; grasping "this" by *likening* it to "that," etc.

Such an approach is an obvious affront to the professional Christian scholar as it requires no technical expertise. While Grandma may not know a *lexicon* from a *Lexus,* she *has* seen a few *trees* in her time; so, when the Holy Spirit wanted to describe a true Bible believer, He moved David to write: *"And he shall be **like a tree** planted by the rivers of water."* (Psalm 1:3) Similitudes are recognized by the words "as" and "like." Jeremiah 23:29 displays both in one verse: *"Is not my word **like as** a fire?"* A similitude is God's bridge that enables the believer to move from the *known* to the *unknown*; from the *tangible* to the *abstract.* It is the supernatural method of *seeing* that which is *invisible*: *"For the **invisible things** of him from the creation of the world are **clearly seen**, being **understood by the things that are made**, even his eternal power and Godhead."* (Romans 1:20)

There are hundreds of similitudes throughout God's word. At least nine *major* ones are used to describe the Bible itself: *honey* (Psalm 119:103); a *light* (Psalm 119:105); a *hammer* (Jeremiah 23:29); *bread* (Matthew 4:4); *meat* (I Corinthians 3:2); a *sword* (Ephesians 6:17); *seed* (I Peter 1:23); *milk* (I Peter 2:2); and, a *mirror* (James 1:22-25).

WEBSTER'S 1828 DICTIONARY

The King James Bible will often provide its own internal definitions of important words and doctrines. Having said this, the 1828 *American Dictionary of the English Language* by Noah Webster constitutes an indispensible supplement to practical Bible study. Sadly, until recently the average Fundamentalist has never even *seen* a copy of this dictionary. Noah Webster was converted to Christianity in 1807 during a winter revival in New Haven, Connecticut. Following weeks of conviction, the future lexicographer was gloriously converted, testifying: "I closed my books, yielded to the influence which could not be resisted or mistaken, and was led by a spontaneous impulse to repentance, prayer, and entire submission and surrender of myself to my Maker and Redeemer. My submission appeared to be cheerful, and was soon followed by that peace of mind which the world can neither give nor take away."

It was Webster's conviction that "the Christian religion is the most important and one of the first things in which all children, under a free government, ought to be instructed." Consequently, he would give the young republic his invaluable *Grammar* and *Reader* along with the *The American Spelling Book* (the famous "Blue Back Speller"). His signature dictionary was produced during the years when the American home, church, and school were grounded upon a biblical and patriotic foundation. Thus, it should come as no surprise, that the finished product contained the greatest number of *scriptural* definitions found in any secular work. Unlike other dictionaries, Mr. Webster's work was formally dedicated to God, "…that great and benevolent being." While the author's labor of love falls short of "inspiration," it commands the recognition afforded similar gifts of providence, such as *Foxe's Book of Martyrs*, *Pilgrim's Progress*, and any conservative hymnal. The 1828 *Webster's* was unquestionably "America's dictionary" for the Philadelphia Church Age. (Note: While his own well-intentioned, though ill-fated, attempt at Bible revision was a bust, his dictionary has displayed the unmistakable sanction of longevity.)

TYPOLOGY

Bible *types* are first cousins to similitudes. The main difference between the two is that typology is primarily *prophetic* in nature. Occasioned by the aforementioned relationship between the Old and New Testaments (the OT being the NT concealed, etc.), types anticipate persons, things, or events. Jesus illustrated their purpose when He cried, *"**And as** Moses lifted up the **serpent** in the wilderness, **even so** must the **Son** of man be lifted up."* (John 3:14) The study of types will always be a spiritually enriching experience.

There are literally hundreds of these prophetic symbols in the Old Testament, thus one can hardly broach the subject. A small sample follows: Adam is the first major type of Christ while Eve is the first type of the Church (the Bride of Christ). The story of Noah's ark foreshadows the Jew being preserved through the Tribulation. With Egypt as a type of the world, the parting of the Red Sea pictures New Testament salvation and eternal security (*we can't part the waters and we sure can't swim back after they close behind us*). In Deuteronomy 18:15-19 Moses is established as a major type of Christ (as confirmed by the words *"that prophet"* in John 1:21). An entire volume could be written on the beautiful symbolism of the Tabernacle. Exodus devotes fifteen chapters to this unassuming "tent." While Aaron prefigures Christ as our High Priest, every lamb would point to *"**the** Lamb of God, which taketh away the sin of the world."* (John 1:29)

One of the most beautiful types in the Bible is the loyal servant of Abraham, Eliezer. He is sent on a special mission to bring back a bride for his master's son, Isaac. Thus, he pictures the Holy Spirit's work in retrieving a bride for *God's* Son. The strength of a type to *reinforce* New Testament doctrine can be seen by Eliezer's commission and Rebekah's response; the heresy of Calvinism being countered by the scriptural position of *free will*. Note how the prospective bride is under no obligation to come: *"And **if the woman will not be willing** to follow thee, then thou shalt be clear from this my oath...And they called Rebekah, and said unto her, **Wilt thou go** with this man? And she said, **I will go.**"* (Genesis 24:58) From a devotional standpoint, the "heart" of the story is when Rebekah says, *"We have both straw and provender enough, and **room to lodge in**"* (Genesis 24:25). This was more than Jesus received in Bethlehem and remains the primary thing He desires today – as in *"give me thine heart."* (Proverbs 23:26)

Joseph is generally recognized as the outstanding type of Christ, the Holy Spirit bearing witness to over 100 specific examples from his life. A tithe would be: 1) his father's love; 2) sent forth to secure the welfare of his brethren; 3) cast into a pit and taken out alive; 4) hated and sold by his brethren; 5) sorely tempted, yet sinned not; 6) thirty years old when he begins his life's work; 7) takes a Gentile

bride; 8) made known to his brethren a second time; 9) brethren
share in his glory; 10) ultimately, saves *"much people alive."*

Bible Names

Another source of spiritual edification can be gained from
studying the biblical *names* of people and places. After 2,000 years,
we name our sons "Paul" and our dogs "Nero." We have already seen
the significance of names in our study on the seven churches of
Revelation: While Ephesus means "desirable one," Egypt means
"black"; while Philadelphia means "brotherly love," Ham means
"warm"; while Pergamos means "marriage and elevation," Capernaum
means "city of comfort"; while Thyatira means "continual sacrifice,"
Bethlehem means "house of bread"; while Laodicea means "rights
of the people," Jerusalem means "city of peace."

Joseph means "he shall add"; thus, he gets a second name,
Zaphnath-paaneah, for "revealer of secret things" (Genesis 41:45).
Other pertinent definitions would include: Adam, "red"; Cain,
"possession"; Sarah, "princess"; Isaac, "laughter"; Jacob, "supplanter";
Israel, "prince of God"; Achan, "trouble"; Job, "desert"; David,
"beloved"; Jezebel, "unmarried"; John, "Jehovah is gracious"; Dodo,
"loving"; Buz, "contempt"; Uz, "fertile"; Huppim "seashore";
Shuppim, "worn out"; and, last but not least, Mahershalalhashbaz,
"the spoil hastens."

There are many valuable lessons that can be gleaned from Bible
names. For instance, the Apostle Paul was the most powerful
Christian in the New Testament. Yet, his name means "little,"
teaching us that God uses *"little* people" to do *"big* things." When
believers lose sight of this truth, God loses sight of *them.* Thus, we
find Paul's original namesake dismissed with the words, *"When
thou wast **little** in thine own sight, wast thou not made the head of
the tribes of Israel, and the LORD anointed thee king over Israel?"*
(I Samuel 15:17) Paul subsequently declares: *"And lest I should
be **exalted** above measure through the abundance of the revelations,
there was given to me a thorn in the flesh."* (II Corinthians 12:7)

With Diotrephes representing the consummate New Testament offender, we are not surprised to learn that the meaning of *his* name is "nourished by Zeus" (III John 9).

Moses records the naming of Lamech's son in Genesis 5:29 – *"And he called his name Noah, saying, This same shall **comfort** us concerning our work and toil of our hands, because of the ground which the LORD hath cursed."* Thus, *Noah* means "rest." The important cross-reference is Matthew 24:37 – *"But as the days of Noe were, so shall also the coming of the Son of man be."* When these verses are compared, a most practical application comes into view. One of the main priorities for a pastor in today's unprecedented, hectic society is to provide *comfort* and *rest* for his frazzled people. As the Lord's remnant in the last days are literally *"running to and fro,"* they are in desperate need of oxygen to avoid spiritual burnout (Isaiah 40:31; Daniel 7:25; 12:4).

Solomon wrote in Proverbs 9:8, *"**rebuke a wise** man, and he will **love** thee."* The writer's own father received one of the harshest rebukes in Scripture. After hiding his adultery with Bathsheba (as well as Uriah's murder), the *king* ran into the long, bony finger of the *prophet*: *"And Nathan said to David, **thou art the man.**"* (II Samuel 12:7) As Nathan means "gift of God," his rebuke was a timely *gift* for David's life (see Psalm 51); and, because *"a **wise** man will hear,"* David immediately repented (Proverbs 1:5). Consequently, after God takes David's illegitimate child, He graciously allows Solomon to be born. Being the "replacement" son, Solomon received a *second* name: *"and the LORD **loved** him. And he sent by the hand of **Nathan** the prophet; and he called his name **Jedidiah,** because of the LORD."* (II Samuel 12:24-25) Jedidiah means "beloved of the LORD."

Among other blessings, Solomon is given three additional brothers to "play" with (which constitutes *another* study in itself, based on the *four-to-one* formula in II Samuel 12:6; David *losing* three children and a nephew through God's *judgment* for his *sin*, yet *gaining* four children through God's *mercy* for his *repentance*). Because of the truth in Proverbs 9:8, David would go on to openly acknowledge his esteem for the one who rebuked him. Note the names of these four boys (listed in reverse order): *"And these were born unto him in Jerusalem; Shimea, and Shobab, and **Nathan**, and Solomon."* (I Chronicles 3:5) And of David's thirteen named sons, who do *you* suppose ends up in the genealogy of Joseph? – *"Which was the son of Melea, which was the son of Menan, which was the son of Mattatha, which was the son of **Nathan**, which was the son of **David**."* (Luke 3:31) And then, with twelve being the number of Israel, we have that prophetic truth in Zechariah 12:12 regarding Nathan's seed in mourning at the end of the Tribulatio.

On a final note, we understand that God's *own* personal name must be very important to Him, as He placed it at *both* ends of the Holy Bible (i.e., *"the beginning and the ending"*). While the *first* word in Genesis begins with the letter "I," the *last* word in Revelation begins with the letters "A - M"; *you* know, as in – "I AM."

NUMEROLOGY

Numerology is the study of numbers in Scripture. (The book of "Numbers" would indicate the obvious importance of this subject to God.) As the concept of Bible numerics has already been surveyed in previous chapters, we will examine only three additional examples. In Revelation 13:18, we learn: *"Here is wisdom. Let him that hath understanding count the **number** of the beast: for it is the **number of a man**; and his number is Six hundred three score and six."* From our study of *Genesis 13:13*, we would expect the greatest *rebel* in history to make his debut in *Revelation 13*. And, because his *number* is 666, we understand that his *verse* is 18 (6+6+6). Thus, the number *six* is established as the number of a *man*. Created from the dust on the *sixth* day, man eventually returns to the same – *"six* feet under," to be exact. The *sixth* book of the Bible is the first book to be named after a *man*. There are *six* letters in "Joshua." The *sixth* book of the New Testament is **Roman**s, also spelled with *six* letters. In one of those KJV-Only "coincidences," the *sixth* word of the *sixth* verse of the *sixth* chapter of the *sixth* book, just "happens" to be – well, take a look for yourself – *"Knowing this, that our old **man** is crucified with him."*

The number *four* has repeated associations with the *earth*. Revelation 7:1 reads: *"And after these things I saw **four** angels standing on the **four corners of the earth**, holding the **four winds of the earth**."* The *four* points of the compass are North, East, South, and West. Then we have the *four* elements: Earth, Air, Fire, and Water. Most of us enjoy *four* seasons: Spring, Summer, Fall, and Winter. The first mention of the word is found in Genesis 2:10 where it describes the river of Eden dividing into *"four* heads" and flowing upon the *earth* in as many directions. In the *fourth* chapter of Genesis, Abel's blood cries unto God *"from the **ground**."* The first man to return to the *ground* has *four* letters in his name. Revelation 14:6 divides those *"that dwell on the **earth**"* into *four* categories – *"every **nation**, and **kindred**, and **tongue**, and **people**."* Daniel 2:37-43 lists the greatest power brokers on *earth* as *four* consecutive kingdoms: Babylon, Medea-Persia, Greece, and Rome. In Matthew 24:6-7, Jesus predicts *four* major judgments upon the *earth*: War, Famine, Pestilence, and Earthquakes.

While the scholar remains baffled by such things, any mother knows that *nine* is the number of *fruit bearing*. The most fruitful king in Israel's history is anointed in I Samuel, the *ninth* book of the Bible. There are *nine* letters in David's capital city, Jerusalem. The most fruit-bearing Christian in the Church Age is *born* again in the *ninth* chapter of Acts. The Apostle Paul goes on to list the nine *"fruit of the spirit"* in the *ninth* book of the New Testament. Located in the fifth chapter of Galatians, they spread over verses 22 and 23 (as in 2+2+2+3 = 9). There are *nine* letters in "Holy Bible," "Scripture," and "word of God." Also, there are *nine* letters in KING JAMES with 1+6+1+1 = (Guess!). The last sermon that Lester Roloff preached at the Southwide Baptist Fellowship was entitled "Don't Mess With My *Mama*." (They say he kept waving his King James Bible in the air in a *most* "undignified" manner.) The birth announcement for the greatest *fruit*-bearing nation in history was given at Genesis 9:27 (*two* nines, as 2+7 = 9). After the cry of "Land Ho" was finally heard on November 9, 1620 (*another* two nines, as 1+6+2+0 = 9), a total of *99* souls disembarked from the Mayflower (*nine* letters).

The Lord told Abraham that his *seed* would eventually be like the *"stars of heaven"* (Genesis 15:5; 22:17). Do you suppose He was serious? Isaiah 9:7 expands on this theme with a truth that is far *too* heavy (and *holy*) for about 99% of the brethren: *"Of the **increase** of his **government** and peace there shall be no end."* Suffice it to say that the number *nine* is the *ultimate* choice for "fruit bearing." Unlike the other eight single-digit numbers, whenever *9* is multiplied by another number the individual figures in the answer will either total 9, or eventually add up to 9, a rather remarkable phenomenon, indeed! Thus, we see that 9 x 3 = 27 (2 + 7 = 9); 9 x 475 = 4,275 (4 + 2 + 7 + 5 =18, and 1 + 8 = 9); 9 x 3,547,248 = 31,925,232 (3 + 1 + 9 + 2 + 5 + 2 + 3 + 2 = 27, and 2 + 7 = 9); *ad infinitum.* Now, how's *that* for "Baptist Bingo?"

THREEFOLD APPLICATION

We learned in a previous chapter that the number *three* points to the Holy Trinity. In addition to man's own nature consisting of *body*, *soul*, and *spirit*, most things in the world can also be grouped into threes. For instance, there are *three* dimensions: *time*, *space*, and *matter*. These, in turn, subdivide accordingly: time into *past*, *present*, and *future*; space into *length*, *width*, and *depth*; and matter into *solid*, *liquid*, and *gas*. Man was designed to survive on *food*, *water*, and *air*. These also breakdown as: energy into *proteins*, *carbohydrates*, and *fats*; water into two parts *hydrogen* and one part *oxygen*; and air into *nitrogen*, *oxygen*, and *argon*.

There are *numbers* of "threes" from the *ridiculous* to the *sublime*, from Goldilocks and the Three Bears, the Three Little Pigs, and the Three Stooges to atmosphere, ionosphere, and stratosphere; light waves, heat rays, and actinic rays; as well as electrons, protons, and neutrons. A sample of everything in-between would include: father, mother, and children; *CBS*, *ABC*, and *NBC*; ready, aim, fire; 1, 2, 3 – repeat after me; yes, no, maybe; ready, set, go; *Veni, Vidi, Vici*; small, medium, large; id, ego, super-ego; Huey, Dewey, and Louie; thesis, antithesis, and synthesis; snap, crackle, and pop; Prince, Paris, and Blanket; the good, the bad, and the ugly; life, liberty, and the pursuit of happiness; of the people, by the people, and for the people; three implosions at the World Trade Center on 9/11; the three R's; three coins in a fountain; three-ring circus; three-time loser; "three strikes and you're out"; "the third time's a charm"; three-bean salad; three sheets to the wind; and the "Three Little Kittens Who Lost Their Mittens."

Of course, the *spiritual* "threes" are the most important groupings. God's personal name is composed of three letters – "I AM." His main attributes are omniscience, omnipotence, and omnipresence. The Old Testament consists of the Law, the prophets, and the writings, while the New Testament contains the Gospels, Acts, and Epistles, collectively written in Hebrew, Greek, and Aramaic. Mankind is divided into Shem, Ham, and Japheth. Israel's three patriarchs are Abraham, Isaac, and Jacob. Moses placed three items in the Ark: the tablets, the golden pot, and Aaron's rod. Jesus, Mary, and Joseph are visited by wise men who bring gold, frankincense, and myrrh. The "Babe" winds up on Calvary's *middle* cross, expiring after three hours in darkness. He then spends three days and three nights in the *"heart of the earth."* The ascended Lord Jesus Christ is now the only *mediator* between God and man. He remains the same yesterday, today, and forever. After the Apostle Paul is saved, baptized, and called to preach, he is sent to Arabia for three years of "study." He then embarks upon his specialized ministry proclaiming Christ's death, burial, and resurrection to the Gentiles. The themes of his epistles include: faith, hope, and charity; justification, sanctification, and glorification; and grace, mercy, and peace. While the words *"thrice was I beaten with rods"* describe a portion of his suffering, his personal revelations included a trip to the third Heaven. At death, his sole possessions consisted of a cloak, books, and parchments. The Apostle John wraps things up by telling us about the three woes, 666, "Holy, Holy, Holy," and the new heavens, new earth, and new city. Once again, many other "threes" could have been cited – the threefold cord; the three Hebrew children; Peter's three denials; Egypt, the Wilderness, and Caanan; natural, carnal, and spiritual; Peter, James, and John; the great commission to go, teach, and baptize; the shout, the voice, and the trump, etc.

Thus, we understand that the number *three* is a picture, or revelation, of the Godhead itself. It follows, therefore, that the proper approach to His word should involve a threefold process. Consequently, every Scripture will have *three* applications: *historical*, *doctrinal*, and *devotional*. The *historical* is simply an accurate rendering of the immediate context of the passage. The *doctrinal* is the most critical application, as it involves the precise *teaching* of the text. I Timothy 3:16 lists *doctrine* as the first purpose for the Scripture itself. Much of the *doctrinal* material in the Old Testament is prophetic, as Israel's future is generally the primary focus. Finally, the *devotional* can be likened to the dessert after a meal. God's children must first determine what their Father has literally said before they can enjoy the blessing of a personal application.

A single illustration will suffice: David wrote, *"Yea, though **I** walk through the valley of the shadow of death, **I** will fear no evil: for thou art with **me**; thy rod and thy staff they comfort **me**."* (Psalm 23:4) The *historical* application would relate to the author's life experience. For instance, a nine-foot giant had undoubtedly turned the "Valley of Elah" into a potential "Valley of *Death*." We are also mindful of the "rod" David *endured* for his *sin*, as well as the "staff" he *embraced* in *forgiveness*. (Note the cross-reference between his *testimony* in Psalm 23:3, *"He **restoreth** my soul,"* and his *prayer* in Psalm 51:12, *"**Restore** unto me the joy of thy salvation."*)

The *doctrinal* application relates to *Israel's* future restoration: *"And I will **restore** to **you** the years that the locust hath eaten."* (Joel 2:25) Peter made reference to this event, stating: *"And he shall send Jesus Christ, which before was preached unto you: Whom the heaven must receive until the times of **restitution** of all things."* (Acts 3:20-21) However, before this *national* restoration can occur, Israel must enter the *"valley of death"* one last time.

After being "reassembled" in the "*valley* of Dry Bones," the time of "Jacob's trouble" finally ends in the "*Valley* of Jezreel" (Ezekiel 37; Revelation 16:16). Thus, the prophet could write: *"Seek him that maketh the seven stars and Orion, and turneth **the shadow of death** into the morning...The LORD is his name."* (Amos 5:8)

Lastly, the *devotional* application is no mystery to seasoned believers. While the *Footprints* poem is beautiful, our text says, *"Yea, though I **walk** through the valley of the shadow of death."* When the waters are *still*, our Shepherd will be found out in front, leading (verse 2). However, when the *shadows* arise, David could affirm: *"I will fear no evil: **for thou art with me.**"* While the Lord may not *carry* us, He will surely walk that last mile *close by our side*.

CROSS-REFERENCING

We have now arrived at the most vital part of this chapter. Without *any* doubt *whatsoever*, the God-given ability to understand *cross-referencing* and *right division* constitutes *the* greatest blessing bestowed upon true Bible believers. (I will always be grateful to Dr. Wendell Runion for teaching me how to cross-reference my Bible.) Conversely, it represents the greatest *forfeiture* to "*Pseudo* King James Onlyites," their only consolation being that "ignorance is bliss." Like the Jews who despised the *living* Word, *TR* Fundamentalists have *no* idea what they are missing, as both share the spiritual epitaph of Luke 19:44 – *"thou knewest not the time of thy visitation."*

Take this matter of Israel's spiritual blindness. A lesson in cross-referencing will illustrate just how close they actually came to their long-awaited Messiah. David wrote in Psalm 23:2, *"He **maketh** me to lie down in **green** pastures."* Beginning in reverse order, the *devotional* application is twofold: Sometimes God *makes* His children lie down in pastures that they would not have chosen for themselves. However, while we may not know the *reason*, we can *always* be certain that it will be a **green** pasture (Romans 8:28).

The *doctrinal* application concerns Israel and is prophetic in nature. Next to Joseph, David is the greatest type of Israel's *shepherd* king, the Lord Jesus Christ. Thus, we find the *"Good Shepherd"* making *His* sheep to lie down in **green** pastures, as well. Being *"moved with compassion toward them, because they were as sheep not having a shepherd...he **commanded** them to make all sit **down** by companies upon the **green** grass."* (Mark 6:34, 39) Unfortunately, many of these same Jews *"went back, and walked no more with him,"* never realizing who Jesus was. (John 6:66; Matthew 21:10-11) Fortunately, however, as Romans 11:19 says, *"The branches were broken off, that I might be graffed in,"* Israel's *loss* became our *gain.* Thus, we turn to the *Song of Solomon* for our next cross-reference. Here, we see the young bride as a type of the Church, longing for the return of her *shepherd* bridegroom. She speaks – *"Behold, thou art fair, my **beloved**, yea, pleasant."* (Having learned that Solomon's second name means "beloved of the Lord," we understand that the *historical* application points to *him.*) Note her specific description of the bridal chamber: *"also our bed is **green**."* (Song of Solomon 1:16) Paul explains this holy truth in Romans 7:4 – *"Wherefore, my brethren, ye also are become dead to the law by the body of Christ; that ye should be **married to another**, even to him who is raised from the dead, **that we should bring forth fruit unto God.**"*

Now, did you happen to notice that Scripture address above – John 6:66? Do you suppose any spiritual bells should be going off by now? With 666 being the *"mark of the beast,"* we understand that the actions described in John 6:66 foreshadow the very defection that will characterize the Tribulation. Ezra 2:13 is the brief cross-reference here: *"The children of Adonikam, **six hundred sixty and six**."* Combining *types*, *numbers*, and *names*, and *cross-referencing* all together, we discern the prophetic significance in the name *Adonikam*, meaning "the lord of *rebellion*," a direct reference to the Antichrist himself. (By the way, did you catch *Adonikam's* verse number?) For the record, as the Devil is a *thief*, he probably stole his idea for marking foreheads *and* using the number 666 from Ezekiel 9:4 (9+4=13) and II Chronicles 9:13 (9+1+3=13).

In a remarkable spiritual paradox, while the prophetic profile in Judges 21:25 describes the end-day Laodicean as doing *"that which was right in his own eyes,"* Revelation 3:17 confirms that in reality, he can't see a thing. However, while *"Pseudo* King James Onlyites" remain blind to what is there for the taking, open apostates have no opportunity for the prize, as multiplied cross-references are eliminated in the modern versions. For example, consider the NIV's rendering of Romans 6:6. Rather than displaying "man" in the sixth word of the sixth verse, we read: "For we know that our old *self* was crucified with him." Not only is the word "man" changed to "self," but it is bumped to the *seventh* word, as well. As the NIV is supposed to make the Bible more readable, the editors also destroyed the cross-reference in Song of Solomon 1:16 by changing *"green"* to "verdant." (*Oy!*)

If we are *saved* by the Cross, *sanctified* by the Cross, and ultimately, *glorified* by the Cross, would it not follow that our *edification* should *also* have something to do with a "cross"? *Cross*-referencing is the Bible's own built-in method for profitable study. Paul wrote: *"Now we have received, not the spirit of the world, but the spirit which is of God; that we might know the things that are freely given to us of God. Which things also we speak, not in the words which man's wisdom teacheth, but which the Holy Ghost teacheth;* **comparing spiritual things with spiritual.** *"* (I Corinthians 2:12-13)

The more that verses are tied together, the more the Bible comes alive; as the wise man wrote, *"Two are better than one... and a threefold cord is not quickly broken."* (Ecclesiastes 4:9, 12) A few examples and I will be through: The key to God using our lives to the fullest can be found by cross-referencing Romans 11:13 with Joshua 3:7; for if *we* will "magnify our *office*," *God* will "magnify our *person*." The explanation for that unmistakable serenity at the deathbed of a godly Christian surrounded by godly family is found in the cross-referencing of Proverbs 16:7 with I Corinthians 15:26 – *"When a man's ways please the LORD, he maketh even his **enemies** to be at peace with him,"* including *"The last **enemy** that shall be destroyed...death."*

The foundation of the Christian home can be traced to a simple cross-reference. Proverbs 17:6 states that *"the **glory** of children are their fathers."* No *normal* boy on any playground ever said to his friends, *"My* mother can wash dishes better than *your* mother"; it was always, *"My* dad can lick *your* dad," etc. This verse confirms what human experience reveals – that the husband's God-given influence is over the *children.* Conversely, I Corinthians 11:7 affirms that the wife's influence is over the husband, as *"the woman is the **glory** of the man."* According to the poet, William Ross Wallace, "The hand that rocks the cradle rules the world." However, I beg to differ; the greatest good any mother can do for her children is to devote her quality time to the one who retains the *greater* influence over them. Thus, the *wife* influences the *husband* so the *husband* can influence the *children.* This is what Solomon meant by the words: *"Every **wise** woman buildeth her house: but the **foolish** plucketh it down with her hands."* (Proverbs 14:1) At the end of the day, the faithful wife will be vindicated, as *her* glory is *delayed* glory. By the time her children are grown, they will have discovered the *real* power behind the throne: *"Her children **arise up** and call **her** blessed."* (Proverbs 31:28; I Kings 1:16, 31; 2:19)

RIGHT DIVISION

The *three* most important verses that define *right division* are II Timothy 2:15, I Corinthians 10:32, and II Timothy 2:7 (in that order). Having enjoined right division in his second pastoral epistle, Paul gave the Corinthians the *threefold* division of humanity: *"Give none offence, neither to the **Jews,** nor to the **Gentiles,** nor to the **church of God.**"* The key to a proper exegesis of any text is understanding whom the writer is addressing; i.e., *Jew, Gentile,* or *Christian.*

One of the biggest stumbling blocks for Christians today is their failure to realize that "their" King James Bible is *not* "theirs" exclusively. The truths contained in the New Testament do *not* stop with the Church Age, as THE BOOK constitutes a *complete* revelation. (I used to tell my students that the A.V. 1611 is only 2/7

Baptist; i.e., based on a 2,000-year Church Age.) As our Bibles do not accompany us at the Rapture, they must serve a purpose for those left behind. The problem is that most Christians have never been taught that the Tribulation is *radically* different from the Church Age. For instance, any genuine believer will acknowledge that the nine books from Hebrews to Revelation generate a *different* spiritual "vibe" than the thirteen Pauline epistles do. However, what is *not* generally understood is – *why*.

The answer to this question has to do with two mutually exclusive subjects: eternal security and the mark of the beast. The word of God clearly teaches that Church Age saints are *"sealed unto the day of redemption."* (Ephesians 4:30; Romans 8:35-39) As such, there is nothing we can do to *break* that seal. Thus, we are going to Heaven whether we "like it or not!" And, though a little heavy for *Pseudos*, while Jewish saints in the Gospel period are said to be *in* the Lord's hand, Church Age saints *literally* morph *into* the hand of God itself. (John 10:28-29; Ephesians 5:30)

(WARNING: What you are about to read was written by a "once-married" preacher, i.e., a preacher who has only been married *one time* and *never* divorced.) However, the same Bible is *just* as clear that Tribulation saints do *not* have eternal security *because of what God has decreed concerning the mark of the beast* – "**IF** *ANY* **MAN** WORSHIP THE BEAST AND HIS IMAGE, AND **RECEIVE HIS MARK**...THE **SAME**...**SHALL BE** TORMENTED WITH FIRE AND BRIMSTONE...IN THE PRESENCE OF THE LAMB: AND THE SMOKE OF THEIR TORMENT ASCENDETH UP FOR EVER AND EVER: AND **THEY** HAVE NO REST DAY NOR NIGHT...*WHOSOEVER* **RECEIVETH THE MARK OF HIS NAME.** " (Revelation 14:9-11)

Now, it is absolutely *amazing* how exasperated Fundamentalists get when confronted by this simple text (as with Luke 18:34 and plenty of others). The only "logic" they can posit is that anyone who was *truly* saved would *never* take the mark, etc. Of course, *this is utter nonsense* given Peter's three denials, followed by 2,000 years of Church history documenting sincere, though weak,

Christians who recanted under persecution (Matthew 26:41). We have all seen the typical modern Christian at a restaurant who would rather sneeze into his napkin, "Bless the food, Lord," than bow his head and pray unashamedly. Can you imagine *this* caliber of believer flat on his back, having that same head *slowly* sawed off at the throat – *Al-Qaeda* style? (Revelation 20:4) Thus, in Matthew 24:13 Jesus said of the Tribulation, *"he that shall* **ENDURE** *unto the end, the same shall be* SAVED. " (While the context of verse 22 points to *physical* salvation, the overriding theme of Revelation 14:9-11 would incorporate the *soul*, as well; i.e., Matthew 10:22, 28.) Conversely, believers in the Church Age are *"confirm*[ed]*...unto the end. "* (I Corinthians 1:7-8)

Thankfully, the English text of the Authorized Version is *more* than capable of handling all matters of final authority. The definitive verse concerning whether genuine Christians can recant under pressure is Acts 26:10-11. Here, the Holy Spirit moved Paul to identify his victims as "saints," testifying, *"and many of the* SAINTS *did I shut up in prison. "* Notice what he says next: *"And I punished them oft in every synagogue,* AND *COMPELLED* THEM TO BLASPHEME. "* Apparently, "saints" *can* be "compelled to blaspheme." To do so in the Church Age is to forfeit eternal *rewards*; to do so in the Tribulation is to forfeit eternal *life*.

Now, because God cares about the Tribulation saints, He has placed certain passages for *them* in the New Testament, as well. Consequently, to avoid confusion, our third verse tells us *exactly* what to do. In II Timothy 2:7, the "apostle to the *Gentiles*" writes: *"*CONSIDER WHAT I SAY AND THE LORD GIVE THEE **UNDERSTANDING** IN *ALL* THINGS. "* The most enlightening truth that you will *ever* hear with regard to finally making sense out of your Bible is simply this: Whenever a verse in the New Testament contradicts a Pauline epistle, go with Paul *every* time! For instance, Ephesians 5:30 says that *"we are members of his body, of his flesh, and of his bones. "* We know that this "spiritual bone graft" occurred at salvation and that Christ *cannot* be divided subsequently (I Corinthians 1:13, 6:17). Hebrews 3:14, however, presents a different situation altogether: *"For we are made* **PARTAKERS** *of Christ,* **IF** WE **HOLD** THE

BEGINNING OF OUR CONFIDENCE **STEADFAST UNTO THE** *END. "* (Note how those last three words cross-reference to Matthew 24:13). As the chief spokesman for the Church Age, Paul gives *no* such conditions as *our* attachment to Christ is predicated on a *done* deal: *"Giving thanks unto the Father, which hath made us meet to be **partakers** of the inheritance of the saints in light: who hath delivered us from the power of darkness, and hath translated us into the kingdom of his dear Son. "* (Colossians 1:12-13)

Then, in the great majority of passages where there is no doctrinal contradiction, *why* – he'p yo'self! And don't let some Bible-correcting "Funnymentalist Nicolaitane" try to back you into a corner with a charge of being a "hyper-dispensationalist," for *"All scripture is given by inspiration of God, and is **profitable**. "* Remember?

So, *now* you know *why* those so-called "Jewish-Christian" epistles (Hebrews through Revelation) resonate a tad *differently* to your spirit. (The very term "Jewish-Christian" epistle is a misnomer in light of Galatians 3:28.) While most of "the brethren" will write you off as a heretic *for accepting what the Bible clearly says about anything* (not to mention *something* that has absolutely *nothing* to do with the Church Age), at *least* you'll have a new approach to those same ol' verses that your *critics* continue to dodge, *especially* when they are being hammered by the cults (i.e., Matthew 6:15, 24:14; Luke 18:31-34, 21:36; Acts 2:38, 10:35, 19:1-7; Romans 2:6-10; Galatians 1:11-12, 2:7; Ephesians 3:1-6; Hebrews 3:6, 14, 6:4-6, 9:28, 10:26, 39, 12:14; James 2:24; I John 2:19, 3:9; Revelation 2:11, 3:5, 14:10, 12, 22:14, 19, etc.).

Allowing the Holy Spirit to speak for Himself, an outline of the entire Bible, rightly divided and in chronological order, would be: Genesis 1-3, *Innocence*; Genesis 3-12, *Gentiles*; Genesis 12 - Exodus 19, *Patriarchs*; Exodus 19 - Matthew 26, *Israel*; Matthew 26 - Acts 2, *Messiah*; Acts 2 - Revelation 4, *Church*; Revelation 4-19, *Tribulation*; Revelation 19-22, *Kingdom* and *Eternity*.

Finally, when Christians heed *right* division, the entire Bible opens up like never before. Other related truths fall *right* in place, such as the importance of *transition* books. Naturally, there are *three*: Matthew takes us from the *Old* Testament to the *New*; Acts moves from *Jews* to *Gentiles*; and Hebrews transitions from the *Church Age* to the *Tribulation*.

Another vista opens by rightly dividing the *literal, physical, material* Kingdom of *Heaven* from the *invisible, spiritual, internal* Kingdom of *God.* (The unmistakable distinction of these two words was established in the very first verse in Scripture, Genesis 1:1.) The reality of a *spiritual* Kingdom that *"cometh not with observation"* (Luke 17:20), consisting of *"righteousness, and peace, and joy in the Holy Ghost"* (Romans 14:17), is in stark contrast to a *material* Kingdom that *"suffereth violence"* at the hands of "wrongly dividing" Fundamentalist Kingdom builders who would *"take it by force"* (Matthew 11:12). Heaven only knows the extent of *spiritual* "violence" attributable to "1-2-3, repeat after me" sinner's prayers being *jerked* out of traumatized "prospects" by soulwinners *"destitute of the truth, supposing that gain is godliness."* (I Timothy 6:5) Consequently, with Jesus Christ destined to rule over *both* realms, the "Kingdom" constitutes the central theme of the Holy Bible (Revelation 11:15 and chapters 20-22).

> *"Let the elders that rule well be counted worthy*
> *of double honour, especially they who*
> *labour in the word and doctrine."*
>
> (I Timothy 5:17)

10

The Old Ship of Alexandria

OVER 2,000 BOOKS and articles have been written about the "Mutiny on the Bounty." No less than five motion pictures, featuring such Hollywood "icons" as Errol Flynn, Clark Gable, Marlon Brando, and Mel Gibson have immortalized the most spectacular naval revolt in history. As a new convert, I was utterly amazed to learn about the lesser-known supernatural aftermath of this highly documented event. In January 1790, after nearly four months at sea, nine mutineers with six native men, twelve native women, and a baby girl eventually put ashore on Pitcairn Island, situated halfway between New Zealand and Peru. The remote tropical paradise soon morphed into a haven of murder and debauchery. The mayhem accelerated when one of the sailors began distilling alcohol from the ti plant. Finally, ten years after their clandestine arrival, only one Englishman remained, surrounded by ten Tahitian women and their half-breed children.

In the providence of God an American whaling ship, the *USS Topaz*, sailed into "Bounty Bay" on February 6, 1808. What the crew uncovered sent shock waves throughout the civilized world. The isolated commune at Pitcairn Island had become a prosperous, moral society with *no* crime, *no* jails, and *no* whiskey. Given the uncanny fact that the lead mutineer had the name of Fletcher *Christian*, we might expect a *spiritual* explanation for his surreal legacy. When the male population had dwindled to just two, Edward Young broke out the ship's Bible and prayer book and spent the last year of his life honing the literary skills of seaman

John Adams. The Holy Spirit took things from there. According to secular accounts, soon after Young succumbed to asthma, Adams "underwent a transformation and became fervently religious." Sunday services were immediately established with Adams officiating. The rest is history.

While this story illustrates the power of the A.V. 1611, the New Testament contains its own maritime narrative, replete with *forty-five* major lessons regarding the modern "Bible" movement. Because "The Book" is a *supernatural* "book," it can teach its truths through any number of scriptural venues. For instance, there are *seven* deacons introduced in Acts 6:5 with their *five* antagonists identified four verses later. Note how one of the deacons is from *"Antioch,"* while *"Alexandrians"* are named among the opposition. Thus, we see the number of *death* stalking the number of *perfection* – precisely as events would later unfold in the arena of textual criticism between *Alexandrian* and *Antiochian* text types.

The Holy Spirit has provided a most remarkable *similitude* in Acts 27 concerning Alexandrian "Bibles." With *twenty-seven* books in the New Testament, we would expect this chapter to have *something* to do with the word of God. Satan was obviously intent on destroying the Scripture, as 1/3 of the New Testament was aboard that storm-tossed ship. While Paul was en route to the very prison where Ephesians, Philippians, Colossians, and Philemon would be composed, the pastoral epistles were destined to follow next. And with that conspicuous "we" in Acts 27:1, *we* understand that Luke was also about to go down with the ship, taking the book of Acts with him, not to mention his yet-to-be-written *"former treatise."* It is fitting, therefore, that verse 38 identifies the commercial freight on board as "wheat."

Thankfully, the Lord intervened and *Leviathan's* wrath was checked (Psalm 104:26; Job 41). However, as the Devil is nobody's fool, he was not *about* to quit after Paul and Luke survived to pen their nine inspired books. Satan would now pursue "Plan B" – corrupt the finished product. As the chapter that catalogued the "great escape" itself, Acts 27 appears to have represented a special target for revenge. Assisted by Westcott and Hort, along with contemporary money changers like Thomas Nelson and Zondervan, the Devil would attempt to make a liar out of God. While verse 22 records the Lord's specific assurance, *"for there shall be no loss of any man's life among you,"* verse 44 confirms the same, *"And so it came to pass, that they escaped **all** safe to land."* Because numbers are important to God, the "inspired" manifest is provided in verse 37: *"And we were in **all** in the ship two hundred threescore and sixteen souls."*

So, what do you suppose the marginal note in practically every modern Bible says about this verse? Even the conservative Scofield Reference Bible states: "Some ancient authorities read, *about threescore and sixteen souls*." The leading "authority" here is the celebrated *Codex B*, "affectionately" known as *Vaticanus*, named after the Vatican Library in Rome (the site of its initial discovery). Thus – according to the "crown jewel" of the *Bibliotheca Apostolica Vaticana* – the Holy Spirit didn't know *what* He was talking about, as 200 passengers and crew apparently disappeared into thin air! (Even the *Titanic* had a better survival percentage than *that*.)

The irony in all of this is that the very passage in question was penned by one of the surviving passengers. We perceive, therefore, that although Satan was unable to *drown* Paul and Luke, he *was* able to eventually send numbers of their salient passages to the bottom by deleting or adulterating them in the modern versions (i.e., Luke 17:36; 23:17; Acts 8:37; 24:7; 28:29; I Timothy 3:16; 6:10, 20; II Timothy 2:15; 3:16, etc.). And, adding insult to injury, he even excised the *last* inspired word the apostle ever dictated; try finding *"Amen"* at the end of II Timothy 4:22 in any modern translation. (Also, this *stolen* "Amen" just "happens" to be the 1,**666**th word in II Timothy – a reflection of the revisers themselves, as well as the Devil's hatred for this word, *especially* with regard to how it is employed during preaching services).

Believed to be one of the fifty royal Bibles commissioned by Emperor Constantine, *Codex Vaticanus* would have been copied at Caesarea under the auspice of Eusebius. However, the older exemplar will be traced to the hand of Origen in third-century Alexandria, Egypt; hence, the expression, "Alexandrian" text type. With this background in mind, we will now commence our journey on the "Old Ship of Alexandria," allowing this Egyptian vessel to represent the *Alexandrian* text type and all related translations that have been spawned in the process.

ALL ABOARD!

1. Paul begins his journey on an *Asian* vessel. Paul and his company embark on a *"...ship of Adramyttium...meaning to sail by the coasts of Asia...."* (27:2) The old port city of Adramyttium was situated on the northwestern coast of Asia Minor (near present-day Edremit, Turkey). The Church began *its* journey with an *Asian* text type, referred to as *Antiochian, Syrian,* or *Byzantine.* As there were *no* autographs produced in Egypt, the story of manuscript corruption must, of necessity, begin with an *Asian* vessel. *"And the disciples were called Christians **first** in **Antioch**."* (Acts 11:26)

2. The apostle has *liberty* at this stage of his trip. *"...And Julius courteously entreated Paul, and gave him **liberty** to go unto his friends to refresh himself."* (27:3) In II Corinthians 3:17, we read: *"and where the Spirit of the Lord is, there is **liberty**."* Consequently, our ancient Baptist heritage of "Soul Liberty" has also stemmed from the proper line of manuscript authority.

3. Paul and his company are subsequently transferred to an *Egyptian* vessel. The Holy Spirit specifies: *"And there the centurion found a ship of **Alexandria**...."* (27:6) Thus, we may view this ship as a *similitude* for the Alexandrian text type. (Note: To head my critics off at the pass, pedagogical methods such as similitudes, types, numbers, and names are never intended to be applied in *every* particular. David, a major type of Christ, committed murder and adultery.)

4. A different *spirit* is discernable at the outset. Compare the words *"And **entering** into a ship of Adramyttium, **we launched**..."* with *"...and he **put** us therein."* (27:2, 6)

5. There is *more than one* Alexandrian ship. *"...the centurion found a ship of Alexandria..."* (27:6) Just as *Codex "B"* is nearly always teamed with its partner in crime *Codex "Aleph"* (also known as *Sinaiticus*), we find that Paul completes his journey in a *second* Alexandrian vessel (28:11). As expected, the two manuscripts vary widely from one another (over three thousand times in the four Gospels alone.)

6. The Egyptian vessel is *found*. *"And there the centurion found a ship of Alexandria..."* (27:6) Both the *Vaticanus* and *Sinaiticus* codices were "found": the *former* in the Pope's library; the *latter* in a monastery trash can. *Alexandrian* manuscripts are always much older than their *Antiochian* counterparts due primarily to neglect and isolation. Just as *our* Bibles wear out through frequent study, any *manuscript* possessing the endorsement of the Holy Spirit would have been thumbed to pieces through similar usage. ("A *Bible* that's falling *apart* is often owned by a *Christian* who's *not*.") Under a natural transmission of the text, successive generations of faithfully executed copies would share a similar fate. Because of this, only a fraction of the 5,000 surviving manuscripts have been granted notoriety for their exceptional antiquity. Like the embarrassed benchwarmer who returns to his locker with an unsoiled uniform, these overrated "ancient authorities" actually owe their unnatural survival to a continuous *abandonment* by God's people. That such is the case may be easily proven by observing both their individual depravities as well as their collective disagreements. If the scholar wants to push that "oldest is best" button, let him start with Job 32:8.

7. The final destination was *Rome*. *"...a ship of Alexandria sailing into Italy..."* (27:6) As the saying goes, "All roads lead to Rome." The modern "Bible" movement is the Devil's main strategy to usher in a one-world church under Vatican control. It is no accident that all Catholic translations of the Bible have followed the *Vaticanus* manuscript. (Well, *duh!*) When the New Testament portion of the Revised Version was finally released on May 17, 1881, there was great rejoicing within the ranks of Roman Catholicism.

The "Very Reverend" Thomas S. Preston of St. Ann's Roman Catholic Church in New York stated: "The brief examination which I have been able to make of the Revised Version of the New Testament has convinced me that the Committee have labored with great sincerity and diligence, and they have produced a translation much more correct than that generally received among Protestants. It is to us a gratification to find that in very many instances *they have adopted the reading of the Catholic Version, and, have thus by their scholarship confirmed the correctness of our Bible.*" (So, *now* you know why Baptist *Pseudos* like Jack Schaap praise Catholic *Popes* like John Paul.)

   8. The Alexandrian ship was *slow*. *"And when we had sailed slowly..."* (27:7) The modern "Bible" movement began *its* voyage by churning *slowly* and with great subtlety. Solomon's warning, *"Remove not the ancient landmark, which thy fathers have set,"* speaks to this satanic stratagem. (Proverbs 22:28) The familiar song, "What's Wrong With the Old Black Book?" contains a most prescient line – "They're making plans in years to come to take God from our minds by giving us new 'Bibles' *changed a little bit each time*."

   9. The *wind* refuses to cooperate. *"...the wind not suffering us..."* (27:7) The most obvious problem with Alexandrian "Bibles" is that the Holy Ghost does not bear witness to their corrupt readings. This is why they are always going in and out of publication. In another major slam against the third member of the Godhead, the preface to the New American Standard Version makes the inane concession regarding the American Standard Version: "Perhaps the most weighty impetus for this undertaking can be attributed to a disturbing awareness that the American Standard Version of 1901 was fast disappearing from the scene....Recognizing a responsibility to posterity, THE LOCKMAN FOUNDATION felt an urgency to *rescue* this noble achievement from an *inevitable demise*, to *preserve* it as a heritage for coming generations...."

   10. The ship approaches *Crete*. *"...we sailed under Crete..."* (27:7) As the story unfolds, the shipwreck can be traced to a decision made on *Crete*. This is *not* insignificant given what the Scripture reveals about this place. Because the Bible is a politically incorrect treatise on the *truth*, it confronts all issues of race, religion, and gender without apology. Conversely, modern translations will pacify the sinner by deleting "sensitive" passages. For instance, while the NIV removed all references to sodomites, the TNIV (Today's New International Version) was "gender friendly," eliminating significant masculine or feminine usage. The presence of Crete is a veiled reference to *race*. While the average Christian may not deny the Lord *per se*, he will often deny what the Lord *says* – *especially* if the subject is perceived as racist in nature. For example, the world decrees that there are no significant differences between ethnic groups. This is just *another* attempt to make a liar out of God, as Exodus 11:7 states: *"But against any of the children of Israel shall not a dog move his tongue, against man or beast: that ye may know how that the LORD doth put a **difference** between the Egyptians and Israel."*

The book of Titus contains one of the worst statements on "hate" in the entire Bible! The Holy Spirit crossed a line at Titus 1:**13** with the definitive statement on racial profiling. After Paul quotes one of the locals as stating, *"The Cretians are always liars, evil beasts, slow bellies,"* his "inspired" response to this intolerant characterization was, *"**This witness is true.** Wherefore rebuke them sharply, that they may be sound in the faith."* Thus, three negative racial traits are ascribed to an entire culture across the board. Unfortunately, anthropology corroborates this "prejudice," acknowledging that the indigenous expression "to act the *Cretian*" was analogous to "play the liar." By the way, don't miss the amazing cross-reference of *"sailing slowly"* (mentioned in the same verse with *"Crete"*) to *"slow bellies"* (in the same verse with *"Cretians"*). For the record, *Crete* is a large island off the coast of North Africa, originally populated by descendants of Ham (Genesis 10:6, 14; Deuteronomy 2:23; I Samuel 30:14; Jeremiah 47:4; Ezekiel 25:16; Amos 9:7; Zephaniah 2:5). In the final analysis, Alexandrian "Bibles" are literally "African-American Bibles" – *produced* in *Africa* and *marketed* in *America* (Jeremiah 42:18; 44:26-30; Titus 1:11). Like

"Sister" P. K. McCary said in her *Black Bible Chronicles* (dubbed the *"Hip Hop Bible"*) – "Now the serpent was one bad dude, one of the baddest of all the animals the Almighty had made."

11. The ship encounters some *hard* places. *"And hardly passing it..."* (27:8) Like Proverbs 13:15 says, *"the way of transgressors is **hard**"*; those who embrace Alexandrian "Bibles" will always be in for a *rough* ride. When the Revised Version was released, Bishop Wordsworth described the transition from the Authorized Version accordingly: "To pass from the one to the other, is, as it were, to alight from a well-built and well-hung carriage which glides easily over a macadamized road, - and to get into one which has bad springs or none at all, and in which you are jolted in ruts with aching bones over the stones of a newly-mended and rarely traversed road, like some of the roads in our North Lincolnshire villages."

All modern translations delete or question the validity of Mark 16:9-20. Yet the *hard* manuscript evidence confirms their existence in 618 out of 620 extant manuscripts. Then, we have that *really* hard rendering of I Samuel 13:1, as given in the original New Scofield Reference Bible – "Saul was...years old." The accompanying footnote explains: "The Hebrew text states 'Saul was...years old,' giving Saul's age. Obviously the numeral before 'years' was lost. Conjectures of thirty or forty years have been made." That *blank* between the words "was" and "years" represents the mentality of a money-hungry publishing company that would induce its customers to put more faith in "human conjecture" than in "divine preservation." Imagine *your* child coming back from DVB, saying: *"Daddy! Mommy!* I learned a new Bible verse today: I Samuel 13:1 – 'Saul was...years old' – I Samuel 13:1."

12. The journey divides into *two* parts. *"Now when much time was spent..."* (27:9) As previously noted, the year 1952 was a spiritual watershed for America. Prior to *that* time, Satan's vanguard translations drew very little attention (Weymouth, Moffatt, Goodspeed, *et al.*).

DANGER

13. The *second* half of the journey would be *life threatening*. *"... and when sailing was **now** dangerous, because the fast was now already past... "* (27:9) The time in our story is late September (the *"fast"* being a reference to the great fast on the Day of Atonement). The ubiquitous "Bible of the Month Club" came to fruition in the *second* half of the twentieth century, beginning with the Revised Standard Version of 1952.

14. Paul *sensed* the danger. *"...Paul admonished them...Sirs, I **perceive** that this voyage will be with **hurt** and **much damage**, not only of the lading and ship, but also of our **lives**."* (27:9-10) Spiritual men perceive the danger posed by modern translations. While *"the times of this ignorance God winked at"* could be applied to deceived Fundamentalists in the "pre-*Cretian*" era, there can be *no* excuse for protracted stupidity *now*. (Acts 17:30) *Any* believer with an ounce of spiritual discernment today knows there's NOTHING wrong with that "Old Back Book."

15. Paul is overruled by the ship's *master* and *owner*. *"Nevertheless the centurion believed the **master** and the **owner** of the ship, more than those things which were spoken by Paul."* (27:11) Alexandrian "Bibles" have "masters" and "owners." While the *former* are in the classrooms of *"Pseudo* King James Only" schools, the *latter* are in the offices of *Zondervan, Holman, Tyndale House, Thomas Nelson, Good News,* and other *"houses* of ill repute." Even Jack Lewis, an outspoken critic of the King James Bible, acknowledged: "As long as there is financial gain in it, publishers will push translations, old or new." Alexandrian "Bibles" are nothing more than *slave* ships that hide their evil behind cargo holds of *grain*.

16. The ship flew various colors. *"...when they had let down the boat into the sea, under **colour**..."* (27:30) *Alexandrian* ships can always be spotted by the *main* flag they fly – ©.

17. The decision to leave is based on a *lie*. *"Nevertheless the centurion **believed**..."* (27:11) As the inspired record of the Holy Ghost confirms that *"sailing was **now** dangerous,"* we can only conclude that the master and owner of the ship must have *lied* to Julius. We are not surprised at this development since they were on the "Isle of Lie" at the time. (Titus 1:12) And, of course, the fateful decision is made at verse 11, the number of *crisis* (i.e., "eleventh-hour reprieve," 9/11, Matthew 20:6-7).

18. They depart because Lasea was not *commodious*. *"And because the haven was not **commodious** to winter in..."* (27:12) According to *Webster's*, "commodious" is simply that which is "convenient" or "suitable" (as in the difference between an outhouse and an indoor *commode*). Laodiceans view the King James Bible as a major *inconvenience*: "I can't understand the archaic words" or "Certain passages offend my sensibilities," etc. And they *surely* don't want the added *strain* of any controversy with family and friends. No sir, that "KJV Only" fanaticism is not *commodious* one bit. (Of course, the words "American Standard" can be found on half the *commodes* in America.)

19. The decision to leave is forced by the *majority*. *"...the **more part** advised to depart thence also..."* (27:12) While the concept of a "majority text" in manuscript theory has considerable merit in most instances, the "majority" is usually wrong elsewhere. While the late Jerry Falwell's "holy hodgepodge" of political conservatives was bad enough, the Scripture clearly warns that the "majority" of end-day Christians would be anything *but* "moral." Though shrouded in a cloak of religiosity (II Timothy 3:5), their prophetic profile depicts them as blinded by materialism (Revelation 3:17), incapable of submission to divine authority (Matthew 6:24), and unwilling to acknowledge the truth (II Timothy 4:3-4). The apex of the "more part" delusion will be manifest at the Great White Throne Judgment (Matthew 7:13-14, 21-23).

20. They depart for *palm trees*. *"...if by any means they might attain to **Phenice**, and there to winter..."* The name *Phenice* means "palm trees" (indigenous to Crete). Though the setting is winter, the imagery is timely. The crowd that has a problem with the "Old Black Book" is a *sensual* crowd that lives for sun and fun; or, as Paul would describe them (*after* his miraculous deliverance), *"lovers of pleasures more than lovers of God."* (II Timothy 3:4) It is rather fitting that the NIV changes *Phenice* to "Phoenix," in honor of the mythological "phoenix rising from the ashes."

But then, Revelation 3:15-16 teaches that the lukewarm *Pseudo* is the most treacherous "bird" of all. For instance, when a prospective student clicks onto the *Pensacola Christian College* website, the first message that appears under the heading of "Campus Life" states – "Modern, multistory residence halls are comfortably furnished, carpeted, and air-conditioned. Every room has a private or adjoining bath, voice mail, and wireless Internet access. Beautiful flowers, PALM TREES, and lots of Florida sunshine give a warm welcome...." (Emphasis mine) The "Sports Center" blurb reads: "Experience the thrill of extreme sports as you climb the 40 and 60 ft. climbing walls....Try the new indoor water park with 3 water slides and 2 surfing waves...." Other appealing amenities feature an indoor ice skating rink, bowling lanes, weight rooms, racquetball courts, miniature golf, and a running track.

With *one* anemic reference to "Outstanding Bible preaching...," *four* separate pitches are made about the "beautiful...snow-white beaches" in the area. In fact, the last line on the page reads: "Summer is typically 'Florida'—sunny, hot, and perfect for the beach!" According to the *Associated Press*, these same beaches attract so many sodomites that the entire area has come to be known as the "Gay Riviera." Over 50,000 sodomites "strut their stuff" at the annual "Gay Memorial Day Weekend." (Of course, a few tar balls from the 2010 *BP* oil spill disaster put a damper on things for awhile; a fitting foretaste of things to come.) Yet, never fear, if you have a daughter at Pensacola "Christian" College, she can avoid these AIDs-infected beaches by simply availing herself of the convenient "Ladies Only" sun-tanning station on the Sports Center roof.

Dr. Horton's "Campus Church" section begins: "You will be part of *our* local church on campus." (Emphasis mine) This is one accurate statement, as the *"Campus* Church" is anything *but* a local *New Testament* Church – *those* assemblies belonging to the Lord

Jesus Christ. If YOUR son attends PCC, *this* is what he will be taught about the "Old Black Book":

> We believe that the Bible is the verbally inspired and infallible, authoritative Word of God and that God gave the words of Scripture by inspiration *without error* **in the original autographs**. God promises that He will preserve His Word; Jesus said, *"my words shall not pass away"* – Matt. 24:35. We believe God has kept that promise by preserving His infallible Word **in the traditional Hebrew and Greek manuscripts** and that the **Authorized Version (KJV) is** *an* **accurate English translation** of the preserved Word of God." (Emphasis mine)

DECEPTION

21. They are misled by a south *wind*. *"And when the south wind blew softly, **supposing** that they had obtained their purpose, loosing thence, they sailed close by Crete."* (27:13) Significantly, while the *decision* is made at verse **11**, the *trouble* begins at verse **13**. Paul wrote that in the last days *"evil men and seducers shall wax worse and worse, deceiving, **and being deceived.**"* (II Timothy 3:13) Modern Christians are too flaky to realize that God *Himself* is often the one *behind* the deception. (Exodus 14:1-4; I Kings 22:22-23; Isaiah 28:13) With regard to the Tribulation, II Thessalonians 2:11-12 states: *"And for this cause, **God shall send them strong delusion**, that they should believe a lie: That they all might be damned who believed not the truth."* There are four references to "wind" in this story. While God's wind is merely *uncooperative* in verses four and seven, it becomes downright *deceptive* in verse thirteen (a theme we will revisit in Chapter 16). Look what it does *next*.

22. The ship is suddenly confronted by a *strong* wind. *"But not long after there arose against it a **tempestuous** wind, called Euroclydon."* (27:14) *Webster's* defines "tempestuous" as: "Very stormy; turbulent; rough with *wind*." While the "breath of God" can *create* for *good*, it can also *destroy* for *bad*: *"and he shall smite the earth with the rod of his mouth, **and with the breath of his lips***

shall he slay the wicked. " (Isaiah 11:4) "Euroclydon" means *"east wave,"* as in the same direction from which the *"the Son of man"* will appear (Matthew 24:27).

23. The ship is *caught.* *"And when the ship was **caught**... "* (27:15) Like the proverbial "hand in the cookie jar," Alexandrian ships eventually get *caught.* The New International Version deletes all references to sodomites; so the sodomites storm America's beaches in their "fairy boats." But then – the NIV gets *caught*: Dr. Virgina Mollenkott, a "stylistic consultant" for the NIV, begins the process by hopping *out* of the closet as one who had changed *"the natural use into that which is against nature."* (Romans 1:26) Then, after Dr. Kenneth Barker, Executive Director of the NIV Translation Center, tried to minimize her involvement, the chairman of the NIV's Old Testament committee itself, Dr. Martin Woudstra, apparently dies *in* the closet; at least, this is the position presented by the longstanding, detailed report of Mr. Michael Penfold of Great Britain. According to him, Woudstra was intimately associated with *Evangelicals Concerned, Inc.*, "a nationwide task force and fellowship for gay and lesbian evangelical Christians," founded by Dr. Ralph Blair, a New York psychologist. Penfold confirms: "Dr. Blair clearly stated to me on the phone on 23rd September 1997 that Dr. Woudstra, a lifelong bachelor, was a homosexual." Lastly, in a classic case of poetic justice, a sodomite brought suit against *Zondervan* and *Thomas Nelson* for causing "mental anguish." (It "almost" makes you want to contribute to the sodomite's legal fund.)

24. The captain *yields* to the wind. *"...and could not bear up into the wind, **we let her drive.**"* (27:15) We have now reached a memorable way mark in our journey. Do you recall that favorite illustration used by all the Greek teachers about *phero* in II Peter 1:21? (The definition that was cited read: "To be conveyed or borne with the suggestion of force or speed: 1. of persons *borne in a ship over the sea.*") Well, don't look now, but *phero* is right under your feet at Acts 27:15, translated as *"we let her drive."* Thus, the Holy Spirit ensured that the *key* illustration used to undermine the

Authorized Version forms the very gust of wind that *smashes* the Alexandrian tub to smithereens!

25. The crew scrambles to *help* the ship. *"...we had much work to come by the boat: Which when they had taken up, they used **helps, undergirding the ship**... "* (27:16-17) Alexandrian "Bibles" cannot float on their own but require the "help" of others. Much of this "help" comes from high-end Madison Avenue ad campaigns. However, most of the "undergirding" comes from within. The preface to the New Scofield Reference Bible declared their product to be a "Holy Bible, Authorized Version with introductions, annotations, subject chain references, and such *word changes* in the text as will *help* the reader." (That's *some* "authorized text" – complete with word changes that change the text.) As the previous quote by Jack Lewis illustrates, Alexandrian vessels take on water *quickly* – "A translation starts to become outdated from the moment it is completed...."

26. The ship is *tossed* about wildly. *"And we being exceedingly **tossed** with a **tempest**... "* (27:18) Christians who ride on Alexandrian ships will eventually find themselves being *"**tossed** to and fro, and carried about with every **wind** of doctrine."* (Ephesians 4:14)

27. The crew *lightens* the ship. *"...the next day they **lightened** the ship."* (27:18) Whereas "helps" imply *additions* made to the text, "lightening" the ship would illustrate *deletions*. According to Dean Burgon, when collated against the *Textus Receptus*, *Codex Vaticanus* deletes 2,877 words from the Gospels alone, while *Codex Sinaiticus* drops 3,455. When it comes to "lightening the ship," *Zondervan* got rid of everything but the kitchen sink! The following verses were tossed overboard in the *original* New International Version: Matthew 17:21; 18:11; 23:24; Mark 7:16; 9:44, 46; 11:26; 15:28; Luke 17:36; 23:17; John 5:4; Acts 8:37; 15:34; 24:7; 28:29; and Romans 16:24. (The Alexandrian propensity for confusion is also exemplified by a break in consecutive verse numbering which corresponds to the excluded Scriptures.) In addition to these 16 *whole* verses, significant *portions* of another 147 verses were tossed in the sea, as well. Having limited this survey to the New Testament alone, the NIV is lighter than the KJV by 1,284 words.

DESPAIR

28. The ship was being driven in *darkness*. *"And when neither sun nor stars in many days appeared…"* (27:20) It was with great foreboding that Dean John Burgon spent the remainder of his life warning his beloved nation of the inevitable storm clouds ahead. Speaking of codices *Vaticanus* and *Sinaiticus*, he prophesied: "Those two documents are caused to cast their sombre shadows a long way ahead, and to *darken* all our future." As the *sun* is a similitude for *Jesus* and the *moon* is a similitude for the *Church*, we understand that Alexandrian "Bibles" sail on in darkness, totally deprived of God's light. (This would make the "Great Lighthouse" in Alexandria, Egypt, one of the "great" paradoxes of the ancient world.)

29. *Despair* covers the passengers and crew. *"…all **hope** that we should be **saved** was then taken away."* (27:20) Paul had written the church in Rome two years earlier: *"For we are **saved** by **hope**"* and *"we through patience and comfort of the **scriptures** might have **hope**."* (Romans 8:24; 15:4) Unfortunately, no such "hope" exists on Alexandrian ships. How can one compare, *"Thou wilt keep him in perfect **peace**, whose mind is stayed on thee"* in Isaiah 26:3 with the NIV's jolting ride, "You will keep in perfect peace him whose mind is steadfast, because he trusts in you"? (Give me a break!)

30. The first sign of approaching land occurs at *midnight*. *"…as we were driven up and down in Adria, about **midnight** the shipmen deemed that they drew near to some country…"* (27:27) As previously mentioned, Rome was ecstatic about the Revised Version. In July 1881, The *Dublin Review* predicted: "The New Version will be the death knell of Protestantism." However, in December 1623, Dr. John Donne, Dean of St. Paul's and Royal Chaplain to King James, had already written his famous verse regarding another "island" scene: "Therefore, send not to know for whom the bell tolls – it tolls for thee."

Just as the *Titanic* struck the iceberg at 11:40 PM, Rome's "Bible" was destined to have its *own* "death knell" near the *midnight* hour. The reference in Acts 27:27 is the *thirteenth* and *last* occurrence of the word "midnight" in Scripture. The "Law of First Mention" brings us to Exodus 11:4 – *"And Moses said, Thus saith the LORD, About **midnight** will I go out in the midst of **Egypt**."* The very *next* verse reads: *"And all the **firstborn** in the land of **Egypt** shall **die**."* Thus, the *first* time the "clock strikes *twelve*," the Lord sets out to destroy the *firstborn* of Egypt; the *last* time it does so, the Lord sets out to destroy the *first* Egyptian *ship* in our chapter.

31. All sense of *direction* is gone. *"...they drew near to **some** country..."* (27:27) As latitude and longitude are set in Greenwich, England, Christians who trade their King James Bibles for Alexandrian counterfeits will eventually succumb to "spiritual vertigo," calling *"evil good, and good evil...darkness for light, and light for darkness."* (Isaiah 5:20) Their life's verse becomes: *"And when it was day, **they knew not the land.**"* (27:39)

32. The ship has *four* anchors. *"...they cast **four** anchors out of the stern..."* (27:29) With "four" being the number of the *earth*, we understand that Alexandrian "Bibles" are *worldly* "Bibles."

33. The crew attempts to *flee*. *"And as the shipmen were about to **flee** out of the ship...under **colour** as though they would have cast **anchors**..."* (27:30) Worldly Alexandrians are *cowards*; as the "colour" of *their* flag is *yellow*. In 1861, Drs. Westcott and Hort were debating whether to publish some of their heresies in the liberal *Essays and Reviews*. They finally came to the conclusion that the anticipated fallout would impair the credibility of their soon-to-be-published Greek New Testament. Writing to Westcott, Dr. Hort reasoned: "Also – but this may be *cowardice* – I have a sort of craving that our text should be cast upon the world *before we deal with matters likely to brand us with suspicion*. I mean, a text, issued by *men already known for what will undoubtedly be treated as dangerous heresy*, will have great difficulties in finding its way to regions which it might otherwise hope to reach, and *whence it would not be easily banished by subsequent alarms*." (What a *snake* in the grass!)

Eleazar became one of David's *mighty* men because *"his hand **clave** unto the **sword**."* (II Samuel 23:10) While courage is a rare commodity in the closing days of Laodicea, Bible believers understand *their* orders – "Hold the Fort, for I am coming." They unashamedly "wave the answer back to Heaven, 'By *Thy* grace we will.'"

34. All will be spared, but only if they listen to *Paul*. *"...Paul stood forth in the midst of them, and said, Sirs, ye should have harkened unto me...Paul said to the centurion and to the soldiers, Except these abide in the ship, ye cannot be saved."* (27:21, 31) As *Paul* is the chief spokesman in the Church Age, deliverance will only come by "harkening" unto *him*. (II Timothy 2:7) Though the Alexandrian *ship* must perish, the passengers and crew will experience *physical* salvation by exercising the apostolic formula of *"repentance* and *faith."* (Acts 20:21) While the captain had ignored Paul's *original* warning regarding the weather, he dare not repeat that mistake regarding the cowardly crew. And so, he "considers" *and* "obeys" what Paul "says" – and *everyone* lives to tell their grandchildren all about it.

35. No one has partaken of any food throughout the ordeal. *"...This day is the fourteenth day that ye have tarried and continued fasting, having taken nothing."* (27:33) Alexandrian "Bibles" can offer no sustenance to God's people, *especially* during storms.

36. Everyone eats at *Paul's* direction. *"...Paul besought them all to take meat...Then were they all of good cheer, and they also took some meat."* (27:33, 36) As the "apostle to the Gentiles," Paul is the *chief* chef for the present age. After finally making it to Rome, he exhorts the Philippians: *"Those things, which ye have both learned, and received, and heard, and seen in me, do: and the God of peace shall be with you."* (Philippians 4:9)

37. They eat *meat*. *"...and they also took some meat."* (27:36) Christians who *submit* to God's word receive the *greater* sustenance. Paul told the carnal Corinthians that he had more to give than they were capable of handling: *"I have fed you with milk, and not with meat: for hitherto ye were not able to bear it."* (I Corinthians 3:2)

38. Paul *prays*. *"And when he had thus spoken, he took bread, and gave thanks to God in presence of them all..."* (27:35) When the Alexandrian ship is exposed for what it is, *prayer* is heard on deck, as well.

39. Their spirits are *lifted*. *"Then were they all of good cheer..."* (27:36) Prayer and a Pauline "meal" will always result in *"good cheer."*

40. The ship *breaks* up. *"...they ran the ship aground; and the forepart stuck fast, and remained unmoveable, but the hinder part was **broken** with the violence of the waves."* (27:41) Although Alexandrian "Bibles" will break, *"the scripture **cannot** be broken."* (John 10:35)

DELIVERANCE

41. Julius intervenes to *spare* Paul's life. *"And the soldiers' counsel was to kill the prisoners... But the centurion, **willing to save Paul**, kept them from their purpose..."* (27:42-43) As a perfect picture of human nature at its best, Satan makes one last effort to destroy those nine unwritten books by moving the soldiers to put *their* interests first, even if it meant killing the one who had ultimately saved *them* (Psalm 39:5).

42. They finally land, though a *long* way from their destination. *"...And so it came to pass, that they escaped all safe to land. And when they were escaped, then they knew that the island was called **Melita**."* (27:44-28:1) One of the most profound lessons in this story can be gleaned from viewing a simple map of the ancient world. What *should* have been a mere *forty*-mile jaunt between the *Fair Havens* and *Phenice*, became a "whirlwind tour" lasting *fourteen* days and covering a total of 600 miles! Alexandrian ships will always take you *farther* than you want to *go*, keep you *longer* than you want to *stay*, and *cost* you more than you want to *pay*.

43. Paul reveals the *means* of their deliverance. *"And now I exhort you to be of good cheer: for there shall be no loss of any man's life among you, but of the ship. **For there stood by me this night the angel of God...**"* (27:22-23) The final lessons of this study present *Paul's* deliverance as a type of the *Bible's* deliverance;

for the way in which God preserved *him* was the way He would go on to preserve his *writings*. Thus, *Paul's* recourse from Alexandrian*s* becomes *our* recourse, as well. The apostle's outline of deliverance is threefold: as indicated above, the *first* was "**Supernatural Intervention**." The Scriptures have been preserved throughout history because God has *supernaturally intervened* to ensure their preservation.

44. The Lord *reassures* Paul of his divine appointment before Nero. *"Fear not, Paul; thou **must** be brought before Cæsar..."* (27:24) The night following his arraignment before the Sanhedrin, Paul had *another* "meeting"; Luke writes: *"the Lord stood by him and said, Be of good cheer, Paul: for as thou hast testified of me in Jerusalem, so **must** thou bear witness also at Rome."* (Acts 23:11) Many years earlier the Lord had instructed Ananias: *"Go thy way: for he is a chosen **vessel** unto me, to bear my name before the Gentiles, and **kings**, and the children of Israel."* Thus, it had *always* been the will of God for Paul to reach the "Eternal City." Note further how the Lord specifically described Paul as *His* "vessel"; thus, ensuring that he could *never* sink (i.e., unlike *Alexandrian* "vessels"). Therefore, the purpose for "Supernatural Intervention" is to fulfill a "**Sovereign Promise**." The primary reason that the *Scriptures* have been *preserved* is because the Lord made promises regarding *their* preservation. The same Jesus who booked Paul's "cruise" to Rome declared of his future writings: *"Heaven and earth shall pass away, but my **words** shall not pass away."* (Matthew 24:35) The debate over "inspired preservation" boils down to a simple question – *"hath he **said**, and shall he not **do** it?"* (Numbers 23:19)

45. Paul then assures everyone else that he *believes* God. *"Wherefore, sirs, be of good cheer: for I **believe** God, that it shall be even as it was told me."* (27:25) The greatest scholar of his age chose to place his trust in the unequivocal promise of God. Hebrews 11:1 says: *"Now **faith** is the **substance** of things hoped for, the **evidence** of things not seen."* The writer goes on to state: *"Through **faith** we understand that the worlds were framed by the* *word of God, so that things which are seen were not made of things which do appear."* If we can exercise *faith* in *Creation*, we can certainly exercise a similar faith in the *Book* that *created* the *Creation*! The threefold way by which we *know* our King James Bible is *perfect* is because of "Supernatural Intervention," a "Supernatural Promise," and "**Simple Faith**." The story is told of an aged theologian who lay dying, surrounded by many of his former students. When asked if he would leave them with the greatest theological discovery he had ever made, his answer took them all by surprise. Rising to the occasion, the departing saint sat up in his bed, leaned upon his bony elbows, and sang at the top of his raspy voice – *"Jesus loves me, this I know, for the Bible tells me so...."*

PITCAIRN REVISITED

When I included the story of "Pitcairn Island" in *Final Authority*, the year was 1993. Up to that point, the tiny island's sole claim to fame had been her association with "Mr. Christian" and the miraculous transformation that followed. Such a legendary notoriety was not bad, given the fact that Pitcairn constitutes the world's smallest island with country status, comprising only 1.75 sq. miles. I mean, what *else* could ever cause this Polynesian islet to become the focus of international attention? A shocking answer to this question would surface only six years later.

In 1999 reports began to circulate about a widespread, decades-long history of multigenerational child sexual abuse. Over the next five years, British detectives conducted an exhaustive investigation, interviewing every woman who had grown up on Pitcairn since 1950. What they uncovered was truly unbelievable. With the entire island boasting only forty-seven inhabitants, the voluminous testimony revealed that nearly every *male* had been implicated, while nearly every *female* had been victimized. Ultimately, seven Pitcairners were tried on *fifty* varied counts of pedophilia; six were convicted. Steve Christian – a former mayor of Pitcairn and a direct descendant of Fletcher Christian – along with *his* son, Randy, began their sentences for rape in the island's prison, a structure they had helped to build. Apparently, Pitcairn Island had returned to her ignominious past. But, what had caused "Paradise Lost"?

The venerable John Adams had passed away in 1829 at the age of 65. Under his direction, the first Christians on Pitcairn Island had embraced the doctrines of the Church of England. However, in 1876 an unassuming package of "religious literature" arrived from the United States advocating a "slightly" different theological position. A decade later, on October 18, 1886, "missionary" John Tay arrived to do some "follow-up." By 1890 the entire population had converted to *Seventh Day Adventism.*

This tragic metamorphosis reveals yet *another* insight about the diabolical ways of Satan (II Corinthians 2:11). As we learned from Acts 27, the Devil's original plan was to destroy the Pauline epistles by drowning the author *before* he could write them. Having failed to do so, he then attempted the next best thing – corrupting the finished product (Acts 27:37). However, as the process of "inspired preservation" had conveyed the true text all the way to the tiny tropical paradise, the Devil was now forced to implement "Plan C." Mr. John Tay was able to re-capture Pitcairn Island by persuading the inhabitants to "consider" what *Ellen* had said rather than *Paul* (i.e., SDA founder, Ellen G. White). Having the *right* Bible is not good enough, unless it's *rightly* divided. The promise remains:

> *"...Fear not Paul; thou must be brought before Cæsar:*
> ***and, lo, God hath given thee all them that sail with thee."***

(ACTS 27:24)

11

Five Smooth Stones in a Shepherd's Bag

𝕿HE ANCIENT TALE of David and Goliath is one of the most popular Bible stories of all time. Recorded in I Samuel 17, the dramatic encounter represents the quintessential contest between might and right; between bully and underdog. For the Christian, David's victory is the main Old Testament illustration of II Corinthians 10:4 – *"For the weapons of our warfare are not carnal, but mighty through God to the pulling down of strong holds."* From a prophetic standpoint, the event transcends the Valley of Elah to that final showdown between Antichrist and Israel in *another* valley. Ultimately, the giant and the stripling are mere surrogates, as the *real* battle is waged between the "gods" of the Philistines and the true God of Israel.

Given the forces currently arrayed against the A.V. 1611, it would be natural that such a famous *chapter* would make a timely contribution to "The Book" that gave it life. In this we are not disappointed, as the similitude of a *shepherd* being confronted by a *giant* resonates with every faithful Bible-preaching *shepherd* today. The application is further strengthened by Eliab's disparaging question: *"and with whom hast thou left those few sheep in the wilderness."* (17:28) Apparently, David did not pastor a "mega flock." Then, there is that remarkable throwback to Elihu and Timothy regarding their age. Whereas Timothy was exhorted, *"Let no man despise thy youth"* – David experienced this very scorn, *"And when the Philistine looked about, and saw David, he disdained him: for he was but a youth."* (17:42)

What we have, therefore, is a picture of a typical scholar trying to intimidate a Bible-believing pastor. Simply put, it is "Dr. Big Bottom" *cursing* "Brother David." (17:43) The spiritual corroboration is remarkable. Consider the "scholar's" qualifications: Goliath was *"a man of war from his youth."* (17:33) Do you recall that profile of the full-time egghead in Proverbs 18:1? Then, note how the giant barks out his rhetoric from a *seated* position (i.e., from behind the "desk of authority"): *"And it came to pass, when the Philistine arose, and came and drew nigh to meet David."* (17:48) David would later write – in the *first* verse of the *first* Psalm – *"Blessed is the man that walketh not in the counsel of the ungodly, nor standeth in the way of sinners, **nor sitteth in the seat of the scornful.**"* Finally, the word of God is the obvious target, as Jeremiah 47:4 traces the giant's *alma mater* to *Crete*: *"for the LORD will spoil the **Philistines**, the remnant of the country of **Caphtor**"* (*Caphtor* being another name for *Crete*). Thus, it is fitting that *Goliath* means "exile," as all opponents of the King James Bible are *exiles* from its blessings – many, from the *Author* Himself.

The main lesson for pastors is found in Saul's initial warning to David: *"**Thou** art not able to go against this Philistine to fight with him: for thou art but a youth, and he a man of war from his youth."* (17:33) Shepherds and scholars live in two different worlds. *Real s*hepherds are called to care for *living* sheep, not to live with *dead* languages. Historically, the healthiest flocks have grazed in "A.V. 1611" pastures. *Real* shepherds also go after those outside of the fold (Luke 15:4). Frankly speaking, the Greek scholar J. Gresham Machen never warranted the police protection afforded the Baptist evangelist, Mordecai Ham. The Devil doesn't care *how* much Hebrew and Greek you *know*, just as long as you don't *spread* any *English* Scripture. Consequently, pastors should never feel inadequate concerning their unfamiliarity with the so-called "biblical languages," for they are certainly in good company. The fishermen *Jesus* chose could barely speak their *own* dialect (Acts 4:13). And the one scholar He *did* use needed a *"thorn in the flesh"* to keep him humble (II Corinthians 12:7).

David sets the pattern concerning how a New Testament pastor is to answer the taunts of professional "Christian" scholars: *"Then said David to the Philistine, Thou comest to me with a sword, and with a spear, and with a shield* [i.e., *linguistic* arguments against the King James Bible]: *but I come to thee in the name of the LORD of hosts, the God of the armies of Israel, whom thou hast defied."* (17:45) As the pastor is just as incapable of engaging the enemy with *his* weapons, a *different* type of armament must be used: *"And He took his staff in his hand, and chose him **five smooth stones** out of the brook, and put them in a **shepherd's bag** which he had, even in a scrip; and his sling was in his hand: and he drew near to the Philistine."* (17:40) We know that someone is fixin' to get *killed* as David chooses "five" stones. (Many a preacher has conjectured from II Samuel 21:22 that the *four* extra stones were for Goliath's brothers.)

Did you catch the nugget hiding in verse forty? David, put his ammo in a *"shepherd's bag."* Notice that the Holy Spirit calls it *"a scrip."* Does the word "scrip" bring to mind anything that applies to a pastor's arsenal? (Hint: The word **scrip** is found *seven* times in the **Scripture**, and its *first* usage is right here.) According to *Webster's*, "scrip" descends from Swedish and Welsh, meaning "a small bag." However, it just so happens that another "scrip" – from the Latin *scriptum* – is also a part of the English language. This "scrip" means "a small *writing*…a piece of paper containing a writing" (i.e., Luke 23:38). Well, what about that! Whereas Daniel 10:21 is the *first* mention of the word "Scripture," the reference in I Samuel 17:40 precedes *that* one by eighteen books. (And don't miss that cross-reference to a "bag" in Proverbs **16:11**)

There are several important observations to make about these "stones." First, they provided David with the spiritual confidence to literally charge Goliath (17:48). Armed only with a slingshot, the "youth" understood that he was now *positioned* for divine deliverance, stating: *"This day will the LORD deliver thee into mine hand…that all the earth may know that there is a God in Israel. And all this assembly shall know that the LORD saveth not with sword and spear: for the battle is the LORD'S, and he will give you into our hands."* (17:46-47)

The lessons we learn in our earliest years will often guide us throughout our lives. Notice how King David was able to trust the Lord in a similar manner when he was accosted by Shimei. He admonished Abishai to *"let him alone, and let him curse; for the LORD hath bidden him. It may be that the LORD will look on mine affliction, and that the LORD will requite me good for his cursing this day."* (II Samuel 16:11-12) Next, these "laser-guided" stones were *so* accurate that David would require only *one* (17:29). Third, Goliath's *head* was David's target (17:46). As a major type of the Antichrist – who is *"wounded to death"* in *his* head (Revelation 13:3) – *Goliath's* head is mentioned *six* times in the chapter. As the giant typifies the *"heady, high minded"* scholar, the *forehead* behind the "bull's eye" was nearly *nine* feet high. Fourth, the power of David's stone was in its ability to *stun* the Philistine. Note the *direction* in which Goliath falls: *"And David put his hand in his bag, and took thence a stone, and slang it, and smote the Philistine in his forehead, that the stone sunk into his forehead; and he fell upon his face to the earth."* (17:49)

We have now arrived at the main juncture of this chapter. The following truths will constitute the "Five Smooth Stones in a Shepherd's Bag." Carried in the *scrip*, they represent five *scriptural* principles that will "smooth out" *any* giant, without recourse to the original Hebrew or Greek. And remember, any *one* of the five will do.

THE STONE OF FINAL AUTHORITY

The *first* stone in the pastor's *scrip* is the stone of "final authority." While a basic precept of logic states, "Things that are different are not the same," the Lord is the *only* authority believers need. How could *Pseudos* oppose "King James Onlyism" when our Saviour plainly declared: *"No man can serve two masters"*? (Matthew 6:24) Thus, to recommend any number of "Bibles" is to call God a liar. In a *Moody Monthly* article entitled "Which Bible Translation Is Best For Me?" John Kohlenberger wrote: "In fact there is no 'best' translation…No translation is perfect, but most are 'for the greatest part true and sufficient.' So the question is not 'Which Bible is best?' But which of the many good translations is best for *you*?"

However, the namesake for this very magazine would have strongly disagreed. Having only a fifth-grade education, D. L. Moody didn't know any better than to believe the A.V. 1611. William E. Dodge, a long-time friend of Mr. Moody, declared:

> But a stronger and greater influence was his beginning in the study of the English Bible. He devoted himself to an intense study of it, and from it got two things: In the first place, he gained that clear-cut, plain, simple Anglo-Saxon of the King James version, that gave him such an immense power over people everywhere. In the second place, he gained an arsenal and armament of promise and warning, which he used through all his life with such magnificent power.

In 1873 Moody was conducting a revival campaign in Great Britain. At the time, Westcott and Hort were two years into their decade-long Revised Version project. As the Lord would have it, the highbrow Dr. Fenton John Anthony Hort decided to take a break and go hear "Crazy Moody" for himself. With the "good Doctor" comfortably seated, Moody simply took "The Book" that Hort and his cronies would eventually alter in 36,191 places – and – *slang* away! Like Goliath of old, the Cambridge professor got more than he had expected, writing: "Think of my going with Gray yesterday afternoon to hear 'Moody and Sankey' at the Hay Market. I am very glad to have been **but should not care to go again**."

When Moody later got into the education business, the "heady" scholars were apparently some of his biggest *headaches*. Quoting his father, Will Moody writes: "**It is a singular fact that few men, otherwise well educated, are acquainted with the English Bible.** I can secure a hundred men who can teach Greek and Latin well where I can find only one that can teach the Bible well." (For the record, Ed Reese and Joe Combs are both products of Moody Bible Institute.)

To promote various Bibles is also a glaring misnomer, as the word "Bible" means "Book." Thus, when you ask for "*The* Bible" you are asking for "*The* Book." So – how can there be *more* than one "*The* Book"? The story is told that when Sir Walter Scott lay dying he asked his son-in-law to bring him "The Book." With astonishment the young man replied, "Father, your library contains thousands of volumes, including your own works. To which *book* are you referring?" The veteran author immediately replied, "There is only *one* book which we *all* call '*The* Book.' Bring me 'The Bible.'" (Someone has rightly observed that "two or more heads make a *monster*"; the Beast of Revelation 13 has *seven*.)

(Note: Moody was a Protestant who never embraced believer's baptism and unwittingly laid the foundation for modern-day ecumenical evangelism. Yet, he represents that substantial assemblage of those within the Body of Christ who were used by God *despite* their doctrinal shortcomings, e.g., John Newton, Fanny Crosby, Hudson Taylor, George Whitefield, et al.; Wycliffe, Tyndale, and the A.V. 1611 translators being the *ultimate* example of this spiritual paradox. As with the *human* family, many of *God's* children "grow up" to make their *own* choices on varying matters of faith [Galatians 3:26; Ephesians 3:15; Philippians 1:15-18; Mark 4:8; Romans 14:4; I Corinthians 4:5]. However, believers must *also* follow their own conscience to "mark" and "avoid" those they *discern* to be *intentional* foes of the Truth [Romans 16:17; Acts 8:21-23; Galatians 2:11-14; II Thessalonians 3:6; I Timothy 5:20; Titus 1:11-13; 3:10; III John 10; Jude 3].)

THE STONE OF HEAVENLY SANCTION

All liberals despise history, as *facts* clash with *fantasy*. Thus, Dr. Westcott wrote: "Poetry is, I think, a thousand times more true than History." After Walt Whitman got a dose of Moody's King James Bible at a Boston crusade, the sodomite poet wrote: "Having heard Moody I am satisfied – But I shall not come to him to be saved. He is not my idea of a Saviour. I do not believe in him – Nor his God."

While Romans 3:15 says of men, *"Their feet are swift to shed blood,"* the religion of secular humanism proclaims the "Fatherhood of God and Brotherhood of Man." However, the historical record agrees with Paul, as reflected by the nineteenth-century Prussian proverb: "In case of rain, the war will be held in the auditorium." The reason that men never learn from history is because the Scripture says they are incapable of doing so: *"There is no remembrance of former things."* (Ecclesiastes 1:11) Thus, the *second* stone in the shepherd's bag is the 400-year track record of the "Old Black Book" itself. No matter *how* many supposed translation problems "Dr. Big Bottom" wants to debate – the *facts* are *in*. The undeniable blessings which have accompanied the preaching of the A.V. 1611 constitute *the* central irrefutable argument for the superiority of our King James Bible. Just like the Lord confirmed Aaron as his personal choice for High Priest by making his rod to bud, the question of "Which Bible" has already been answered in a similar manner.

When David declined Saul's armor, he informed the king: *"I cannot go with these; for I have not **proved** them."* (17:39) Though that slingshot may not have looked all that impressive, it *had* killed a lion *and* a bear. Christians would be wise to follow David's example by sticking with the Bible that's been *proved*. Remember that it was the Church in *Philadelphia* that "kept the word." To illustrate, in 1755 Elder Shubal Stearns led eight families into the wilderness of Orange County, North Carolina, to establish the Sandy Creek Baptist Church. At that time, there were relatively few Baptist churches south of the Mason-Dixon Line. However, by the end of the century the "Bible Belt" was born, with over 1,000 Separate Baptist works tracing their lineage to the mother church at Sandy Creek. That King James *rod* was "budding" in America.

By contrast, what has the modern Bible movement produced? While the *Philadelphia* Church Age produced "fruit," the *Laodicean* Age has produced "fruits," nut jobs like Benny Hinn, Rod Parsley, Kenneth Copeland, Peter Popoff, Jim Bakker, Jimmy Swaggart, Oral Roberts, Jr., and Creflo Dollar, along with slick psycho-babblers like Robert Schuller, James Dobson, Bill Hybels, Rick Warren, Joel Osteen, and others. Jesus said, *"a corrupt tree bringeth forth evil fruit."* (Matthew 7:17) For example, the Bay Area Fellowship "Church" in Corpus Christi, Texas, awarded "lucky" visitors more than a million dollars in prizes over Easter weekend 2010. Enticed by the church's website to "come on down" for the "Ultimate Giveaway," a horde of religious fools did just that, with many "winning" everything from laptop computers and giant screen televisions to

several automobiles, including a brand new BMW (John 19:24).
Bill Cornelius, senior pastor of the 7,500-member mega-church,
explained: "Jesus said to be fishers of men and we just got big bait
at the end of our hooks." In an interview with T. J. Holmes of *CNN*,
Cornelius compared his shindig to a typical Easter egg hunt for
kiddies, stating: "We just couldn't find any eggs big enough for
cars." It was enough to make Lester Roloff "roll over in his grave"
(just a few miles away).

THE STONE OF SANCTIFICATION

The entire modern "Bible" movement is invalidated by a single
verse of Scripture: *"Who can bring a clean thing out of an unclean?
not one."* (Job 14:4) Alarmingly, the average Christian who uses
any English translation other than the Authorized Version is
completely unacquainted with the *men, manuscripts,* and *methods*
that brought them into existence. (Generic offspring from the *Textus
Receptus,* like the New King James Version, remain in a class by
themselves.) Once again, regardless of remonstrances by the
scholars' union, the historical record confirms that the Revised
Version of 1871-1885 violated Job 14:4 in all of the aforementioned
particulars. This is a crucial issue, for one *cannot* endorse the
modern "Bibles" without tacitly ascribing a divine sanction to the
original Revision Committee, as well.

With the climacteric rescue of the Holy Scriptures at stake
(according to Westcott-Hort theory), one would think that these
self-appointed saviors would have displayed a minimum conformity
to the text they were *supposed* to be salvaging; yet, the very opposite
is true. Having carefully read both two-volume sets of the *Life and
Letters of Brooke Foss Westcott* by his son, Arthur Westcott (1903),
and the *Life and Letters of Fenton John Anthony Hort* (1896) by
his son, Arthur Fenton Hort, I am firmly convinced that the celebrated
Cambridge professors were anything *but* what they professed to
be. (In my chapter in *Final Authority* entitled "Vessels of Dishonour,"
I document this conviction with 140 endnotes.) While Drs. Westcott

and Hort are venerated as spiritual giants, the testimony from their personal correspondence confirms that both men endorsed evolution, spiritism, socialism, globalism, communalism, disarmament, baptismal regeneration, popery, Purgatory, and Mariology, while deprecating the inspiration of *any* Scripture, salvation by grace, Heaven and Hell, a literal Devil, Bible miracles, and the United States of America.

Unfortunately, as the scope of this chapter precludes me from doing justice to the subject, only a few of their incriminating statements can be referenced. For instance, if you know someone who owns an NIV, ask them for their opinion of Dr. Hort's position on the doctrine of imputation: **"The fact is, I do not see how God's justice can be satisfied without every man's suffering in his own person the full penalty for his sins."** (*Hort, Volume I,* p. 120) In a letter addressed to Reverend John Ellerton, Dr. Hort openly acknowledged his unorthodox views; having been invited to become an Examining Chaplain for Reverend Harold Brown, Hort states: "I wrote to **warn** him that **I was not safe or traditional in my theology**, and that I **could not** give up association with **heretics** and such like." (*H, II,* p.165) Dr. Westcott made a similar concession, writing in a letter to Bishop Lightfoot about a particular book on the canon: "...all the **questionable doctrines** which I have ever maintained are in it." (*Westcott, Volume I,* p. 290)

Then, we have the most embarrassing indictment of all. An old expression goes: "You've got a face only a *mother* can love." Dr. Hort's own *mama* had no use for his heretical ways. (Even the mother of notorious serial killer John Wayne Gacy stuck with *her* boy until the end.) With reference to his grandmother, Annie (Collett) Hort, the daughter of a Suffolk preacher, Arthur Hort confirms:

> Her religious feelings were deep and strong...She was unable to enter into his theological views, which to her school and generation seemed a desertion of the ancient ways; thus, pathetically enough, there came to be a barrier between mother and son...She studied and knew her Bible well, and her own religious life was most carefully regulated. (*H, I,* p. 7-8)

The second source of "uncleanness" concerns the *manuscripts* employed in the revision. Should we be surprised that they would reflect the depravity of their sponsors? As mentioned in the previous chapter, codices *Vaticanus* and *Sinaiticus* disagree with each other over 3,000 times in the Gospels alone (constituting an average of *nineteen* disagreements per page). Such textual perjury would be natural, given the testimony arrayed against the *living* Word: *"At the last came two false witnesses...But neither so did their witness agree together."* (Matthew 26:60; Mark 14:59)

Dean Burgon wrote: "The impurity of the text exhibited by these codices in not a question of opinion but of fact...In the Gospels...Codex B (Vatican) leaves out words or clauses...It bears traces of careless transcription on every page." His analysis of *Aleph* was more of the same:

> On many occasions 10, 20, 30, 40 words are dropped through very carelessness. Letters and words, even whole sentences, are frequently written twice over, or begun and immediately cancelled; while that gross blunder, whereby a clause is omitted because it happens to end in the same words as the clause preceding, occurs no less than 115 times in the New Testament.

Housed at the British Museum, *Sinaiticus* is recognized as one of the most defaced manuscripts "in captivity." Phillip Mauro writes: "...since this document was first inscribed, it has been the subject of no less than *ten* different attempts of revision and correction." These repeated efforts at salvaging *Aleph* continued through the sixth and seventh centuries. Mauro then concludes with the noteworthy observation that the sole purpose of the alterations was "to make the Ms. conform to manuscripts in vogue at that time which were 'far nearer to our modern *Textus Receptus.*'" Now you know why this ancient "treasure" was found in the "trash." (For the sake of historical preciseness – while the German textual "scholar" Constantin von Tischendorf was snooping around St. Catherine's monastery in 1844, he discovered 129 leaves of the Old Testament in Greek crammed in a receptacle of discarded parchments used to light the monastery's ovens.)

To add insult to injury, the scribe of *Codex Vaticanus* included nearly all of the Roman Catholic Apocrypha (lacking only the *Prayer of Manasses*, along with *I and II Maccabees*); *Codex Sinaiticus* contained the *entire* set with the *New Testament* Apocryphal books, *Shepherd of Hermas* and the *Epistle of Barnabas*, thrown in as a "bonus." (For the record, the A.V. 1611 translators segregated the Old Testament Apocrypha *between* the Testaments, while Origen and company imbedded the spurious books *amidst* the canonical ones.)

Finally, the third source of "uncleanness" involves the *methods* that were used in the revision process. Corrupt *men* promoting corrupt *manuscripts* will inevitably lead to corrupt *methods*, for *"Who can bring a clean thing out of an unclean?"* The decade-long project that began in 1871, producing the Revised New Testament in 1881 (the Revised Old Testament being released in 1885), was fraught with unethical and surreptitious activity throughout. Again, there is far too much material to condense here, so only a sample of the abuse can be presented.

The Revision Committee was formally sanctioned by the Church of England in 1870 with a strict set of guidelines being adopted from the outset. (Of course, the very idea of making even the slightest "improvements" to the Authorized Version was an accident waiting to happen.) The Church's Southern Convocation passed resolutions – in the strongest possible language – limiting the revision activity to "PLAIN AND CLEAR ERRORS." However, with Westcott and Hort at the helm, over *36,000 changes* would eventually be made. Unbeknown to the naïve company of revisers, the "diabolical duo" had been plotting an immediate takeover of the proceedings. On the eve of the historic occasion, Westcott wrote to Hort: "The rules though liberal are vague, and the interpretation of them will depend upon action at the first."

True to form, the biggest shock of all occurred at the very *first* meeting. (You see, for eighteen long years, Westcott and Hort had kept a "dirty little secret.") After securing a uniform pledge of silence with regard to all internal committee procedures, the two professors surprised their 100-plus colleagues with a special gift – their very own copy of the brand new – never-before-seen – hot-off-the-press – Westcott and Hort Greek New Testament. (My, my, how thoughtful!) Arthur Hort confirms: "Each member of the Company had been supplied with a *private* copy of Westcott and Hort's Text...." (*H, II,* p. 237) Talk about a "monkey wrench" – What were they supposed to do with *that*? The first rule of the Committee, passed on May 25, had enjoined the revisers: "To introduce as *few* alterations as possible *into the Text of the Authorized Version*, consistently with faithfulness." And *now* an unfamiliar Greek text was being introduced; and no one could tell the outside world about it? Benjamin G. Wilkinson writes: "When the English New Testament Committee met, it was immediately apparent what was going to happen. Though **for ten long years the iron rule of silence kept the public ignorant** of what was going on behind closed doors, the story is now known."

The distinguished Samuel Wilberforce, Bishop of Oxford, the committee's original chairman, *quit* after only *one* meeting, bemoaning to an associate: "What can be done in this most miserable business?" Dean Burgon was understandably livid, writing: "...to construct a new Greek Text formed no part of the Instructions which the Revisionists received...Rather were they warned against venturing on such an experiment...." An exodus followed Wilberforce, with the average attendance dwindling to about sixteen persons. The domineering Westcott and Hort played the stereotypical bullies, described by Wilkinson as being "constantly at their elbow." In a letter to his wife dated 24 May 1871, Westcott wrote: "We have had hard fighting during these last two days, and a battle-royal is announced for tomorrow." (*W, I,* p. 396) One unnamed detractor calculated that "Dr. Hort talked for three years out of the ten!"

And so, over the *ten-year* period, *tens of thousands* of readings from a predominantly *Majority Text* were systematically removed by a simple *majority vote*, the "theological thugs" being "constantly at their elbow," etc. When the smoke finally cleared, the underlying Greek of the *Textus Receptus* was found to be changed by the Westcott and Hort Greek Text in approximately 5,337 instances. But, why should anyone be surprised when Dr. Hort had already stated at the outset of his epoch-making project: "Think of that **vile** *Textus Receptus* leaning entirely on late MSS.; it is a blessing there are such early ones." (*H, I,* p. 211)

The end result was a consummate disaster! Burgon's summary of the Revised Version was succinct: "To speak plainly, the book has been made *unreadable.*" Westcott and Hort had *definitely* "left the building" as *their* "House of Wisdom" imploded on impact:

> Yea, and for this very cause adding on your part all diligence, in your faith supply virtue; and in your virtue knowledge; and in your knowledge temperance; and in your temperance patience; and in your patience godliness; and in your godliness love of the brethren; and in your love of the brethren love. (R. V. II Peter 1:5-7)

Perhaps the most startling quote of all comes from a letter Dr. Hort wrote to his wife after receiving his appointment to the "prestigious" Revision Committee. Not even *he* could fathom the evil his *unclean* "Bible" would bring upon mankind. "I have just written to Ellicott to accept! This makes it a memorable day; the **beginning of one knows not what changes or events in one's life, to say nothing of public results. IT IS NO LONGER A SECRET.**" (*H, II,* p. 133)

THE STONE OF SPIRITUAL ILLUMINATION

One of the most common complaints against the King James Bible is that it is too hard to read. This charge is entirely unfounded, as acclaimed language labs have rated the text at a 5th-grade reading level. The famed deist Benjamin Franklin once remarked that it wasn't the selections of the Bible of which he was ignorant that worried him as much as it was the Scripture he already knew. God's words have always been easy to understand for those seeking the truth. The wisest man in history quoted the divine Author as saying: *"All the words of my mouth are in righteousness; there is nothing froward or perverse in them. **They are all plain to him that understandeth, and right to them that find knowledge.**"* (Proverbs 8:8-9) The next time some Bible corrector wants to whine about the "Elizabethan English," remind him that the eternal destiny of all mankind will one day be determined by nineteen *one-syllable* words – *"He that hath the Son hath life; and he that hath not the Son of God hath not life."* (I John 5:12) How much "plainer" can you get?

The following exposé of "Christian scholarship" will serve as an apropos illustration for this portion of our chapter. The same year that I was saved (1974), a so-called "Christian film" took the churches by storm. While *The Burning Hell* certainly had a number of hokey moments (angels talking with Southern accents, etc.), it apparently scared the "burning Hell" out of many a sinner, both at home and abroad. Now, fast-forward to 1993: Having just opened my Post Office box in Schererville, Indiana, I pulled out the very first mail order for my new book, *Final Authority*. Was I ever surprised *and* honored when I read the name on the personal check – Dr. Estus W. Pirkle. Why, this was the famous Baptist evangelist who had produced *The Burning Hell*! I immediately tore up his check and sent the "man of God" a free copy. Then, I got *another* surprise the following year; Dr. Pirkle sent *me* a *gratis* copy of *his* new book, *The 1611 King James Bible: A Study*. However, there was only *one* problem; *his* book was an *attack* on the Authorized Version.

It all must have started when "Brother Estus," a native of Mississippi, acquired a taste for higher Christian education; *unfortunately*, it "took." To illustrate what years and years of classroom *Hebrew* and *Greek* will do to one's *common sense*, consider "Dr. Pirkle's" section on "difficult" words in the King James Bible (the *same* "Bible" that mentions a "burning Hell" 54 times). In his book, an imaginary dope-head named "Joe" has just gotten saved. According to the author's innuendo, Joe's problems begin when some idiot gives him an A.V. 1611. Beginning to read at Genesis 1:1, it doesn't take long before Joe is in trouble. Pirkle begins: "He continues to verse 21. Here he meets the word *'moveth.'* Since he has never heard this word, he ponders what it means." (Now brethren, I don't want to dredge up *my* past, but I once had a lifestyle similar to Joe; and let me tell ya' – I knew *exactly* what *"moveth"* meant!) "He looks the word up, but cannot find it in the dictionary; it is not there. Finally, he gives up the search and continues reading, still not knowing what *'moveth'* means." The Doctor continues: "He gets along fine until he comes to the word *'creepeth,'* in verse 25. Again, he goes to the dictionary, only to find that it is not there." (Again, let *me* assure *you* – I knew exactly what *"creepeth"* meant, too; *all* of us creeps did!)

Pirkle then gives a long list of "archaic" words, supposedly rendering the A.V. 1611 obsolete. The first word on the list is "aileth." *Give me a break* – a good ol' boy from New Albany, Mississippi, would have a problem with *"aileth"*? Why, even *I* was able to decipher that word as a ten-year-old boy growing up in Manhattan just by watching "Granny" get after Jethro on the *Beverly Hillbillies*. (*"Boy*, what's *ailin'* you?")

One of the most powerful "Hell-fire-and-brimstone preachers" in Bible Belt history was Dr. Percy Ray, late founder and director of Camp Zion in Myrtle, Mississippi. Untold thousands were converted under his signature sermon "The Red Light of Hell" (during which he would wave an ominous lantern of warning). Dr. Ray went to his reward on April 11, 1991. Seven years later, the King's Press published *The Official Biography of Percy Ray: A Ray for God* written by none other than – Estus W. Pirkle! We are thus confronted by the disconcerting fact that Dr. Pirkle's "study" undermining the King James Bible (1994) was sandwiched between *The Burning Hell* (1974) and Percy Ray's life story (1998). On March 3, 2005, Estus went on to his *own* reward, having spent the last *eleven* years of his ministry discrediting the only book God ever wrote.

However, notwithstanding all of the above, who ever said that the ability to *understand* the Bible was determined by the reading level of the text? This is what devils like Dr. Hort believe; that the word of God is assimilated through the *intellect*. In a letter to his son after the Revised Version was released, Dr. Hort smugly asserted: "It is impossible not to hope that there are multitudes of quiet people who will be able to read their Bible a little more **intelligently** now." (*H, II,* p. 283) Hence, all scholars think they are aiding the Body of Christ with their "reader friendly" perversions. Dr. Luke would strongly disagree, writing of Jesus in his recording of the Emmaus Road encounter: *"Then opened he their understanding, that they might understand the scriptures."* (Luke 24:45) How could any Bible critic *understand* what Jesus was talking about in John 6:63? ***"It is the spirit that quickeneth;*** *the flesh profiteth nothing: the* **words** *that I speak unto you, they are* **spirit***, and they are life."* The fourth stone in the shepherd's *scrip* has "Job 32:8" inscribed upon it and *no* scholar on earth can withstand its force!

THE STONE OF FAITH

This *last* stone is like to the previous one: a *spiritual* concept *totally* beyond the grasp of the worldly-wise scholar. The evangelist Gypsy Smith crossed the Atlantic Ocean forty-five times in his quest for souls. He summarized his antipathy for the cult of intellectualism, stating: "I didn't go through your colleges and seminaries. They wouldn't have me...but I have been to the feet of Jesus where the only true scholarship is learned." When the "Old Ship of Alexandria" was about to go under, Paul's sole plan for survival rested on three simple words: *"I believe God."* (Acts 27:25) There is simply no rejoinder to *"I believe God,"* for *"the natural man receiveth not the things of the Spirit of God: for they are foolishness unto him: neither can he know them, because they are spiritually discerned."* (I Corinthians 2:14)

And isn't it amazing how much wisdom the Holy Spirit can impart to those "ignorant and unlearned" among us? For instance, one of the greatest "nuggets" I ever heard opposing evolution came from a North Carolina redneck. He said (and I quote): "Dr. Grady, you know *why* I don't believe in dat dere Big Bang Theory?" He then put his hand in that scrip and let 'er sling – *"'Cause, ain't no round things come outta explosions!"*

As previously mentioned, after hearing D. L. Moody at the Hay Market in London, Dr. Hort had remarked: "...but [I] should not care to go again." The attendance figures from Mr. Moody's closing services in London would have rattled *any* dry scholar: Agricultural

Hall – 60 meetings attended by 333,000; Bow Road Hall – 60 meetings attended by 600,000; Camberwell Hall – 60 meetings attended by 480,000. In all, *285 meetings were attended by 2.5 million people* (including Dr. Hort). Not bad for a Bible in need of revision! For all his weaknesses, the Protestant Moody possessed the right attitude toward "The Old Black Book," stating: "If you ask, do I understand what is revealed in Scripture, I say no, **but my faith bows down before the inspired Word**, and I unhesitatingly believe the great things of God even when reason is blinded and the intellect is confused."

The problem with Westcott and Hort is the same problem shared by *all* Bible correctors. One cannot effectively preach from a "Book" he doesn't really believe (I Thessalonians 2:13). Do you recall Dr. Schaap's number one headache of trying to find three new "sermon" ideas each week? Does this handicap sound familiar? Hort wrote of his father: "It was in the production of sermons that the difficulty of finding expression for his thoughts was most felt." (*H, I,* p. 360) Westcott wasn't much better, his son stating: "It had always been a great physical effort to him to preach." (*W, I,* p. 302)

The stone of *faith* is the most precious stone of all, for *"without faith it is impossible to please him."* (Hebrews 11:6) Never let the giants of scholarship intimidate you, for at the end of the day they are finished off by their own swords: *"Therefore David ran, and stood upon the Philistine, and took his sword, and drew it out of the sheath thereof, and slew him, and cut off his head therewith."* (17:51) Just ask the next person who wants to sell you on the merits of the New International Version to answer one question: "Who killed Goliath?"

"In another battle with the Philistines at Gob,
Elhanan of Jaare-oregim the Bethlehemite **killed Goliath**
the Gittite who had a spear with a shaft like a weaver's rod."

(II SAMUEL 21:19 **NIV**)

12

Nuggets From the English

IT SHOULD BE evident by now that the text of the Authorized Version is truly inexhaustible. Consequently, we have a lot to shout about. As my good friend, Evangelist Jerry Monday, pointed out in one of his many songs, the *first* word of the Bible is "In," while the *last* word is "Amen"; thus, we can *all* rejoice as, "We're *in*! *Amen*?" Arthur Pink has written:

> In creation we are surrounded with both that which is useful and that which is ornamental. The earth produces a wealth of lovely flowers as well as grain and vegetables for our diet. The Creator has graciously provided things which charm our eyes and ears as well as supply our bodies with food and raiment. The same feature marks God's Word. The Scriptures contain something more than doctrine and precept: there are wonderful types which display the wisdom of their Author and delight those who are able to trace the merging of the shadow into the substance, and there are mysterious prophecies which demonstrate the foreknowledge of their giver, and minister pleasure to those granted the privilege of beholding their fulfillment. These types and prophecies form part of the internal evidence which the Bible furnishes of its divine inspiration, for they give proof of a wisdom which immeasurably transcends that of the wisest of mortals.

The purpose of this chapter is to invite you to a smorgasbord of spiritual "nuggets" taken *exclusively* from the "archaic Elizabethan English." As these delicacies are served "family style," no additional "study aids" will be needed for their understanding – *"Come and dine."* (John 21:12)

THE SCARIEST VERSE IN SCRIPTURE

There are certainly many examples that could warrant the title "Scariest Verse in Scripture": Leviticus 26:29, where God told the Jews He would cause them to eat their own children; Numbers 16:32, where the earth opens her mouth and swallows up Korah and his confederates *alive*; Revelation 9:3-5, where locusts ascend out of the same pit to *torture* men for five months, without recourse to suicide; Revelation 19:11, where sinners stand before God at the "Great White Thrown Judgment"; Matthew 7:23, where the same hear those fateful last words, *"I never knew you: depart from me, ye that work iniquity."* No doubt, the list could go on and on. Any one of them would empty Joel Osteen's Houston coliseum in a New York minute!

My own choice for "scariest verse in Scripture" is Deuteronomy 28:63. The Nazi Holocaust is universally recognized as the greatest illustration of man's inhumanity to his fellow man. (When I was only 19 years old, I had the sobering experience of touring the infamous Auschwitz death camp.) What could possibly compare to a towering SS officer informing a cowering Jewish mother that her only way out of camp was through the chimney? While any "sane" person would attribute such ghastly atrocities to Satan, the Old Testament points to *Jehovah* as the ultimate architect. Though shocking to most, the matter is quite clear, given the Lord's repeated promises to punish Israel in the future. While the Holy Spirit repeatedly described Nebuchadrezzar as "God's servant" with regard to his conquest of Israel, an unwitting Adolph Hitler simply filled that same role in the twentieth century (Jeremiah 25:8-9; 27:6; 43:10; Ezekiel 29:19-21). However, the *fact* of God's "complicity" in the genocide of 6,000,000 Jews is not *nearly* as scary as the *attitude* He professed to have exhibited throughout the Holocaust itself. Have you ever read *The Diary of Anne Frank*? Well, keep the pathos of her ordeal in mind as you examine the following bloodcurdling statement, made by the God of her people: *"And it shall come to pass, that as the* LORD *rejoiced over you to do you good, and to multiply you;* **so the** LORD **will rejoice over you to destroy you, and** *to bring you to nought: and ye shall be plucked from off the land whither thou goest to possess it.* " (Deuteronomy 28:63) Proverbs 1:26 adds: *"I also will laugh at your calamity; I will mock when your fear cometh.* " Is it any wonder that the Lord cries, *"O that there were such an heart in them, that they would fear me"*? (Deuteronomy 5:29)

CHECKS AND BALANCES

The religion of secular humanism is devoted to suppressing America's Judeo-Christian heritage, especially in the public school arena. For instance, a prominent historical marker at the city limits of Portsmouth, Rhode Island, reads: *"Birthplace of American Democracy Est. 1638.* " Do you suppose that any of our nation's young people have ever learned that Portsmouth was founded by the Baptist pastor, Dr. John Clarke, according to the Bible precept of "Soul Liberty"? Regardless of whatever political philosophers the founding fathers may have studied, they *all* possessed a copy of the Holy Bible. The genius of the government they created is revealed in the separation of powers. Do you recall that *Jewish* key from Revelation 3:7? Note how the *judicial, legislative*, and *executive* branches of our political framework were outlined by a Hebrew prophet over two millenniums before Christopher Columbus could crawl: *"For the LORD is our judge, the LORD is our lawgiver, the LORD is our king; he will save us.* " (Isaiah 33:22) And, for the record, the same prophet was also aware that the earth was *round*, writing: *"It is he that sitteth upon the circle of the earth.* " (Isaiah 40:22)

INSPIRED BLUEPRINTS

In recent years, word began to spread like wildfire that a certain Christian philanthropist was dolling out hundreds of thousands of dollars to pastors who wanted to build new church auditoriums. In many cases, a simple letter of request would be followed by a prompt check in the mail. I learned about this gentleman from a former student of mine who had already made a six-figure deposit into *his* church's account. This was no joke. (In fact, the guy was practically a neighbor, living less than an hour from my church.) However, after extensive probing, I finally uncovered the proverbial "fly in the ointment." The only "string" to getting the cash was that a picture of the benefactor had to be displayed in the new building along with the following inscription: "As the Lord gave Solomon wisdom to build the Temple, he gave (donor's name) wisdom to build God's churches." A more fitting text would be: *"But when thou doest alms, let not thy left hand know what thy right hand doeth: That thine alms may be in secret: and thy Father which seeth in secret himself shall reward thee openly."* (Matthew 6:3-4)

As it turns out, the well-meaning egomaniac had it all wrong about Solomon's blueprints anyway. According to I Chronicles 28:11-12, Solomon received the plans from his daddy, *not* the Lord: ***"Then David gave to Solomon his son the pattern*** *of the porch, and of the houses thereof, and of the treasuries thereof, and of the upper chambers thereof, and of the inner parlours thereof, and of the place of the mercy seat.* ***And the pattern of all that he had by the spirit****, of the courts of the house of the LORD, and of all the chambers round about, of the treasuries of the house of God, and of the treasuries of the dedicated things."*

This story also represents an insightful illustration of "inspiration" in action: *"All this, said David, the LORD made me **understand in writing by his hand upon me**, even all the works of this **pattern**."* (I Chronicles 28:19) As an "added bonus," the Holy Spirit inserted five references to "candlesticks" between verses 12 and 19 (along with three others to "lamps") for *"there is a **spirit** in man"* and *"[t]he **spirit** of man is the **candle** of the LORD."* (Job 32:8; Proverbs 20:27) Moral of the story: Should you ever come across a similar "out of the box" fundraiser idea, remember the old adage: "If it seems too good to be true, it probably is." And another thing – *Woe unto any pastor who would dare to compromise the integrity of a local New Testament church for filthy lucre's sake!*

THREEFOLD POWER OF SCRIPTURE

The issue concerning the King James Bible is much greater than any of us realize. The importance that God places on His word can be seen by a unique *three*-point outline that He has given us in Scripture. *First*, the Holy Spirit tells us that God's word is greater than His name: *"for thou hast magnified thy word **above** all thy name."* (Psalm 138:2) This is rather significant in light of Philippians 2:9 – *"Wherefore God hath highly exalted him, and given him a name which is above every name."* *Second*, the Holy Spirit tells us that God's word is greater than His *voice*: *"And this voice which came from heaven we heard, when we were with him in the holy mount. We have also a **more sure** word of prophecy."* (II Peter 1:18-19) *Third*, the Holy Spirit tells us that God's word is greater than His *miracles*: *"If they hear not Moses and the prophets, neither will they be persuaded, though one rose from the dead."* (Luke 16:31)

THE LIVING WORD

In Psalm 119:160, we read: *"Thy word is true from the beginning."* The Holy Spirit moved John to take the first five verses of his Gospel to introduce the Lord Jesus Christ as the *living* Word of God: *"In the beginning was the Word, and the Word was with God, and the Word was God. The same was in the beginning with God. All things were made by him; and without him was not any thing made that was made. In him was life; and the life was the light of men. And the light shineth in darkness; and the darkness comprehended it not."* With Jesus constituting the ultimate type of the *written* "word of God" – being specifically called *"The Word of God"* in Revelation 19:13 – how many "words" do you suppose were used in His introduction?

II TIMOTHY 3:16

With all the doctrinal haranguing about II Timothy 3:16, four *practical* applications are often overlooked. The text plainly states that the Scripture *is* given to us *"for **doctrine**, for **reproof**, for* *correction, for* **instruction** *in righteousness."* As we have learned, the *first* purpose for the Bible is always *doctrinal*. Here, we have the preacher doing *his* part by communicating God's truth through preaching. For the sake of illustration, the sermon can be likened to a "spiritual hand grenade" that is hurled from the pulpit. Thus, the *second* stage in the process occurs whenever the grenade goes off, as in "reproof." Now it is the job of the Holy Spirit to make application and bring conviction. The *third* stage of "correction" follows as the responsibility of the hearer – to "pull out the shrapnel" at an old-fashioned altar. Finally, to employ a further illustration of a baseball diamond, having cleared third base, the believer can now head for home plate to receive what he needs the most – *"instruction in righteousness."*

"AUSTIN 3:16"

Following in the spirit of Jim Carrey's *Bruce Almighty*, the pagan professional wrestler, "Stone Cold" Steve Austin, adopted the promotional moniker "Austin 3:16" as a mockery of John 3:16. What this blasphemer didn't know, however, is that the Bible contains more than one salient "3:16." (If I'm not mistaken, the very subject of this book deals with one.) In addition to *II Timothy* **3:16**, a sample of seven others would include: *Genesis* **3:16** – where the relationship between husband and wife is established; *Matthew* **3:16** – where the Holy Spirit descends upon Jesus; *I Corinthians* **3:16** – where the same Spirit is declared to be *within* the believer; *Colossians* **3:16** – the most important New Testament verse on music; *I Timothy* **3:16** – the greatest proof text on the deity of Christ; *II Peter* **3:16** – containing a secondary, latent warning in *reverse* for Tribulation saints that wresting *Pauline* passages on eternal security from their Church Age context *could* result in their *own* destruction (i.e., should they disregard Matthew 24:13 and violate Revelation 14:9-11); and finally, *Revelation* **3:16** – where the Lord's *ultimate* indictment on Laodicean end-day apostasy is given: *"I will spue thee out of my mouth."*

NUMBER 13

As mentioned previously, the number "13" stands for *sin* and *rebellion*. Consequently, Genesis 1:13, the *first* Scripture address to employ this numeric, "just happens" to be the *first* verse in the Bible where God's name is made conspicuous by its *absence*: *"And the evening and the morning were the third day."* (Note further how it reappears in verse 14). The *first* mention of the word "thirteen" itself is found in Genesis 17:25 – *"And **Ishmael** his son was **thirteen** years old, when he was circumcised in the flesh of his foreskin."* The cross-reference here is Genesis 16:12, where the Holy Spirit employs racial profiling when forecasting the lad's genetic posterity: *"And he will be a **wild man**; his hand will be against every man, and every man's hand against him; and he shall dwell in the presence of his brethren."* The "prophet" Mohammed claimed descent from Ishmael. (See Moammar Kadafi's 75-minute rambling diatribe at the UN, September 23, 2009, causing his *own* translator to collapse, screaming in Arabic, "I just can't *take* it anymore!" – the breakdown occurring at the *precise* moment that "Mo" began his attack on Israel; notice the 13 letters in *this* version of his name.) Finally, the *first* mention of the word "thirteenth" is found in Genesis 14:4, *"Twelve years they served Chedorlaomer, and in the **thirteenth** year they **rebelled**."* In the New Testament, Jesus lists *thirteen* things that proceed out of the heart and defile men (Mark 7:21-22). Judas Iscariot has *thirteen* letters in his name. The Antichrist shows up in Revelation *thirteen*. There are *thirteen* words in the harlot's title in Revelation 17:5, etc.

While about 85% of the "thirteens" in Scripture refer to something *bad*, one can be a "rebel" *for* God. In II Kings 18:7, we read of Hezekiah: *"And the LORD was with him; and he prospered whithersoever he went forth: **and he rebelled against the king of Assyria, and served him not.**"* Paul was the ultimate rebel in the New Testament, being the *thirteenth* apostle, called in the *thirteenth* chapter of Acts, taking the leadership (from Barnabas) at the *thirteenth* verse, who goes on to write *thirteen* epistles, with I Corinthians 13:13 constituting the heart of his ministry. There were *thirteen* colonies that rebelled against Great Britain to form the United States of America. One of America's earliest flags had *thirteen* stripes, *thirteen* stars, and *thirteen* letters – "DON'T TREAD ON ME." In the closing days of Laodicean apostasy, the Church needs some rebels *"with* a cause" – *especially* regarding the A.V. 1611. And after we are gone, a remnant of Tribulation saints will carry on the rebellion, being rallied by those *thirteen* words in the *thirteenth* verse of the *thirteenth* chapter of the book of Hebrews: *"Let us go forth therefore unto him without the camp, bearing his reproach."*

NUMBER 5

Students who sit under *"Pseudo* King James Only" professors in Fundamentalist Bible *colleges* are taught that *five* is the scriptural number for *grace*. Meanwhile, their counterparts, in local church Bible *institutes*, learn that *five* is actually the scriptural number of *death*. The divide between these two views is as pronounced as the doctrinal statements of the respective institutions. While David may have received a measure of *grace* in the "Valley of Elah," his nemesis received a sentence of *death* related to *"five* smooth stones." Even the world appears to recognize this truth. When ships are in trouble, the captain issues a "Mayday" (*fifth* month), taken from the French term *venez m'aider*, meaning, "Come help me." The *second* biggest gang of killers in modern history, international Communism traditionally celebrates May 1 as their "high and holy" day. As for the *largest* bunch – an image of the "Blessed Virgin Mary" is ceremonially crowned on a global scale, on or around May 1, signifying Mary as "Queen of Heaven" and the veritable "Mother of God."

The Scripture is replete with illustrations of the number *five* representing *death*: The "night" (*five* letters) – a picture of *death* – is created as a separate entity in the *fifth* verse of the Bible. As the *dying* process begins at birth, life appears on the *"fifth* day," being identified as such in verse 23 (2+3=5). With Adam's name mentioned *five* times in *five* verses, the first man "to *die*" kicks the bucket at the *fifth* verse of the *fifth* chapter of Genesis. (Abel's "death" was a *homicide.*) The first mention of the word *"five"* itself occurs in the very next verse: *"And Seth lived an hundred and **five** years,"* though only two verses later we read, *"and he **died"*** (the reoccurring phrase of the chapter). As Romans 3:15 declares, *"Their **feet** are swift to shed blood,"* men have *five* toes on each foot; and, as Isaiah 59:3 states, *"your **hands** are defiled with blood, and your **fingers** with iniquity,"* a man has *five* fingers on each hand (representing a last reminder of his mortality, as they will eventually lay folded across his chest in death.)

According to Hebrews 2:14, the "Devil" (*five* letters), named "Satan" (*five* letters)—formerly, the *fifth* cherub who *five* times proclaimed *"I will"* in Isaiah 14:13-14—has had the *"power of **death"*** (*five* letters) or the ability to put men in their "grave" (*five* letters). But, praise God, the Holy Ghost also tells us in verse nine that *"Jesus"* (*five* letters) came into this world *"for the suffering of **death"*** and to *"taste **death** for every man."* This holy event was prefigured throughout the Old Testament as thousands of animals were sacrificed on a brazen altar measuring *five* cubits by *five* cubits. Then, having finally arrived, *God's* Lamb was led to the slaughter at an old rugged altar called Calvary; His *five* meager garments being subsequently exchanged for *five* major wounds. While the *fifth* chapter of Romans compares Christ's *death* to Adam's *death*, the *fifth* chapter of Revelation records that angelic pronouncement, *"Worthy is the Lamb that was **slain."***

Finally, while Stephen is considered to be the first Christian martyr, he is *not* the first professing believer to be *killed* in the New Testament. That honor goes to "Brother Ananias" who is slain by his personal Lord and Saviour, Jesus Christ. If there is any doubt about the number *five*, you might want to meditate on *this* obituary entry, listed in the *fifth* verse of the *fifth* chapter of the *fifth* book of the New Testament: *"And Ananias hearing these **words** fell down, and gave up the ghost: and great fear came on all them that heard these things."* The *fifth* word – "words" (*five* letters) – is a reference to the death sentence itself. And, for what it's worth, "Sister Sapphira" dies *five* verses later at verse *ten* (2 x 5).

FOOLISH VOWS

Many sincere Christians share the common experience of having made foolish vows under various circumstances. The typical setting would be a high-pressure altar call where the "layperson" was browbeaten into promising God to read the Bible three hours a day, or fast three days a week for the rest of his/her life, etc. After floundering for awhile, the despondent believer goes from bad to worse when some "well-meaning brother" (usually in the same boat) blocks all hope of escape by citing Ecclesiastes 5:4-5: *"When thou vowest a vow unto God, defer not to pay it; for he hath no pleasure in fools: pay that which thou hast vowed. Better is it that thou shouldest not vow, than that thou shouldest vow and not pay."* In the final analysis, the blood-bought believer is subject to the same psychological bondage as that of a Mason or Jesuit priest. Thankfully, however, a spiritual antidote for foolish vows is given in Leviticus 4:27-28 and 5:4-10. As most "vows" are a violation of James 4:13-15, the solution is simple: *"If we confess our sins, he is faithful and just to forgive us our sins, and to cleanse us from all unrighteousness."* (I John 1:9) Sadly, as a major player in the book of Judges, Jephthah was prone to miss this scriptural solution to his own dilemma (Judges 11:34-39)

"ROAD RAGE"

Henry Ford devoted much of his energies to attacking the Jew on a worldwide scale. In 1920 he purchased a small Michigan newspaper, the *Dearborn Independent*, and subsequently published 91 consecutive issues of anti-Semitic rhetoric. He then released a four-volume series of books entitled *The International Jew: the World's Foremost Problem*. The set sold millions of copies and was eventually translated into 16 languages, including German. Adolph Hitler was so inspired by Ford's hatred of the Jews that on July 31, 1938 (in honor of Ford's 75th birthday), Henry was awarded the *Grand Cross of the German Eagle* (the "Fatherland's" highest honor for a non-citizen). According to the *New York Times*, a life-size portrait of the automobile titan hung in Hitler's private office in Berlin.

As the *"curse causeless shall not come,"* Ford's legacy speaks for itself. Detroit is 67% black with a 50% illiteracy rate, a 75% dropout rate, and an unemployment rate nearing 30%. Recently, the Motor City led the nation with a *violent* crime rate of 1,924 and a *property* crime rate of 5,861 per 100,000 people. For instance, in a single "normal" week in "da hood," Mayor Dave Bing's GMC Yukon and the visiting "Reverend" Jesse Jackson's Cadillac Escalade were "borrowed" by the *bruthas* in separate incidents (two weeks later, Aretha Franklin's son was mugged on the northwest side). Last, but not least, 250,000 Muslims now inhabit Ford's boyhood home of Dearborn, comprising one of the *largest* assemblies of rag-heads outside of an Islamic country (second only to Paris, France).

Of the many "shocks" that must have greeted Henry in Hell, the fact that a *Jew* had described the combustible engine over 2,500 years before *his* birth would have constituted the *ultimate* "V8" moment: *"the **chariots** shall be with **flaming torches** in the day of his preparation, and the fir trees shall be terribly shaken. The **chariots** shall **rage** in the streets, they shall justle one against another in the **broad ways**: they shall seem like **torches**, they shall run like the **lightnings**."* (Nahum 2:3-4)

OBEYING JESUS *CAN* SEND YOU TO HELL

What you are about to read has *nothing* to do with a Greek lexicon and is rendered in the spirit of "spiritual facetiousness." While Jesus is certainly *"the way, the truth, and the life,"* and His further assertion that *"no man cometh unto the Father, but by me"* is likewise correct, He did make *other* statements that would send a person to Hell who assayed to comply with them – *in the wrong dispensation.* For instance: *"And, behold, one came and said unto him, Good Master, **what good thing shall I do, that I may have eternal life**? And he said unto him...**if thou wilt enter into life, keep the commandments**."* (Matthew 19:16-17) Try claiming *that* approach on Judgment Day! *"Many will say to me in that day, Lord, Lord, have we not prophesied in thy name? and in thy name have cast out devils? and in thy name done many wonderful works? And then will I profess unto them, I never knew you: depart from me, ye that work iniquity."* (Matthew 7:22-23) You see, on *this* side of the Cross, *Paul* is your primary guide. Better "Twitter" *him* (I Corinthians 4:16; 11:1; Philippians 3:17; I Thessalonians 1:6; II Thessalonians 3:7, 9; II Timothy 1:13; 2:7).

PREACHING OUTLAWED IN MILLENNIUM

Another scriptural reality that boggles the Fundamentalist concerns the banishment of "soul-winning" in the Millennium. Having been taught that all ages are basically the same, *Pseudos* are incapable of rightly dividing passages like Jeremiah 31:33-34: *"But this shall be the covenant that I will make with the house of Israel; After those days, saith the LORD, I will put my law in their inward parts, and write it in their hearts; and will be their God, and they shall be my people. And they shall teach no more every man his neighbour, and every man his brother, saying, Know the LORD: for they shall all know me, from the least of them unto the greatest of them."* Zechariah 13:3 adds the bizarre twist: *"And it shall come to pass, that when any shall yet prophesy, then his father and his mother that begat him shall say unto him, Thou shalt not live; for thou speakest lies in the name of the LORD: and his father and his mother that begat him shall thrust him through when he prophesieth."* Can you even imagine how flabbergasted the Bible corrector must feel? First, he is told that Old Testament saints were not "looking *forward* to the Cross," and now he is told that Millennium saints will not be "looking *backward* to the Cross." But, really, how many PhDs are necessary to understand that *faith* and *sight* are mutually exclusive (Hebrews 11:1)? As the words to *Sweet Beulah Land* go, "I'm looking now across the river – where my *faith* will **end** in *sight*."

"HELL ON EARTH"

For years unregenerate men have been popping off about "Hell on Earth," etc. General William T. Sherman said, "War is Hell." Alfred Lord Tennyson described those who had survived the "Charge of the Light Brigade" as having ridden "Back from the mouth of Hell." Audie Murphy, the most decorated soldier of World War II, titled his memoirs "To Hell and Back." However, with all due respect to these noble souls, they didn't have a *clue*. While Hell is currently located in the *center* of the earth, during the Millennium, King Jesus will give man what he has always envisioned – a literal place of fire and brimstone *on* the earth. According to Isaiah 34:4-10, Edom will be transformed into a surreal lake of fire for 1,000 years: *"And the streams thereof shall be turned into pitch, and the dust thereof into brimstone, and the land thereof shall become burning pitch. **It shall not be quenched night nor day; the smoke thereof shall go up for ever.**"* (34:9-10) Here, the obvious cross-reference is Revelation 14:10-11.

While a Bible *college* will inform you that the Lord will *"rule with a rod of iron,"* a Bible *institute* will tell you *how* this will be done. Anyone who disregards the "Sermon on the Mount" gets tossed into this place *alive* (Matthew 5:22, 29-30). In fact, the "EDOM LAKE OF FIRE" will constitute a major "tourist attraction" during the annual Holy Land pilgrimages: *"And it shall come to pass, that from one new moon to another, and from one sabbath to another, shall all flesh come to worship before me, saith the LORD. And they shall go forth, and look upon the carcases of the men that have transgressed against me: for their worm shall not die, **neither shall their fire be quenched;** and they shall be an abhorring unto all flesh."* (Isaiah 66:23-24; Mark 9:44, 46)

UNDERSTANDING AT A PREMIUM

In I Chronicles 12:32, the children of Issachar were commended for having an *"**understanding** of the times."* Obviously, God places a high premium on spiritual "understanding." Contained within this passage is a subtle, though powerful, truth that illustrates this principle. The *military* strength of the tribes is given by number: *Judah*, first, with **6,800** *"ready armed to the war"*; followed by *Simeon*, with **7,100** *"mighty men of valour for the war"*; *Levi* (and the Aaronites), **8,300**; *Benjamin*, **3,000**; *Ephraim*, **20,800**; ½ *Manasseh*, **18,000**; *Zebulun*, **50,000**; *Naphtali*, **38,000**; *Dan*, **28,600**; *Asher*, **40,000**; *Reuben, Gad*, and ½ *Manasseh*, **120,000**. However, when we come to *Issachar*, there is no mention made of any military prowess, with the only statistic given as follows: *"And of the children of Issachar, which were men that had **understanding** of the times, to know what **Israel** ought to do; the heads of them were **two hundred**; and all their brethren were at their commandment."* The *only* people who are numbered are the **200** *leaders* of these *"men that had **understanding**."* Given the thesis of this book (regarding Job 32:8), one of the main purposes for *inspiration* in the last days would relate to a Bible believer *"know*[ing] *what **Israel** ought to do."* Thus, to heed the admonition of Luke 21:28 – *"And when these things begin to come to pass, then look up, and lift up your heads; for your redemption draweth nigh"* – remember to keep *your* eye on *"the apple of **his** eye."* (Zechariah 2:8) All other "current events" are *less* than meaningless.

A STORY WITHOUT AN END

The account of the "Prodigal Son" is one of the most recognized stories in all of literature. Known as the "Pearl of Parables," it consists of only 504 words comprising 22 verses. Such enduring acclaim is made even more remarkable by the fact that the reader is left hanging without a conclusion to the narrative. The catalyst for the parable is found in Luke 15:1-2, where the Pharisees are criticizing Jesus for rubbing shoulders with the common man. These self-righteous religious leaders could not endure the prospect of sharing the joys of the world to come with those whom they despised as hopeless transgressors here. Thus, as our Lord's subtle rebuke unfolds, the younger son represents the publicans and sinners – the elder son, the Pharisees and Scribes – and their father, the God of Israel.

There are many beautiful themes in this chapter which have been preached down through the ages. A sample outline would be: *Rebellion* (11-13); *Ruination* (14-16); *Repentance* (17-21); *Restoration* (22-24); and *Reunion* (25-32). The essence of the prodigal's *rebellion* is captured in the words *"and took **his** journey into a far country."* The depth of his subsequent *ruin* is revealed by that repulsive "trip to the trough," bringing the *Jewish* profligate lower than the *swine*, as the "slop" was their *natural* habitat (and contrary to popular preaching – as a careful reading of the text reveals – by ultimately being *deprived* of the desired "husks," as well). The outstanding truth concerning *repentance* is conveyed by the statement, *"and when he **came to himself"*** (indicating that a lost man is *"beside* himself"), leading to the words, *"and he arose and **came to his father.**"* The exhilaration of the *restoration* itself can be seen by the father *running* to meet his wayward son, illustrating the promise in James 4:8, *"Draw nigh to God, and he will draw nigh to you."*

However, it is at the final point of this outline that our *English* nugget appears. While the "fatted calf" was being killed (a reminder that something has to die in order for life to be restored), the elder brother returns from the rigors of "the field" (a type of the meaningless, debilitating, and spirit-deadening effects of legalism, alluded to in verse 29). Thus, predictably, when he learns about his younger brother's "welcome home" celebration, he becomes angry and refuses to go in, whereupon the father goes out to personally entreat him (a holy glimpse into the burden that Jesus carried for the proud Pharisee.) Their emotional exchange continues over the next four verses, but then *suddenly* – the text comes to an incongruous *halt* with the father affirming, *"It was meet that we should make merry, and be glad: for this thy brother was dead, and is alive again; and was lost, and is found."*

So, what *was* the end of this strange scene? Did the elder boy go *in* and embrace his repentant brother – or did he stay *out* and pout? The closing scene, so full of forgiveness and joy, leaves the reader with the hopeful impression that the divided household would be reconciled. *However, when Jesus taught the parable, the story was not yet played out.* It remained to be seen how the religious leaders would react, for *they* were the only ones who could determine the "end of the story." What occurred at Calvary after only a few weeks, and then a generation later when the entire city was destroyed, reveals what *ultimately* happened to the elder son in our story. (The doctrinal implications are *off the chart*; for, although the *immediate* context has the younger son representing the dregs of Jewish society, the *greater* antitype of the Prodigal was destined to become the predominantly *Gentile* New Testament Church.) But, praise the Lord, there *will* be an end to this parable some day! We shall *yet* see the two brothers *in the same house,* "making merry" with their father *"in the presence of the angels of God."* And, oh, *what* a day that will be! *"For if the casting away of them be the reconciling of the world, what shall the receiving of them be, but life from the dead?"* (Romans 11:15)

REPLACEMENT THEOLOGY

The Vatican Harlot (along with her rebellious Protestant offspring) has insisted over the centuries that God is *through* with that "elder son." Because of this supposed disenfranchisement, every pope has viewed Rome as the New Jerusalem, claiming all of Jehovah's original promises to Israel in the process (e.g., Augustine's *City of God*). Thus, *Rome's* "replacement" of Israel has come to be known as *Replacement Theology*. Once again, note how this eventuality was forecast in the "archaic" English of the Authorized Version when the paranoid Pharisees prophesied: *"If we let him thus alone, all men will believe on him: and the **Romans** shall come and take away both our **place** and nation."* (John 11:48)

JERUSALEM

Jerusalem means "City of Peace." Yet, ironically, the Holy City has been destroyed and rebuilt *seventeen* times throughout her turbulent history. King David would prophesy accordingly: *"Pray for the peace of Jerusalem: they shall prosper that love thee."* (Psalm 122:6) With reference to a brighter future to come, Paul reminds the Church: *"But Jerusalem which is above is free, which is the mother of us all."* (Galatians 4:26) In our own brief history as a nation, Americans have experienced the blessings of Psalm 122:6 firsthand, having stood by Jehovah's covenant people from the outset. As Haym Solomon repeatedly saved the Continental Army from certain defeat, *another* patriotic American Jew would do the same for *Israel's* War of Independence.

Colonel David "Mickey" Marcus was born February 22, 1902, on New York's Lower East Side, the fifth child of Romanian immigrants, Mordecai and Leah Marcus. When David was eight years old, his father died suddenly. He later learned to box in order to survive the tough streets. Having applied himself academically, Marcus entered West Point when Douglas MacArthur was the commandant, graduating with honors in 1924. After resigning his Regular commission, he earned a doctorate at Brooklyn Law College in 1934. That same year, Mayor LaGuardia appointed him Deputy Commissioner of Corrections. Having maintained a Reserve commission, Marcus utilized his legal expertise by joining the Judge Advocate General's Corps (JAG). After Pearl Harbor, he was recalled to active duty and organized and commanded an army ranger school, training 8,000 men for combat. Over the years, Colonel Marcus was intimately involved in nearly every wartime conference, including Cairo, Dumbarton Oaks, Teheran, Yalta, and Potsdam. In one of his more "controversial" moves, Marcus broke away from his desk responsibilities and clandestinely parachuted into France with the 101st Airborne on D-Day. After leading several firefights against the Germans, Marcus was located by Major General Maxwell Taylor who asked him, "What the ____ are you doing here?" With his casual reply, "Oh, just looking around," Marcus was promptly sent back to Washington with a stern reprimand.

In the closing year of the British mandate in Palestine, Colonel Marcus was "drafted" by Israel's future Prime Minister, David Ben-Gurion, to become the leading military advisor to his Jewish underground defense forces known as the *Haganah*. In roughly 200 days, Marcus was able to transform the fragmented freedom fighters into a disciplined unit that would defeat five Arab armies in less than a month. He constantly exhorted his poorly supplied troops, "Act with what you have. Don't forget, David did it with a slingshot." The Manhattan-born native was awarded the sacred rank of *"Aluf,"* making him the first Jewish general since Yehuda Ha-Maccabi, over 2,000 years before. His last accomplishment in the war was to rescue Jerusalem from a deadly Arab siege.

On June 11, 1948, Colonel Marcus was accidently killed by a sentry only hours before a negotiated truce went into effect. He is considered to be the last Jewish fatality of the war. Ben-Gurion said of Marcus, "He was the best man we had." Colonel Marcus is the only American soldier buried at West Point who died while fighting for a foreign country. His life was portrayed in the 1966 Hollywood film "Cast a Giant Shadow." In the interim since his death, God's people have taken up the mantle, giving rise to the adage, "America's Bible Belt is Israel's Safety Belt." But then, all of this *should* have been anticipated from the *English*, given those three center letters in JER*USA*LEM.

MESHECH AND TUBAL

The Holy Spirit devotes two entire chapters in the book of Ezekiel to Russia's incursion *"against the mountains of Israel"* in the great Tribulation (Ezekiel 38:8). Russia's contemporary, unorthodox alignment with both Iran (Persia) and Turkey (Togarmah) against Israel was forecast in back-to-back verses (Ezekiel 38:5-6). Over eighty years of Communism, atheism, gulags, oligarchies, famine, drunkenness, and Russian Mafia hits have coalesced to prepare the former Soviet Union for this denouement of all mankind. According to most secular historians (including the esteemed Russian author, Edvard Radzinsky), the major catalyst for the fall of old Russia was the Siberian *staret* ("holy man"), Gregory Rasputin, "affectionately" known as the "Holy Devil." Alexander Kerensky once remarked, "…without Rasputin there would have been no Lenin." Basically, Gregory was able to capture a country with 11 times zones (9 as of March 2010), stretching over 1/6 of the earth's surface, through the power of satanic manipulation.

Rasputin got his "hoof" in the palace door by convincing the neurotic Empress Alexandra that he could treat her son's hemophilia. He then persuaded the woman to send her wimpy husband to the German front. With Nicholas off the scene, the Czarina's favorite advisor was able to take over. His brief "reign" was characterized by influence peddling and political corruption, exacerbated by public intoxication and scandalous encounters with the leading women of St. Petersburg. Even more outrageous was the monk's "theological" explanation for his blatant debauchery. Reasoning that *revival* requires *repentance* and *repentance* requires *sin*, Gregory "preached" a perverted message advocating fornication as a catalyst for "spiritual renewal." The bottom line was that the public outrage played into the hands of Lenin's revolutionaries. Having served his purpose, Rasputin was "eliminated" on December 17, 1916, by a sodomite prince named Felix Yusupov. (I once had the macabre experience of visiting the very room where the murder occurred.) The rest is history: Nicholas abdicated the following March; the Russian Revolution occurred in October; and the Czar's entire family was massacred on July 17, 1918.

The "English" nugget related to this story is truly amazing. Ezekiel 38:1-2 reads: *"And the word of the LORD came unto me, saying, Son of man, set thy face against Gog, the land of Magog, the chief prince of **Meshech** and **Tubal**, and prophesy against him."* The applicable note in the Scofield Reference Bible accurately identified these cites as modern-day "Moscow" and "Tobolsk," while further stating that the intention of their inhabitants was to make a "last mad attempt to exterminate the remnant of Israel in Jerusalem." It is significant that these notes were published in 1909, almost three decades before "dispersed Israel" was granted statehood by the British mandate. Dr. Scofield would also have been unaware of his Russian contemporary, Gregory Rasputin.

While many subjects within the sphere of eschatology may foster debate, the simple facts of geography are stable by comparison. With thousands of cities destined to blanket the Russian landscape, the Holy Spirit moved Ezekiel in 597 BC to designate two for significant end-time activity regarding Israel. Founded in AD 1147, Moscow's role as the capital of the current Russian Foundation is a remarkable fulfillment of the prophet's words concerning *Meshech*. But what about *Tubal*, or Tobolsk, founded later yet in AD 1587? Regarding Kerensky's statement, "…without Rasputin there would be no Lenin" – should we be surprised that the "Holy Devil's" birthplace and childhood village of Pokrovskoye just *happened* to be situated in the Siberian province of Tobolsk, a mere 120 miles to the north of the city of Tobolsk itself? Thus, the scriptural version of Kerensky's statement would translate, "…without *Tubal* there would have been no *Meshech*"; better yet, "…without Ras*putin* there would have been no *Putin*!" – as in *Vladimir* Putin (or "Pootie Poot," as his pal, President George W. Bush, liked to call him).

THE PALESTINIAN PROBLEM

There is nothing as phony as the so-called "Palestinian Problem." The historical "Palestinians" were Jews, Greeks, Arabs, Turks, Egyptians, Frenchmen, Italians, Persians, and even some Americans. Prior to *these* "Palestinians" taking over the region, the land was occupied by Jebusites, Ammorites, Moabites, Hittites, Perizzites, Hivites, Edomites, etc. At *no* time in 3,400 years was it ever a Muslim religious state run by Arabs who were born in "Palestine." This is typical news media propaganda. Even the secular *World Book Encyclopedia* (2003) concedes, "Many peoples have invaded the region, and there has *never* been an independent Palestinian state." Thus, note how the Holy Spirit anticipated this very deception by moving Moses to record the prophecy: *"I will hide my face from them, I will see what their **end** shall be...They have moved me to jealousy with that which is not God; they have provoked me to anger with their vanities: and I will move them to jealousy with **those which are not a people**; I will provoke them to anger with **a foolish nation.**"* (Deuteronomy 32:20-21) While the immediate, doctrinal application is to the Body of Christ (as cross-referenced by Romans 10:19; 11:11 and I Peter 2:9-10), the later, contemporary fulfillment is striking. In the providence of God, Israel's end-time *"jealousy"* would be caused by her number one ally, the United States of America, *crawfishing* over Muslim *oil* and being forced to placate the *foolish* Palestinian "nation" in the process – a people *"which are not a people."*

"HEDGED UP"

While most Bible believers are passionate in their support of the State of Israel, few understand the unique dilemma that the Jewish people face regarding the so-called "Road Map" to peace. Simply put, from a geo-political standpoint Israel is "hedged up." This scenario was forecast over 2,700 years ago in the Lord's rebuke concerning Gomer's unfaithfulness to Hosea, a type of Israel's own spiritual adultery: *"I will **hedge up thy way with thorns**, and make a wall, that she shall not find her paths."* (Hosea 2:6) Having presented their Messiah with a crown of *thorns*, the Jews would experience nothing *but* thorns in a perennial "hedged up" existence ("hedge" being defined in *Webster's* as "...to obstruct in any manner; To enclose for preventing escape").

Because of Israel's unwillingness to accept their *new* covenant, Jehovah literally "fixed things" so they would not be *able* to obey the commandments of the *first* covenant – by *evicting* them from their covenant land – *the very place where they were obligated to worship*. Henceforth, the Jew would be snared by the words of Deuteronomy 12:11 – *"**Then there shall be a place** which the LORD* *your God shall choose to cause his name to dwell there;* **thither shall ye bring all that I command you;** *your burnt-offerings, and your sacrifices, your tithes, and the heave-offering of your hand, and all your choice vows which ye vow unto the* LORD." (This "place" was purchased by King David in II Samuel 24:18-25.)

Hosea 3:4 records the specifics of their approaching "Catch-22": *"For the children of Israel shall abide many days without a king, and without a prince,* **and without a sacrifice,** *and without an image, and without an ephod, and without teraphim."* The preliminary stage of Israel's separation from her land was the Babylonian *captivity* in 586 BC, vicariously described through Jeremiah's pen in Lamentations 3:7 – *"He hath* **hedged** *me about, that I cannot get out."* Psalm 137:4 epitomizes their predicament: *"How shall we sing the* LORD*'s song in a strange land?"* The second phase was inaugurated by the siege and destruction of Jerusalem by the Roman general, Titus, in AD 70. This was the "hedging up" that Jesus foretold in Luke 21:20 – *"And when ye shall see Jerusalem* **compassed** *with armies, then know that the desolation thereof is nigh."* The view from the city wall in the closing days of the siege left no doubt as to what the word "hedge" meant. Josephus records that 500 Jews a day were being caught trying to escape and summarily crucified, "till owing to the vast numbers there was no room for the crosses, and no crosses for the bodies" (an eerie fulfillment of their own prophecy in Matthew 27:25 – *"His* **blood** *be on us, and on* **our children,"** uttered a *generation* earlier). With the eventual expulsion of the survivors, the *really* heavy judgments (and "rejoicing") of Deuteronomy 28:63 would begin.

Then, after twenty centuries of being "hedged up" in a worldwide Diaspora of pogroms and genocide, a Jewish remnant miraculously found itself back in the land – though as "hedged up" as ever. About the size of New Jersey, the modern State of Israel is bordered by four Arab nations, with the Mediterranean Sea to her back. And, with "Allah's" flunkies in charge of the Temple Mount, Israel *still* cannot pursue her ancient worship. However, her greatest quandary has now become the focus of relentless international scrutiny.

Christians find it disconcerting that *any* Israeli (much less *many*) would endorse a two-state solution for the contrived Palestinian "problem." For example, in a July 7, 2010 interview on *Larry King Live*, Israeli Prime Minister Benjamin Netanyahu said that he spends an hour-and-a-half every Sabbath reading "from the Bible" with his younger son, gaining "enormous reservoirs of strength and relaxation." (Earlier that year, fifteen-year-old Avner Netanyahu won the prestigious National Bible Quiz for youth, stating: "The Bible is the very essence and foundation of the existence and spirit of the Jewish people.") And yet, the Prime Minister stands committed to a Palestinian state *within the historic boundaries of Israel*. Ironically, one of the *many* pertinent texts that this famous father and son would have encountered is Joel 3:2, where Israel's God explains that one day He will wipe out most of the world (including millions of Jews) for the unpardonable sin of having *"parted my land."*

Should Israel go with the "Road Map," her national security could be compromised even further by another demand that is never discussed by the liberal media. In his first address to the United Nations General Assembly on September 22, 2009, Barak Obama called for a "viable, independent Palestinian state with *contiguous* territory." What this translates to is that Gaza and the West Bank would have to be joined by a meaningful corridor, or easement. Thus, not only would the sole Jewish state in the world be downsized to a land mass smaller than Rhode Island, but the remaining territory would be split in half, effectively creating *two* separate cantons.

Now, the reason why this untenable concession is practically inevitable is because "Gomer" is "hedged up" even further. The way that the Lord has arranged things this time is simple: The Knesset has only *three* possible options: She can reject a two-state solution and continue the status quo, denying citizenship to the 4.2 million "Palestinians" in the West Bank and Gaza. However, this would only accelerate the already widening international condemnation from *without*, as the "crisis" is perceived as Middle East apartheid. Her second choice would be to reject a two-state solution while granting citizenship to her Arab residents. However, this would invite destruction from *within*, as Israel's continued existence as a "Jewish State" relies upon a sustained Jewish demographic majority. Of Israel's 7.5 million citizens (as of July 2010), approximately 75% are Jewish; 20%, Arab; and 5%, other. However, if everyone were suddenly lumped together into one big "happy" family, Israel's "voter edge" would drop to about 52% to 48%, a tenuous margin, indeed. And all experts agree that the non-Jewish population *will* tip the scale in the immediate future. Then, as if all of this were not enough, the satanic United Nations wants to include *another* 4-5 million Palestinian "refugees" from outside of the country, *vis-à-vis* the "Right of Return" mandate in Resolution 194, specifically – "Article 11" (how appropriate).

Thus, we can discern why Israel will come to believe that her only solution is option number 3 – *accepting* a two-state solution; eliminating threats from both *within* and *without* in the process. Unfortunately, the only problem is that *this* time the destruction will come from *above*: In 586 BC, the Jews were *taken* out of their land; in AD 70, they were *thrust* out of their land; however, in 20??, they will *walk* out of their land, *voluntarily*, for perceived self-preservation. Consequently, we see God "hedging up" His own people for the final slaughter described in Ezekiel 9 and Revelation 4-19. As Job is the greatest type of Israel in the Tribulation, we now *understand* the significance of his dilemma – *"Why is light given to a man whose way is hid, and whom God hath **hedged** in?"* (Job 3:23)

9/11

Many sermons have been preached on the horrors of September 11, 2001. According to the highly documented *New York Times* best seller, *House of Bush, House of Saud: The Secret Relationship Between the World's Two Most Powerful Dynasties* by Craig Unger, the Bush administration spent September 8-10 finalizing discussions with Saudi Arabia concerning a forthcoming public statement by either Colin Powell or President Bush advocating a Palestinian state within the historic boundaries of Israel. One of the more portentous verses that anticipated the 9/11 catastrophe is Isaiah 26:5, *"For he bringeth **down** them that dwell on high; the lofty **city**, he layeth it low; he layeth it low, even to the ground; he bringeth it even to the dust."* As the text indicates that an *entire* city is razed, the *primary* doctrinal context would probably apply to Rome's destruction in the Tribulation, as prefigured by the words, *"Thus with violence shall that great **city** Babylon be thrown **down**."* (Revelation 18:21) However, as your King James Bible is as current as tomorrow's news headlines, the verse *also* contains a precise four-part similitude related to the implosion of the Twin Towers: *"For he bringeth **down** them that dwell on **high**,"* for **high**-rise buildings brought **down**; in *"the **lofty city**,"* for "**The Big Apple**," or, more specifically for Manhattan – "**The City**"; *"even to the **ground**,"* as in "**Ground** Zero"; and, *"even to the **dust**,"* as in 10,000 plaintiffs being awarded $657 million in damages for their exposure to *toxic* **dust** during rescue-related efforts. Applying the "Law of First Mention" to a lethal implosion orchestrated by Satan, we find an exact type in the oldest chapter in the Bible: *"And, behold, there came a great wind from the wilderness, **and smote the four corners of the house**, and **it fell upon the young men**, and they are **dead**."* (Job 1:19) Why mess around with "Hebrew Codes" when the *real* action is in the *English*? (You might want to take a *second* look at that unassuming Scripture address in Job.)

EZEKIEL 9

I have always believed in the pre-Tribulation Rapture of the Church. Paul wrote: *"For God hath not appointed us to **wrath**, but to obtain salvation by our Lord Jesus Christ."* (I Thessalonians 5:9) However, while I do not anticipate the *eruption* of God's wrath – primarily because of that *interruption* promised in I Thessalonians 4:16 – I am *not* so sure as to whether believers may experience some level of *disruption* on *this* side of the *interruption* because of all the *corruption* sown by the modern Bible movement (Matthew 5:13). The same apostle also prophesied: *"This know also, that in the last days **perilous** times shall come."* (II Timothy 3:1) *Webster's* first definition for "perilous," reads: "Dangerous; hazardous; full of risk...." For instance, according to Federal crime statistics, 68% of all hate crimes committed in the United States in 2007 were against Jewish people, even though they constitute only 1.7% of the population; prompting New Jersey Representative Chris Smith to remark that anti-Semitism is "back with a vengeance." This cannot bode well for the country as a whole (Genesis 12:3).

In view of this sober warning, it would behoove God's people to acquaint themselves with a timely survival principle tucked away in Ezekiel 9. Though the *doctrinal* application relates to Israel in the Tribulation, the *devotional* application could literally save *your* life as *well* as the lives of *your loved ones* amidst the closing chaos of the Laodicean Church Age. In the context, Jehovah is preparing to dispatch *six* angels armed with *"slaughter weapons"* to wipe out the majority of Jerusalem's wicked inhabitants. However, before they're unleashed, a *seventh* angel with a *"writer's inkhorn"* is given a preliminary assignment. Verse four reads, *"And the LORD said unto him, Go through the midst of the city, through the midst of Jerusalem, and set a mark upon the foreheads of the men that **sigh** and that **cry** for all the abominations that be done in the midst thereof."* (Now you know where the Antichrist gets the inspiration for *his* mark.) Note the all-important spiritual criteria for obtaining *God's* mark – "sighing" and "crying" for the abominations of the land. The text continues with details reminiscent of Joshua's horrific invasion of Canaan: *"And to the others he said in mine hearing, Go ye after him through the city, and smite: let not your eye spare, neither have ye pity: Slay utterly old and young, both maids, and little children, and women: **but come not near any man upon whom is the mark**... And they went forth, and slew in the city."*

Now, while the Lord is under no *obligation* to extend this Tribulation arrangement to Church Age saints, He *might* be so inclined should we exhibit a *similar* burden for the abominations of our *own* country. (We know that He honored it in the Old Testament for the "weeping prophet" in Jeremiah 39:11-18) It is hard to tell the two nations apart. *The iniquity of* [America] *is exceeding great, and the land is full of blood, and the city full of perverseness: for they say, The LORD hath forsaken the earth, and the LORD seeth not."* (Ezekiel 9:9) I have often said that the three most practical hymns to sing in the last days would be "Hold the Fort," "Keep On the Firing Line," and, especially, "Till the Storm Passes By."

It has been my privilege to experience the providential protection of God on several occasions. One night, while conducting a revival meeting in San Antonio, Texas, I was sleeping in an RV in the church parking lot when a burglar broke in and ransacked the entire place, *including my bedroom.* By the grace of God, I snored through the whole thing (Psalm 127:2). As the song "He's in the Midst" reminds us, "And every night as you lay down, angels are camping all around." Ezekiel's bloodcurdling account of this future event concludes with the words: *"And, behold, the man clothed with linen, which had the inkhorn by his side, reported the matter, saying, I have done as thou hast commanded me."* So, if an angel was passing out the same marks tonight, would he give one to *you*? By the way, this has nothing to do with the Hebrew – but, do you suppose we should take note that this last Scripture address is 9:11?

"LIGHTS, CAMERA, ACTION"

Sitting unnoticed in the Genesis account of the Flood is one of the most profound eschatological truths in all of Scripture. Most Bible teachers believe that the *"sons of God"* in chapter six were fallen angels that cohabited with women. Their mutant offspring became the catalyst for the decadent conditions described in Genesis 6:5 – *"And God saw that the wickedness of man was great in the earth, and that every imagination of the thoughts of his heart was only evil continually."* The unpardonable sin of these supernatural *"men of renown"* equated to the original cult of "Man Worship." Obviously, something would have "to give," as the God of the universe declares in Isaiah 42:8 – *"I am the LORD: that is my name: and my glory will I not give to another."*

While the resultant Flood wiped out the entire population except for Noah's family, those ominous words in Genesis 6:4 – *"and also after that"* – ensured that the *"giants"* would be back. The relevance of this topic is seen in the Lord's statement in Matthew 24:37, *"But as the days of Noe were, so shall also the coming of the Son of man be."* Thus, one of the major end-day signs would be *"mighty men... men of renown."* Unfortunately, Laodicean Christians have been so preoccupied watching the "boob tube" that they've failed to discern that the professional entertainment industry is the world's foremost manufacturer of "human gods," appropriately known as "stars." The headquarters for this blasphemous operation is the hellhole known as "Hollywood" (get this), located in the "City of *Angels*." If one doubts that celebrities are "filled with *a* spirit," just watch what happens when "mere mortals" come into their awe-inspiring presence ("O, *my* G-d – it's Lady Ga Ga!")

One of the most profound, yet, least understood reasons why a national revival is utterly impossible (no matter *what* your Fundamentalist guru thinks) is because the great majority of prospects have rendered themselves *unreachable* by their willful addiction to the cult of god-making (i.e., "American Idol"). While there *was* a day when sinners could be reached by telling them that Jesus Christ is *"the resurrection, and the life,"* as well as *"the way, the truth, and the life,"* and thus, the one who *"giveth life"* – the *silver* screen would now *project* mere humans as *"bigger* than **life**." With "silver" portrayed in Scripture as a major type of redemption, "stars" such as Robert DeNiro, Madonna, Brad Pitt, Angelina Jolie, Russell Crowe, and George Clooney have become America's new saviors (e.g., Morgan Freeman shocked Charlie Rose during his June 4, 2010, interview, declaring, matter-of-factly: "*I* am God.")

However, believers can *still* praise the Lord, as a subtle prophetic connection could yet exist between the history of motion pictures and the Rapture of the church. The era began in **1891** with Thomas Edison and his epoch-making Kinetograph camera and Kinetoscope viewing apparatus. Following a decade of primitive clips, the first movie with an actual story debuted in 1903, known as "The Great Train Robbery." By the eve of World War I, ten million Americans were going to the movies daily. The *"gods"* had finally come down *"in the likeness of men."* (Acts 14:11) As for *how* this filth relates to the Second Advent, it all has to do with what our long-suffering God said when those *first* "stars" began showing up in 2553 BC. *"And the LORD said, My spirit shall not always strive with man, for that he also is flesh: yet his days shall be **an hundred and twenty years**."* (Genesis 6:3) Do the math! As *America's* "giants" have now been around for nearly the same amount of time (from the "Gay Nineties" to the "*Gay* Nineties," and *then* some), you *might* say that we are at *least* in the general vicinity. *"Even so, come, Lord Jesus."* (Revelation 22:20)

DEFINITIVE VERSES

- Fallacy of "works" salvation – *Galatians 2:21*
- Global Warming – *Genesis 8:22; Isaiah 5:14*
- The Road Map to Peace – *Joel 3:12; Amos 9:15*
- *Facebook, MySpace,* and *Twitter – Psalm 94:11; Proverbs 10:19; Ecclesiastes 5:1-3; John 1:22; 7:18*
- Women's pants issue – *Job 38:3*
- Feminism – *Leviticus 27:4; I Peter 3:7*
- NASCAR, PGA, NBA, NFL, MLB, NHL, WWF, MMA, etc. – *Luke 16:15*

MISCELLANEOUS

- Prophetic reference to the colonization of America – *Genesis 9:27*
- The New Testament does *not* begin *until* the death of Jesus Christ – *Hebrews 9:16-17*
- Prophetic reference to "information highway" (*transportation* and *knowledge*) – *Daniel 12:4*
- The *"sop"* as a veiled reference to the *"Son of Perdition"* – *John 13:26; 17:12*
- Epitaph for Pope John Paul II and Billy Graham – *John 15:19*
- Existence of a *postdiluvian* "water canopy" between 2nd and 3rd heavens – *Genesis 1:7; Psalm 148:4*

- Prophetic reference to Alexander the Great "goring" Darius at Gaugamela – *Daniel 8:7*
- God's remedy for gaining *immediate* peace of mind under *any* circumstance – *Job 22:21; I Thessalonians 5:18*
- Type of a mother's heart when serving God, separated from her children – *I Samuel 6:10, 12*
- Prophetic reference to the globalism and race-mixing policies of Antichrist – *Isaiah 10:12-14*
- The most likely candidates who carried the staff of grapes from Canaan – *Numbers 14:6*
- *Separate* head wrap exposes *singular* "Shroud of Turin" as a fraud – *John 20:7*
- Refuting Rome's claim that Jesus' siblings were cousins – *Mark 6:3; John 2:17; Psalm 69:8*
- A biblical command that is often a sin to obey (due to lack of self acceptance) – *Mark 12:31*
- As God's *pattern* of longsuffering, Paul had the *worst* past but *most* fruit – *I Timothy 1:15-16*
- The greatest thing God ever did *for* David was what He *didn't* do *to* David – *Psalm 18:35*
- Why no tears will be shed for unsaved loved ones throughout Eternity – *Job 20:8; 24:20; Isaiah 26:14; 65:17*
- The greatest "mystery" of all, Mary changing *God's* diaper – *I Timothy 3:16*

"O SACRED HEAD SO WOUNDED"

We have now arrived at the *fiftieth* "English" nugget in our chapter. If Deuteronomy 28:63 represents the *scariest* text in Scripture, Exodus 17:6 may constitute the *holiest* text. As the chapter unfolds, all three members of the Trinity come into view: God the Father appears to Moses in response to his cry for help; the "rock" that is smitten is a type of Christ being crucified for the sins of the world (I Corinthians 10:4); while the water that gushes forth pictures the Holy Spirit that is subsequently made available (John 7:37-39). Now, certainly, there is no way that any of us can even *begin* to comprehend what our Lord endured on the Cross. The last three hours must have been ineffably horrendous, for Matthew 27:45 states: *"Now from the sixth hour there was darkness over all the land until the ninth hour."* In Bible college we "learned" that Jesus bruised the serpent's head at *this* time (Genesis 3:15). However, it has been noted previously that Satan's head will not be bruised *until* the Second Advent (Psalm 68:19-22; Habakkuk 3:13; Romans 16:20). Once again, the English text of the A.V. 1611 will rescue the Bible believer from Fundamentalist tradition. Only, in this case, the truth may be *too* holy for words.

In John 3:14, Jesus identifies Himself with the brazen serpent, stating: *"And as Moses lifted up the **serpent** in the wilderness, even so must the Son of man be lifted up."* When II Corinthians 5:21 says, *"For he hath **made** him to **be sin** for us, who knew no sin"* – this is precisely what the Holy Spirit means. Paul adds: *"Christ hath redeemed us from the curse of the law, **being made a curse for us: for it is written, Cursed is every one that hangeth on a tree.**"* (Galatians 3:13) Having become sin for us in a *literal* sense – bearing a vicarious responsibility for *every* sin that would *ever* be committed in history – the *best*-case scenario was that the lovely Lord Jesus took on the appearance of the brazen serpent itself – *"that old **serpent**, called the **Devil**."* (Revelation 12:9) Thus, while Isaiah tells us that He would have *"**no form** nor comeliness,"* Jesus prophesied through David: *"But I am a **worm**, and **no man**."* (Isaiah 53:2; Psalm 22:6)

And yet, there is something even *more* unspeakable than this spiritual metamorphosis; and it's staring right off the page at us in Exodus 17:6. Long before the *serpent's* head is bruised at *Armageddon*, the *Saviour's* head is bruised at *Calvary* – Isaiah 53:5 declaring that *"he was **bruised** for our iniquities."* The part that is *too* surreal for spiritual comprehension has to do with *WHERE* GOD WAS STANDING when Moses smote the rock. *"And the* LORD *said unto Moses, Go on before the people, and take with thee of the elders of Israel; and thy rod, wherewith thou smotest the river, take in thine hand, and go.* **BEHOLD, I WILL *STAND***

BEFORE THEE THERE *UPON THE ROCK* IN HOREB; *and thou shalt smite the rock, and there shall come water out of it, that the people may drink. And Moses did so in the sight of the elders of Israel."* Thus, according to the solemn typology suggested in Exodus 17:6, the "Light of the World" went out at high noon – because the Father **STOMPED** it out! While Moses had warned Israel that *"the LORD will **rejoice** over you to **destroy** you,"* Isaiah 53:10 affirmed that their Messiah would be treated no differently – *"Yet it **pleased** the LORD to **bruise** him."* Having been informed that *"Thy **bruise** is incurable,"* how *else* could Israel be *"set at liberty"*? (Jeremiah 30:12; Luke 4:18)

> *"There be three things which are too wonderful for me, yea, four which I know not...the way of **a serpent upon a rock**."*
>
> (PROVERBS 30:18-19)

13

Seeing His Days

𝔄N ALLUSION TO the disconcerting reality that, ultimately, numbers of Christians would be void of "understanding" regarding Job 32:8 was provided by the Holy Ghost in a previous truth in Job 24:1. The question with which Job remonstrated his three "friends" goes to the very heart of the matter, as it confirms that God's own children can be *totally* clueless regarding any number of crucial matters, the King James Bible issue being paramount – *"Why, seeing times are not hidden from the Almighty, do they that know him not **see** his days?"* Once again, we *see* that "the problem" is an *eye* problem (i.e., Revelation 3:17).

Job was frustrated by the fact that people who supposedly "know" God, for some reason are not able to *see* what he is doing at any given time or place. The explanation is that knowing *God* is one thing; knowing God's *mind* is something else altogether. As Paul instructed the Philippians to *"Let **this mind** be in you, which was also in **Christ Jesus**,"* believers who *have* the mind of Christ *will* be able *"see his days"* by their ability to discern what is going on around them. (Philippians 2:5) Unfortunately, the average Christian today knows more about the *Mind of Mencia.*

To summarize several truths in this volume: The unprecedented materialism of the Laodicean Church Age has led the majority of professing Christians to place *mammon* ahead of *God*. As *"no man can serve two masters,"* selling out to *money* has rendered these apostates *incapable* of submission to God. This, in turn, has caused spiritual blindness, for according to John 7:17, a direct correlation exists between a believer's willingness to *obey* God's *will* and his ability to *understand* God's *word*. Consequently, John counseled the Laodiceans to *"anoint thine eyes with eyesalve, that thou mayest see."* (Revelation 3:18) Such a state of irremediable deterioration can lead to only one destination, the Lord declaring in Hosea 4:6, **"My people are destroyed for lack of knowledge**: *because thou hast rejected knowledge, I will also reject thee."* Thus, like Samson of old, Christians in the seventh, and final, period of Church history are destined to commit spiritual suicide; though they themselves *"shall be saved; yet so as by fire."* (I Corinthians 3:15) For instance, after Heisman Trophy winner Tim Tebow gained national attention for placing John 3:16 on his eye black, those same Southern Baptist eyes made their eventual fixation on *mammon* as the "consecrated MK" signed a lucrative endorsement contract with *Jockey*, known as the "tighty-whitey" underwear company (so much for the *fruit* of the Holman "Christian" Standard "Bible").

Applying this "inability to see" to the A.V. 1611 controversy, we observe that the very next thing Job mentions is that *"some remove the **landmarks**"* (i.e., *"the ancient landmark"* of Proverbs 22:28). I have always been convinced that a Bible believer needs more than just a handle on the standard arguments involving the Authorized Version. What is often lacking is that *"understanding of the **times**"* spoken of in I Chronicles 12:32. Consequently, as the greater part of the Body of Christ in end-day America is as "blind as a bat," why should we be surprised that they would oppose the very "Book" that birthed them into the Kingdom of God? Jesus said, *"And if the blind lead the blind, both shall fall into the ditch."* (Matthew 15:14) Unfortunately, brethren, "there's nobody home upstairs," and very little that you or I can do about it. Truth is, we have come full circle – Peter's admonition to the *Hebrew* remnant at the end of the *Jewish* Age to *"**save yourselves** from this **untoward** generation"* having a peculiar application to the *Gentile* remnant at the end of the *Church* Age. (Acts 2:40) The timeliness of employing this text in reverse should not be underestimated. *Webster's* defines "untoward" as "Froward; perverse; refractory; *not easily guided or taught.*" Thus, an "untoward generation" is an "*untowable* generation"; like a car that not even a "repo man" can tow away. While the typical Bible-correcting Fundamentalist will wrest II Chronicles 7:14 to "prove" that a national revival is "just a prayer away," etc., the following subject matter will reveal the calculated, catastrophic, and *irrevocable* damage that America has sustained through the modern "Bible" movement.

REVISERS' SUBLIMINAL AGENDA

Opponents of the "King James Only" position will often accuse Bible believers of causing "unnecessary division" within the Body, etc. Of course, the fact that "we wuz here *foist*," means nothing. And because *they* have the proverbial microphones, *we* remain the villains – *despite* the historical reality that the "**Old** Black Book" **(1611)** was here *long* before the **New** World Translation **(1961)**, the **New** American Bible **(1970)**, the **New** English Bible **(1970)**, the **New** American Standard Bible **(1971)**, the **New** International Version **(1978)**, the **New** Scofield Reference Bible **(1967)**, the **New** King James Version **(1982)**, the **New** Jerusalem Bible **(1985)**, the **New** Century Version **(1987)**, the **New** Revised Standard Version **(1989)**, and the **New** Living Translation **(1996)**.

As Laodicean Christians have *trashed* the Bible of the Philadelphia Church Age, preferring any number of generic translations traced in part to that "dumpster dive" at St. Catherine's Monastery, our once-blessed nation has likewise degenerated in the process. Unbeknown to most, the diabolical patriarchs of the modern "Bible" movement would have greatly rejoiced to see such a day. As I documented in *Final Authority*, Westcott and Hort despised *everything* about America. While that historical marker in Portsmouth, Rhode Island states, "Birthplace of American Democracy," Dr. Hort wrote, "I...cannot say that I see much as yet to soften my **deep *hatred* of democracy in all its forms**." (*H, II*, p. 234) In one particular diatribe he ranted: "...the American empire is a standing menace to the whole civilization of Europe, and sooner or later one or the other must perish...American doctrine...destroys the root of everything vitally precious which man has by painful growth been learning from the earliest times till now, and tends only to reduce us to the *gorilla* state." With regard to causing "division," these Darwinian heretics literally *prayed* for the rupture of the United States, Hort concluding: "Surely, if ever Babylon or Rome were rightly cursed, **it cannot be wrong to desire and pray from the bottom of one's heart that the American Union may be *shivered* to pieces.**" (*H, I,* p. 459) Westcott chimes in: "**I suppose I am a *communist* by nature.**" (*W, I,* p. 309)

And my, *what* a job they have done! Who could have *possibly* envisioned the "America" that we have today? Thanks to a growing array of federal, state, and local statutes, "gender confused" males may now enter public ladies' restrooms whenever they feel "confused." While one school district in Helena, Montana, proposes teaching "family planning techniques" to *kindergartners*, another in Provincetown, Massachusetts, wants to supply the "necessary means" to *elementary* students. For the first time in the history of our free republic, a law is on the books that actually *requires* citizens to purchase a product whether or not they *want* it, or can *afford* it (health insurance). When visiting our nation's capital, motorists must contend with the prominent six-spire, bright white "Moron Temple" (Hatch, Romney, Reid, Cleaver, Beck, et al.) that rises 288 feet above the skyline of the westbound Beltway traffic. (Maryland state police are constantly erasing the words "Surrender Dorothy" from the girders of an adjacent railroad bridge that crosses the expressway.) The "Black Farmers Association" continues to demand exorbitant compensation for alleged discrimination; Mexican flags fly *right-side up* alongside *upside-down* American flags, while a *Dollar General* store in Dallas, Texas, was exposed during the 2010 Fourth of July weekend for selling American flags with 61 stars (no worse than Obama's claim of having campaigned in 57 states).

New Black Panther Party Chairman "Dr." Malik Zulu Shabazz declared war on the "Tea Party," affirming that the *bruthas* are "ready to rumble." Muslim states *within* the United States based solely on Islam and Sharia law (known as "no-go zones," like

Gwynn Oak in Baltimore, Maryland), are building the American caliphate one enclave at a time. Islamic "foot baths" for ritual washing are being installed in taxpayer funded airports and colleges. First Amendment rights are flagrantly suspended in Muslim-controlled Dearborn, Michigan. (In the face of all the politically correct rhetoric about burkas and veils, one of Dearborn's own, Rima Fakih, was crowned the nation's first "*Arab*-American" Miss USA.) With over 1,500 mosques currently dotting the land, Hamtramck, Michigan, became the first American city to allow the Muslim "call to prayer" siren to invade local airwaves. While a "Christian" nation cannot erect a Nativity scene in public, Manhattan Muslims citing "overcrowding" at area mosques gained approval to move their Friday "prayer" meetings out onto the public streets, closing traffic down for two hours at a time. In a nearly unanimous vote, the Lower Manhattan Community Board approved the construction of a 15-story, $100 million mosque and Islamic "cultural center" – *500 feet from Ground Zero*. (This was later followed by an even *more* incredible 9-0 "go ahead" by the New York City Landmarks Preservation Commission.) Finally, the first Islamic "honor" killings on American soil occurred in Irving, Texas, when a Muslim father shot his two teenage daughters upon learning that they had boyfriends.

Then, we have professional *women* cage fighters; energy drinks; balance bracelets; marijuana referendums; ads for medical marijuana; Prozac for preschoolers; "zombie walks" (8,000 participants in Grand Rapids, Michigan alone); the *Dante's Inferno* video game commercial during the 2010 Super Bowl showing a knight graphically plunging into Hell to save his woman; the saga of "Balloon Boy"; the "acid attack" hoax; *T.G.I. Friday's* restaurants taking God's name in vain; "Rent-a-Friend" web sites (hourly rates and "strictly platonic"); access to *500 million* pornography web pages (described by secular pundits as a "runaway train"); Hugh Heffner sending his "*prayers* and thoughts" to the family of Anna Nicole Smith; 50,000 new cases of AIDS each year; the Metropolitan Community "Church" and other sodomite "ministries" like the "Gay Christian Network"; *Mattel's* new sodomite Ken doll – "Palm Beach Sugar

Daddy Ken" – complete with pink polo shirt and a little white dog on a pink leash; Steven Slater, a sodomite flight attendant, becoming an instant folk hero for throwing a "tarmac tirade," receiving over twenty-five offers for reality television programs; the gate-crashing Salahis and their *own* reality TV show appearances; over 716,000 registered sex offenders nationwide (not including *thousands* of pedophile Catholic "Fathers"); five murders and a suicide in Kentucky, purportedly instigated by "cold eggs"; and, the infamous Amish school shooting where five little girls, aged 6-13, were gunned down while they stood at the blackboard.

Being *"lovers of pleasures more than lovers of God,"* a growing number of end-day Americans have convinced themselves that they can keep right on partying *after* death. Country singer Joe Diffie put it this way: "Prop me up beside the jukebox if I die; Lord, I wanna go to heaven but I don't wanna go tonight; Fill my boots up with sand, put a *stiff* drink in my hand; Prop me up beside beside the jukebox if I die." The late James Henry Smith, a fanatical Pittsburg Steelers fan, was "laid out" at the local funeral home – in a *recliner* in front of a high definition television, remote in hand, "watching" a continuous loop of Steelers highlights. Jim was last seen in a pair of dark sunglasses, decked out in his black and gold silk pajamas, slippers, and robe, his beer and cigarettes within "arm's reach." (Now *that's* a "zombie walk!")

Even *Burger King* is fraught with controversy: their highly suggestive "Sponge Bob Square Pants" video, featuring "The King" rapping with five dancers *to market $0.99 "Sponge Bob" Kids Meals*; followed by an entire marketing program built around the satanic *Twilight* saga; their new "Whopper Bar" outlets adding *beer* to the menu; and, let's not forget that idiotic employee who took a bath in a sink after-hours and racked up over a million hits on YouTube.

While my generation grew up profiting from the "It Pays to Enrich Your Word Power" vocabulary tests in *Reader's Digest*, 42 million Americans in the "post-*Reader's Digest Bible* era" are unable to read at *all*. Come-and-go inane colloquialisms that define modern American "culture" include: "To continue in English, press one"; "Whoever dies with the most toys wins"; "Bells and Whistles"; "Are we havin' fun yet?"; *"Fuhgedaboudit!"*; "Talk to da hand!"; "Scrait Up!"; "Leave Britney alone!"; "Whazzup?"; "Wussup?"; "'S'up?"; "Know'm sayin'?"; and, "Don't *tase* me, Bro....*Aggggh!"* Other "indispensible" buzz words would include: *Dude!*; *chillin'*; *space*; *crib*; *bling-bling*; *"da bom' diggity"*; *Whatever!*; *LOL*; and, rebellious man's *ultimate* blasphemy – *OMG!*

Of course, our political leaders are a *joke* (some, *more* literally than others): former *SNL* comedian, Minnesota Senator Al Franken, whose filthy language can only be surpassed by Hillary Clinton and Rahm Emanuel (in that order), being investigated for stealing his contested election with over 1,000 illegal votes from federal prisoners; Elvis impersonator, Elvis D. Presley, running for governor of Arkansas as a write-in candidate; Linda McMahon, wife of current Chairman and CEO of the satanic *World Wrestling Entertainment*, Vince McMahon, Jr. (a.k.a. "The Genetic Jackhammer," "The Boss," "The Mac Attack," "The Mac Daddy," "Daddy Mac," "Vinnie Mac," "No Chance," "Junior," "VKM," "Mr. McMahon," *and* "Higher Power"), spending over *$50 million* of her *own* money to pursue a *$200,000-a-year* position as a U.S. senator from Connecticut; Levi Johnston (Sarah Palin's "almost" son-in-law) *hinting* at a potential run for mayor of Wasilla, Alaska; Madame Speaker of the House Nancy Pelosi's airhead, jaw-dropping, logic-defying one-liner regarding the mysterious 2,000-page Health Care package: "We have to *pass* the bill – *so you can see what's in it*"; and Massachusetts Representative "Barney" Frank (enough said).

And then, there is the *really* bizarre case of Alvin Greene, an unemployed *"African-*American" living in his parents' basement, with "only" a pending felony obscenity charge to his name, *who would make Forrest Gump look like Albert Einstein* – who *somehow* "captures" the South Carolina Democratic senate primary with a 59% margin (nearly 100,000 votes), defeating four-term state lawmaker Vic Rawl, a well-known former judge – and he does so (get *this*) with no *resumé*, no *experience*, no *campaign*, no *funds*, and no *web site*. Responding to "Big Al's" proposal that unemployment could be reduced by making action figure dolls of *himself*, the Charleston RiverDogs minor league baseball team decided to start the ball rolling with a promotional Alvin Greene doll for their fans. Produced by *Raph*co, the doll's instructions say, "Pull my string! Hear me say, 'Yes,' 'No,' 'Good,' 'Busy,' and 'What you doin' here so early?'" The RiverDogs' General Manager, Dave Echols, put it all in perspective, stating: "Who better pictures the American dream that *anything* is possible than Mr. Greene?" (Now you know the meaning of the political aphorism – "South Carolina: too small to be a nation; too big to be an insane asylum.")

Turning to the Empire State for a more "distinguished" delegation, we have: former Governor Eliot Spitzer, resigning over a prostitution scandal (now co-hosting *CNN's* "Parker Spitzer"); Spitzer's legally blind Lieutenant Governor, David Paterson (New York's first "African-American" Governor), "feeling" his way through a myriad of corruption charges, resulting in a 19% approval rating; Representative "Charlie" Rangel, the embattled eighty-year-old former Chairman of the House Ways and Means Committee, facing a similar array of ethics violations; and "Gotham City" Mayor Michael Bloomberg endorsing the mosque at Ground Zero (while also doing *his* part to entice free-agent LeBron "King James" to play for the Knicks).

Out in the "Wild West" there is the *"Austrian*-American" former body builder and Governor Arnold Schwarzenegger (a.k.a. "The Governator") looking for new "challenges" after leading "Cawlifornia" to the brink of bankruptcy; Meg Whitman, spending *$100 million* of *her* personal fortune to replace him (a "smack down" of Linda McMahon by comparison); California Representative Maxine Waters, outspoken member of the Congressional Black Caucus, rated one of the most corrupt members of Congress by Citizens for Responsibility and Ethics in Washington; and, busted former Idaho Senator Larry Craig, explaining his now-famous "wide stance" to his incredulous constituents.

Moving right along, we have former Bush advisor, Karl "MC" Rove, dancing and rapping at the White House Correspondents Dinner; Detroit's former "African-American" mayor, Kwame

Kilpatrick, dubbed the "Hip-Hop Mayor," indicted on 19 federal charges (currently doing *his* "rapping" as prisoner #702408 at the Oakes Correctional Facility in Manistee, Michigan); former Ohio Representative Jim Traficant, back on the ballot seeking to retrieve his old seat, having served *seven* years in federal prison for bribery, racketeering, and tax evasion; John Conyers, the "African-American" Congressman from Michigan *still* advocating reparations for the descendants of slaves; *Skull & Bones* alumnus, Senator John "Swift Boat" Kerry, taking on water for $500,000 in unpaid taxes on his $7 million yacht; disgraced "*Serbian*-American" former Illinois Governor Rod Blagojevich (impeached by a vote of 114-1) suffering the added "indignity" of hearing those fateful words – "*You're fired!*" – from "The Donald" on *Celebrity Apprentice* (Was he jealous of "Blago's" hairdo?); the ponytailed former wrestler and Minnesota Governor Jesse Ventura, fulminating his paranoia on his off-the-wall reality show, *Conspiracy Theory*; another "Minnesotan," Keith Ellison, posing with his hand on the "Holy Koran" after becoming the first Muslim to be elected to the U.S. Congress; and, South Carolina Governor Mark Sanford disappearing for four days of adultery in Argentina.

Talk about the "New South": In another "Palmetto Land" victory, Nikki Haley, born *Nimrata Randhawa*, positioned herself to become the country's first "*Indian*-American" *female* governor, despite her *Sikh* background of meditation and reincarnation, not to mention two different allegations of marital infidelity. (To Nikki's "credit," she *did* join up with the liberal United Methodist Church.) Meanwhile, during the formal hearings into the Deepwater oil spill, when it was suggested that BP executive Lamar McKay resign, Louisiana representative *Anh* "Joseph" *Cao*, the nation's first "*Vietnamese*-American" Congressman, stoically replied, "Well, in the Asian culture, we do things differently; during the *Samurai* days, we just give you a knife and ask you to commit *hara-kiri*"; finally, the man that continues to be touted as America's first *black* president – *somehow* – had a *white* mother (though this is not *nearly* as confusing as the late Mike Jackson's *all-white* children).

Returning to the "real world," while Christians can be arrested for disciplining *their* children, *heathen* parents can subject *their* daughters (some, barely out of kindergarten) to everything from exotic dancing to beauty pageants to enhance their "self esteem." Plenty of "mentors" are also available, running the gamut from teenage tramps like Miley Cyrus to novelty dance troupes of "cheerleading grannies" performing at local school pep rallies. Break-dancing baby videos flood the Internet. In 2010 a father was killed, along with his daughter and a flight instructor, when the *seven*-year-old crashed the plane she was attempting to use to become the youngest pilot to fly across the country. Later that same year, another idiot played it safe by coaxing his sixteen-year-old daughter to attempt a sailboat ride around the world – *alone*. (Of course, rumor had it that a reality show was in the works.) To help teenage girls "cope," *Zondervan* published the *True Images* "Bible" (New International Version), featuring over 1,000 notes that profile fictional teens discussing – in the most *graphic* manner – topics such as fornication, flirting, sodomy, and other subjects too explicit to include here.

Concerning the *males* of our nation, boy beauty pageants have become the latest fad. Time-honored "macho" toys like BB guns and pocket knives are now considered politically incorrect. Football and other traditional contact sports are slowly being replaced by the "rigors" of cup stacking and skateboarding along with Wii games and other virtual reality innovations, contributing to unprecedented levels of childhood obesity. While some educators have lobbied to ban swing sets from school playgrounds for being "too dangerous" others want to eliminate recess altogether. Soccer (and the ubiquitous "soccer mom") remains the subtle exception, as imbedding the *"world's* biggest sport" *here* continues to be a serious cultural goal of the New World Order. Finally, untold spiritual, emotional, and psychological damage continues to be inflicted on our young people through the medium of Harry Potter; video games; and other occult venues. *Zondervan's* answer for the teen boy "market" is their perverted 90-day NIV devotional, *Revolution*.

With the age of *Father Knows Best* having been eclipsed by *Hogan Knows Best* (not to mention programs featuring *rock star* dads, *mobster* dads, and even *sodomite* dads) the current teen culture, identified as "Generation Y" (also known as the "Millennial Generation" and "Generation Next") has devolved to a nightmare of surreal proportions: alcohol and drugs (including all-night marathons known as "raves"), along with fornication and the resultant venereal diseases; attention-deficit hyperactivity disorder (ADHD), obsessive-compulsive disorder (OCD), oppositional defiant disorder (ODD), and the panacea of Ritalin "therapy"; texting (now reaching *addiction* levels according to *The American Journal of Psychiatry*), "sexting," and online predators; melodic metalcore, metallic hardcore, and melodic death metal "music"; bulimia and anorexia disorders; depression, panic attacks, and suicide; the *Twilight Saga*-inspired, vampire-like blood drawing (known as "love bites," with many being posted on YouTube); tattoos, gender-change operations, and body modifications – *specifically* – ritual scarification, 3D art implants, stretching and cutting, transdermal implants, facial sculpture, tooth art, tongue splitting, branding, and amputations. Some of the more out of the box stuff would include "suspensions" (hanging from hooks) and "bug chasing" (*intentionally* contracting and succumbing to AIDS). Many other "common practices" are too vile to add to this list.

Our tax-funded public schools resemble everything from *prisons* and *zoos* to *psych wards* and *war zones*, "featuring" gangs, Goth cults, and cyber bullying; fantasy battles between vampires and werewolves; zero tolerance, metal detectors, and mass shootings; socialism, globalism, and anti-Americanism; recruitment centers for sodomite and transgender students; diversity, tolerance, and race-mixing indoctrination; science textbooks shifting the "cradle of evolution" to Africa – all moving to the continuous beat of sensual jungle music, not to mention a dysfunctional dance team of "Hammite Hip-Hoppers" with their "EMINEM wannabe" protégés shuffling down the halls with their trousers drooping down – inspiring that "international rap video sensation," *Pants on the Ground* (i.e., "I'm jus' sayin,' man, I'm sick o' seein' yo' underwear.")

At the top of this sick pyramid, the education system continues throwing "good" money after bad. With the State of California at a *$19.1 billion* deficit, *3,000* teachers laid off over two years, the school district facing a *$640 million* shortfall, and "showcasing" several schools with students persistently ranking among the lowest academic performers in the land – Robert F. Kennedy Community Schools opened its doors in the fall of 2010 at a final price tag of *$578 million*, the *costliest* in the nation! But don't think this was a fluke. While Governor Schwarzenegger may not be very fluent in English, nothing was too good for the students in *his* state; the Edward R. Roybal Learning Center debuted in 2008 at $377 million, followed by the Visual and Performing Arts High School in 2009 at "only" $232 million. ("Hasta la vista, baby!")

A pretty good indication of the present state of affairs is the now-famous answer (over ten million hits on YouTube) given by Lauren Upton, Miss South Carolina (Alvin Greene country), in the 2007 Miss Teen USA pageant. Her question was: "Recent polls have shown that a fifth of Americans can't locate the U.S. on a world map. Why do you think this is?" She answered (and I quote):

> I personally believe that, U.S. Americans are unable to do so, because...uhmmm, some people out there in our nation don't have maps. (*going...*) And uh, I believe that our education, like such as in South Africa, and uh, the Iraq, everywhere, like, such as, and, I believe that they should, uh, (*going......*) our education over here, in the U.S. should help the U.S., err, should help South Africa; it should help the Iraq and the Asian countries so we will be able to build up our future, for us. (*GONE!*)

While the *Millennials* divide *their* escape mechanisms between all things electronic and the ever-widening *drug* of social networking sites, their parents are mostly content to remain with the more familiar "boob tube" for *their* excursions into fantasy land. As a television program is only as strong as the advertising revenue it can generate, the abject buffoonery currently permeating the airwaves

constitutes one of the *scariest* social indicators of our time. Believe
it or not, folks in *your* neighborhoods are actually spending "quality"
time watching shows about such "enriching" subjects as: autopsies;
tattoos; sodomy; fornication; adultery; magic; speeding tickets;
midget wrestlers; lumber jacks; bully beatdowns; drug interventions;
losing weight; playing poker; repossessing cars; stealing cars;
busting child predators; filming ghosts; baking cakes; marrying
millionaires; hoarding junk; hunting scrap metal; and *last,* but not
least, spraying bugs with good ol' *Billy the Exterminator.* Many of
the other program titles speak for themselves: *Gary and Tony Have
a Baby*; *Teen Moms*; *Bridezilla*; *Growing up Twisted*; *How Do
I Look?*; *Neighbors From Hell*; *Headbangers Ball*; *Diners, Drive-
ins and Dives*; *Man vs Food*; *Biggest Loser*; *MTV Cribs*; *Clean
House: Search for the Messiest Home*; *Dirty Jobs*; *Paranormal
State*; *Criss Angel Mindfreak*; *Swamp People*; *Chasing Mummies*;
1,000 Ways To Die; *Vampire Diaries*; and the hands-down, all-time
scariest show in television history – *Geraldo At Large.* (Another two
dozen "household name" shows, once again, are *too* filthy to list.)

Moral degenerates like Ellen *Degeneres*, Jerry Springer, Madonna,
"Flavor Flav," Gene Simmons, "Snoop Dog," Bill Maher, Tiger
Woods, and Kathy Griffin, rule the day. Other mentally challenged
"role models" would include the Osbournes, Paris Hilton, "Lady
Ga Ga," Joy Behar, Danny Bonaduce, Courtney Love, Lindsay Lohan,
Tyra Banks, Whoopie Goldberg, Bret Michaels, Tonya Harding, and
Joan Rivers, to name a *few.* And who wouldn't sell their soul to
the Devil to be on *American Idol*? (The nation practically went into
mourning when Simon Cowell announced he was leaving the show.)
On a "serious" note, Baby Boomers have had a really hard time
making the adjustment to such programming. Having cut my own
teeth on shows like *Paladin* – "Have Gun, Will Travel" (1957-63),
I was dumbfounded to discover a show called *Saw For Hire* about
a tree-trimming service in Tulsa, Oklahoma. Then, we have 82-year-
old Cloris Leachman – *Dancing with the Stars.* (What's *really* wrong
with this picture?) In any event, from *Cupcake Wars* to *Hamburger
Paradise*, the theme is the same – America is *toast* (Proverbs 14:34).

"PROUD INTERNATIONALIST"

To whatever degree God's *people* abandon God's *word* – God's *protection* will diminish accordingly (Proverbs 16:7). While America was once the envy of the world, standing strong and independent, sadly, that is no longer the case. The United States is now the world's greatest *debtor* nation, the ubiquitous *Dollar Stores* representing an ominous sign to the more "ancient" generation (Ezra 3:12). With all of the red ink amassed, a final economic blow is inevitable to enable the global elite to *yank* America into the coming world government of Antichrist.

Having documented these treacherous developments since 1993, I recently came across one of the most audacious "in your face" admissions that I have ever seen in print. One of the telling signs that a scam is just about over is when the villains start removing their masks (like the Devil does at the end of the *Chick* tract, "Somebody Goofed"). For instance, after courting the gullible *Religious Right* for years, President George W. Bush waited until the last possible moment to come out of *his* closet. When asked in an *ABC Nightline* interview on December 8, 2008, whether he believed the Bible was *literally* true, "Brother" Bush replied, "Probably not; no, I'm not a literalist, but I think you can learn a lot from it...." (Do you suppose *Fundamentalist* politicians like Dr. Schaap and Dr. Sexton *still* display those silly publicity photos of themselves, posing with the greatest charlatan who ever duped a generation of spiritual blanks?)

At the turn of the millennium, David Rockefeller reigned as the ranking member of the "House of Rockefeller," America's premier elitist dynasty. Founded by the industrialist-philanthropist, John D. Rockefeller – a tithing "Baptist" and the nation's first billionaire – the Rockefeller name has long been synonymous with wealth and the power it buys. For example, when I was a child, my father worked as a doorman at 740 Park Avenue in Manhattan. According to the book *740 Park: The Story of the World's Richest Apartment Building*, a 31-unit "apartment" previously belonging to John D., Jr., sold for nearly *$30 million* in 2000, a record even for Park Avenue.

For several decades, the Rockefeller "empire" has been viewed as the embodiment of globalism and international intrigue. While the family public relations firm consistently took the "pay no attention to that man behind the curtain" approach, thinking people had plenty of reason for their suspicions. After all, didn't the patriarch himself coin the phrase that "competition is a sin"? (For the record, the "old man" was about as "spiritual" as his son, John D., Jr., who brought the notorious liberal, Dr. Harry Emerson Fosdick, to Manhattan's Riverside Church in the early 1920s.) Under Junior's leadership, the Rockefellers donated the land for the United Nations building and funded the refurbishing of the prestigious *Pratt House*, the new headquarters of the Council on Foreign Relations (CFR).

Throughout his long career, grandson David held and/or established over sixty major positions and institutions. The most *un-American* would include: Co-founder of the *Bilderbergers* (1954); Founder of the *Trilateral Commission* (1973); Chairman of the CFR (1970-1985); Chairman of Chase Manhattan Bank (1969-1981); and Class A Director of the Federal Reserve Bank in New York. He caused considerable outrage among the political Right when he told the *New York Times*, August 10, 1973: "The social experiment in China under Chairman Mao's leadership is one of the most important and successful in human history." In case you're not up on your history, this was the "social experiment" that resulted in the deaths of *sixty million human beings*, and it didn't have a *thing* to do with "leadership." (To illustrate the prevailing oppression within the ROC: A Christian businessman once informed me that after leaving his personal copy of my book *What Hath God Wrought!* on a bus in Tianjin, he was unable to retrieve it before departing the country because the local courier refused to ship a "religious" book.)

That quote *had* been one of the most outlandish statements in "Rockefeller history" – that is, until *now*. In 2002 David Rockefeller's *Memoirs* were published; at age 87 it was finally time to come clean. In his chapter entitled "Proud Internationalist," Dave wrote:

For more than a century ideological extremists at either end of the political spectrum have seized upon well-publicized incidents such as my encounter with Castro to attack the Rockefeller family for the inordinate influence they claim we wield over American political and economic institutions. Some even believe we are part of a secret cabal working against the best interests of the United States, characterizing my family and me as "internationalists" and of conspiring with others around the world to build a more integrated global political and economic structure – **one world**, if you will. **If that's the charge, I stand guilty, and I'm *proud* of it.**

For the record, the original idea for a "**World** Trade Center" in lower Manhattan is generally credited to David Rockefeller – *"**Pride** goeth before **destruction**, and an haughty spirit before a **fall**."* (Proverbs 16:18)

"LET NOT YOUR HEART BE TROUBLED"

A major part of the spiritual blindness in our time is a lingering optimism that secular patriotic conservatives will be able to save America from the "bad guys." After all, everyone knows that *country* music is better than *rock* music, right? Unfortunately, however, the only choices that exist today are between "bad guys" and "*bad* good guys"; like "Dexter," the action figure doll based on the TV show of the same name, featuring a "good" serial killer who kills "bad" serial killers. (The "*bad* good guy" paradox is also a perfect depiction of a typical "*TR* Man.") For example, Sean Hannity of *Fox News* proudly testifies (and believes) that he is a "*Roman Catholic* Christian" (i.e., "square circle"). And why *shouldn't* he, having received the "*right* hand of fellowship" from such Evangelical and Fundamentalist leaders as James Dobson and the late Jerry Falwell? Consequently, as one of the leading "subliminal messiahs" for the religious Right and tea partiers alike, the charismatic host of the *Sean Hannity Show* faithfully reassures his flock every night – "Let not your heart be troubled." Of course, the only problem is that these words are from the lips of our Lord Jesus Christ as found in John 14:1. Is this any less blasphemous than "Austin 3:16," when the rest of the verse says, *"ye believe in God, believe also in me"*? (For the record, as prefigured by *Deborah* and prophesied by *Isaiah*, confused Americans in search of leadership today must *also* include an array of "bad good *girls*," running the gamut from Sarah Palin and Ann Coulter to Carrie Prejean.)

Bill O'Reilly, the tough-talking creator of the "No Spin Zone," is another loyal son of Rome. In his book, *A Bold Piece of Humanity*, Bill credits his third-grade nun, Sister Mary Lurana, as being one of the major players in his life. The "folksy" Glenn Beck (a recovering alcoholic) would have made it a Catholic trinity, but he jumped ship to become a *Mormon*. (Beck's confrontation with the "Reverend" Al Sharpton at the Washington Mall on August 28, 2010, was *the* quintessential illustration of "*bad* good guys" vs. "bad guys".) Then, by virtue of Dr. Falwell's lingering influence of compromised pragmatism (i.e., *The Moral Majority*), blood-bought, born-again Baptists are supposed to be "encouraged" by the fact that four of the *six Roman Catholics* on the Supreme Court consistently vote conservatively, especially Chief Justice Roberts. (Boy, do *I* ever feel relieved, particularly given Rome's 1,500-year track record involving tolerance of "hate crimes," as documented in *Foxe's Book of Martyrs*.)

Karl Christian Rove was Senior Advisor and Deputy Chief of Staff for President George W. Bush for seven years. *Fox News* consistently touts Rove as their number one political pundit. Does anyone remember that his relationship with Bush rivaled the nefarious team of "Colonel" Edward Mandel House and President Woodrow Wilson? Does anyone remember that the record GOP spending under Bush was so bad that Obama literally became "Dubya's" legacy? For instance, while *Fox* jumped on the $144,541 Obama stimulus grant to Wake Forest University to study monkeys on cocaine, some of us can *still* recall the exaggerated American-led "coalition" in "Operation Iraqi Freedom" that included 2,000 Moroccan monkeys to help detonate land mines. The fact that Rove can be given such a positive "spin" so quickly can only be understood as an accelerated fulfillment of Ecclesiastes 1:11 – *"There is no remembrance of former things."*

Former Speaker of the House Newt Gingrich is viewed by many Republican insiders as a leading presidential hopeful for 2012. One of the sharpest critics of Bill Clinton's immorality, Newt has experienced a few "bad days" himself. At age sixteen, he began secretly dating his high school geometry teacher, Jackie Battley, marrying her three years later. After a marriage of nearly twenty years, resulting in two daughters, Newt set his eyes on Marianne Ginther. According to Battley, while she was in the hospital recovering from cancer surgery her husband "stopped by" to discuss the details of their divorce. Then, after fifteen years of marriage with Marianne, Newt the narcissist began an adulterous relationship with staffer Callista Bisek, 23 years his junior (which continued throughout President Clinton's impeachment proceedings). Newt divorced Marianne in 1999, marrying Callista the following year. Given the spirit of the age, the liberal Southern Baptist *quickly* converted to the faith of his Roman Catholic bride. "Their" latest project is hosting the propaganda documentary "Nine Days That Changed the World," promoting the ministry of Jack Schaap's buddy, the late, "great" Pope John Paul II.

If a poll were taken among serious conservatives, Dr. Ron Paul would be the most popular candidate of all. Ironically, however, his strength is considered to be his main liability; he's so "right on the money," *literally* (gold standard, balanced budget, etc.), that he could never be elected by a sizable majority. In a 2007 interview with John Stossel, the "professing" Christian said that he was in favor of "gay marriage." On March 13, 2009, Congressman Paul appeared on *Larry King Live* for a debate with Hollywood actor, Stephen Baldwin. (The loud-mouth, Catholic liberal Joy Behar was Larry's substitute host that evening.) The topic was whether marijuana should be legalized. Now take a deep breath – the *heathen* Baldwin argued *against*, while the *libertarian* Paul – "your friend and mine" – argued *for*. (Why, even "Slick Willy" knew better than that!) Finally, Dr. Paul *really* shocked his GOP constituents on August 19, 2010, by coming out in *favor* of the mosque at Ground Zero, labeling the opposition as "Hate."

Then, we have Mr. Rush Limbaugh, the "inspiration" for one of my favorite myth-busting, reality-check illustrations ever. On June 5, 2010, Limbaugh paid *Sir Elton John $1,000,000 to perform during the reception of his fourth wedding* (to Kathryn Rogers). Now, how could *anyone* find a *freakier* "Odd Couple" than *El Rushbo* – the legendary *ultra*-conservative radio talk show commentator and decades-long standard bearer for old-time American values – and the iconic sodomite – *Rocket Man* himself? (By the grace of God, I had this phony's number *years* ago, as documented on pages 222-253 of *How Satan Turned America Against God*.) Back from his honeymoon, Rush was *so* "ecstatic" (*his* word) that he devoted fifteen minutes of air time to a glowing recap of the controversial gig (i.e., "damage control" with the "ditto heads"). The bottom line was that *Kathryn* had made booking the filthy sodomite her number one goal for the big day, and Rush, the self-proclaimed "harmless little fuzzball" (as well as a *three*-time loser already), was not *about* to frustrate her fantasy (Genesis 3:12).

According to Rush, his big opportunity came when he and Kathryn checked in to the Kahala Hotel & Resort on the island of Oahu and were told that Elton John was staying in the suite directly above them. (And, if you can believe it, Barak Obama was also in town at that time.) Realizing that "he who hesitates is lost," Rush stepped out onto the patio deck and started serenading Elton with his own material ("Little Jeanie," etc.). He then had Kathryn send her hero a quick note through the hotel manager. However, their plotting was abruptly interrupted when Rush suffered a mysterious "medical emergency" serious enough to keep him hospitalized for a few days. (Hey, Rush! Like – *duh!* Remember when your hearing went out after you slandered the book of Revelation?) After his release (and the doctors *still* don't know what took him out), he discovered that Elton had been "touched" by it all and would be only too happy to perform at their reception.

In a private ice-breaker before the concert, *Elton* and *El* Rushbo embraced in a warm ceremonial hug (a real *rush* for EJ). The British rocker then went on to play 13 numbers (how appropriate) and received almost as many standing ovations from the 400-plus "conservative" guests in attendance. The highlight of the evening was when Elton addressed the 800-pound gorilla in the room, "You might be surprised to see me here...I want to build bridges... I don't want to erect walls." (Of course, that *million-dollar check* can buy a lot of cement, no matter *what* you build, etc.) His encore was "Can You Feel The Love Tonight?" The only downer was that David Furnish, Elton's own "husband" (*civil partner* in the UK), was unable to share in the historic rapprochement. However, he did comment afterwards, "We have to *bring the world together*, not apart." (Spoken like a true disciple of David Rockefeller.)

As the *EIB* network prides itself on insightful *analysis* of all things conservative, let *me* give *you* some parting perspective on *why* the controversial "Army of One" was willing to "come out of his *own* closet" to *openly* abandon "Don't ask, don't tell" so everyone could enjoy "Benny and the Jets." For years Rush has been labeled the most "polarizing" figure in American politics and the undisputed leader of the "fringe element" within the Republican Party. By hiring that sodomite, Rush sent an important signal. You see, he really *is* a "harmless fuzzball," after all (i.e., he's got feelings like anyone else). Rush is an unsaved version of the Laodicean Christian who wants to keep reproach to a minimum. While he doesn't mind drawing a line in the sand regarding the basics (taxes, Obama, Pelosi, etc.), he has now made an open break with the "moral police." As evidenced by the increasing use of jungle music on his show, Rush will now appear more as the "Doctor of Democracy," limiting his money-making influence to *fiscal* conservatism only.

To the shock of numerous (and *stupid*) "Christian ditto heads," many of the lieutenants within the new "*Pragmatic* Majority" followed Limbaugh's lead practically overnight. On August 7, word leaked out that Ann Coulter, the "Queen of Conservatism," would be headlining "Homocon 2010" in New York City, on September 25 – the first annual convention of "conservative" sodomites. "We wanted to have a fun party, and we couldn't think of anyone more fun than Ann," said Jimmy LaSalvia, president of

GOProud, a group of "funny" Republicans who promote "same-sex marriage" and "gays" in the military. A promotional poster labeling Coulter as "the rightwing Judy Garland" declares: "Our gays are more macho than their straights." Then, only five days later, Bill O'Reilly asked Glenn Beck, "Do *you* believe that gay marriage is a threat to the country IN ANY WAY?" The "patriotic" Mormon "family man" answered, "NO, I DON'T," adding, "I think we've got bigger fish to fry." (For the record, if Beck doesn't replace Moroni with Jesus – *he'll* be the one *frying* – along with "Joey" Smith; Donnie and Marie; the Marriotts; "Reverend" Eldridge; Butch Cassidy; Ted Bundy; the Mormon Tabernacle Choir; and all the *rest* of those Christ-rejecting infidels!) Even the "No Spin Zone" host *acted* startled, replying, "That's interesting, because I don't think a lot of people understand that about you." (Well, DUH!) The sodomite magazine, *Washington Blade*, summed things up, stating: "...conservatives have taken the leadership role in achieving marriage equality." (Meanwhile, back at the ranch, Barak Obama's "official" position remains, "I do not support gay marriage. Marriage has religious and social connotations, and I consider marriage to be between a man and a woman.")

The fact that the majority of *normal* Americans are totally clueless as to the depth of depravity that is practiced in the sodomite community remains entirely irrelevant. (Any "straight" policeman or emergency room attendant can provide the *revolting* details.) In a related paradox, one *could* say that the Devil's crowd has been able to keep the entire movement "under the radar" by exploiting a single *Christian* teaching – *"For it is a shame even to speak of those things which are done of them in secret."* (Ephesians 5:12)

As the fire and brimstone that fell in Genesis 19 reveals, the sin of sodomy rates right behind the perversion described in Genesis 6. Next to our abandoning of Israel, the growing acceptance of the so-called "gay" agenda is probably the second greatest cause for God's escalating judgment on America. However, the good news is that such decadence is another clear sign that the Rapture is just about here (Luke 17:28-30). And "just one more thing" (as my old

hero, Lieutenant Colombo, used to say), the next time you hear
Rush yelling about "feminazis," *why* – don't you believe a *word*
of it – he's just as "hen-pecked" as Todd Palin. While Kathryn may
be a direct descendant of John Adams, she is every bit a picture of
modern-day feminism as Kim Winslow, the first female referee to
enter the octagon in UFC history.

A LITTLE "ROCK" FROM LITTLE ROCK

No survey of our "conservative saviors" would be complete
without a reference to former Arkansas governor, Mike Huckabee.
If *this* guy's resumé is taken seriously, he belongs in a category all
by himself. While Bill O'Reilly graduated from *Marist College* in
Poughkeepsie, New York, established in 1905 by the Marist Brothers
(a Roman Catholic order founded in France by "Saint" Marcellin),
Huckabee earned *his* bachelor's degree in religion from *Ouachita
Baptist University* in Arkadelphia, Arkansas. He then earned his
MA at *Southwestern Baptist Theological Seminary* in Fort Worth,
Texas (founded three years after *Marist College* by Baptist patriarchs
Dr. B. H. Carroll and Dr. J. Frank Norris). While Glenn Beck was
in Utah "coping with Dr. Jack Daniels" (as he has stated), and Sean
Hannity was tending bar and working as a general contractor in
Santa Barbara, California, *Pastor* Huckabee was busy overseeing
Baptist congregations in the Bible Belt – *Beech Street Baptist Church*
in Texarkana (1980-1986) and *Immanuel Baptist Church* in Pine Bluff
(1986-1992). Before Rush ever "founded" the mythical *Limbaugh
Institute for Advanced Conservative Studies*, Dr. Mike Huckabee
was president of the *Arkansas Baptist Convention* (1989-1991).

The bottom line in all of this is that Michael Huckabee is *the*
guy who *should* be closer to the truth than any of his colleagues
(John 17:17). Surely, if *anyone* was qualified to be president it
would have to be "Brother Mike." Former "Texas Ranger," Chuck
Norris, now a "devout Christian," wrote in 2007: "I believe the
only one who has all the characteristics to lead America forward into
the future is ex-Arkansas Governor Mike Huckabee." But, here is

where it all breaks down; the truth is to whatever degree the "preacher's" resumé *is* taken seriously – he would be the *last* man that anyone should trust! This assessment is based on a simple question – What exactly led Mike Huckabee to assume those two pastorates? There are only two possible answers for the *ordained* Baptist minister – either he *was* divinely called, or he was *not*. As I am not aware of any concession regarding the latter, the most pertinent Scripture that will forever define the "charming" host of *Huckabee* is Romans 11:29 – *"For the gifts and calling of God are **without repentance.**" If* God ever calls a man into the ministry, that call is *never* retracted. While the *man* himself may be called home early, the Lord will never "recall the call" *from* the man (I Kings 13:24).

Now this leaves Mikey in a "Catch-22," for if he *was* called – then *why* did he step *down* to become Governor of Arkansas, and if he was *not* called – *why* did he pretend to be something he was not for twelve long years? Mike Huckabee is *the* personification of the lukewarm Laodicean Christian described in Revelation 3:15, *"I know thy works, that thou art neither cold nor hot: I would thou wert cold or hot."* If you want to know what this guy is *really* all about, just check out what he does with his "free time." In II Timothy 3:4, Paul described end-day apostates as being *"lovers of pleasures more than lovers of God."* Soon after becoming governor, Huckabee formed a rock band with seven members of his executive staff. The name *Capitol Offense* was chosen because they all worked at the Capitol, and, according to Mike, "In the course of our playing we offend just about everybody."

After a failed bid for the White House in 2008, Mike reappeared on the *Fox* network to host his own weekend show, *Huckabee*. As the format developed, he would end each program by personally jamming with guest musicians, working in various *Fox* employees as an added novelty (known as the "Little Rockers"). At first, the only thing that "offended" *me* was how down-right *hokey* it all appeared: the balding former governor "rocking it out" in a suit and tie with a semi-mediocre hodgepodge of Blue Grass-Country-

Christian-Patriotic numbers to a comatose audience of Lawrence Welk holdovers. (Having attended many rock concerts in my own heathen days, including the Rolling Stones, believe me – I *know* "corny" when I see it.) And then we have that verse in I Corinthians 13:11 – *"when I became a man, I put away childish things."* However, my antenna suddenly shot up one evening when I caught Mike *really* "kicking it" as he played "Sweet Home Alabama" with the legendary Southern rock band, *Lynyrd Skynyrd,* led by the tattooed, long-haired, cross-wearing Gary Rossington.

With my curiosity piqued, the more I researched the history of *Capitol Offense,* the more "offended" I became. Their first performance was at the governor's staff Christmas party in 1996. *Less than six years after resigning the pulpit at Immanuel Baptist Church –* "ex-pastor" Huckabee began his professional music career with the following *three*-song set: "Rock and Roll Music" by the Hammite deviant and ex-con, Chuck "Duck Walk" Berry; Barnett Strong's "Money – That's What I Want"; and David Rockefeller's favorite theme, "Come Together" by the Beatles. According to Mike, Paul McCartney was his primary inspiration from youth, often stating that "music was life changing for me."

It only gets worse from here. Apparently, *Capitol Offense* has done pretty well for being just a bunch of conservative, "semi-Christian" good ol' boys from the hills of Arkansas. They have opened for such headliners as Percy Sledge, *The Charlie Daniels Band*, Willie Nelson, *38 Special*, and *Grand Funk Railroad*. In an interview with Lisa Ryan of *CBN*, Mike bragged that they had even performed for Dionne Warwick (former host of the *Psychic Friends Network*, currently living in Brazil with a $2,185,901.08 U.S. tax liability). He also told Lisa, "I got to play with *Grand Funk Railroad*; that was a trip." (I can *still* remember the "trip" I was on at the 1969 Atlantic City Pop Festival when I heard *Grand Funk Railroad* "play" under a mushroom cloud of "Paul's pot.")

In September 2004 Huckabee's group entertained for the Republican Governors Association festivities at Brooklyn's Fulton Landing. *The New York Times* quoted Mike as saying, "Some of you are going to have to lose some jackets and loosen up," adding, "We want you to prove today that Republicans can rock." The following January, *Capitol Offense* performed at the Free Republic Inaugural Ball for President George W. Bush. (G. W. was not as musically inclined as his predecessor, Bill Clinton, another Southern Baptist former Arkansas governor, who played the sax at his own inauguration to the tune of "Your Mama Don't Dance and Your Daddy Don't Rock and Roll.") Their three-hour set included hits by *Creedence Clearwater Revival*, the *Animals*, the *Eagles*, and the *Rolling Stones*. In an interview with Don Imus, Mike listed "Purple Haze" (by the departed "African-American" doper, Jimmy Hendricks) as one of his all-time personal favorites.

On the band's *MySpace* page, fans are encouraged to register their own requests under the heading, "What songs should Capitol Offense play?" As of this writing, a sample of their featured "hits" included: "Honky Tonk Women" (a song about *whores*); "House of the Rising Sun" (a song about a *whore* house); "Mustang Sally" (a term for crack *whores*); "Devil With A Blue Dress On" (*Duh*); "Born to be Wild" (take a *wild* guess); "Midnight Hour" (guess again...) "Louie Louie" (one of the *most* disreputable songs in rock-and-roll history). Other "classics" include "Jailhouse Rock"; "Ain't Too Proud to Beg"; "Roll Over Beethoven"; "Takin' Care of Business"; and "A Whiter Shade of Pale."

Thankfully, however, there is *some* "good" news to report concerning Mr. Huckabee. When asked by *Newsweek's* Holly Bailey during the *CNN*/YouTube presidential debate – "Do you believe the Bible is inerrant?" – "Brother" Mike replied, unashamedly, "I believe it is." My only response to this statement would be that it has a particular relevance to the title of that last song listed above. While the meaning behind the nonsensical lyrics of *this* dope-era tune by *Procol Harum* continues to be debated by fans, there is a partial consensus that when the characters in the song find themselves on the verge of *vomiting* – their faces "turn a whiter shade of pale." As the Scripture implies in Revelation 3:16, the caliber of "Christianity" that could mix "Honky Tonk Women" with biblical inerrancy makes

God puke: *"So then because thou art lukewarm, and neither cold nor hot, I **will spue thee out of my mouth**."*

Furthermore, on the basis of our Lord's preference – *"I would thou wert **cold** or hot"* – I'm afraid that if push ever came to shove, I would have to vote for the Democratic pornographer Alvin Greene over a professing Christian who spurns *"the **offence** of the cross."* (Galatians 5:11) For, as "sick" as this spiritual reasoning sounds, at least you know where you stand with the "Stone *Cold"* Steve Austins of this world; it's the *lukewarm* Laodicean wackos holding up the John 3:16 signs that you have to keep your eyes on! (Ditto: Umar Farouk Abdulmutallab, alias Umar Abdul Mutallab and Omar Farooq al-Nigeri a.k.a. "The Underwear Bomber"; and, Timmy "Tighty Whitey" Tebow.)

> "The wicked return to the grave,
> all the nations that forget God."
>
> (PSALM 9:17 NIV)

> *"The wicked shall be turned into hell,*
> *and all the nations that forget God."*
>
> (PSALM 9:17 KJV)

14

BN, BO, BP & "The BOP"

HE GREATEST "FRUIT" of Westcott and Hort's Revised
Version would have to be the 2008 Presidential election.
Talk about God sending a recalcitrant people *"strong
delusion that they should believe a lie"* – in the middle of America's
so-called "War on Terrorism," with two hot wars being fought
simultaneously in two Islamic countries – an anti-Semitic closet
Muslim with three Middle Eastern names is elected to the White
House! *Go figure.* (The only silver lining in the whole nightmare
is the knowledge that Mr. Obama "got in" *solely* by the sovereign
will of God as an instrument of divine judgment, reflecting how *low*
this wicked nation has fallen.) With America having rejected the
scriptural admonition in Proverbs 24:21 to *"meddle not with them that
are given to **change,"*** the handwriting was on the wall as early as
inauguration week. The festivities kicked off on *Sunday*, January 14,
2009, with a gala "We Are One" *rock concert* at the Lincoln Memorial
(taking precedence over "Church"). Headliners included Beyoncé,
Bono, Stevie Wonder, Sheryl Crow, Garth Brooks, and Mr. Patriotism
himself, Bruce Springsteen – a.k.a. "The Boss." So-called "historical
readings" were given by Jamie Foxx, Denzel Washington, Martin
Luther King III, and the "incomparable" Queen Latifah.

However, because it was the Lord's Day, an opening "prayer"
was in order. After batting *0* for *1* in the ministerial department
with "Reverend" Jeremiah Wright damning America in God's name,
Obama's next pick was the "Right Reverend" Gene Robinson, New
Hampshire's first openly *sodomite* Episcopal Bishop. As Obama

promised "change," let the record state that HIS ADMINISTRATION WAS THE FIRST IN AMERICAN HISTORY TO FORMALLY INVOKE THE BLESSING OF *LUCIFER* UPON OUR BELEAGUERED NATION! Robinson's petition began with the words, "O God of our many understandings." With those six memorable words, the filthy pervert invoked the god of the *Buddhists*, the god of the *Muslims*, the "gods" of the *Hindus*, and *the* god of the *Satanists*. Such blasphemous proceedings were anticipated by Paul's words in I Corinthians 10:20 – *"But I say, that the things which the Gentiles sacrifice, **they sacrifice to devils, and not to God**: and I would not that ye should have fellowship with devils."*

The inauguration ceremony the following Tuesday was filled with insightful imagery for those who *"have their senses exercised to discern both good and evil."* (Hebrews 5:14) This time the invocation was given by an evangelical apostate, the *lukewarm* Rick Warren (again, far more dangerous than the *limp-wrist* Gene Robinson). The national anthem followed, sung by *"The Queen of Soul,"* Aretha Franklin. This was only "fitting," as she had helped to draw a crowd when Barak campaigned in Detroit, whereupon the grateful politician started singing – "Chain, Chain, Chain… *Chain of Fools*…." (How appropriate, considering the electorate that went on to vote for "Change, Change, Change…*Change of Fools*," etc.) Next came the swearing-in of our Roman Catholic Vice President, Joe Biden, by our Roman Catholic Chief Justice, John Roberts.

The "highlight" of the affair was the distinct *possibility* that a *foreign-born usurper* was sworn into the highest office of the land, contrary to Article Two, Section One, of the United States Constitution. (Having campaigned on "openness," Mr. Obama has *yet* to surrender, among other pertinent documents – his *long-form birth certificate*, his U.S. passport, his medical records, his school records, his Illinois Bar Association records, his Illinois state representative records, etc. – while *conversely* misappropriating well over $1.5 million for legal expenses to block their release; thus, putting a *serious* "hold" on Romans 13:7.)

After Yo-Yo Ma and company finished "lip synching" their instrumental gig, the First Lady Elect held out Abraham Lincoln's 1861 inauguration Bible (Authorized Version). Then, with everyone holding their breath, *Barak Hussein Obama* placed his unworthy hand on the Holy word of the living God. What happened next was truly remarkable (as well as an omen of the future). The intellectual Roman Catholic Chief Justice and the articulate Muslim President *stumbled through the thirty-second ceremony, making three mistakes in 35 words*! The same God who confounded the speech at the "Tower of Babel" did it *again* at the "Inauguration of Barak." The prevailing *confusion* led presidential lawyers to strongly recommend a "re-do," which took place the following evening in a private ceremony in the White House Map Room. However, this time there was *no* Bible involved, as Abe's copy was safely back at the Smithsonian and, apparently, no one had thought to bring another. Obviously, the God of Israel was not *about* to let America's first Muslim president be sworn into office on the Holy Bible – *period*.

Obama's third "preacher" of choice, the racist agitator "Reverend" Joseph Lowery, brought the dramatic benediction. The close of Joe's "prayer" was a reprehensible insult to every white man in the United States of America: "Lord, we ask you to help us work for that day when *black* will not be asked to get *back*; when *brown* can stick *around*; when *yellow* will be *mellow*; when the *red man* can get *ahead, man*; **and when *white* will embrace what is *right*...** Amen!" The new president (whose *mama* was white) smiled and nodded approvingly. Within hours of that fiasco, the Lord added His own "Amen" – two of the most liberal senators in Washington having to be *carried* out of the inaugural luncheon – Ted Kennedy, with a seizure, and Robert Byrd, with digestion complications (both of whom would die before mid-term elections). In retrospect, no wonder our *last* super-patriot, Senator Jessie Helms of North Carolina, was called home to Glory on July 4, 2008 – the *last* Fourth of July *before* America "changed" *forever*!

There would be many "changes" throughout the Obama years, for sure (like there will be under the Antichrist, according to Daniel 7:25).

For example, at the *first* State of the Union address on January 27, 2010, over 175 years of USMC tradition was *trashed* as the "Commander-in-Chief" expressed his disdain for "Hail to the Chief," preferring a piano bar solo of *Sting's* Arab melody, "Desert Rose," instead. Then, there was that *first* "bas'etball" court in the White House. The United States would "change" from *capitalism* to *socialism* with "Obama Care." His successful appointment of the Jewish *closet* sodomite, Elena Kagan, to the Supreme Court brought about a *really* significant "change" – the *first* time in American history that the highest court in the land would be void of *any* Protestants (their diminished, token status notwithstanding). Our quagmire in Afghanistan became the longest war in American history on Obama's watch, another "change" from his campaign promises to "bring the troops home," etc.

Our national security would also experience serious "change." When I was a year old (1953), an American couple, Julius and Ethel Rosenberg, were electrocuted in Sing Sing Prison, New York, for passing atomic secrets to the former Soviet Union. On June 27, 2010, *ten* Russian spies were arrested in four states for spying on the United States for a decade. (The bust occurred only three days after Obama and Russian President Dmitry Medvedev, a Putin puppet, held their "Hamburger Summit" photo-op at Barak's favorite gourmet joint in Arlington, Virginia.) On July 8, the ten secret agents were sent back to "*Meshech*," having been sentenced to "time served" (*eleven* days). According to the *Associated Press*, "The spies left for Moscow *hours* after pleading guilty to conspiracy in a Manhattan courtroom...." A conspicuous media blackout, *including* our "friends" at *Fox News* has prevailed from the outset. (Less than a month later, Michigan Congressman Mike Rogers recommended *execution* as an appropriate punishment for Pfc. Bradley Manning if he was to be found guilty of passing classified military documents to the online whistleblower site *WikiLeaks*, stating: "If *that's* not a *capital* offense, I don't know what is.")

A major "change" in NASA was signaled when Charles Bolden, the agency's first "African-American" administrator, told an *Al Jazeera* correspondent that his "foremost" mission as the head of America's space exploration agency was to improve relations with the people of the "Crescent Moon." An Obama appointee, Charlie made it clear that his boss wanted Muslims "to feel good about their historic contributions to science and math and engineering." Obama also installed "*Egyptian*-American" Ahmed Zewail and "*Algerian*-American" Elias Zerhouni as our first "Science Envoys" to the Middle East, whatever *that* means. (Neil Armstrong – Where are you when we need you?)

Given all the "Islamaphobia" (being generated by all the "Obamaphobia") another "change" occurred on August 19, 2010, when "person of color" Deputy White House Press Secretary Bill Burton issued the *first* formal clarification in American history that the president was *definitely* a "devout Christian…and prays every day" (i.e., "He's definitely *not* a devout Muslim who prays every day"). Five days later, "Zaytuna College" (located in liberal Berkley, California) opened its doors to become the *first* "accredited" institute of higher education in the nation that defines itself as "Moooslem." Founded by Imam Zaid Shakir, Shaykh Hamza Yusuf, and "Dr." Hatem Bazian, the school motto is "Where Islam meets America." One of the purported goals is to make Zaytuna the Islamic version of Notre Dame ("Touchdown Mohammed," etc.)

Concerning "Obamanomics," six months after that sodomite's "prayer" at the Lincoln Memorial, General Motors filed for bankruptcy. (You might want to check with places like Greece, Iceland, Spain, Portugal, and Ireland about that old saying, "As goes General Motors, so goes the world.") The national debt was "only" 40% of GDP in 2008. Since day *one* of the Obama administration the total figure itself has increased at a rate of $4.8 *billion* per *day*. On March 24, 2010, House Minority Leader John Boehner of Ohio made a startling prediction in an op-ed piece in the *Des Moines Register*: "Our national debt…is on track to exceed the size of our entire economy…in just two more years." This would mean that the entire country would be "under water." Thus, one more "change" that the "change" agent will likely make at the "change" of his administration is to leave us with nothing *but* "change."

"MAY DAY! MAY DAY! MAY DAY!"

Now, all *these* "changes" would rate as mere "*chump* change" when compared to what Mr. Barak Hussein Obama would eventually do to the State of Israel. Many Christians have begun to notice the astonishing cause-and-effect relationship between adverse U.S. policies against Israel followed by immediate divine repercussion. (To my knowledge, the first book to document this unfolding phenomenon was the 2002 release *Israel: The Blessing or the Curse* by John McTernan and Bill Koenig.) I incorporated twenty of these documented incidents in the first chapter of *How Satan Turned America Against God.* I then concluded the chapter with the following unequivocal warning: "If you're still undecided about standing with the Lord, just start watching the Weather Channel before retiring each night...Then pull those covers snugly against your chin. You won't have to worry about anything stirring out there in the dark—*until* the next mile marker is reached on the 'Road Map to Peace.' *Nighty-night!*"

The first printing of my book was in April 2005. That same month, Israeli Prime Minister Ariel Sharon, *under pressure* from President Bush, set a timetable for the highly controversial withdrawal of 25 contested Jewish "settlements" (21 in Gaza and 4 in the West Bank). On August 16, a force of 40,000 IDF troops began the unprecedented eviction of their *own* citizens, a blatant violation of Amos 9:15 – *"And I will plant them upon their land, **and they shall no more be pulled up out of their land** which I have given them, saith the LORD thy God."* The final holdouts in Gaza were forcibly removed on August 23, with the last of their counterparts in Samaria being ousted the following day. All told, approximately *10,000* Israelis became homeless within a week. Every building was leveled to the ground except for 21 synagogues and several huge vegetable greenhouses (the latter being left as a goodwill gesture, though both were immediately destroyed by the new "residents").

On August 24 – the very *day* the last Jew in Samaria was evicted – Tropical Depression *Twelve* (the number of Israel) formed over the Bahamas and then upgraded to a tropical storm named *Katrina* (meaning "to purify"). By August 29 Katrina had intensified into a Category 5 (the number of death) *hurricane*, smashing ashore with a tidal surge of nearly 35 feet (the highest ever recorded). The rest is history: Over 1,700 killed; 500,000 homes destroyed or seriously damaged; costs in excess of $100 billion; and *1.3 million* "homeless" *Americans*! (That's a ratio of 130 to 1.)

So, what does "Barry" Obama do in the face of this surreal object lesson? On March 23, 2010, the day before Senator Boehner's prediction regarding America going under water, our "President" initiated the most egregious diplomatic snub in the history of U.S.-Israeli relations. Having arrived at the White House on an official state visit, Israeli Prime Minister Benjamin Netanyahu was unceremoniously slipped *in* through a *side* door and later sent *out* through a *back* door with *no* photographs allowed. However, what took place inside Obama's "crib" just may have "changed" our nation's destiny *forever*.

Once again, *our* "problem" with Israel has to do with *their* covenant homeland; this time, the amount of settlements *we* feel *they* can build in *their* capital city. (Now *that's* a "*capital* offense.") When their tense negotiations stalled, Obama rose from his chair and tersely informed America's number one ally in the Middle East – "I'm going to the residential wing to have dinner with Michelle and the girls." (Roughly translated, his parting remarks equated to "Consider the error of your ways," etc.) Such treatment is without historical precedent. Not even Israel's accidental attack on the USS *Liberty* in 1967 (resulting in 204 total casualties) could evoke a negative response from then-President Johnson. As Mr. Netanyahu was unmoved when Barak returned *over an hour later*, the "Road Map" was in obvious trouble. (Incidentally, regarding that *Jewish* key in Revelation 3:7, "Bibi" Netanyahu just "happens" to be a graduate of Cheltenham High School, located in Cheltenham, Pennsylvania – a suburb of PHILADELPHIA; though the seventeen-year-old missed his June 7, 1967, commencement, having returned to Israel to fight in the Six-Day War with his elite special forces unit, the *Sayeret Matkal*.)

Initially, the Lord appeared to "clear His throat" with those two apocalyptic volcano eruptions at Eyjafjallajökull glacier near Kirkjubæjarklaustur, Iceland; but this was merely the preliminaries. Back in Zion, the disgraced prime minister spent April 19 with his fellow countrymen celebrating Israel's sixty-second birthday as a nation. (Similar to Passover and Yom Kippur, Israelis recognize their Independence Day according to the lunar calendar, causing the annual date to fluctuate.) As only the Lord can arrange such matters, that same evening *Fox News* issued a stunning article entitled "Obama and Israel: Showdown at the UN?" (The content of which would directly involve Susan Rice, Barak's "African-American" UN Ambassador). An excerpt follows:

> The Obama administration is reportedly signaling another major shift in policy towards one of its staunchest allies, Israel, and this shift could change the way it votes at the Security Council. The change would mean an end to the US' use of its veto power in the United Nations Security Council when certain anti-Israel resolutions are introduced for a vote.

> Reports surfaced a couple of weeks ago, that a senior US diplomat met with Qatar's foreign minister in Paris. They discussed the possibility that the US was giving serious consideration to not using its veto if a vote on Israeli settlements was to come up. It has been the policy of successive administrations to veto virtually all anti-Israel resolutions at the Security Council....Anne Bayefsky is a senior fellow at the Hudson Institute and Touro College and says **the administration, like none other before them, appears prepared to blackmail Israel at the UN**.

Well, what do you suppose happened next? As that "snub heard 'round the world" would ultimately relate to our suicidal addiction to Muslim oil from the *Persian* Gulf – *America's* Gulf oil "spill" began *the very next day* with the catastrophic explosion of the *British Petroleum* Deepwater Horizon offshore drilling rig. Similar to the September 11 terrorist attacks, the incineration of *eleven* workers (whose bodies were never recovered) would represent a subtle reminder that America was in *crisis* mode once again (the repeated *"May* Day" calls only adding to the macabre imagery of the number *five*). Billy Nungesser, president of Plaquemines Parish, Louisiana, would tell *CNN*, "This oil spill is 100 times worse than Katrina." (For those who can *"see his days,"* that innocuous political term "parish" is a *another* reminder that the target zone for these back-to-back judgments is the Vatican's historic stronghold in the Bible Belt – not to mention the voodoo-practicing, race-mixing, African music-generating debauchery capital of the nation, as epitomized by the annual satanic *Mardi Gras* perversion in the "Big Easy.")

Built in 2001 at a cost of $350 million, the Deepwater Horizon semi-submersible mobile offshore drilling rig had dug the deepest well in human history, going to a depth of 35,000 feet. As Hurricane Katrina had a fixed timeline tracing *back* to a tropical depression, the BP explosion had a similar "paper trail." In a dramatic *60 Minutes* episode entitled "The Deepwater Horizon Disaster," Scott Pelley conducted an exclusive interview with Mike Williams, the chief electronics technician on the platform, and one of the last men to escape the inferno. According to Williams, the disaster was ultimately linked to a critical *preliminary* accident that involved the blowout preventer (BOP). The BOP is a large valve or series of valves (standing 53 feet tall and weighing 325 tons) designed to seal off the well whenever necessary, especially in an emergency. Situated on the seabed, it is the single-most important safety feature for both the workers and the natural environment.

Williams told *60 Minutes* that the initial mishap occurred after a worker accidently nudged a control lever when the BOP was *closed*, resulting in hundreds of thousands of pounds of pressure *forcing* 15 feet of drill pipe *through* the *sealed* apparatus. The large rubber gasket (called an *annular*) was shredded in the process. Handfuls of rubbery chunks were recovered topside and reported to officials. However, the damage was never properly repaired and the BOP subsequently failed on April 20.

The relevance of this calamity to our overall thesis concerning Israel has to do with the actual date that it occurred. According to Williams "...the accident happened *four* weeks before the explosion." Now, we certainly realize that the words "four weeks" could mean a *rough* "four weeks" (i.e., give-or-take a day or two on either side). However, the amazing observation to make is that counting back *four* Tuesdays from April 20 brings us to March 23 – the *exact* day that Mr. Obama *intentionally* activated his *own* "control lever," treacherously ramming fifteen feet of pipe through *America's* "Blow Out Preventer" – THE GOD-GIVEN BLESSING AND SECURITY AFFORDED *ANY* NATION THAT WOULD BEFRIEND THE "APPLE OF HIS EYE" (Zechariah 2:8).

Do you suppose that Mr. Obama and his Communist cronies know anything about the holy Judeo-Christian heritage of our once-great land? Do you recall that *Jewish* key to the *Gentile* door in the Church at Philadelphia? Well, about two months after *How Satan Turned America Against God* was published, I read an intriguing article in the April 15, 2005, issue of *The Jewish Forward*, the oldest Jewish newspaper in America. (It was sent to me by Bob Militello, a preacher friend and editor of *The Righteous Gentile* newsletter.) The article chronicled the brief life of the Jewish poet, Emma Lazarus (previously mentioned as the author of "The New Colossus"). If you want to know where America is presently headed, consider the following two lines about the woman whose writings adorn the Statue of Liberty: "In her early work, Lazarus worried that the United States had no past and the Jews had no future. She came to resolve this dilemma by claiming that it was the singular destiny of the United States to secure the fate of the Jews." (This is what that expression, "America's *Bible* Belt became Israel's *Safety* Belt," means.)

While April 19 has been shown to have great significance in 2010 as Israel's sixty-second birthday, the *Fox News* article concerning U.S. policy at the UN, and the eve of the historic "blowout" – it is also a date wrought with deep spiritual import for America. It was on April 19, 1783, that General George Washington assembled his army in New Windsor, New York, to announce a formal cessation of hostilities. This was exactly *eight* years to the day that the fighting began at Lexington and Concord. To recognize the hallowed occasion of America's "new beginning," Washington decreed that a special "prayer of thanksgiving" be offered to "The Almighty Ruler of the World." That prayer was made before 7,000 troops by the general's favorite preacher, John Gano, known as "The Fighting Chaplain," and founding pastor of the First Baptist Church of New York City.

As an *unbelievable* final illustration of the "Westcott and Hort Effect," a holiday poll that was taken on July 2, 2010, by Bill O'Reilly's alma mater, Marist College, asked the simple question: "From what country did the United States win its independence?" Of the 18-to-29-year-olds who participated, 40% did *not* know the answer! (Sadly, Baptists are just as ignorant of their *own* history; probably *less* than 40% ever having heard of John Gano.) Yet, on that same Friday (day 75 of the oil spill) the exciting announcement *was* made that "Lady Ga Ga" had beaten "President" Obama to the ten-million-"fans" mark on *Facebook* (though at that time she was *still* trailing the *late* Michael Jackson with his fourteen million followers).

Meanwhile, five days before the Deepwater Horizon got "bopped," Obama unveiled dramatic plans for a manned landing on an *asteroid* by 2025! However, as *Given By Inspiration* was nearing completion, the former *community organizer* was "up to his eyeballs in tar balls" just trying to *organize* the necessary clean-up in America's own "Dead Sea." (He would spend Day 100 of the oil spill taping an appearance on *The View*, constituting yet *another* "change," being the first sitting American president to appear on a daytime talk show, *and* one of the *tackiest* to boot.)

It is estimated that 4.9 million barrels of oil (205 million gallons) ultimately spewed out of the ruptured well. And wouldn't you *just* know it – while everyone was asking later that summer where all the oil went – on August 7, 2010, the State of Israel announced the "miracle" discovery of a potential 1.5 billion barrels of oil near Rosh Ha Ayin, followed by a *second* announcement on August 29 of *another* 4.2 billion barrels *off the coast* of Haifa, making a total of 5.7 billion barrels, not to mention a potential 850 billion cubic meters of natural gas thrown in as a bonus!

While even the experts cannot project the final cost of the Gulf Coast disaster, the figure will surely accelerate the foreboding economic forecast that Senator Boehner made the day *before* Obama slam-dunked Mr. Netanyahu. Like those ever-encroaching oil slicks, America's day of fiscal reckoning is inevitable (regardless of how long it takes to transpire). Of the thousands of photographs that document the greatest oil spill in U.S. history, one in particular represents a prescient image regarding our nation "going under water." Posted on *Al.com*, the picture shows an American flag and a speckled crab lying side-by-side off-shore near the Bon Secour National Wildlife Refuge in Baldwin County, Alabama (you know, "Sweet Home Alabama"). Like the dead creature, "Old Glory" is encrusted with the thick, brown, goopy oil found hugging the sea floor. (Thus, from the *top* of Mount Suribachi to the *surface* of the Moon to the *bottom* of the Gulf of Mexico, it's – "*Change* you can believe in.")

SNEAK PREVIEW

An old adage says that "Truth is stranger than fiction." This means that Hollywood cannot begin to touch reality. Take the Tribulation, for instance – even Stephen Spielberg would be incapable of giving mankind a sneak preview of the horrors that will soon descend upon this planet. However, God, in His mercy, has done this very thing. In Revelation 16:3, we read: *"And the second angel poured out his vial upon the sea; and it became **as the blood of a dead man**: and every living soul died in the sea."* While living blood is bright red, blood that is out of the body turns reddish brown. *This is the very color of the oil that invaded the Gulf of Mexico in the aftermath of the Deepwater Horizon explosion.* In another allusion to Matthew 24:37, the oil itself was formed by the catastrophic sedimentation of human, animal, and plant matter resulting from the Flood; thus, we read in Job 26:5, *"Dead things are formed from under the waters."* Among the complex mixture of organic compounds in petroleum, *porphyrin* is one that is found in crude oil, as well as in plants and *blood*. Thus, in a rather macabre way – the gas you pump in your car *may* have come from your great, great, great...grandpa (i.e., *"the blood of a dead man"*). The dead marine life that dotted the coastlines of *five* states is a mere foretaste of that *ultimate* "environmental disaster" described in the apostle's words, *"and every living soul died in the sea."* And, as for *how* all of this may come about, bear in mind that there are nearly *seven hundred* off-shore oil rigs worldwide. Do you suppose that any one of the *five* major earthquakes described in the book of Revelation could cause a few more "spills"? (Perhaps a global oil shortage would also explain those *horses* in Ezekiel 38:15).

NUGGETS FROM THE "GEEK"

In closing, let me say that the only thing any scarier than *these* "changes" is the "spiritual" perspective of Fundamentalist, kingdom-building critics of the King James Bible like Dr. Jack Schaap, as reflected in the following sermon excerpt to his brain-dead congregation, August 2, **2009**:

> **I think he's a born-again Christian**, if you want to know the truth of the matter...**I'm kind of excited** about him getting into office....**I'm kind of looking forward to Mr. Obama. This is historic; I think it's wonderful**; I'm glad for him, glad for his family...I'm happy for them; I want them to enjoy it. He won, man, let him celebrate. **This is historic.**"

Then, after pooh-poohing all the "**negative** talk," he added: "Everybody's unhappy; ya' know, 'What's gonna happen? **What's gonna happen?**' – **Probably pretty much like last year**" (i.e., *no* "change"). Well, besides being a poor *prophet*, "Dr. Schaap" has also proven himself to be a poor *student* of the word of God, Proverbs 29:2 declaring: *"When the righteous are in authority, the people rejoice: **but when the wicked beareth rule, the people mourn.**"*

At 1:35 PM on Friday, July 30, 2010, Barak Hussein Obama was back in "Motown" touring a General Motors plant in Hamtramck, Michigan. *At that precise moment*, America's *first* formally approved Muslim prayer siren was *blaring* from the *Al Islah* Mosque just 3.19 miles away! How "picturesque" could you get, given Obama's statement to *The New York Times* on February 27, 2007 – **"The Muslim call to prayer is one of the *prettiest* sounds on earth..."**? According to *Times* reporter Nicholas Kristof, our "Christian president" recited the satanic *Adhan* flawlessly, in a first-class Arabic accent (a better job than he did when taking the oath of office). Two weeks later, while hosting his **Friday the 13th** *Ramadan* dinner at the White House, the "tone deaf" Obama *personally* endorsed the controversial mosque at Ground Zero, drawing the applause of his fellow rag-heads – despite nearly 70% opposition across the political spectrum. And then, to add insult to injury, the State Department announced the following Tuesday that Imam Feisal Abdul Rauf, executive director of the Cordoba Initiative, would be going on an all-expense-paid "goodwill" trip to Qatar, Bahrain, and the United Arab Emirates. (After all, a $500-million mosque could always use a little capitalistic fundraising, especially when the junket is being underwritten by the American taxpayers.)

For the record, *and solely by the grace of God*, Bible believers are generally privy to a greater "understanding" with regard to such matters. As Job put it, they are able to *"see his days."*

> "The God I serve isn't worried about *anything*!
> From *Osama* to *Obama*,
> He's got everything under control...."
>
> (*How Satan Turned America Against God*, 2005)

15

Gleaning in the Fields

𝕿HE PRESENT CHAPTER will serve as a final insightful illustration of the thesis of this book – the *fruit* of "inspiration" being an exclusive *understanding* of the *"word of truth,"* as preserved in the English text of the Authorized Version. In plainer words, as *"the **inspiration** of the Almighty giveth them **understanding**,"* the *ultimate* evidence of "inspiration" (traditionally limited to the process of creating autographs) will be the Spirit-led capacity to *recognize* the final authority of the A.V. 1611, *and* to *understand* its truths by employing the scriptural mandate of "right division." As *something* must ultimately account for the power of *that* "Book," that *something* might just as well be "inspiration." Thus, to a genuine Bible believer, the *Holy Scriptures* and the *King James Bible* are one and the same, for Ecclesiastes 8:4 reminds us that *"Where the **word** of a **king** is, there is **power**"* (Hebrews 4:12).

As established earlier, the disastrous conditions of the previous two chapters were anticipated in the Old Testament book of Judges. Like ancient Israel, the problem with end-day Christianity is a problem with *centralized* authority; i.e., with the *King James Bible* discredited in America, the average Laodicean Christian now uses *"that* [translation] *which* [is] *right in his own eyes."* Consequently, because *"the salt have lost his savour,"* the inhabitants of *our* land have chosen to allow *other* "kings" (alive *or* dead) to rule over them, as well, such as: Elvis Presley; Michael Jackson; James Brown; Budweiser; Pat's King of Steaks; King Kong; Martin Luther King, Jr.; The Lion King; Don King; B. B. King; Burger

King; Rodney King; Larry King; and, especially – "His Highness" LeBron James, a.k.a. "King James" himself. (And, for those who want it *both* ways, there's the *Holy Bible: Martin Luther King, Jr., Remembrance Edition*, King James Version, which includes King's biography, his *I Have a Dream* speech, and "Letter from Birmingham Jail.") Then, just as Jesus is the "*King* of kings," these *generic* "kings" are likewise installed by *their* sovereign – *King Apollyon* – ruler of the bottomless pit. (Matthew 5:13; Revelation 9:11; Luke 4:5-6)

However, there is a timely truth just beyond the anarchy described in Judges 21:25. When those twenty words comprising the *last* sentence in the book of *Judges* are compared to the twenty words comprising the *first* sentence in the book of *Ruth*, we note the amazing historical nexus between the two: *"Now it came to pass **in the days when the judges ruled**, that there was a famine in the land."* (Ruth 1:1) This observation is not without significance, as Ruth's original place in the Hebrew text was among the poetic books; the Holy Spirit repositioning it to the *historical* section in our *English* Bible (though not just *anywhere* within that twelve-book arrangement, but immediately *after* Judges). The important point to note is that the events recorded in Ruth occur during the time of the Judges. When this basic sequential context is considered in the light of chapter three of this book, the spiritual implications are astounding! While the book of *Judges* constitutes the greatest Old Testament picture of *Laodicean* apostasy – the book of *Ruth* is the greatest Old Testament picture of a *Philadelphia* remnant contending *for* the faith *within* Laodicea. Thus, the story of *Ruth* is as *beautiful* as the content of *Judges* is *barbaric*. Appropriately enough, "Ruth" means *friendship* (John 15:15).

Ruth is one of only two books in the Bible named after a woman (thirty-eight being named after men). While the Jewess *Esther* is a type of *Israel*, the restored Wife of Jehovah – the Gentile *Ruth* is a type of the *Church*, the espoused Bride of Christ. As the Church must pass the time of *her* betrothal on *earth*, we note that there are *four* letters in *Ruth's* name; *four* letters in the name of her spouse; *four* letters in the name of her son; and *four* chapters in the book itself, the opening scene in verse one depicting the *fourth* famine in Scripture. With a honeymoon cottage awaiting her in the *"New Jerusalem"* (not to mention her *new* life to follow), we also discern that Ruth is the *eighth* book in Scripture, the number of *new* beginnings. Thus, if you want to know *how* to serve God in the closing days of the Church Age – *Ruth is your pattern.*

There is so much spiritual imagery in the story that we can barely scratch the surface. Naomi pictures modern-day Israel, returning to her land after a bitter period of divine chastisement (1:13, 20-21). With *five* letters in *her* name, we find the *deaths* of her husband and sons recorded in verse *five*. As Luke 21:24 implies that *ultimate* "aliyah" (emigration) could only be realized *after "the times of the Gentiles be fulfilled,"* we note that Naomi reappears after a *ten-year* "sojourn" in a Gentile land – *ten* being the number of the *Gentiles.* (1:4) Next, Mahlon is a type of the Law, as his *death* freed Ruth to be *"married to another, even to him who is raised from the dead."* (Romans 7:4) With the Law described in Romans 8:3 as being *"weak through the flesh,"* we note that *Mahlon* means "sickly." Then, as *"a wild olive tree"* cannot *"partakest of the root and the fatness"* of the *natural* tree unless *"some of the branches be broken off,"* Naomi's entire line had to *die* so that Ruth the Moabitess could be *"graffed in."* (Romans 11:17)

The hero of our story makes his entrance in the opening verse of chapter two: *"And Naomi had a kinsman of her husband's, **a mighty man of wealth**, of the family of Elimelech; and his name was **Boaz**."* As a type of the Lord Jesus Christ, Boaz is a Judean *Jew*, from the tribe of *Judah*, who was born in *Bethlehem*. Within *one* verse of the mention of his *name*, the word "grace" appears; for as soon as Ruth "hears" of *him*, "faith" wells up in her heart, *inspiring* her to "believe" that *he* is surely the one *"in whose sight I shall find **grace**."* (2:2; Romans 10:17) Because *she* is seeking *him* (in the spirit of Hebrews 11:6), we find that amazing statement in the very next verse: *"and her **hap** was to light on a part of the field belonging unto Boaz"* ("hap" being Old English for "happened," i.e., *"**H**is **a**ppointed **p**lace"*; or as the Rabbis say, *"Coincidence is* not a kosher word"). As James 4:8 states, *"Draw nigh to God, and he will draw nigh to you,"* the *next* verse states, *"And, behold, **Boaz** came from Beth-lehem."* Ruth is then introduced to *"the **Lord** of the harvest"* by an *unnamed "servant,"* a beautiful type of the Holy Spirit. (2:5; Luke 10:2; John 16:13) Finally, over fourteen centuries before Philippians 2:10-11 is written, the Gentile Ruth both *"**bowed** herself to the ground"* and addressed Boaz as *"my **lord**."* (2:10,13) Her confession, *"I am a **stranger**...not like unto one of thine handmaidens,"* was a holy precursor to Paul's words: *"That at that time ye were without Christ, being aliens from the commonwealth of Israel, and **strangers** from the covenants of promise, having no hope, and without God in the world."* (Ephesians 2:12)

The main focus of the book is the manner in which Boaz and Ruth are brought together as husband and wife. The procedure that governed Naomi's need for a "kinsman redeemer" was based on local tradition, influenced in part by the custom of *Levirate* marriage (Deuteronomy 25:7-9). Thus, to make a complicated story simple – whenever a widow was constrained by poverty to sell the property of her late husband, a relative of the deceased could "redeem" the land in her behalf (either by buying it from *her*, or buying it *back* from another *for* her). More importantly, if the widow was childless and still young enough to bear children, the kinsman would also be expected to marry her so that a male heir could re-enter the family of the first husband, in order to perpetuate the family name and inherit the land.

Being past the age of childbearing, Naomi counsels her daughter-in-law to pursue Boaz as her own kinsman redeemer, as the estate would eventually be hers (3:1-6; 4:3). While Ruth's subsequent nocturnal visit to Boaz may appear objectionable to some, it was not so when judged by the social mores of the people of Israel at that time. The important doctrinal application is that Ruth *initiated* the final stage of their relationship – *"For whosoever shall call upon the name of the Lord shall be saved."* (Romans 10:13) As our Saviour promised in John 6:37, *"him that cometh to me **I will** in no* *wise cast out,"* Boaz likewise assured Ruth, *"And now, my daughter, fear not; **I will do** to thee all that thou requirest."* (3:11)

In the interim, *whatever* sustenance Naomi receives (i.e., the *"six measures of barley"*) can only come *through* Ruth, reflecting how Jews in the Church Age (the *"present time"* of Romans 11:5) can only be saved *through* the *"gospel of the grace of God,"* forming that *"remnant according to the election of grace."* (3:17; Acts 20:24) As Amos 3:3 states, *"Can two walk together, except they be agreed?"* – Ruth and Naomi are likewise seen to *"walk together"* no further than *Bethlehem*, a picture of Israel's historic rejection of the Virgin Birth (John Hagee's dual-covenant, ethnic-salvation heresy notwithstanding).

There was, however, a potential impediment that leads to yet another powerful truth. Although Boaz was a kinsman of Elimelech, he was not the *nearest* of kin. Thus, he would have to offer "the deal" (which included Ruth) to the *"kinsman nearer than I."* (3:12) When the presentation is formally made in the presence of the city elders (numbering *ten*, as Christ's "Bride" would be primarily *Gentile* in nature), a startling response is given by the nearer redeemer. While he was *initially* willing to accept the offer on behalf of *Naomi*, he was forced to decline when *Ruth* entered the arrangement: *"And the kinsman said, I cannot redeem it for myself, **lest I mar mine own inheritance**: redeem thou my right to thyself; for I cannot redeem it."* (3:6) Here, we find the *nearest* of kin being a type of God the Father, who already has His inheritance – *"For the LORD's portion is his people; **Jacob** is the lot of his **inheritance**."* (Deuteronomy 32:9)

Though *technically* "related" to the Moabitess through *Creation* (Ruth being the *"offspring of God"* described in Acts 17:29), Jehovah was not *about* to violate His own principle of "right division" by acknowledging Jew and Gentile as *one* – prior to Calvary. Only "Boaz" could accomplish this, *"For **he** is our peace, **who hath made both one**, and hath broken down the middle wall of partition between us."* (Ephesians 2:14) Thus, we read the greatest statement confirming Boaz as a type of the Lord Jesus Christ: *"Moreover **Ruth the Moabitess, the wife of Mahlon, have I purchased to be my wife**."* (4:10) Again, as Ruth is a "Gentile" bride, the declaration is made in verse *ten*. The obvious cross-reference here is Acts 20:28 where Paul exhorted the Ephesian elders to *"feed **the church of God**, which **he hath purchased** with his own blood."* As Naomi had assured Ruth that *"this man will not be in rest, until he hath **finished** the thing this day,"* we understand the import of those words, *"It is **finished**."* (3:18; John 19:30) And, for an added devotional nugget, this "restlessness" *also* depicts our Lord's intense desire to return for *His* Bride.

Yet, praise the Lord, the purchase price encompassed more than the property of Ruth the *Gentile* (going back to her Hebrew in-laws, as well): *"And Boaz said unto the elders, and unto all the people, Ye are witnesses this day, that I have bought **all that was Elimelech's**, and all that was Chilion's and Mahlon's, of the hand of Naomi."* (4:9) Because the *greater* "Boaz" would one day come *"up* from the grave," He would also be able to transport all of those Old Testament saints *up* from Paradise and *into* Heaven (Ephesians 4:8). Thus, we have that significant postscript: *"Moreover Ruth...have I purchased to be my wife, **to raise up** the name of **the dead** upon his inheritance, that the name of **the dead be not cut off from among his brethren**."* (4:10)

Once again, the contrast between Judges and Ruth is pronounced. While the *former* ends with a concubine *from* Bethlehem being violated, murdered, and dismembered, the *latter* ends with another woman receiving a beautiful baby boy from the Lord *in* Bethlehem; but not just *any* boy. The last *eight* words of the book give the genealogy of her son – *"And Obed begat Jesse, and Jesse begat **David**"* (the *ultimate* type of that One who would provide a "new beginning" for Jew and Gentile alike). Thus, we find that a destitute widow from a foreign land, whose only hope for survival was to labor in the fields as a common peasant ends up married to the richest man in Bethlehem, in the royal line of Jesus Christ, and has a book in the Jewish Old Testament named after her, as well. With the lineage of her own people traced back to Lot's unnatural relationship with his elder daughter (as well as the prohibitive injunction of Deuteronomy 23:3), we gain a new appreciation for the words: *"But where sin abounded, grace did much more abound."* (Romans 5:20)

"HANDFULS OF PURPOSE"

We have now arrived at the most important application for the faithful remnant laboring in Laodicea. As I have repeatedly said throughout this volume – to fully appreciate the doctrine of inspiration, as well as the A.V. 1611 debate itself, an *"understanding of the times"* is absolutely essential. For instance, throughout the length and breadth of this land, numbers of faithful, separated, King James Bible-believing Baptist pastors are facing increasing opposition *whenever* and *wherever* they preach "The Book." A profile of these men can be found in our Lord's commendation: *"Yet I have left me seven thousand in Israel, all the knees which have not bowed unto Baal, and every mouth which hath not kissed him."* (I Kings 19:18) Having spoken in scores of their churches over the past thirty-plus years, I can testify that some of the most spiritual men I have ever met pastor flocks no bigger than David must have had when his brethren asked, derisively, *"and with whom hast thou left those **few sheep** in the wilderness?"* (I Samuel 17:28)

From a practical point of view, prospects for churches that are built on old-fashioned holiness are dwindling in unprecedented fashion; the flighty religious consumers of our nation being *"tossed to and fro, and carried about with every wind of doctrine."* (Ephesians 4:14) One might call it a spiritual "free for all" in "free fall." First, it was the "seeker friendly" church; then, it was the "purpose driven" church; then, the "emergent" church; now it is the "Internet" church; tomorrow, it will be something else. Consequently, many an isolated prophet struggles with that soul-wrenching question in Job 3:23 – *"Why is light given to a man whose way is hid, and whom God hath hedged in?"* The answer to this dilemma is found in the book of Ruth. As you recall, a *famine* is mentioned in the opening verse. In Amos 8:11, the Lord warns of a far greater threat on the horizon, using a famine as a similitude for *scriptural* deprivation – *"Behold, the days come, saith the Lord GOD, that I will send a famine in the land, **not a famine of bread**, nor a thirst for water, **but of hearing the words of the LORD.**"* I also believe that the *spiritual* famine of the last days – as represented by the modern "Bible" movement – will be *the* primary catalyst for a possible *physical* famine consistent with II Timothy 3:1 (that "disruption" on *this* side of the "interruption.")

With all of the above in mind, the single-most important truth to grasp about spiritual conditions in the *last* days has to do with the *last* activity Ruth is seen performing just prior to her wedding day. I'll give you a *big* hint – she wasn't building a mega-church, *"supposing that gain is godliness"* (I Timothy 6:5) – *"And Ruth the Moabitess said unto Naomi, Let me now go to the field, and* **glean** *ears of corn"* (2:2); *"And she said, I pray you, let me* **glean** *and gather after the reapers among the sheaves"* (2:7); *"So she* **gleaned** *in the field until even, and beat out that she had* **gleaned***"* (2:17); *"So she kept fast by the maidens of Boaz to* **glean** *unto the end of barley harvest and of wheat harvest"* (2:23).

As a final example of the number "three" in Scripture, the harvest of the New Testament Church has followed the threefold stage of a growing season, as illustrated by the doctrine of the Resurrection in I Corinthians 15:23-24: *"But every man in his own order: Christ the* **firstfruits***; **afterward** they that are Christ's at his coming. **Then** cometh **the end**"* (i.e., Garden Tomb/Rapture/Tribulation Saints). Likewise, with respect to the reaping of lost mankind, the firstfruits were gathered between Pentecost and Hampton Court; the main harvest commenced with the A.V. 1611; while the blatant rejection of the King James Bible for any number of generic challengers has ushered in the final stage of gleanings. Thus, we have *Ephesus* to *Sardis* as the firstfruits; *Philadelphia* as the main harvest; and *Laodicea* as the gleanings. With regard to the parallel forecast given in *Genesis* through *Judges*, the obvious teaching of the book of Ruth is that the Church is now in her final stage of "gleanings." And whether we like it or not, there is *nothing* that you or I can do about it *but* follow Ruth's example, who *"**continued** even from the morning until now, that she tarried a little in the house"* and *"unto the end."* (2:7, 23) Note the amazing cross-reference to Paul's *end*-day directive in II Timothy 3:14 – *"But **continue** thou* *in the things which thou hast learned and hast been assured of."*

While Christians sing *"We'll Work Till Jesus Comes,"* they must *never* get discouraged when their results seem less substantial than the main harvest of Philadelphia. (In some ways, it may require even *more* devotion and tenacity to glean than otherwise; the majority of professing Christians turning to fables at this time.) Thus, against this backdrop of famine and gleaning, the whole "Bible of the Month Club" garbage should certainly stand out for what it is – Satan's *last attempt to destroy the Bible* of the Philadelphia Church Age. To draw a timely application from a Tribulation context – *"Woe to the inhabiters of the earth...for the **devil** is come down unto you, **having great wrath, because he knoweth that he hath but a short time.**"* (Revelation 12:12) Consequently, what Fundamentalist in his right mind would want to spend his time attacking the A.V. 1611 when "Boaz" will be here *any minute* (his very name meaning "fleetness," as in I Corinthians 15:52)?

Like I said earlier, if pastors would only embrace the A.V. 1611 as their *real* "final authority," they could trash all those sermon-idea books and simply *"preach the word."* Consequently, it just so "happed" that the definitive set of these so-called "homiletical helps" was named after a text from the book of Ruth, and more specifically, from a text about "gleaning." Published in 1943, *Handfuls On Purpose* (by Smith and Lee) flourished during the second leg of that ill-fated Alexandrian journey in Acts 27. According to *Christianbook.com*, "When you're *stuck for sermon ideas*, you'll be glad you have this unique, time-tested commentary on your reference shelf!" Of course, there's only one problem – the authors got the verse wrong: *"And when she was risen up to glean, Boaz commanded his young men, saying, Let her glean even among the sheaves, and reproach her not: And let fall also some of the handfuls **of** purpose for her, and leave them, that she may glean them, and rebuke her not."* (2:15-16) Talk about a timely illustration – for over half-a-century, Fundamentalists like Jack Schaap have been searching for "sermon ideas" in a set of books that can't even get a three-word portion of Scripture correct on the cover! (Sounds a little like that inauguration fiasco.) Thus, the crowd that wants to nit-pick *your* King James Bible apparently doesn't recognize the grammatical difference between "handfuls *on* purpose" and "handfuls *of* purpose."

Finally, as if to prepare young preachers for the end-day squabbles over the integrity of the Authorized Version – in the providence of God – the most famous "error" in the history of the King James Bible is also traced to the book of Ruth. In fact, the "mistake" in question involved our heroine personally. There were two printings of the new Bible in 1611; both were folio editions made in Oxford by Robert Barker. Printing conditions in the seventeenth century were extremely primitive, with each letter (of some 775,000 words) having to be set by hand – backwards, and by candlelight! Consequently, mistakes were inevitable, averaging about one in ten pages. The first folio came to be known as the *"He* Bible" because of a confusion of pronouns in Ruth 3:15. Whereas the correct reading for the end of the verse should have been *"and she went into the city,"* a distracted printer left off the "s" making it *"he went."* Corrected in the second folio, *it* became known as the *"She* Bible."

Now, although Ruth 3:15 *did* contain a legitimate printing error that *did* require correction, the enduring *hype* behind the *type* that has attached itself to this vanguard "mistake" is ridiculous. As the truth in Psalm 2:4 states, *"He that sitteth in the heavens shall laugh,"* in the final analysis, it was just as true that Boaz *"went into the city"* as it was regarding Ruth. Furthermore, from a doctrinal standpoint, by the time the reader arrives at verse 15, Boaz has already made the commitment, *"I **will** do to thee all that thou requirest."* Consequently, Paul tells us that *"we are members of **his** body, of **his** flesh, and of **his** bones. For this cause shall a man leave his father and mother, and shall be joined unto his wife, **and they two shall be one flesh.**"* (Ephesians 5:30-31) Thus, Ruth the "she," was destined to become Ruth the "he," as in *"Male and female created he them...and called **their** name **Adam**."* (Genesis 5:2)

While pointing out these tell-tale "errors" in the Holy Scriptures, *Pseudos* continue to treat their *Greek* and *Hebrew* study guides as the *infallible* "final authority." Take the matter of "Ho, Ho, Ho," Santa's favorite one-liner. According to the *Strong's Exhaustive Concordance of the Bible* that I have had for over twenty years (Hendrickson Publishers; Peabody, Massachusetts), the word "ho" is limited to *three* references – one in Isaiah 55:1, and two in Zechariah 2:6. Jehovah is the speaker in each case, making this a profound "nugget" that further illustrates how SANTA/SATAN attempts to usurp God's place in the hearts of children. However, notice what is said just four verses from the "catastrophe" at Ruth 3:15 when God the Father shows us at Ruth 4:1 – *"Then went Boaz up to the gate, and sat him down there: and, behold, **the kinsman of whom Boaz spake** came by: unto whom he said, **Ho**, such a one! turn aside, sit down here. And he turned aside, and sat down."* While the "error" has been corrected in the *Strong's* online version, I believe the point has been made. Whether it's a "he" or a "Ho," printers are only human; or, according to the *Online Urban Dictionary*, "'He ho' is a slang term to describe *nothing*." (For the record – our Christmas "nugget" is still intact, as "Ho" number 4 is not "technically" uttered by God, but rather by Boaz.)

"THE REST OF THE STORY"

As noted in chapter three, *Oprah* Winfrey was supposed to have been named after the biblical *Orpah*, but the name was misspelled on the birth certificate. Why would any mother want to name her daughter after this loser in the first place? Orpah goes down in history as the great antithesis of Ruth; her telling legacy – *"thy sister in law is **gone back** unto her people"* – constituting a major type of end-day, Laodicean defection. (1:15)

When Naomi's attempt to dissuade Ruth from remaining with her proved unsuccessful, *four* prescient words follow: *"**So they two went** until they came to Beth-lehem."* (**1:19**) Taking note of that now-familiar Scripture address, we understand that in our ever-darkening, post-**911** world, these same two "women" – the *tenuous State of Israel* and the *remnant Body of Christ* – will *share* the increasing hostility of Satan and his minions. As prefigured in

Ruth 1:22, and prophesied in II Timothy 3:1, the final stretch of their journey will be fraught with danger and uncertainty for both. But then, suddenly – *"in the twinkling of an eye"* – the pair will be separated by the words, *"So Boaz **took** Ruth"* (4:13; I Corinthians 15:52; Genesis 5:24; Matthew 24:36, 40; I Thessalonians 4:16). As *this* marriage was occasioned by Israel's *rebellious* refusal to receive her national Messiah, the "wedding announcement" is made in verse 13. However, the *parting* will not be permanent, as Jehovah declares in Isaiah 54:7, *"For a small moment have I forsaken thee; but with great mercies will I **gather** thee"* (Matthew 24:31). For "Israel" (as anticipated in Job 42:13) the glorious reunion *seven* years later will be *"better to thee than **seven** sons."* (4:15)

With the birth of Naomi's *grandson*, who would become the *grandfather* of King David (and, ultimately, the ancestor of Joseph), the women prophesy in the Holy Ghost: *"And he shall be unto thee a **restorer of thy life**."* (4:15) The Apostle Paul provides the *doctrinal* cross-reference in Romans 11:15 – *"For if the casting away of them be the reconciling of the world, what shall the receiving of them be, **but life from the dead**?"* (For a *devotional* application – As Naomi gains the unforeseen blessing in Romans 11:26 that *"all Israel shall be saved,"* when the redemption of her husband's parcel was all that she had initially desired, the truth of Ephesians 3:20 comes to mind: *"Now unto him that is able to do exceeding abundantly above all that we ask or think, according to the power that worketh in us."*)

Thus, the great love story ends with Boaz and Ruth "living happily ever after." But, what of Naomi; how did *she* spend the remaining years of *her* life? The last glimpse we have of her in Scripture shows her caring for Obed. (4:16) Consequently, the *fullest* extent of her "restoration of life" and "nourishment in old age" must be left to conjecture. However, while we cannot know what happened to the *historical* Naomi, the Bible *does* reveal what *will* happen to her *antitype*, the nation of Israel.

The Old Testament frequently identifies Israel as the "Wife of Jehovah" (e.g., Jeremiah 31:32, *"I was an **husband** unto them, saith the LORD."*) While the average Fundamentalist has been programmed to consign divorced Christians to "outer darkness," the Lord declares in Jeremiah 3:8, *"for all the causes whereby backsliding Israel committed adultery I had put her away, and given her a **bill of divorce**.*" And while Malachi 2:16 states that *"the LORD, the God of Israel, saith that he **hateth putting away**,"* Jehovah's divorce from Israel was reaffirmed in Hosea 2:2 – *"Plead with your mother, plead: **for she is not my wife, neither am I her husband**.*" According to the Mosaic Law concerning divorce, the *former* wife *"may go and be another man's wife."* (Deuteronomy 24:2) From the words attributed to Israel in Hosea 2:7, it would appear that the divorced wife of Jehovah did that very thing: *"And she shall follow after her lovers, but she shall not overtake them; and she shall seek them, but shall not find them: then shall she say, I will go and return to **my first husband**; for then was it better with me than now."* (Thus, we find the implication of a *second* husband replicated in the wording of Matthew 1:25, *"And knew her not till she had brought forth her **firstborn son**.*")

A further indication that Israel had remarried, *symbolically*, is the Lord's own statement to her in Isaiah 54:4 concerning *"the reproach of thy **widowhood**.*" While Lamentations 1:2 states that the Babylonian captivity had caused Israel to become *"as a widow,"* Hosea 2:7 implies that she became a widow through the *desertion* and *disappearance* of her lovers – *"and she shall seek them, **but shall not find them**.*" In any event, *three* separate Scriptures – Jeremiah 3:8, Hosea 2:7, and Isaiah 54:4 – identify Israel as *divorced*, *remarried*, and *widowed*.

But, praise God, the story doesn't end here! The same prophets who record Jehovah's *divorce* from Israel *also* record their future glorious *reconciliation*. In Hosea 2:14 and 19-20, the Lord declares: *"Therefore, behold, I will allure her, and bring her into the wilderness, and speak comfortably unto her…And I will **betroth** thee unto me forever; yea, I will **betroth** thee unto me in righteousness, and in judgment, and in lovingkindness, and in mercies. I will even **betroth** thee unto me in faithfulness: and thou shalt know the LORD."* In Isaiah 54:4-6, He states: *"Fear not; for thou shalt not be ashamed:*

neither be thou confounded; for thou shalt not be put to shame: for thou shalt forget the shame of thy youth, and shalt not remember the reproach of thy widowhood any more. ***For thy Maker is thine husband;*** *the* LORD *of hosts is his name; and thy Redeemer the Holy One of Israel."*

Now, *if* all of the above were to be applied, or read, back to the original types of our story – *for the sake of illustration alone* – a most remarkable event "would have" occurred. With the widow Naomi as a type of *Israel*, and the nearer redeemer as a type of *Jehovah*, we understand that *their* eventual *reconciliation* "would have" constituted the *ultimate* "Rest of the Story." (Remember that this kinsman *had* initially *agreed* to rescue Naomi's parcel, declaring, *"I will redeem it,"* and declining only when Ruth the *Gentile* entered the picture.) Thus, if we "read in the white," as they say (i.e., "between the lines") – Elimelech "would have" represented Naomi's *second* husband, the one responsible for that costly sojourn in Moab (i.e., *"We have no king but Cæsar"*). While no type plays out in *every* particular, the important truth to "glean" from this purely illustrative scenario is that the *Church's* marriage to *Jesus* will be followed by *Israel's* remarriage to *Jehovah*. (Moral of story: *Replacement Theology is out of Hell*.)

WAITING FOR THE SHOE TO DROP

The final type in our story is a solitary *shoe*. When the kinsman-redeemer waived his right of redemption, he removed his shoe and gave it to Boaz as a means of solemnizing the transaction. *"Now this was the manner in former time in Israel concerning redeeming and concerning changing, for to confirm all things;* ***a man plucked off his shoe, and gave it to his neighbor****: and this was a testimony in Israel. Therefore the kinsman said unto Boaz, Buy it for thee. So he drew off his shoe."* (4:7-8) As previously noted, this rite is not to be confounded with the law that dealt with levirate marriages in Deuteronomy 25:5-10. It probably originated with the idea that the right to "tread the soil" belonged "solely" to the owner; thus, the transfer of a sandal would serve as an appropriate object lesson for the relinquishment of this right.

Once again, the related typology is profound! As the anti-type of the nearer redeemer, God the Father would also have to remove *His* shoe as the symbolic sign of deferring to the Lord Jesus Christ, the anti-type of Boaz. And, in this holy supposition we are not left without appropriate cross-references, for twice the Lord declares in Psalms 60:8 and 108:9: *"**Moab** is my washpot; over Edom **will I cast out my shoe**."* (Note that unmistakable allusion to Ruth the **Moabitess**.) According to the context in both passages, the Father will kick off His shoe somewhere over Edom in the Tribulation – *just in time* for those Heavenly festivities described by John: *"Let us be glad and rejoice, and give honour to him: for the marriage of the Lamb is come, and his wife hath made herself ready."* (Revelation 19:7) In the meantime, as *we* await that glorious day, may we glean *our* fields with patience, being ever mindful of that definitive pledge of selfless fidelity:

"And Ruth said, Intreat me not to
leave thee, or to return from following
after thee: for whither thou goest,
I will go; and where thou lodgest,
I will lodge: thy people shall be
my people, and thy God my God:
Where thou diest, will I die, and
there will I be buried: the LORD do
so to me, and more also, if ought
but death part thee and me."

(RUTH 1:16-17)

16

The Good Fight of Faith

IT HAS OFTEN been stated throughout this volume that faith *must* work in tandem with the King James Bible issue. We will therefore bring our study to a close by devoting the final chapter to this vital subject. The same apostle who instructed Timothy about the doctrine of inspiration also exhorted him to *"Fight the good fight of faith."* (I Timothy 6:12) While Paul mentioned inspiration only *once* in his epistles to Timothy he spoke of faith *twenty-seven* times. It is no coincidence that one of these references is II Timothy 3:15. The Holy Spirit moved Paul to "write" *theopneustos* a grand total of *one* time in all of his autographs, while he led him to employ *pistis* (the Greek word for faith) 138 times. When a Bible-wide comparison is made, the final score is: Inspiration - 2; Faith - 244.

And yet, as the controversy *drags* on regarding the trustworthiness of our Authorized Version, the sole criteria continues to mandate a defense by *sight* (i.e., through demonstrable data, argumentation, manuscript evidence – *"science falsely so called"*). Though there have been times when the Church has needed to *"stop the mouths of gainsayers"* while *"earnestly contending for the faith,"* given our present cultural addiction to narcissism ("talking heads," "turning heads," etc.), it may behoove us to *"Fight the good fight of faith"* – by spending *more* time in Romans 1:4 *"declaring* the truth" – and *less* time in Romans 1:29 *"debating* the truth" (Isaiah 53:7; John 19:9). We *know* that people benefit from *hearing* God's word, while *"foolish and unlearned questions…gender strifes"* (Romans 10:17; II Timothy 2:23).

For example, despite the many spiritual blessings attributed to the English text of the A.V. 1611 that were surveyed in the previous chapters, an array of satanic anti-KJB books and websites continue to abound *solely* to *"overthrow the faith of some."* (II Timothy 2:18) Like that *"vale of Siddim"* in Genesis 14:10 these *"slime pits"* are designed to mire the Bible believer in a morass of ambiguities, half-truths, and general disinformation overload. While one scholar desires to acquaint you with "awkward syntax," "unclear statements," and "archaic terms," another deals in "basic translation errors," with special emphasis on "passages in the King James Bible having no Greek manuscript support," etc. The heaviest concentration of "slime" concerns that worn-out cliché which they all delight in springing upon fledgling KJV Onlyites – "Exactly *which* A.V. 1611 do you mean?" This, of course, is an indirect reference to the many changes that were necessitated by a transition from Gothic to Roman type, various printing errors, and a protracted fluidity concerning spelling, punctuation, and grammar (much of which was not standardized until the mid-nineteenth century.)

Now, amidst all the ruckus over your Bible, a profound truth often goes unnoticed. On a website called "KJV Only advocates refuted," readers are *assured*: "Only a very *tiny* fraction of people who use the KJV actually believe that the translation process was inspired by the Holy Ghost." *Wikipedia* makes reference to this "tiny fraction" in their article, stating : "...but groups do exist – sometimes termed the King James Only movement – that distrust anything not in agreement with ("that changes") the Authorized Version." But this supposition begs the question – *"Why do the heathen rage?"* (Psalm 2:1) If there *are* just a "few" of us "King James *Wackos*" out there – *why* are so many "experts" spending such a *disproportionate* amount of time and money to shut us up? Thus, the best "evidence" that we have the right Bible is confirmed by the degree of satanic hostility that continues to be directed against it!

It is fitting that the word "inspiration" has *eleven* letters, as the Bible-believing Philadelphia remnant in Laodicea is currently facing an eleventh-hour crisis concerning the integrity of "The Old

Black Book." I am convinced that the Devil's number one strategy today is to deceive believers into abandoning a *faith*-based conviction in favor of some perceived *intellectual* defense. Sadly, whenever this occurs, the Christian is usually half-way out on the proverbial limb before he realizes that *no such position exists*. Having crossed a spiritual *Rubicon*, many of these unfortunate brethren never return, as *"he that doubteth is damned...for whatsoever is not of faith is sin."* (Romans 14:23) Dr. Clarence Sexton once asked me, "How do we defend the King James Bible on an *intellectual* level; as the head of a college I am expected to do so." I answered that this was impossible and that he would have to be willing to be a "fool for Christ" (as Lester Roloff would often say, *"I'm a fool for Christ; whose fool are you?"*).

Though we may not be able to understand the full gravity of the words *"overthrow the faith of some,"* we *can* discern the application to a novice who finds himself overwhelmed in Bunyan's "Slough of Despond." (That kindhearted deacon who blew his own brains out after leading me to Christ *must* have been troubled about *something*.) As the old black preacher put it, "You may be *saved* down here, but you ain't necessarily *safe* down here." In the course of writing this book, I received a telephone message from a hard-working pastor that is typical of many. The preacher was troubled about a speaker he had who corrected the King James Bible in the pulpit and later sent him a long list of supposed "errors." The spirit of the frustrated pastor is evident and goes to the heart of this chapter: "I believe that God preserved his word; I believe I can hold the word of God in my hand. *However, I'm ashamed that I cannot deal with some of the questions he deals with in his e-mail.*" In a follow-up email he stated: "I would like to be more proficient in rebutting these critics than I am. *I need some help....*" (The list of "errors" that he forwarded to me was pure "slime.")

While opponents of the King James Bible will denounce Bishop Blayney's standard-setting 1769 *Oxford* edition for supposedly deviating from the original A.V. 1611 in "at least 75,000 details," F. H. A. Scrivener alludes to less than 200 as noteworthy of mention. (A significant portion of these "75,000 details" were nothing more than changing "darke" to "dark" or "rann" to "ran".) However, to delve into the *particulars* of this issue, one would have to trace the 400-year printing history of the Authorized Version. Such a journey would make "Mr. Toad's Wild Ride" appear *tame* by comparison. For instance, does the name *Eyre & Spottiswoode, Ltd.*, ring any bells? This is the former London-based printing house that holds the dubious distinction of being the *first* company to print (in 1920) the highly inflammatory, and grossly fabricated, anti-Semitic *Protocols of the Learned Elders of Zion* (also known as the *Jewish Peril*). Many believe that the anonymous document played a significant role in the Holocaust. However, this same firm *also* held the prestigious title of *King's Printer* – being one of three licensed printers of the Authorized Version (Cambridge and Oxford Universities being the other two) until they were bought out by *Cambridge University Press* in 1990.

The original printing of the A.V. 1611 was assigned to Robert Barker, his official title duly noted on the finely engraved title page – "Printer to the Kings most excellent Maiestie." However, due to extenuating circumstances (primarily a substantial personal debt load), Barker was constrained to share the work with other rival printers in London (his two principle partners being John Bill and Bonham Norton, father-in-law to his son, Christopher). With *the* opportunity of history before him, Barker declared, "I do yet groan under the burden of this book." As the Devil was surely on the prowl, significant financial disputes and protracted litigation ensued. Add to this the aforementioned escalation of the English language itself and it is easy to see how many competing editions would have surfaced. The *increasing* demand for these early King James Bibles, offset by the *decreasing* quality of their production, led the Crown to include Cambridge and Oxford Universities within the printing monopoly. Two early landmark editions were subsequently produced at *Cambridge* in 1629 and 1638. Other conscientious efforts appeared in 1644, 1676, 1680, and 1701. An important milestone was reached when the 1762 *Cambridge* edition by F. S. Harris was followed by Blayney's watershed Oxford standard seven years later. (At least four other editions were made in the nineteenth century.)

When we survey the twenty-first century, the trek is no less mindboggling. While eight editions of the *Cambridge* King James Bible are still being printed in London, the majority of their *Oxford* counterparts have been *outsourced to South Korea*! As each printing house retains its longstanding option to introduce alterations in spelling, punctuation, and capitalization on an ebb-and-flow basis, slight variations continue to be seen on occasion. For example, while many of my pastor friends preach out of a *Cambridge* King James Bible, an equal number of others prefer the *Old Scofield Reference Bible* published by *Oxford*. When they speak on Genesis 24:57, the *Cambridge* edition reads "enquire," while the *Oxford* reads "inquire." While the former places a *comma* after "nations" in Romans 4:18, the latter places a *semicolon*. (Other editions have differed over such inconsequential matters as *ankle*, or *ancle*; *soap*, or *sope*; etc., causing many believers unnecessary anxiety.)

In a technical sense, the Authorized Version has been the object of a superintending providence that has preserved it through the plates of one secular printer after another. Appropriately, a typographical error in the now famous "Printers Bible" of 1612 made Psalm 119:161 read, "*Printers* have persecuted me without a cause," instead of "Princes." There is no way to account for this potentially unsettling phenomenon apart from simple faith. Personally, I have *never* been the least bit troubled regarding the issue of "human error" in either the *manuscript* or the *printing* era. My reasoning is quite elementary— The Holy Spirit has *obviously* permitted this convergence of the human and the divine. As I understand the manuscript tradition, nearly *all* extant copies of any sizeable length display *some* variant readings, while the printing record speaks for itself. Thus, with the Rapture hopefully near, the bottom line at the close of the Church Age regarding the legacy of legitimate textual errors is simple – "It *is* what it *is*." God the Holy Ghost has already spent 3,500 years displaying His willingness to empower both His written *and* printed Scripture – *despite* whatever degree of human deficiencies may have accompanied the process.

For example, the 1631 edition by Robert Barker and Martin Lucas left the word "not" out of Exodus 20:14, producing the untenable reading – *"Thou **shalt** commit adultery."* This copy of the Holy Scripture went on to be labeled as the "Wicked Bible," the "Sinners Bible," and even the "Adulterous Bible." Yet, despite this egregious mistake, resulting in the printers being heavily fined and their license suspended (triggering a flurry of unsubstantiated rumors that Barker's press had been sabotaged), the Holy Spirit *would* have borne witness to everything *else* within the covers had there not been an emergency recall by King Charles I (James' son). One of the more bizarre episodes from the printing history of the Authorized Version involves Barker himself. By 1635 the "venerable" printer of the King James Bible had succumbed to his personal debts and was remanded to the King's Bench Prison where he remained until his death a *decade* later! (I *told* you it would be a wild ride!)

The same spirit of "divine resiliency" would apply to other "classic" editions of Bible errata such as the 1635 "Unrighteous Bible," omitting the word "not" in I Corinthians 6:9; the 1716 "Sin On Bible," reversing the letters "n-o" to "o-n" in John 8:11; the 1810 "Wife-hater Bible," changing "life" to "wife" in Luke 14:26; the 1613 "Judas Bible," confusing *Judas* for *Jesus* in Matthew 26:36; the 1763 "Fools Bible," substituting the word "a" for "no" in Psalm 14:1 (Joe Combs' favorite text); and even a 1611 "Basketball Bible" in "honor" of Lebron James and Barak Obama that reads, *"hoopes of the pillars"* instead of *"hookes"* in Exodus 38:11.

Once again, the only two options that we have are to exercise child-like faith, or to fall *off* that limb, quoting *"the honor of kings is to search out a matter."* (Proverbs 25:2) I'm sure God *must* have known what He was doing when he allowed such disconcerting aberrations. Thus, rather than lose sleep down *here* over whether Ecclesiastes 8:17, Matthew 26:39, and Mark 1:19 should read *"farther,"* as in the 1945 Oxford Old Scofield, or *"further,"* as in the 1996 Old Scofield and 2009 Cambridge – *at this late stage of the game* – we may just have to content ourselves with the words of that timeless hymn, *"Farther along* we'll know all about it, *Farther along* we'll understand why...."

"HIS NAME IS CALLED THE WORD OF GOD"

I have gained a great deal of spiritual insight on this issue by comparing the *"written* word of God" to the *"living* word of God." As previously referenced, the Greek translation committee at Oxford, under the leadership of Dr. Thomas Ravis, employed the first 66 words in the Gospel of John to introduce Jesus Christ as *the* "Word" of God. While Luke and Matthew tell us *where* the Christ-child was born, the *date* of his arrival has remained a mystery. About the only thing we know for sure is that the shepherds would not have been *"keeping watch over their flock"* on a cold December night, etc. Obviously then, the Heavenly Father must *not* have wanted us to know *when* His Son arrived. The same would apply to the *written* word of God. In preparation for the 400th anniversary of the A.V. 1611, many pastors had intended to mark the exact anniversary with a Bible conference. However, these plans eventually had to be "adjusted," as the Lord imposed a similar information blackout regarding the arrival date of His word in *printed* form.

While one KJB website "confirms" that the publication date of the Authorized Version was, "in fact," May 2, 1611, the truth of the matter is – *nobody* knows for sure, because the first edition of the King James Bible was never formally entered by the "Worshipful Company of Stationers and Newspaper Makers" (better known as the Stationers' Company). David Norton writes in *A Textual History of the King James Bible*: "The printing history of the KJB is plagued throughout by inadequate publishing records. Presumably because it was considered a revision [of the Bishops' Bible] rather than a new book, the first edition was not entered on the Stationers' Registers, **so we do not know when in 1611 it appeared**." There is a great spiritual lesson here: The King James 1611 Authorized Version of the Holy Bible is the most printed book *in the history* *of the world*, as well as the *only* book with over *one billion copies in print* – **AND WE DON'T EVEN HAVE A FORMAL RECORD THAT IT WAS EVER PUBLISHED!** This *could* have something to do with the fact that it is *also* the only book in the *history* of the world that was written by the *Creator* of the world. Like the blind man said in John 9:30 *"Why herein is a marvelous thing, that ye know not from whence he is, and yet he hath opened mine eyes."*

But there is more. It appears that the Lord was quite intent on keeping this milestone date a secret. In his oft-referenced *Records of the English Bible*, Alfred W. Pollard states: "…if the [King James] version was 'appointed to be read in churches' (as is expressly stated on the title-page of 1611), at the time of its first publication, nothing is more probable than that this may have been done by Order in Council. If so, the authentic record of that order would now be lost, because all the Council books and registers from the year 1600 to 1613 inclusive were destroyed by a fire at Whitehall, on the 12th of January, 1618."

There is also evidence lacking with regard to the much-celebrated status of the "Authorized Version" having been *formally* authorized. While Olga S. Opfell states in *The King James Bible Translators*, "Admittedly, the translation was prepared with the approval of the highest authorities" and "No king other than James had ever shown so much interest in a Bible translation," the author also confirms – "But in spite of the fact that Barlow in his 'Sum and Substance of the Hampton Court Conference' had quoted King James as saying that a 'uniform translation' was to be 'presented to the Privy Council, and lastly ratified by Royal Authority,' no Act of Parliament or Convocation, no royal proclamation or degree of Privy Council ever conferred legal authority. The word 'authorized' never appears."

Now, if this *were* so, it would only make the issuance of the King James Bible that much more in conformity to Baptist principles (i.e., separation of Church and State). Yet, what does it matter anyway? Opfell goes *on* to acknowledge the *more* important sanction: "Actually, the lack of formal authorization of the King James Bible never proved to be any handicap. As Geddes MacGregor has observed, universal acceptance gave this version 'greater authority than it could have acquired through any…formality.' Ultimately its authority 'sprang from the hearts of the people. It was authorized by popular acclamation.'" While there *may* very well have been a "formal decree," the *point* is that the historical proceedings were shrouded in a *providential* cloud of obscurity, Norton reaffirming: "The surviving evidence about the making of the KJB is patchy and tantalising." Thus, we are confronted once again with the absolute necessity of *faith*. Such a view will also accommodate our model of the "unaccredited" *living* Word of God, of whom it was said, *"How knoweth this man letters, having never learned?"* along with the equally unexplainable endorsement that *"the common people heard him gladly."* (John 7:15; Mark 12:37)

Also, just as we have never had a *physical* description of Jesus, scholars are likewise in the dark as to a precise understanding of *what* Mr. Barker received from the translators. Opfell asks: "What exactly *was* given to the printer?" An anonymous pamphlet printed in London (circa 1660) entitled *The London Printer, His Lamentation: or, The Press Oppressed, or Overpressed*, makes a nebulous reference to "the Manuscript Copy of the last Translation of the holy Bible in English (attested with the hands of the Venerable and learned translators in King James his time)." So the "pressing" question is – what *kind* of a "final manuscript" did the translators deliver to Barker? (The simple reality of what I am about to suggest would hardly occur to a normal Bible believer, instinctively focused on the infinitely more important *message* of the text.) David Daniell asks in *The Bible in English*: "…did such a document exist? Barker in 1611 had to set up from *something*, whether a manuscript OR *a revised Bishops' Bible….*" (Emphasis mine). Thus, while it *may* have been a rough manuscript, comprised exclusively of the *handwritten* pages submitted by the six companies of translators – *more than likely* – it was a final, collated "manuscript" of loose *annotated* sheets from the forty *Bishops' Bibles* that the translators received at the start (i.e., given their fundamental charge to produce a "revision of the 1602 Bishops' Bible," the simplest method would have been to record their individual corrections on the applicable printed leaves from their Bishops' Bible working masters, rather than "reinvent the wheel," etc.)

Only one complete annotated Bishops' Bible has survived (from an early stage of the translation process), being housed at the Bodleian Library at the University of Oxford. While this Bible (known as Bod 1602) is currently bound in a single volume, Norton writes: "But when the translators worked on it, it was unbound: the annotations frequently disappear into the fold of the leaf, which would have been impossible if the sheets were already bound. Consequently, it is possible that Bod 1602 represents not one of the forty Bishops' Bibles supplied by Barker, but a combination of two or more of them." (Remember that the various companies traded their work back and forth for critique, resulting in various levels of progress.)

This would illustrate the thinking behind the words of Dr. Miles Smith in his Preface to the Authorized Version: "Truly (good Christian Reader) wee neuer thought from the beginning, that we should neede to make a new Translation, nor yet to make of a bad one a good one...but to make a good one better, or out of many good ones, one principall good one..." While Bible critics love to exploit that word "good," they fail to realize that the translators' *non-inspired* personal opinions about the work God was leading them to perform – *at the moment* – had *nothing* to do with *God's* "opinion" of the work, especially concerning the yet-to-be-revealed manner in which He would employ it – *over the long haul*. Just as Paul had no idea that *his* epistles would exist for such a protracted period (expecting the Rapture at any moment according to I Thessalonians 4:16), the 1611 translators were likewise oblivious that *their* latest "good" translation would be sustained through four centuries of providential preeminence. All were totally unaware that the Hampton Court Conference would become *the* major watershed event of the post-Reformation Era where the Bishops' Bible – the sixth, and *last*, translation of an 86-year period of "prep work" (beginning with Tyndale in 1525) – would be eclipsed by the *King* James Bible, destined to rule as the "KING" of English translations for over 400 years!

Yet, the conditions employed in Barker's landmark project could have been even *more* chaotic, thus requiring *more* providence on *God's* part and *more* faith on *our* part. As Isaiah 53:2 states, *"he hath no form nor comeliness,"* Norton writes, "...it [the original manuscript] may never have existed in a single, final *form*: annotations and summaries, for instance, may have been separate from the main text...." Historians also postulate that either a fire or a serious accident occurred at the print shop near the completion of the first edition. Would it not be safe to assume that the same Devil who was able to toss Paul and Luke into the Mediterranean could *also* have "figured out a way" to access *Barker's* facilities?

However, far more intriguing than *what* was used, is the question – Whatever *happened* to the "original" 1611 manuscript (*whatever* "it" was)? Norton writes: "Only a little is known of what happened to it...." According to Henry R. Plomer in *The King's Printing House under the Stuarts*, a 1651 pamphlet by William Ball made the claim that "...the sole right of printing of the Bible was Matthew Barker's, in regard that his father paid for the amended or corrected translation £3,500, 'by reason whereof the translated copy did of right belong to him.'" The anonymous author of *The London Printer* accused the Barkers of keeping the original manuscript in their possession. However, this scenario would appear inconsistent with the fact that Robert Barker spent the last decade of his life in debtors' prison. Consequently, Adam Nicolson makes the assertion in *God's Secretaries*: "What was said to be the 'manuscript copy of the Bible' was *sold* twice in the seventeenth century, once to Cambridge University Press, once to a firm of London printers, but has now disappeared."

Having submitted my own inquiry to the British Library in London, I received an e-mail from the Rare-Books Reference Service confirming: "Records relating to an original manuscript of the King James Bible are seemingly as scarce and ambiguous as those relating to its precise date of publication....As you suggest, most scholars agree with Daniell in suggesting that the printer's copy (in whatever form) perished in the Fire of London. **Ultimately,** *no*

one can know what happened to it." Once *again*, the Holy Spirit has decreed that we operate by *faith*. **THIS SHOULD SETTLE THE MATTER ONCE AND FOR ALL HOW GOD FEELS ABOUT ENSHRINING "THINGS" LIKE AARON'S ROD, MOSES' TOMB, AND ORIGINAL MANUSCRIPTS – HEBREW, GREEK, *OR* ENGLISH!** In *A Transcript of the Registers of the Company of Stationers of London*, Edward Arber makes the concession that scholars have about as much access to the original *English* as they do the autographs of *Moses* and *Paul*: "…unless therefore the autographic-attested manuscript of our present common Version be hidden away in some recess awaiting its future happy recovery; **it probably perished in the great Fire of London in 1666 A.D.**" (You *did* catch that uncanny date, *didn't you*, the one matching the number of that last *deleted* word in II Timothy 4:22?)

There are many other analogies to make between the *living* and *written* word that will dispel Satan's confusion. For instance, Exodus 2:9 states: *"And Pharaoh's daughter said unto her, Take this child away, and **nurse it for me.**"* Roughly sixteen centuries later we find the beautiful anti-type in Luke 1:35, where God entrusted *His* Son (*"that holy **thing**"*) to *another* Jewish maiden for the *same* purpose (*"nurse **it for me**"*). After the eternal Word of God is introduced in John1:1-5, verse 14 states: *"And the Word was made flesh, and dwelt among us"* (or, as The Message "Bible" says, "The Word became flesh and blood, and moved into the neighborhood"). Paul called it *"the **mystery** of godliness."* (I Timothy 3:16) The application to the printed text of the A.V. 1611 is striking! Just as God allowed His *Son* to enter the world in the vulnerable state of an infant, requiring – *nursing, burping*, and *changing* – sixteen centuries after *that*, He would entrust His *written* word to the primitive, unpredictable, and lucre-oriented printing industry of seventeenth-century England. Consequently, just as the Lord hung *naked* before His mother at Calvary, the *printed* text (as previously noted) would also suffer many indignities. (One such occurrence that initially went undetected in the infamous 1631 edition in the book of Deuteronomy was *so* blasphemous that I *cannot* reproduce it here, as it would make the error at Exodus 20:14 seem like John 3:16 by comparison.)

Then, we have the matter of the Saviour's *human* "weaknesses." Luke 8:23 shows us that Jesus *"fell asleep"* in the boat after spending a full day ministering to the people. In fact, *God* was so "exhausted" that he was able to *remain* asleep though the ship was awash. However, once He was "aroused," it didn't take Him *any* time to put the *storm* to bed! So, why should *Christians* expect some 700,000 words, spread over 2,000 pages of paper, measuring 17" x 12" x 5", and weighing nearly thirty pounds – to be any *less* susceptible to the imperfect conditions of *this* sin-cursed time than the *Creator's* own Son was to *His*?

Throughout our Lord's three-year public ministry He was hated, maligned, and plotted against. However, the *worst* attacks on His *person* occurred at the *close* of His life, being ended by the same with untold brutality (Isaiah 52:14). Typically, the ones who orchestrated His passion were "religious scholars" who professed to understand the Scriptures more *accurately* than He. Thus, we observe the precise pattern for the *accelerating* attack on the *written* word of God in our own lifetime (even the pagans at *Wikipedia* date the final assault on the "Old Black Book" from about 1950). While Jesus' warning in Matthew 24:23-24 is primarily a Tribulation passage, it also speaks to the unprecedented proliferation of false "Bibles" at the end of the Church Age: *"Then if any man shall say unto you, Lo, here is Christ, or there; believe it not. **For there shall arise false Christs**, and false prophets, and…if it were possible, they shall deceive the very elect."*

If you want a *graphic* insight as to how Kingdom-building Fundamentalists (unwittingly aligned with the Devil himself) are currently assailing the *"written* word of God" in the closing days of *its* public ministry – then lend your ear to that deserted, marred, and suffocating *worm* who cries out from the darkness – *"All they that see me laugh me to scorn…trouble is near…there is none to help…Many bulls have compassed me…They gaped upon me with their mouths, as a ravening and a roaring lion…**My strength is*** *dried up...thou hast brought me into the dust of death.* FOR **DOGS HAVE COMPASSED ME....** *"* (Psalm 22:6-16) In Matthew 15:26, the "dog" is cast as a major type of the *Gentile* (i.e., our soldiers are identified by "*dog* tags"). So – how many Gentile "dogs" do *you* know who take delight in ravaging *the* "Book" about which Psalm 138:2 declares: *"thou hast magnified thy word above all thy name"*? (And we thought Tammy Faye Bakker's air-conditioned doghouse made God vomit!)

"THE WORD OF GOD IS NOT BOUND"

The beloved hymn "Ten Thousand Angels" begins with the words: "They *bound* the hands of Jesus in the garden where he prayed...." These lyrics are certainly scriptural, as John 18:12 states: *"Then the band and the captain and officers of the Jews took Jesus, and **bound** him."* However, there is a subtle paradox related to this truth that has everything to do with the theme of this chapter. Did they *really* bind the hands of Jesus? Or should I put it this way – Did *they* really bind the hands of Jesus? (Do you discern the difference in the italics?) John 19:1 says: *"Then Pilate therefore took Jesus, and scourged him."* Did *Pilate* really take him? The answer to this spiritual conundrum is found in the dramatic encounter between Pilate and Jesus: *"Then saith Pilate unto him, Speaketh thou not unto me? knowest thou not that I have power to crucify thee, and have power to release thee?"* Jesus answered, "THOU COULDEST HAVE *NO* POWER AT *ALL* AGAINST ME, **EXCEPT IT WERE GIVEN THEE FROM ABOVE....** *"* (John 19:10-11) Thus, while the hands of Jesus *were* "bound" by Pilate's soldiers, in a *technical* sense – the same goons could not have done a *thing* to Him *without* the Father's approval. In fact, that is the very theme of our hymn: "He *COULD* HAVE called ten thousand angels to destroy the world and set Him free...*BUT* HE DIED ALONE."

In the discourse on the Good Shepherd, Jesus said, *"I lay down my life, that I might take it again. **No man taketh it from me**, but I lay it down of myself. I have power to lay it down, and I have* *power to take it again.* " (John 10:17-18) The Lord proved these words on the Cross when he *"yielded up the ghost"* as an act of His own volition (Matthew 27:50). Of course, the great cross-reference here involving the King James Bible "debate" is II Timothy 2:9 – *"BUT THE WORD OF GOD IS NOT BOUND.* " (Note the close proximity to II Timothy 3:16.) While *Robert Barker* may have died behind bars – the "word" that "he" bound – *"is not bound,"* has *never been* bound, nor *will ever be* bound! The bottom line is that *whatever* marring, disfigurement, or reproach may have fallen upon the A.V. 1611 – rest assured that in *this* context – it *was* "formally *authorized,*" and by the King of kings Himself!

Finally, at our Lord's Ascension, His *physical* presence disappeared from this world. However, with the *descent* of the Holy "Ghost" ten days later, the glorified Christ *reentered* His Creation invisibly through the vehicle of the Church (John 14:16-18). The Apostle Paul makes reference to this miracle in II Corinthians 4:7, *"But we have this **treasure** in **earthen** vessels, that the excellency of the power may be of God, and not of us."* Once again, the *Eternal* has chosen to inhabit the *temporal.* Conversely, while the original King James manuscript has long since disappeared, *this* treasure has likewise reappeared in the *earthen* copies that we possess today. This process is made complete when the "indwelling Word" of II Corinthians 4:7 becomes the "manifested Word" of II Corinthians 3:3 – *"Forasmuch as **ye** are manifestly declared to be the epistle of Christ ministered by us, written not with ink, but with the Spirit of the living God; not in tables of stone, but in fleshy tables of the heart."* Thus, a spirit-filled believer is a similitude for the preserved copies of the Holy Scripture that he believes!

A "DECEPTIVE" BOOK

When I was a new Christian, I came upon a Bible verse that really threw me. In the middle of the story concerning Jesus and the Emmaus disciples, Luke 24:28 states: *"And they drew nigh unto the village, whither they went: **and he made as though he** *would have gone further."* Without thinking, I blurted out to my new bride, "Honey, look how Jesus *conned* these guys." Boy, did she ever let me have it! "Don't you call *my* Saviour a con artist!" Whereupon, I quickly revised my earlier assessment, *"Honey* – look how Jesus *fooled* these guys." Of course, the obvious focus of the text is the sensitive nature of the Godhead (Psalm 50:12; Ephesians 4:30). Though Jesus desired fellowship with these brethren, He would not impose upon them. Thus, it was only after *"they constrained him"* that He "yielded" and *"went in to tarry with them."* Yet, a greater truth exists.

Over two decades would pass before I would gain a renewed insight to my original "thesis." One of the deeper concepts that I have ever heard about the Bible is almost too difficult to explain. It constitutes yet another parallel between the *living* and *written* word. While a normal Christian naturally loves the Scripture, especially as the Father makes it an "open book" to him – *"All the words of my mouth are...plain to him that understandeth"* – this is *not* the case with the unsaved world. (Proverbs 8:8-9; I Corinthians 2:14) In fact, the same Bible is so designed that any Christ-rejecting sinner can find a convenient place to "hide" *if* he desires one. When the dying infidel, W. C. Fields, was asked why he was reading the Bible, he purportedly replied, *"Loopholes;* I'm looking for *loopholes."* (He would have loved Deuteronomy 14:26.) This is easy to see from the vantage point of right division. As previously noted, if your "religious" friend or loved one does not *really* want the Gospel, the Lord will *allow* him to justify himself by clinging to such "*wrongly* divided" passages as Matthew 19:16-17 – only to crash and *burn* at Matthew 7:22-23. Another famous "loophole" is Acts 2:38 (II Peter 3:16 anticipating the same abuse in reverse during the Tribulation).

Thus, we *understand* that the Bible *can* be an extremely DECEPTIVE book to examine – *unless* one is sincerely looking for the truth. While this will surely sound like blasphemy to Bible-correcting Fundamentalists, Isaiah 28:13 says, *"But the word of the* LORD *was unto them precept upon precept, precept upon precept; line upon line, line upon line; here a little, and there a little;* THAT THEY MIGHT GO, AND *FALL* BACKWARD, AND BE *BROKEN,*

AND *SNARED, AND TAKEN.*" (See also: Exodus 4:21; 14:17; I Kings 22:20-23; Proverbs 13:13; Isaiah 6:10; 29:10-14; Jeremiah 4:10; Ezekiel 14:9; Mark 4:11-12; Romans 7:11; I Corinthians 2:14; and II Thessalonians 2:11-12.)

Though beyond the comprehension of many, the Holy Bible is a *Jewish* book, consisting of 66 individual books (6+6=12, the number of Israel) written by Jews, that revolves around the heritage of Abraham as represented in the lineage of the twelve sons of Jacob. Given our thesis of the Bible having a "deceptive" side, we understand that the name "Jacob" just *happens* to mean "heel-catcher" or "supplanter" (i.e., *deceiver*). Applying this principle to the King *James* controversy can be most enlightening. For instance, as noted in chapter two, it is no coincidence that the English name "James" is the English equivalent of "Jacob". Thus, we have a *Jewish* book, named after an *English* king, with a *Hebrew* name, for – *"Where the word of a **king** is, there is **power**"* (Ecclesiastes 8:4). This, in turn, leads me to believe that the Lord has providentially *allowed* a number of so-called "problem texts" to exist in the Holy Scriptures – *just so the heathen can have something to rage about* (as in the story of the ignorant skeptic who tried to corner a little Sunday school girl by asking her, "How could the Israelites carry Noah's Ark through the wilderness for 40 long years?"). Consequently, whenever the King James Bible *appears* to be "defective," in *reality* – it is only being "deceptive."

However, I *also* believe that these same passages exist to *test the believer*, for *"without faith it is impossible to please him"* (Hebrews 11:6). The words to *another* beautiful hymn "Until Then" remind us – "And things of earth that cause the heart to *tremble*, remembered *there*, will only bring a smile." Just as the pillar of fire that *separated* Pharaoh's army from the escaping Hebrews at the Red Sea, the Lord's "two-edged sword" is designed to function as Jacob "the supplanter" with the *critic* – while simultaneously appearing as Israel, a "Prince with God," to the *believer* (Genesis 32:28). The moral of the story is that God's people must continually *"Fight the good fight of faith,"* as the King James Bible will most assuredly be vindicated *someday* – no matter *how* "weakened" it may *appear* on the Internet *today*. While John 4:6 has the eternal *"living* Word" *leaning* on a well, *"being **wearied** with his journey,"* you wouldn't want to let that "holy perspiration" fool you; for, although *God* got a "little winded," he could *still* tell the Samaritan woman *"all that* [she] *ever did."* And wouldn't you know that "the Word" was leaning on *Jacob's* well?

Just because we cannot *understand* every single problem – at the *moment* – doesn't mean that we will not *eventually* gain the desired light. For instance, while I was speaking in a camp meeting in Connecticut, a Bible believer asked me about a verse in the Old Testament that had long confused him. *"And Urijah the priest built an altar according to all that king Ahaz had sent from Damascus: so Urijah the priest made it **against** king Ahaz came from Damascus."* My first reaction was that I didn't have a clue as to how the word "against" fit the text. It also sounded incongruous to the ear. However, when I got home I simply referenced my *Webster's* and discovered that while the first seven definitions described "against" in the familiar sense of "opposition," etc. – the *eighth* definition stated: "In provision for; in preparation for…." Thus, the meaning of the passage is that Urijah finished his assignment *in time for* the King's return from Damascus. So don't let the Devil play with your mind; even Yogi Berra knew that "It ain't *over* till it's *over*." By the way, the Scripture address for this illustration just "happens" to be II Kings 16:11.

"GOD SAVE THE KING!"

When I wrote *Final Authority* in 1993, I was much more impressed with the *technical* side of the "argument" than I am today. For one thing, like the attitude Lester Roloff conveyed in his sermon "Don't Mess with My Mama!" – the King James Bible has so enriched *my* life that I am no longer willing to dignify each and every challenge to its moral authority with a response. Paul wrote in II Corinthians 5:20, *"Now then we are **ambassadors** for Christ."* I doubt that many secular emissaries would feel compelled to entertain (much less respond to) the repeated character assassination of *their* kings. As an enlightened Bible believer, I can relate to the blind man in John 9:25. When modern-day Pharisees want to challenge the credentials of *my* gracious benefactor (call "Him" the *"word of God,"* as identified in Hebrews 4:12-13), the scriptural reply remains unassailable: *"Whether he be a sinner or no, I know not: one thing I know, that, **whereas I was blind, now I see.**"* I mean, really, is it *my* fault that after 36 years I cannot recall a *single* Hebrew or Greek "nugget" that has resonated with my spirit, while the English text of the A.V. 1611 has totally transformed my life? The scholars just don't get it.

Then, one day I suddenly began to experience a *whole new attitude* toward the never-ending barrage of "slime." The *more* the enemy attempted to *separate* my A.V. 1611 from the Hebrew and Greek autographs, the *more* they made me feel as though my Bible was even *more* UNIQUE than ever. I have now come to believe that the longer one "weighs the evidence" *against* that "Book," the *more* that "Book" will manifest a distinctive profile of its own. For instance, when I was introduced to the "King James Only" movement (in 1988) the first principle I learned was that the Authorized Version is superior to all other "Bibles" because it was translated from the *Textus Receptus* – its ideological strength being established by a *majority* of readings. Mark 16:9-20 was presented as *the* classic illustration, bearing witness in 618 of the 620 extant manuscripts, missing only in the "corrupt" codices *Vaticanus* and *Sinaiticus* (I Timothy 3:16 was given as another example, "God" being found in 252 of 254 manuscripts). So far, so good.

However, about the time I became emboldened with *this* impressive approach, I stumbled upon the disconcerting manuscript evidence for I John 5:7 – confirming *its* existence in only *four* Greek manuscripts (*Codex Wianburgensis*, and the miniscules 61, 88, and 629). Now, while my "faith" *in* "The Book" never wavered, an adjustment to my "understanding" *about* "The Book" was suddenly in need of a little tweaking. Apparently, *some* verses with only a *minority* of attestation *could* be just as authentic as verses represented in a *majority* of readings. (While I probably didn't grasp it at the time, my initial perplexities were boiling down to this: either I would allow the *Devil* to *overthrow* my faith, or I would allow the *Lord* to *grow* my faith!)

The next discovery I made (as mentioned in Chapter 4) was that the sacrosanct term – "The" *Textus Receptus* – was actually an "unfortunate misnomer," there being at *least* sixteen "*TRs*" in circulation during the Reformation, and *all* differing *slightly* from one another. This, in turn, led to my understanding that the King James Bible was *not* a direct translation of any *one* edition of the *Textus Receptus*, but rather embodied an *eclectic* text (i.e., constructed from several sources). Edward F. Hills articulated this unique truth in *Believing Bible Study*: "Hence the King James Version ought to be regarded not merely as a translation of the Textus Receptus but also as an independent variety of the Textus Receptus." Then, one day I saw those *ten* italicized words in I John 2:23 indicating that *the whole second half of the verse* was missing in the Greek manuscripts employed by the translators. My faith was *really* put to the test when I subsequently learned that the entire reading *was* eventually vindicated – though by less than twenty mostly older manuscripts, led by *Vaticanus, Sinaiticus*, and *Alexandrinus*. (Like I said, the longer one views this thing – *through the eyes of faith alone* – the more that King James Bible will appear as the designer's model that it literally *is*.)

My favorite illustration of these "faith enhancing texts" (FETs) is the phrase *"God save the King,"* found in I Samuel 10:24, II Samuel 16:16 and I Kings 1:25. One Internet critic dogmatically asserts that this is a *major* ERROR, as the correct reading should be – "May the King live," further stating: "God's not in the TR [I'm sure he meant the Hebrew *Masoretic* text] but reflects British culture of the 1600s. Proof that the translators used dynamic equivalents." With my first acquaintance of the term "dynamic equivalence" (i.e., the theoretical antithesis of a literal, word-for-word translation) being ascribed to the villainous New International Version, my faith was tried yet again. However, *this* time I said, "Forget this!" Either the Lord wanted me to have a "Book" that

I could hold in my hand and trust without ANY hesitation – or He didn't – it was as *simple* as that!

No sooner had I crossed this line in my spirit than the Holy Ghost reminded me of the *historical* application of this text to the A.V. 1611 itself. But let me first digress. Like his Hebrew namesake *before* him – and the Bible that would bear his name *after* him – James I of England (and Ireland) would persevere through various and sundry *physical* afflictions. On Monday, January 16, 1604 (day two of the Hampton Court Conference), Dr. John Rainolds moved "...his Maiestie, that there might bee a newe *translation* of the *Bible,* because, those which were allowed in the raigns of *Henrie* the eight, and *Edward* the sixt, were corrupt and were not aunswerable to the truth of the Originall." It was highly symbolic that both Rainolds *and* his Sovereign were suffering with *gout.* Thus, we understand that *Jacob* limped, *James* limped, and *John* limped (Genesis 32:25). It was fitting, therefore, that Dr. Rainolds, revered as "a living library and a third university," would join the eight-man Old Testament committee at Oxford (assigned Isaiah through Malachi) and eventually translate, among other phrases – *"the lame take the prey."* (Isaiah 23:23)

The frail monarch suffered from a variety of chronic ailments (including crippling arthritis, and abdominal colic). Ironically, this made James an excellent illustration of the Bible that would define his reign. While the former would literally *"halt upon his thigh,"* the latter (once again) would only *appear* to do the same (Genesis 32:31). However, there is a marked difference between God granting a king "life" (particularly *long* life, as in Daniel 6:21, *"O King, live forever"*) – and God actually "saving" the life of a king. Though it does not appear that James received the former, dying at the age of 58, he *was* the object of a timely divine intervention, having been "saved" from the "Gunpowder Plot" on November 4, 1605. The night before the new King was to make his first address to the Parliamentary body at Westminster Palace, royal agents discovered *thirty-six barrels of gunpowder* hidden in the basement directly below the spot where he was to speak. In the ensuing investigation, the Vatican was directly implicated through the lead conspirator, Henry Garnet, Provincial of the English Jesuits. Garnet's main flunky, a self-proclaimed "Catholic soldier of fortune" named Guy Fawkes, had been apprehended outside the cellar door with the match (fuse) in his hand. He and several of his accomplices were put to death on January 31, 1606. ("Guy Fawkes Day" continues to be commemorated in England to this day.)

On the morning of Garnet's execution, May 3, 1606, Dr. John Overall, Dean of St. Paul's Cathedral, interrupted his translation work to visit the condemned priest, urging upon him "a true and lively faith to God-ward." However, "Father" Henry wasn't interested and was subsequently hanged, drawn, and quartered. After witnessing the macabre ordeal, Dr. Overall's Westminster committee on the Old Testament would go on to translate those four immortal words – *"God save the king."* Thus, we understand the great spiritual paradox – had it *not* been for the "literal fulfillment" of this despised "dynamic equivalent" there would have been *no* "King James" Bible in the first place! The same God who would "save the King" of Glory after hearing his cry in Psalm 22:21 – *"Save me from the lion's mouth"* – would likewise do the same for the King of England and the Bible that would issue from his reign.

FAITH FOR THE LAST DAYS

As the world pays ever more attention to the ticking seconds of the infamous "Doomsday Clock," a timely article appeared in the July 28, 2010, *USA Today* entitled "Doomsday shelters making a comeback." (A related story in *Popular Mechanics* declared, "The bomb shelter business is booming.") Apparently, one of the few sectors of the economy that *has* experienced growth under the Obama administration is the *survival* industry. The *USA Today* reporter wrote: "The Vivos Network [of Del Mar, California], which offers partial ownerships similar to a timeshare in underground shelter communities, is one of several ventures touting escape from a surface level calamity." Interestingly, the company website pitches *eleven* potential global catastrophes, ranging from nuclear wars to solar flares and comets. Founder Robert Vicino bristles at the notion that he's profiting from people's fears, stating: "We're not creating the fear; the fear is already out there. We're creating a solution." Thus, one *more* "change" that Americans have come to believe in is *burrowing underground*. On a "positive" note, at *least* we're *right on schedule*, for Jesus said that a sure sign of the end would be *"Men's hearts failing them for fear...."* (Luke 21:26) Unfortunately, however, sinners aren't the *only* ones who are panicking.

A final parallel between the *living* and *written* word would be the "desertion" that "both" would experience at the close of "their" respective ministries (don't forget that subtle *personal* pronoun in Hebrews 4:13). As Matthew 26:56 confirms – *"Then all the disciples forsook him and fled"* – many "professing" Bible believers today have likewise *forsaken* the A.V. 1611 and *fled*, no longer willing to be identified with its "apparently" untenable position. While in both cases the basic cause would *appear* to be the sudden and overwhelming hostility of the enemy, the *greater* reason was (and is) the Saviour's disconcerting acquiesce to His antagonists. When Peter bravely rose to his Master's defense in Gethsemane, Jesus rebuked him, saying, *"Put up thy sword into the sheath"* (John 18:11). This had to confound the disciples for He had just *told* them to buy a sword (Luke 22:36).

As Israel's Messiah was subsequently "bound" and led away *without the slightest resistance*, His followers suddenly experience an unprecedented "mood swing" – from consternation to *anger*. While the Holy Spirit graciously chose to conceal their venting, we know that it happened because the Lord *said* that it would in His warning just a few hours before: *"All ye shall be **offended** because of me this night: for it is written, I will **smite** the shepherd, and the sheep of the flock shall be **scattered** abroad."* (Matthew 26:31) Consequently, the disciples would pass the time between the Crucifixion and the Resurrection in severe depression, having allowed *their* "faith" to be temporally "overthrown" by Christ's unexplainable passivity. Thus, as the Father now *appears* to be allowing His *written* word to be "smitten" by widespread attacks via books, Christian higher education, the Internet, etc., many believers have likewise been "offended" and "scattered." While the *"offence of the Cross"* has always been a vital part of the Christian experience, a peculiar "offence" of the last days appears to involve a "Sword" (*peculiar* in the fact that the resentment remains focused on that Sword's "Creator").

However, this could not have come at a worse possible time! While God's people have *always* needed the comfort and direction of the Holy Bible, the end of the Laodicean Church Age is fraught with *"perilous times"* (II Timothy 3:1-7). Any number of potential scenarios could play out in the immediate future: amnesty for illegal aliens; Islamic demographical encroachment; hate crime persecution; economic collapse; race riots; martial law; suicide bombers; not to mention the inevitable nuclear showdown between Israel and Iran. (On Thursday, August 19, 2010, at 9:19 am CDT – *the precise moment* when Secretary of State Hillary Clinton was convening the first session of "peace" talks between Palestinian Authority President Mahmoud Abbas and Israeli Prime Minister Benjamin Netanyahu – a *second* oil rig in the Gulf of Mexico *exploded in flames*; during the live coverage on *C-Span*, the caption – ALERT: GULF OIL RIG EXPLODES OFF LOUISIANA COAST – actually appeared as Mr. Netanyahu was speaking.)

As this book was going to press, the *"Bad* Good Guys" ("death by slow gas leak while you're asleep" *Republicans*) were preparing to clobber the "Bad Guys" ("death by frontal chain saw attack in broad daylight" *Democrats*) in the 2010 mid-term elections. Assuming that there's life *after* Obama, and that the Lord tarries His coming, the Devil will have *plenty* of others waiting in the wings to carry on his infernal agenda. Thus, if Bible believers *ever* needed to *"Fight the good fight of faith"* and rally around "The Book" – that time is NOW!

A "LOONY" EXPERIENCE

I will now bring my remarks to a close by relating a most unusual incident that happened to me during the writing of this book. I was speaking for a Bible-believing pastor in the New England area. He was a *very* gracious host who provided me with a vehicle and a lovely private cabin on a scenic lake. (The only "drawback" for this *city* boy was the eerie shrieking of the *loons* throughout the night!)

When I informed the preacher that I was researching the printing history of the Authorized Version, he showed me a genuine 1613 octavo edition that he had purchased several years ago. It appeared in excellent condition and was bound in a beautiful wooden cover. He asked me if I would like to take the Bible back to the cottage to examine it more thoroughly. Since "my mamma didn't raise no dummy," I gladly took the pastor up on his timely offer. As this was the last night of the meeting, and I was fairly exhausted, I decided that I would pack up, hit the hay, and then drive to the church an hour earlier so I could have a fresh look at the book there (i.e., before the pastor would arrive to take me to the airport).

The next morning, when I was about to carry my two bags and the pastor's Bible out to the truck, I noticed a slight drizzle in the air. Although it was only a few feet to the vehicle, I felt that such a valuable spiritual antique should not be exposed to the elements. So I tucked that blessed Holy Book inside my snug, buttoned-down shirt and walked out the door with a bag in each hand. (Like I said, "my mama didn't raise no dummy," etc.) I can still recall thinking how "heavenly" it seemed to have such an ancient treasure, *literally*, next to my heart.

When I got to the back of the truck, I opened the window above the tail gate and tossed my smaller bag in first. As I hoisted the larger, heavier bag *up*, *over*, and *in*, the "looniest" thing happened. (Wait till I get there!) That 397-year-old King James Bible *somehow* slipped right on down through my shirt and hit the ground with a thud! When I finally peaked, to my shock I saw the wooden front cover laying *next* to the Bible, having detached at impact. (Like I said, "my mama....") Thankfully, the rest of "The Book" was intact. Let me tell ya' – this was *not* one of my better moments!

The thirty-minute drive to the Church was a total blur. I kept trying to think – *how* could I explain such a colossal disaster to my generous host? After pulling into the parking lot, I just sat there, oblivious to everything. Finally, I decided to utilize the brief time that I had by following the original plan. So I picked up the "broken" Bible and began turning the pages, *ever so delicately.* Suddenly, the Holy Ghost put a verse on my heart. Sitting in the front seat of that truck, I looked down at II Corinthians 4:7 and read, with holy awe – *"BUT WE HAVE THIS TREASURE IN EARTHEN VESSELS...."* The Author seemed to say, "That cover was made from one of the trees on my *earth* and doesn't have a *thing* to do with the *truth* conveyed on the pages."

It dawned on me that I was having a bona fide *"religious* experience," as *one* treasure in an earthen vessel had unintentionally mishandled *another* treasure in *another* earthen vessel. And the whole fiasco *must* have been approved by the Lord Himself, for *"the word of God is not bound."* Then, just before the pastor arrived, the Spirit of God also prepared my heart for the encounter by impressing me that my *"yokefellow"* was a Bible believer, *not* a Fundamentalist. While the latter would have gone into *hysterics* because of *aesthetics*, the former was more *enamored* with the *treasure* itself. And sure enough, when the man of God finally did appear, he could not have been *more* thoughtful and empathetic of *my* embarrassing predicament.

My concluding reflection was that the Lord *really* doesn't have much to work with down here. And then I realized...

> *"...we have this treasure in earthen vessels,*
> ***that the excellency of the power may***
> ***be of God, and not of us.***"
>
> (II CORINTHIANS 4:7)

The Translators to the Reader

...It remaineth, that we commend thee to God, and to the Spirit of his grace, which is able to build further then we can aske or thinke. Hee removeth the scales from our eyes, the baile from our hearts, opening our wits that wee may understand his word, enlarging our hearts, yea correcting our affections, that we may love it above gold and silver, yea that we may love it to the end. Ye are brought unto fountains of living water which yee digged not; doe not cast earth into them with the Philistines, neither preferre broken pits before them with the wicked Jewes. Others have laboured, and you may enter into their labours; O receive not so great things in vaine, O despise not so great salvation!...It is a fearefull thing to fall into the hands of the living God; but a blessed thing it is, and will bring us to everlasting blessednes in the end, when God speaketh unto us, to hearken; when he setteth his word before us, to reade it; when hee stretcheth out his hand and calleth, to answere, Here am I; here we are to doe thy will, O God. The Lord worke a care and conscience in us to know him and serve him, that we may be acknowledged of him at the appearing of our Lord Jesus Christ, to whom with the holy Ghost, be all prayse and thankesgiving. Amen.